HIS DIVINE GRACE A.C. BHAKTIVEDANTA SWAMI PRABHUPADA
FOUNDER ACHARYA OF THE INTERNATIONAL SOCIETY FOR
KRISHNA CONSCIOUSNESS AND THE GREATEST EXPONENT OF
KRISHNA CONSCIOUSNESS IN THE WESTERN WORLD.

SRILA BHAKTISIDDHANTA SARASWATI GOSWAMI MAHARAJ
THE SPIRITUAL MASTER OF SRILA A.C. BHAKTIVEDANTA SWAMI
AND FOREMOST SCHOLAR AND DEVOTEE IN THE RECENT AGE.

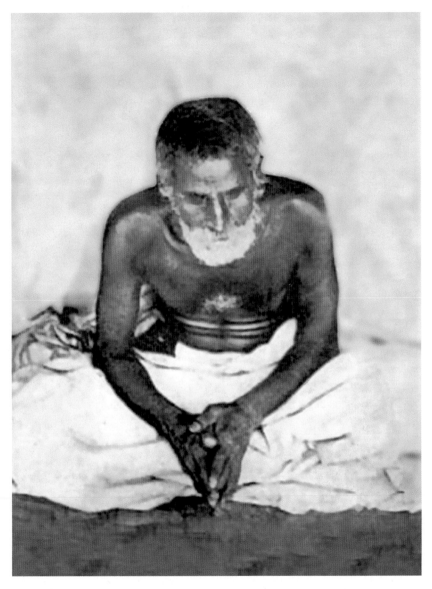

SRILA GOUR KISORE DAS BABAJI MAHARAJ
THE SPIRITUAL MASTER OF SRILA BHAKTISIDDHANTA SARASWATI
GOSWAMI AND INTIMATE STUDENT OF SRILA THAKUR BHAKTIVINODE.

SRILA THAKUR BHAKTIVINODE
THE PIONEER OF THE PROGRAM FOR BENEDICTING
THE ENTIRE WORLD WITH KRISNHA CONSCIOUSNESS
BY THE INSTRUCTIONS OF LORD CHAITANYA.

SRILA JAGANNATH DAS BABAJI
INSTRUCTING SPIRITUAL MASTER OF SRILA THAKUR BHAKTIVINODE
AND THE DISCOVERER OF THE ACTUAL BIRTHSITE OF
SRI CHAITANYA MAHAPRABHU.

SRIDHAMA MAYAPUR
THE BIRTHPLACE OF THE SUPREME LORD SRI KRISHNA CHAITANYA
IN THE PROVINCE OF GAUDA IN BENGAL.

The great temple at Jagannatha Puri, where **Lord Chaitanya** displayed many of His transcendental pastimes.

SRI PANCHA TATTVA

Lord Krishna Chaitanya surrounded (From left to right) by His Avatar (Adwaita Acharya),
His Expansion (Lord Nityananda), His Manifest Internal Energy (Sri Gadadhar),
and His Perfect Devotee (Sri Srinivas).

PLATE 1 "Mahaprabhu was a beautiful child and the ladies of the town came to see Him with presents." *(P.XXVII)*

PLATE 2 "It has also been stated that when His mother gave him sweetmeats to eat, He ate clay instead of the food." *(P.XXVIII)*

PLATE 3 "...on His arrival at the Kazi's house, He held a long conversation with the Kazi, and in the end communicated into his heart His Vaisnava influence by touching his body." *(P.XXXI)*

PLATE 4 "He worked another miracle by touching (making them immediately disappear) the seven Tal trees, through which Ramchandra, the son of Dasarath, had shot His arrow and killed the great Bali Raj." *(P.XXXIII)*

PLATE 5 "...Mahaprabhu had shown a good many miracles on His way to Puri, such as making tigers and elephants dance, on hearing the name of Krishna." *(P.XXXV)*

PLATE 6 "O Govinda! Feeling Your separation I am considering a moment twelve years or more, and tears are flowing from my eyes like torrents of rain. I am feeling all vacant in the world, in the absence of You." *(p. XXXIX)*

PLATE 7 "Chaitanya Mahaprabhu takes the part of Radharani and tries to love Krishna as Radharani loved Him....This is the secret of Lord Chaitanya's incarnation." *(p. 8)*

PLATE 8-9 "We have information that beyond this cosmic manifestatio[n] one-fourth of the manifestation." *(p. 12)*

here are very extensive *Vaikunthas*. This material manifestation is only

PLATE 10 "...underneath one of the desire trees of Vrindaban there is a nice throne decorated with valuable jewels on which Radharani and Krishna are seated." *(p.17)*

PLATE 11 "Here one associates with the Supreme on an equal level with love and respect. That stage is further developed in the matter of joking...laughing, and so forth." *(p.33)*

PLATE 12 "When Sanatan entered the courtyard of the house, Lord Chaitanya hurriedly came to receive him and embraced him." *(p.43)*

PLATE 13 "The necessity of approaching a spiritual master is not a fashion, but is for he who is seriously conscious of the material miseries, and who wants to be free of them." *(p.49)*

PLATE 14 "...Krishna originally is the Son of Nanda Maharaj...He is the Origin of all emanations and all incarnations, yet there in Vraja or Goloka Vrindaban He is just like a young boy." *(p.60)*

PLATE 15 "The Lord appears in this age in yellowish color, and he teaches people love of God by chanting the Name of Krishna..." *(p.78)*

PLATE 16 "The body of Krishna, the ocean of the eternal beauty of youth, can be seen as moving in waves of beauty. And there is a whirlwind at the sound of his Flute." *(p 91)*

PLATE 17 "The inhabitants of Vrindaban, Vrajabhumi, are practical living examples of devotional service. Theirs is ideal devotional service with attachment..." *(p.114)*

PLATE 18 "If you are hunting all these poor animals, why don't you kill them at once?...they are flapping in death pains... If you want to kill any animal, why don't you kill it completely?" *(p.147)*

PLATE 19 "Is it not wonderful for a devotee of the Lord, that he is not inclined to give any sort of pain, even to the ant?" *(p. 149)*

PLATE 20 "...one must be anxious to hear about the transcendental message. And this qualification of hearing with interest is the prime qualification for assimilating transcendental knowledge." *(p.219)*

PLATE 21 "For this purpose, human society may be divided into four classes: namely, the intelligent class, or the Brahmins, the administrative class, or the Kshatriyas, the mercantile class, or productive class, called Vaishyas, and the laborer class or the helping class, the Sudras." *(p.246)*

PLATE 22 "…although Krishna the son of Devaki is Superexcellence and the last word of beauty, still, when He is amongst the Gopis, it appears that He is a sublime Jewel set amongst divine golden craftsmanship." *(p.262)*

PLATE 23 "I am the Selfsame Krishna—Son of Maharaja Nanda, and due to contact with the body of Srimati Radharani I have now assumed this Form." *(p.290)*

PLATE 24 "...Mahaprabhu continually lived in Puri...until His disappearance in His forty-eighth year at the time of samkirtan in the temple of Tota Gopinath. *(P. XXXV)*

TEACHINGS OF
LORD CHAITANYA

BOOKS by His Divine Grace
A.C. Bhaktivedanta Swami Prabhupāda
published by Krishna Books Inc:

Bhagavad-gītā As It Is

Śrīmad Bhāgavatam, First Canto

Kṛṣṇa, the Supreme Personality of Godhead

Teachings of Lord Chaitanya

Śrī Īśopaniṣad

The Science of Self-Realization

Easy Journey to Other Planets

Kṛṣṇa, the Reservoir of Pleasure

The Perfection of Yoga

Beyond Birth and Death

On Chanting Hare Krishna

TEACHINGS

of

LORD CHAITANYA

A TREATISE ON FACTUAL SPIRITUAL LIFE

His Divine Grace
A.C. Bhaktivedanta Swami Prabhupāda
Founder-*Ācārya* of the International Society for Krishna Consciousness

TEACHINGS OF
LORD CHAITANYA

uses the original text found in the first edition which
was published by ISKCON BOOKS in 1968.

Krishna Books Inc is licensed by the Bhaktivedanta Book Trust
to print and publish the pre-1978 literary works of
His Divine Grace A. C. Bhaktivedanta Swami Prabhupāda

To obtain other titles by the author, readers
are invited to correspond with Krishna Books Inc

http://www.krishnabooks.org
email: info@krishnabooks.org

Krishna Books Inc

578 Washington Blvd. Suite 808
Marina del Rey, CA 90292 USA

Library of Congress Catalog Card Number: 68-29320
1968 English Edition ISBN: 978-1-60293-002-5

First printing 2008

Printed and bound by Thomson Press (India) Ltd.

Namah om vishnu padaya krishna presthaya bhutale
Srimate bhaktivedanta swamin iti namine

We offer our respectful obeisances to Bhaktivedanta Swami
Who is so dear unto Krishna on this earth due to His
taking shelter unto the Lord's Lotus Feet.

We prostrate ourselves at the Lotus Feet of our Beloved Spiritual Master and offer this treasured book to His Divine Grace on our bowed heads. We came to Him looking for broken pieces of glass, and He has bestowed upon us a priceless gem. He has opened our eyes, which were blinded by the darkness of atheism, mental speculation, and sense gratification, to the glorious light of Lord Chaitanya Mahaprabhu. His transcendental words are seeds which in our hearts have bloomed into the perfection of human life—the discovery that God lives and that we can live with Him—Krishna Consciousness.

The Publishers

DEDICATED TO

The Sacred Service

of

SRILA SACHCHIDANANDA BHAKTIVINODE THAKUR

Who Initiated The Teachings of Lord Chaitanya

in

The Western World

(McGill University, Canada)

in 1896

The Year Of My Birth

A. C. BHAKTIVEDANTA SWAMI

The 40th Anniversary
Commemorative Edition
1968 - 2008

We thank you, Srila Prabhupada, for giving the people of this planet the opportunity to follow the path of the *mahajan Vaisnava acharyas*. You have presented the teachings of the Supreme Personality of Godhead, Sri Krishna, without addition, subtraction, or alteration, as you are specifically empowered by Him to do this. These books are our Deities and if there is to be peace and love anywhere in the world, then it will come by faithfully following Their instructions.

Our thanks also to Bhakta Charles for donating photos from his collection.

The end plate is an 18th century watercolor of the Dasaswamedha Ghat in Benares where Lord Chaitanya instructed Srila Rupa Goswami.

This 2008 printing of the *Teachings Of Lord Chaitanya*, 1968 version, is humbly presented to you in memory of your disciple Gangamayee devi dasi by her friends and family.

Annada devi dasi

March 21, 2008

Gaur Purnima, Vrindavan

ACKNOWLEDGEMENT

My thankful acknowledgement is due to Sriman Brahmananda Brahmachary (Mr. Bruce Scharf), Sriman Gargamuni Brahmachary (Mr. Gregory Scharf) and Sriman Satyabrata Brahmachary (Mr. Stanley Moskowitz) for their financial help for this publication, and I beg to thank Sriman Rayarama Brahmachary (Mr. Raymond Marais), Sriman Satsvarupa Brahmachary (Mr. Stephen Guarino) and Sriman Madhusudan Brahmachary (Mr. Michael Blumert) for editing and typing the manuscript, and Sriman Goursundar Das Adhikary (Mr. Gary McElroy) and his good wife, Srimati Govinda Dasi (Mrs. Bonnie McElroy) who are always engaged to see to my personal comforts and I am so much obliged to them for their drawing all the nice pictures contained in this great publication.

All glories to the devotees engaged in the matter of Krishna Consciousness. I am sure that Lord Sri Krishna Chaitanya Mahaprabhu will bestow His Causeless Mercy upon everyone who is engaged in pushing the cause of Krishna Consciousness.

A.C.B

TABLE OF CONTENTS

PART I

PART II

ILLUSTRATIONS

The Author

A. C. Bhaktivedanta Swami was born Abhay Charan De on September 1, 1896 in Calcutta. In 1920 he finished his education, majoring in philosophy, English, and economics, at the University of Calcutta. Because of his involvement in Gandhi's national non-cooperation movement, however, he rejected any formal diploma. Soon afterward Abhay Charan De took up the duties of manager of a large chemical concern. Then, in 1922, he met His Divine Grace Sri Srimad Bhakti Siddhanta Saraswati Goswami Maharaj, the founder of 64 Goudiya Vaishnava Maths in India, Berlin, and London. His Divine Grace liked this educated young man and injected in him the idea of preaching Lord Chaitanya's message all over the world.

At Allahabad in 1933, Abhay Charan De was formally initiated, and in 1936, just days before His Divine Grace's departure from this mortal world, he was specifically ordered to spread Krishna Consciousness in the English language and to the West.

Thus, *Back To Godhead* magazine was started in 1944 with Abhay Charan De serving as editor-in-chief. *Back To Godhead* is now being published monthly in America by his American disciples.

The Goudiya Vaishnava Society recognised him as BHAKTIVEDANTA in 1947. In 1954 he became *Vanaprastha*, retired from family life. In 1959 he took *Sannyasa*, the renounced order of spiritual life and is now known as A. C. Bhaktivedanta Swami.

In September 1965, at the advanced age of 70, A. C. Bhaktivedanta Swami arrived in New York City to fulfil his master's sacred mission. Immediately, young Americans were attracted to him, and in July 1966, the International Society for Krishna Consciousness was formally incorporated.

A. C. Bhaktivedanta Swami is the author of the remarkable *Bhagavad-Gita As It Is*, published in 1968 by the Macmillan Company. Presently he is working on his masterpiece, a projected 60 volume work of translation and elaborate commentary of the *Srimad Bhagwatam*, three volumes of which have already been published. He has also recorded a unique 33 1/3 r.p.m. record album of the mystical mantra *HARE KRISHNA*, entitled "Krishna Consciousness," which has met with extraordinary popularity in India and America.

PREFACE

There is no difference between the teachings of Lord Chaitanya presented here and the teachings of Lord Krishna in the *Bhagavad Gita*. The teaching of Lord Chaitanya is a practical demonstration of the teaching of Lord Krishna. In the *Bhagavad Gita* the last word of the Lord is that everyone should surrender unto Him, Lord Krishna, and that He will take immediate charge of such a surrendered soul. The Lord, the Supreme Personality of Godhead, is already in charge of the maintenance of this Creation by His plenary expansion as Kshirodakashayee Vishnu. But such maintenance by the Lord is not specific. When, therefore, the Lord takes charge, it means that He takes particular charge of a pure devotee. A pure devotee is a soul ever surrendered to the Lord, like a child to his parents or an animal to its master. This surrendering process is manifested in six different stages, namely: (1) to accept things favorable for discharging devotional service, (2) to reject things unfavorable for discharging devotional service, (3) to believe firmly that the Lord will protect His devotee always, (4) to feel exclusively dependent on the Mercy of the Lord, (5) to have no separate interest besides the interest of the Lord, and (6) always to feel oneself meek and humble.

Therefore Lord Krishna demanded that one should surrender unto Him through the above-mentioned six phases of the surrendering process; but the less intelligent class of men and so-called scholars of the world misunderstood these demands of the Lord, and thus misguided the general mass of people to reject them. In the *Bhagavad Gita*, at the end of the Ninth Chapter, the Lord directly orders one to always think of Him, become His devotee, worship Him only, offer obeisances unto Him only—and by doing so one is sure to come to Him in His Transcendental Abode. But so-called scholarly demons misguide the mass of people, directing them not to surrender like that to the Personality of Godhead, but rather to the impersonal, non-manifested, eternal, unborn Truth. The *Mayavadi*, impersonalist, philosophers do not accept that the last word in the matter of understanding the Absolute Truth is the Supreme Personality of Godhead. If one desires to understand the Sun as he is, one faces first of all the sunshine, and then the Sun globe, and at last if one is able to enter into that globe, there is the possibility of seeing face-to-face the predominating Deity of the Sun. The *Mayavadi* philosophers, due to a poor fund of knowledge, cannot go beyond the Brahman effulgence which is like the sunshine. The *Upanishads* confirm that one has to penetrate the dazzling effulgence of Brahman, and then one can see the real Face of the Personality of Godhead.

Lord Chaitanya therefore teaches us directly that one has to worship Lord Krishna, Who appeared as the foster Child of the King of Braja. He also recommends that the place known as Vrindaban is as good as Lord Krishna because, Lord Krishna being the Absolute Truth, the Personality of Godhead, there is no difference between His Name, Quality, Form, Pastimes, Entourage, and Paraphernalia.

Lord Chaitanya also recommended that the mode of worshipping the Lord in the highest perfectional stage is the method of worship conceived by the Damsels of Braja. The Damsels of Braja, the Gopis, simply loved Krishna without any motive for material or spiritual gain. He also recommended that *Srimad Bhagwatam* is the spotless narration of transcendental knowledge and that the highest gain in the human form of life is to develop unalloyed love of Krishna, the Supreme Personality of Godhead.

Lord Chaitanya's teachings are exactly the same as those given by Lord Kapila, the original propounder of the *Samkhya Yoga*, or the *Samkhya* system of philosophy. This authorized system of Yoga is practiced on the principle of meditation on the Transcendental Form of the Lord. There is no meditating on something Void or impersonal involved. When one is practiced to meditate upon the Transcendental Form of Lord Vishnu, even without the sitting posture in a particular place and atmosphere, the stage is called perfect *Samadhi*. This perfect *Samadhi* of *Samkhya Yoga* is confirmed in the *Bhagavad Gita* at the end of the Sixth Chapter, where the Lord says that of all the yogis, one who constantly thinks of the Lord within the core of his heart with love and devotion is the greatest.

Lord Chaitanya instructed this *Samkhya Yoga*, or system of philosophy—called

Achintya Bhedabheda Tattwa (simultaneously one and different)—most practically for everyone among the mass of people, simply by chanting the Holy Name of the Lord. He says that the Holy Name of the Lord is the Sound Vibration Form of the Lord. The Lord being the Absolute Whole, there is no difference between His Holy Name and His Transcendental Form. Therefore, by chanting the Holy Name of the Lord, one can directly associate with the Supreme Lord by Sound Vibration. This Sound Vibration of the Lord has three stages of development, namely: (1) offensive stage, (2) clearing stage, and (3) transcendental stage. In the offensive stage one may desire all kinds of material happiness or distress as one acts, but in the second stage of chanting, one becomes cleared from all material contamination. But when one is situated on the transcendental stage, one achieves the most covetable perfection, the stage of loving God. Lord Chaitanya recommended that this is the highest stage of perfection for the human being.

Yoga practice is essentially meant for controlling the senses. Mind is the central controlling factor of all senses; and therefore one has to practice first controlling the mind by engaging the mind in the matter of Krishna Consciousness. The gross activities of the mind are expressed through the external senses, either for acquiring knowledge or functioning under the will, and the subtle activities of the mind are thinking, feeling, and willing, according to the different attitudes of consciousness. This consciousness is either polluted or clear. If the mind is fixed up in Krishna (His Name, Quality, Form, Pastimes, Entourage, and Paraphernalia), then the whole of the activities, subtle and gross, is changed favorably. The *Bhagavad Gita's* process of purifying consciousness is to fix the mind on Krishna—to talk of His Transcendental Activities, to cleanse the Temple of the Lord, to walk to the Temple of the Lord, to see the Beautiful Transcendental Form of the Lord nicely decorated, to hear His Transcendental Glories, to taste foodstuffs offered to the Lord, to smell the flowers and Tulsi leaves offered to the Lord, to associate with the Lord's devotees, to engage oneself in the activities for the interest of the Lord, and to become angry also at those who are envious of the devotees. No one can stop the activities of the mind or the senses, but one can purify such activities by changing the account. This change of account is recommended in the *Bhagavad Gita* (Chapter II/39). A human being is sometimes restricted in the matter of sense-gratification under certain circumstances of disease, etc. But that prescription or regulative principle is for the less intelligent class of men. Such less intelligent men, without knowing the actual process of controlling the mind and senses, either want to stop them by force, or to give them up or to be carried away by the waves of sense-gratification.

The eight formulas of practicing Yoga—regulative principles, following the rules, practicing the different sitting postures, breathing exercise, and thus to withdraw the senses from the sense objects, etc.—are meant for the persons who are too engrossed in the bodily concept of life. But the intelligent man who is situated in Krishna Consciousness, does not forcibly stop his senses from acting on behalf of Krishna.

You cannot stop a child from his playful activities and leave him inactive, but you can stop him by engaging him in superior activities. Similarly, the forceful restraint of the sense activities, by following the eight principles of Yoga practice, is recommended for an inferior class of men; but the superior class of men, being engaged in the better activities of Krishna Consciousness, naturally retire from the inferior activities of material existence.

Lord Chaitanya in this way teaches us the science of Krishna Consciousness, which is absolute. Dry mental speculators try to restrain themselves from material attachment, but it is generally found that the mind, being too strong to be controlled, sometimes drags such speculators down in the matter of sensual activities; but there is no such chance for persons in Krishna Consciousness. Therefore, one has to engage one's mind and senses in Krishna conscious activities, and how this is practically possible is taught by the Lord, Sri Krishna Chaitanya.

Before His acceptance of the *Sannyas*, or renounced order of life, Lord Chaitanya was known as Viswambhar. *Viswambhar* means the one who maintains the whole Universe as leader of all living entities. The very same maintainer and leader of all living entities appeared as Lord Sri Krishna Chaitanya to give us the sublime teachings of life, and was the ideal Teacher of the prime necessities of life. He is the most munificent Giver of the love of Krishna. He is the complete Reservoir of all mercies and auspiciousness. Although He is the Supreme Personality of Godhead, Krishna, as is confirmed in the *Srimad Bhagwatam*, *Bhagavad Gita*, *Mahabharata* and *Upanishads*, He appeared as worshipable by everyone in this age of disagreement. Everyone can join in His Samkirtan movement without any previous qualification, and everyone can become the most perfect human being by following His teachings. If anyone is fortunate enough to be attracted by all His Features of manifestation, one is sure to be successful in the mission of one's life. In one word, those who are interested in being situated in spiritual existence can get easily relieved from the clutches of Maya by the Grace of Lord Chaitanya, now presented in the book form of *Teachings of Lord Chaitanya*, non-different from the Lord.

The conditioned soul, being engrossed in the material body, increases the pages of history of all kinds of material activities. But the Teachings of Lord Chaitanya can help the human society to stop such unnecessary and temporary activities, and can elevate one to the topmost platform of spiritual activities, which begin after liberation from material bondage. Such liberated activities in Krishna Consciousness are the goal of human perfection. The false prestige of acquiring lordship over the material Nature is illusion only, and one can get illuminating knowledge from the Teachings of Lord Chaitanya, in order to advance in one's spiritual existence.

One has to suffer or enjoy the fruits of one's activity, and nobody can check the laws of material Nature which govern such things. So long as one is engaged in such activities, one is sure to be baffled in attempting to achieve the ultimate goal of life. I hope therefore most sincerely that by understanding the Teachings of Lord

Chaitanya human society will have a new light of spiritual life, opening the field of activities of the pure soul.

Om Tat Sat

A. C. Bhaktivedanta Swami

A. C. Bhaktivedanta Swami

14 March 1968
(Birthday of Lord Chaitanya)
Sri Sri Radha Krishna Temple
New York, N.Y.

PROLOGUE

THE LIFE OF CHAITANYA MAHAPRABHU

by

Srila Thakur Bhaktivinode

reprinted from *Chaitanya - His Life and Precepts*
by Srila Thakur Bhaktivinode, Calcutta India (1895)

Chaitanya Mahaprabhu was born in Mayapur in the town of Nadia, just after sunset on the evening of the 23rd Falgoon 1407 Sakabda, answering to the 18th February 1486 of the Christian Era. The moon was eclipsed at the time of His birth, and the people of Nadia were then engaged, as is usual on such occasions, in bathing in the Bhagirathi with loud cheers of *Haribol*. His father, Jagannath Misra, was a poor Brahmin of the Vaidic order, and His mother, Sachi Devi, was a model good woman, both descended from Brahmin stocks originally residing in Sylhet. Mahaprabhu was a beautiful child and the ladies of the town came to see Him with presents. His mother's father, Pandit Nilambar Chakravarti, a renowned astrologer, foretold that the Child would be a great personage in time; and he, therefore, gave Him the name Vishwambhar. The ladies of the neighbourhood styled Him Gour Hari on account of His golden complexion, and His mother called Him Nimai on account of the Nim tree near which He was born. Beautiful as the Lad was, everyone heartily loved to see Him every day. As He grew up He became a whimsical and frolicsome Lad. After His fifth year, He was admitted into a school where He picked up Bengali in a very short time.

Most of His contemporary biographers have mentioned certain anecdotes regarding Chaitanya which are simply records of His early miracles. It is said that when He was an infant in His mother's arms, He wept continually, and when the neighbouring ladies and His mother cried *Haribol!* He used to stop. Thus there was a continuation of the utterance of *Haribol* in the house, foreshowing the future mission of the Hero. It has also been stated that when His mother once gave Him sweetmeats to eat, He ate clay instead of the food. His mother asking for the reason, He stated that as every sweetmeat was nothing but clay transformed, He could eat clay as well. His mother, who was the consort of a pandit, explained that every article in a special state was adapted to a special use. Earth, while in the state of a jug, could be used as a water pot, but in the state of a brick such a use was not possible. Clay, therefore, in the form of sweetmeats was usable as food and not clay in its other states. The Lad was convinced and admitted His stupidity in eating clay, and agreed to avoid the mistake in future.

Another miraculous act has been related. It is said that a Brahmin on pilgrimage became a guest in His house, and cooked his food and read his grace with meditation on Krishna. In the meantime, the Lad came and ate up the cooked rice. The Brahmin, astonished at the Lad's act, cooked again at the request of Jagannath Misra. The Lad again ate up the cooked rice while the Brahmin was offering the rice to Krishna with meditation. The Brahmin was persuaded to cook for a third time. This time all the inmates of the house had fallen asleep, and the Lad showed Himself as Krishna to the traveller, and blessed him. The Brahmin was then lost in ecstasy at the appearance of the Object of his worship.

It has also been stated that two thieves stole away the Lad from His father's door with a view to purloin His jewels and gave Him sweetmeats on the way. The Lad exercised His illusory energy and deceived the thieves back towards His own house. The thieves, for fear of detection, left the Boy there and fled.

Another miraculous act has been described of the Lad's demanding and getting from Hiranya and Jagadisha all the offerings they had collected for worshipping Krishna on the day of Ekadashi. When only four years of age He sat on rejected cooking pots which were considered unholy by His mother. He explained to His mother that there was no question of holiness and unholiness as regards earthen pots thrown away after the cooking was over. These anecdotes relate to the tender age up to the fifth year.

In His eighth year, He was admitted into the *tol* of Gangadas Pandit in

Ganganagar close by the village of Mayapur. In two years He became well read in Sanskrit Grammar and Rhetoric. His readings after that were of the nature of self-study in His own house, where He had found all-important books belonging to His father, who was a pandit himself. It appears that He read the *Smriti* in His own study and the *Nyaya* also, in competition with His friends who were then studying under the celebrated Pandit Raghunath Shiromani.

Now, after the tenth year of His age, Chaitanya became a passable scholar in Grammar, Rhetoric, the *Smriti* and the *Nyaya*. It was after this that His elder brother Vishwarup left his house and accepted the asram (status) of a sanyasi (ascetic). Chaitanya, though a very young Boy, consoled His parents, saying that He would serve them with a view to please God. Just after that, His father left this world. His mother was exceedingly sorry, and Mahaprabhu, with His usually contented appearance, consoled his widowed mother.

It was at the age of 14 or 15 that Mahaprabhu was married to Lakshmi Devi, the daughter of Ballabha Acharya, also of Nadia. He was at this age considered one of the best scholars of Nadia, the renowned seat of *Nyaya* philosophy and Sanskrit learning. Not to speak of the *smarta* pandits, the *naiyaiks* were all afraid of confronting Him in literary discussions. Being a married man, He went to Eastern Bengal on the banks of the Padma for acquirement of wealth. There He displayed His learning and obtained a good sum of money.

It was at this time that He preached Vaishnavism at intervals. After teaching him the principles of Vaishnavism, He ordered Tapan Misra to go and live in Benares. During His residence in East Bengal, His wife Lakshmi Devi left this world from the effects of snake-bite. On returning home, He found His mother in a mourning state. He consoled her with a lecture on the uncertainty of human affairs. It was at His mother's request that He married Vishnupriya, the daughter of Raj pandit Sanatan Misra. His comrades joined Him on His return from *pravas*, or sojourn.

He was now so renowned that He was considered to be the best pandit in Nadia. Keshab Misra of Kashmere, who had called himself the Great Digvijayi, came to Nadia with a view to discuss with the pandits of that place. Afraid of the so-called conquering pandit, the *tol* professors of Nadia left their town on pretence of invitation, and Keshab met Mahaprabhu at the Barokonaghat in Mayapur and, after a very short discussion with Him, he got defeated by the Boy and mortification obliged him to decamp. Nimai Pandit was now the most important pandit of His times.

It was at the age of 16 or 17 that He travelled to Gaya with a host of His students, and there took His spiritual initiation from Iswara Puri, a Vaishnava sanyasi and a disciple of the renowned Madhavendra Puri. Upon His return to Nadia, Nimai Pandit turned religious preacher, and His religious nature became so strongly represented that Advaita Prabhu, Srivasa and others, who had before the birth of Chaitanya already accepted the Vaishnava faith, were astonished at the change in the young Man. He was then no more a contending *naiyaika*, a wrangling *smarta* and a criticizing rhetorician. He swooned at the Name of Krishna, and behaved as an inspired man under the influence of His religious sentiment. It has been described by Murari Gupta, an eyewitness, that He showed His heavenly powers in the house of Srivasa Pandit in the presence of hundreds of His followers, who were mostly well-read scholars.

It was at this time that He opened a nocturnal school of kirtan in the compound of Srivasa Pandit with His sincere followers. There He preached, there He sang, there He danced, and there He expressed all sorts of religious feelings. Nityananda Prabhu, who was then a preacher of Vaishnavism, and who had then completed his travels all over India, joined Him by that time. In fact a host of pandit preachers of Vaishnavism, all sincere at heart, came and joined Him from different parts of Bengal. Nadia now became the regular seat of a host of Vaishnava *acharyas*, saintly teachers, whose mission it was to spiritualize Mankind with the highest influence of the Vaishnava, devotional, creed.

The first mandate that He issued to Prabhu Nityananda and Haridas, His close associates, was this: "Go, friends, go through the streets of the town, meet every man at his door and ask him to sing the Name of Hari with a holy life, and you then come and report to Me every evening the result of your preaching." Thus ordered, the two preachers went on and met Jagai and Madhai, the two most abominable characters. They insulted the preachers on hearing Mahaprabhu's mandate, but were soon converted by the influence of bhakti, inculcated by their Lord.

The people of Nadia were now surprised. They said, "Nimai Pandit is not only a gigantic genius, but He is certainly a missionary from God Almighty." From this time to His 23rd year, Mahaprabhu preached His principles not only in Nadia but in all important towns and villages around His city. In the houses of His followers He showed miracles, taught the esoteric principles of bhakti, and sang His samkirtan with other *bhaktas*, or devotees. His followers of the town of Nadia commenced to sing the Holy Name of Hari in the streets and bazaars. This created a sensation and roused different feelings in different quarters. The bhaktas were highly pleased. The *smarta*, caste-conscious Brahmins, became jealous of Nimai Pandit's success, and complained to Chand Kazi against the character of Chaitanya as un-Hindu. The Kazi came to Srivas Pandit's house and broke a mridanga (drum used in samkirtan) there, and declared that unless Nimai Pandit ceased to make noise about His queer religion, he should be obliged to enforce Mohamedanism on Him and His followers.

This was brought to Mahaprabhu's notice. He ordered the town-people to appear in the evening, each with a torch in his hand. This they did, and Nimai marched out with His samkirtan divided into 14 groups, and on His arrival at the Kazi's house, He held a long conversation with the Kazi, and in the end communicated into his heart His Vaishnava influence by touching his body. The Kazi then wept and admitted that he had felt a keen spiritual influence which had cleared up his doubts and produced in him a religious sentiment which gave him the highest ecstasy. The Kazi then joined the samkirtan party. The world was astonished at the spiritual power of the Great Lord, and hundreds and hundreds of heretics converted, joining the banner of Vishwambhar after this affair.

It was after this that some of the jealous and low-minded Brahmins of Kulia picked a quarrel with Mahaprabhu and collected a party to oppose Him. Nimai Pandit was naturally a soft-hearted Person, though strong in His principles. He declared that party feeling and sectarianism were the two great enemies of progress, and as long as He should continue to be an inhabitant of Nadia, belonging to a certain family, His mission would not meet with complete success. He then resolved to be a citizen of the world by cutting off His connection with a particular family, caste and creed; and, with this resolution, He embraced the position of a sanyasi at Kutwa, under the guidance of Keshab Bharati of that town, in the 24th year of His life. His mother and wife wept bitterly for His separation, but our Hero, though soft in heart, was a strong Person in principle. He left His little world in His house for the unlimited spiritual world of Krishna with Man in general.

After His sanyasa, He was induced to visit the house of Advaitaprabhu in Santipur. Advaita managed to invite all His friends and admirers from Nadia and brought Sachi Devi to see her Son. Both pleasure and pain invaded her heart when she saw her Son in the attire of a sanyasi. As a sanyasi Krishna Chaitanya put up nothing but a kaupin and a bahirbas (outer covering). His head was without hair and His hands bore a danda (stick) and a kamandalu (hermit's water pot).

The holy Son fell at the feet of His beloved mother and said, "Mother! this Body is yours and I must obey your orders. Permit Me to go to Vrindaban for My spiritual attainments." The mother, in consultation with Advaita and others, asked her Son to reside in Puri, the town of Lord Jagannath, so that she might obtain His information now and then. Mahaprabhu agreed to that proposition, and in a few days left Santipur for Orissa.

His biographers have described the journey of Krishna Chaitanya (that was the name He got after His sanyasa) from Santipur to Puri in great detail. He travelled along the side of the Bhagirathi as far as Chhatrabhog, situated now in Thana Mathurapur, Diamond Harbour 24 Pergs. There He took a boat and went as far as Pryag Ghat in the Midnapur District. Thence He walked through Balasore and Cuttack to Puri, seeing the temple of Bhubaneswar on His way. Upon His arrival at Puri, He saw Jagannath in the temple, and put up with Sarvabhauma at the request of the latter.

Sarvabhauma was a gigantic pandit of the day. His readings knew no bounds. He was the best *Naiyaik* of the times, and was known as the most erudite scholar in the Vedanta Philosophy of the school of Shankaracharya. He was born in Nadia (Vidyanagar) and taught innumerable pupils in the *Nyaya* Philosophy in his *tol* there. He had left for Puri sometime before the birth of Nimai Pandit. His brother-in-law, Gopinath Misra, introduced our new Sanyasi to Sarvabhauma, who was astonished at His personal beauty, and feared that it would be difficult for the young Man to maintain sanyasdharma during the long run of His life. Gopinath, who had known Mahaprabhu from Nadia, had a great reverence for Him and gave out that the Sanyasi was not a common human being. On this point Gopinath and Sarvabhauma had a hot discussion. Sarvabhauma then requested Mahaprabhu to hear his recitation of the *Vedanta Sutras*, to which the latter tacitly submitted.

Chaitanya heard with silence what the great Sarvabhauma uttered with gravity, for seven days, at the end of which the latter said, "Krishna Chaitanya! I think You do not understand the *Vedanta*, as You do not say anything after hearing my recitation and explanations."

The reply of Chaitanya was that He understood the *sutras* very well, but He could not make out what Shankaracharya meant by his commentaries.

Astonished at this, Sarvabhauma said, "How is it that You understand the meanings of the *sutras* and do not understand the commentaries which explain the *sutras*? All well! If You understand the *sutras*, please let me have Your interpretations!"

Mahaprabhu thereupon explained all the *sutras* in His own way, without touching the pantheistic commentary of Shankara. The keen understanding of Sarvabhauma saw the truth, beauty and harmony of arguments in the explanations given by Chaitanya, and obliged him to utter that it was the first time that he had found one who could explain the *Brahma Sutras* in such a simple manner. He admitted also that the commentaries of Shankara never gave such natural explanations of the *Vedanta Sutras* as he had obtained from Mahaprabhu. He then submitted himself as an advocate and follower. In a few days Sarvabhauma turned out as one of the best Vaishnavas of the time. Report ran out, and the whole of Orissa sang the praise of Krishna Chaitanya, and hundreds and hundreds came to Him and became His followers. In the meantime, Mahaprabhu thought of visiting Southern India, and He started with one Krishnadas Brahmin for the journey.

His biographers have given us a detail of the journey. He first went to Kurmakshetra, where He did a miracle by curing a leper named Vasudev. He met Ramananda Rai, the governor of Vidyanagar on the banks of the Godavari, and had a philosophical conversation with him on the subject of *Prembhakti*, loving devotion. He worked another miracle by touching (making them immediately disappear) the seven Tal trees, through which Ramchandra, the son of Dasarath, had shot His arrow and killed the great Bali Raj. He preached Vaishnavism and nam-samkirtan, chanting of the Holy Names of God, throughout the journey. At Rangakshetra He stayed for four months in the house of one Venkata Bhatta in order to spend the rainy season. There He converted the whole family of Venkata from Ramanuji Vaishnavism into Krishna bhakta, along with the son of Venkata, a boy of ten years named Gopal, who afterwards came to Vrindaban and became one of the six Gosvamins or Prophets serving under their leader Sri Krishna Chaitanya. Trained up in Sanskrit by his uncle Probodhananda Saraswati, Gopal wrote several books on Vaishnavism.

Chaitanya visited numerous places in Southern India as far as Cape Comorin and returned to Puri in two years by Panderpur on the Bhima. In this latter place He spiritualized one Tukaram, who became from that time a religious preacher himself. This fact has been admitted in his *abhangas*, which have been collected in a volume by Mr. Satyendra Nath Tagore of the Bombay Civil Service. During His journey He had discussions with the Buddhists, the Jains and the *Mayavadis* in several places, and converted His opponents to Vaishnavism, the worship of God as a Person.

Upon His return to Puri, Raja Prataprudra Dev and several pandit Brahmins joined the banners of Chaitanya Mahaprabhu. He was now twenty-seven years of age. In His 28th year He went to Bengal as far as Gaud in Maldah. There He picked up two great personages named Rupa and Sanatan. Though descended from the lines of the Karnatic Brahmins, these two brothers turned out demi-Moslems by their continual contact with Hossain Shah, the then-Emperor of Gaud. Their names had been changed by the Emperor into Dabirkhash and Saker Mallik, and their master loved them heartily as they were both learned in Persian, Arabic and Sanskrit, and were loyal servants of the state. The two gentlemen had found no way to come back as regular Hindus, and had written to Mahaprabhu while He was at Puri, for spiritual help. Mahaprabhu had written in reply that He would come to them and extricate them out of their spiritual difficulties. Now that He had come to Gaud both the brothers appeared before Him with their longstanding prayer. Mahaprabhu ordered them to go to Vrindaban and meet Him there.

Chaitanya returned to Puri through Santipur, where He again met His dear mother. After a short stay at Puri He left for Vrindaban. This time He was accompanied by one Balabhadra Bhattacharya. He visited Vrindaban and came down to Prayag (Allahabad), converting a large number of Mohamedans to Vaishnavism by argument from the *Koran*. The descendants of those converts are still known as Pathan Vaishnavas. Rupa Goswami met Him at Allahabad, and Chaitanya trained him up in spirituality in ten days, and directed him to go to Vrindaban on missions. His first mission was to write theological works explaining scientifically pure *bhakti* and *prema*, devotional service, and love of Godhead. The second mission was to revive the places where Krishna Chandra had in the end of Dvapara Yuga, the previous Age, exhibited His *lila*, or Pastimes, for the benefit of the religious world. Rupa Goswami left Allahabad for Vrindaban, and Mahaprabhu came down to Benares. There He put up in the house of Chandrasekhar, and accepted His daily *bhiksha* (meal) in the house of Tapan Misra. Here it was that Sanatan Goswami joined Him, and took instruction for two months in spiritual matters.

The biographers, especially Krishnadas Kaviraj, have given us details of Chaitanya's teachings to Rupa and Sanatan. Krishnadas was not a contemporary writer, but he gathered his information from the Goswamins themselves, the direct disciples of Mahaprabhu. Jiva Goswami, who was the nephew of Sanatan and Rupa, and who has left us his invaluable work the *Sad-sandarbha* has philosophized on the precepts of his great leader. We have gathered and summarized the precepts of Chaitanya from the books of those great writers.

While at Benares, Chaitanya had an interview with the learned sanyasis of that town in the house of a Marhatta Brahmin, who had invited all the sanyasis for an entertainment. At this interview, Chaitanya showed a miracle which attracted all the sanyasis to Him. Then ensued reciprocal conversation. The sanyasis were headed by their most learned leader Prakasananda Saraswati. After a short controversy, they submitted to Mahaprabhu, and admitted that they had been misled by the commentaries of Shankaracharya. It was impossible even for learned scholars to oppose Chaitanya for a long time, as there was some spell in Him which touched their hearts and made them weep for their spiritual improvement. The sanyasis of Benares soon fell at the Feet of Chaitanya and asked for His grace (*kripa*). Chaitanya then preached pure bhakti, and instilled into their hearts spiritual love for Krishna which obliged them to give up sectarian feelings. The whole of Benares, on this wonderful conversion of the sanyasis, turned Vaishnava, and they made a master samkirtan with their new Lord.

After sending Sanatan to Vrindaban, Mahaprabhu went to Puri again by the jungles, with His comrade Balabhadra. Balabhadra reported that Mahaprabhu had shown a good many miracles on His way to Puri, such as making tigers and elephants dance, on hearing the name of Krishna.

From this time, that is, from His 31st year, Mahaprabhu continually lived in Puri in the house of Kasi Misra, until His disappearance in His forty-eighth year at the time of samkirtan in the temple of Tota Gopinath. During these 18 years, His life was one of settled love and piety. He was surrounded by numerous followers, all of whom were of the highest order of the Vaishnavas, and distinguished from the common people by their purest character and learning, firm religious principles and spiritual love of Radha Krishna.

Svarup-Damodar, who had been known by the name of Purushottamacharya while Mahaprabhu was in Nadia, joined Him from Benares and accepted His service as His secretary. No production of any poet or philosopher could be laid before Mahaprabhu unless Svarup had passed it as pure and useful. Rai Ramananda was his second mate. Both he and Svarup sang while Mahaprabhu expressed His sentiment on a certain point of worship. Paramananda Puri was His minister in matters of religion. There are hundreds of anecdotes described by His biographers which we do not think it meet here to reproduce. Mahaprabhu slept short. His sentiments carried him farther and farther in the firmament of spirituality every day and night, and all His admirers and followers watched Him throughout. He worshipped, communicated with his missionaries at Vrindaban, and conversed with those religious men who newly came to visit Him. He sang and danced, took no care of Himself and oft-times lost Himself in religious beatitude. All who came to Him believed Him as the All-beautiful God appearing in the netherworld for the benefit of Mankind. He loved His mother all along, and sent her Mahaprasad, spiritual foods, now and then with those who went to Nadia. He was most amiable in nature. Humility was personified in Him. His sweet appearance gave cheer to all who came in contact with Him. He appointed Prabhu Nityananda as the missionary in charge of Bengal. He despatched six disciples, the Goswamis, to Vrindaban to preach love in the upcountry. He punished all of His disciples who deviated from a holy life. This He markedly did in the case of junior Haridas. He never lacked in giving proper instructions in life to those who solicited them. This will be seen in His teachings to Raghunath Das Goswami. His treatment of Haridas (senior) shows how He loved spiritual men, and how He defied caste distinction in the cause of spiritual brotherhood.

Lord Chaitanya's Mission

Lord Chaitanya Mahaprabhu instructed His disciples to write books on the Science of Krishna, a task which those who follow Him have continued to carry out down to the present day. The elaborations and expositions on the philosophy taught by Lord Chaitanya are in fact the most voluminous, exacting and consistent—due to the unbreakable system of disciplic succession—of any religious culture in the world. Yet Lord Chaitanya, in His youth widely renowned as a scholar, Himself left us only eight verses, called *Sikshastak*, in which His mission and precepts are revealed. Here, rendered by A.C. Bhaktivedanta Swami, are these eight supremely valuable prayers:

I.

Glory to the Sri Krishna Samkirtan which cleanses the heart of all the dust accumulated for years together. Thus the fire of conditional life, of repeated birth and death, is extinguished. This Samkirtan movement is the prime benediction for humanity at large because it spreads the rays of the benediction Moon. It is the life of all transcendental knowledge, it increases the ocean of transcendental bliss, and it helps to have a taste of the full nectar for which we are always anxious.

2.

O my Lord! Your Holy Name alone can render all benediction upon the living beings, and therefore You have hundreds and millions of Names, like Krishna, Govinda, etc. In these transcendental Names You have invested all Your transcendental energies, and there is no hard and fast rule for chanting these Holy Names. O my Lord! You have so kindly made approach to You easy by Your Holy Names, but, unfortunate as I am, I have no attraction for Them.

3.

One can chant the Holy Name of the Lord in a humble state of mind, thinking himself lower than the straw in the street, more tolerant than the tree, devoid of all sense of false prestige, and ready to offer all respects to others. In such a state of mind one can chant the Holy Name of the Lord constantly.

4.

O almighty Lord! I have no desire to accumulate wealth, nor I have any desire to enjoy beautiful women; neither do I want any number of followers of mine. What I want only is that I may have Your causeless devotional service in my life—birth after birth.

5.

O Son of Maharaj Nanda, I am Your eternal servitor, and although I am so, somehow or other I have fallen in the ocean of birth and death. Please, therefore, pick me up from this ocean of death, and fix me as one of the atoms of Your Lotus Feet.

6.

O my Lord! when shall my eyes be decorated with tears of love, flowing constantly while I chant Your Holy Name? When will my words be choked up when uttering the Holy Name? And when will all the holes of hair on my body have eruptions by the recitation of Your Name?

7.

O Govinda! Feeling Your separation I am considering a moment twelve years or more, and tears are flowing from my eyes like torrents of rain. I am feeling all vacant in the world, in the absence of You.

8.

I do not know anyone except Krishna as my Lord, and He shall always remain as such, even if He handles me roughly by His embrace; or He may make me broken-hearted by not being present before me. He is completely free to do anything and everything, but He is always my worshipful Lord, unconditionally.

INTRODUCTION

Delivered as five morning lectures on the **Chaitanya Charitamrita;** *the authoritative biography of Lord Chaitanya Mahaprabhu, written by Krishna Das Kaviraj; before the International Society for Krishna Consciousness, New York City, April 10–14, 1967.*

Chaitanya means the living force. You and I can move, but a table cannot because it has no living force. Not only movement, but resistance is also a sign of living force. *Chaitanya* means activities, *Amrita* means immortal, and *Charitra* means character. There is no activity without living force. The material condition has living force but is not *Amrita,* immortal. *Chaitanya Charitamrita,* then, means the Character of the Living Force in Immortality.

But how is this displayed? It is not displayed by you or I—none of us are immortal in these bodies. We have living force and activities, and we are immortal by nature and constitution. But the material condition into which we have been put doesn't allow these qualities to be displayed. It is stated in the *Katha Upanishad* that eternality and living force are characteristic of both ourselves and God. But God and ourselves, although both immortal, are different. The living entities have many activities, but have a tendency to fall down. God has no such tendency. He is All-powerful. He never comes under the control of material Nature, because material Nature is only a display of His energy.

There is a nice example of this: When I was flying from San Francisco, the plane was above the cloud ocean. Above the cloud was the sun; and though we came down through the cloud and everything in New York was dim, still, above the cloud, the sun was shining. A cloud cannot cover the whole world—it can't even cover the whole United States, which is not more than a speck in the universe. From the sky the skyscrapers are very tiny, just as from God's position all this nonsense becomes insignificant. I, the living entity, am very insignificant, and my tendency is to come down; but God hasn't got this tendency. The Supreme Lord doesn't come down to Maya, and more than the sun comes under the cloud. But we have the tendency to be controlled by Maya. *Mayavadis*, impersonalist philosophers, say that because we are under the control of Maya in this world, when God comes, He is also put under the control of Maya. This is the fallacy of their philosophy.

Lord Chaitanya therefore is not one of us. He is Krishna Himself, the Supreme Living Entity. He doesn't come under the cloud of Maya. Krishna and His expansions, or even His higher devotees, are never in the clutches of Maya. Lord Chaitanya came to preach *Krishna Bhakti*: Lord Krishna Himself is teaching us how to approach Krishna; just as the teacher, seeing a student not doing well, takes the pencil and says, "Do it like this, write like this: A, B, C." But we must not mistakenly think that the teacher is learning the ABC's. Teaching us how to become Krishna conscious is Lord Chaitanya's position, and we must study Him in that light.

In *Bhagavad Gita* the Lord says, "Give up all this nonsense and surrender to Me." And we say "Oh—surrender? Give up? But I have so many responsibilities." And Maya says to us, "Don't do it, or you'll be out of my clutches. Stay in my clutches, and I'll kick you." It's true; you are being kicked by Maya. Do you know how Maya kicks? The she-ass kicks the male-ass in the face when he comes for sex. Among the cats, they fight and whine. These are the teachings of Nature. She tricks. It is like the capture of an elephant. He is caught in the forest by the use of a trained she-elephant, who leads him and makes him fall into a pit. Maya has many activities, and her shackle is the female. Of course, male and female means this outer dress—we are all actually Krishna's servants. But we are shackled by iron chains which are beautiful women. Every male is bound up by sex life; and therefore sex life should be controlled. Unrestricted sex life puts you fully in the clutches of Maya. Lord Chaitanya got away from this Maya at the age of twenty-four—His wife was sixteen and his mother seventy, and He was the only male of the family; He was a Brahmin, and not rich—but He took *Sannyasa*, the renounced order, and didn't care for the Maya of wife and mother.

If you want to become fully Krishna conscious, you have to give up the shackles of Maya. Or, if you remain with Maya, you should live in such a way that there is no illusion. Lord Chaitanya had many house-holders among His closest devotees. Yet one renounced devotee of His, Junior Haridas, who was important for being a good *Kirtan* singer, glanced lustfully at a young woman, and he was at once rejected by Lord Chaitanya: "You are living with Me in the renounced order, and yet looking at a woman with lust." This Junior Haridas later committed suicide in despair over his separation from Chaitanya. Other devotees had approached Chaitanya and asked Him to forgive Junior Haridas, but Chaitanya replied, "You all go live with him and forgive him. I'll stay alone." And when the news of Junior Haridas' suicide reached Him, Lord Chaitanya, Who was aware of everything that was happening, said, "Very good, that is very good." A householder devotee of His pleased Chaitanya, and Chaitanya, on learning of the devotee's wife being pregnant, asked that the baby be given a certain auspicious name. So He approved of householders, having sex in a regulated way; but He was strict—like a thunderbolt—with those of the renounced order who cheated by the method known as "drinking water underwater while taking a bath on a fast day."

From *Chaitanya Charitamrita* we learn how Chaitanya has taught people to become immortal. Krishna and all reformers also taught this to people; They are mortified that people should prolong their mortal life, instead of arranging it so as to make the next life immortal.

So *Chaitanya Charitamrita* means the Immortal Character of the Living Force. The Supreme Living Force is the Supreme Personality of Godhead. There are innumerable living entities, all individual. This is very easy to understand: We are all different, in thought, in desires—and the Supreme Lord is also an individual Person, like you and me. But He is the Leader. No one can excel Him. Among us, one can excel another in one capacity or another. Similarly, the Lord is individual, but He is Supreme. *Achyuta* is another name for Krishna—The Infallible. In the *Bhagavad Gita*, Arjuna had a delusion, but Krishna had none. God is infalliable. In the *Gita* He states:

"I appear in My own internal potency." He is not overpowered by the material potency when He is in the material world; Krishna and the incarnations are not under its control—They are free. In *Srimad Bhagwatam* this is the definition of godly nature—one is not affected although in material Nature. Even a devotee can attain this freedom. Rupa Goswami explains that, if you want to remain unattached to material contamination, the formula is to make your ambition to serve Krishna. How to serve? It is not done by simply meditating, which is just an activity of the mind, but by practical work. It is achieved by working for Krishna. No resource should be left unused; whatever is there, whatever you have, should be used for Krishna by practical work. We can use everything: airplanes, the atom bomb, anything. If you speak to an audience of Krishna Consciousness, that is also service. If your mind, senses, speech, money, and energy are engaged, then you are not in material Nature. Krishna and His expansions and His devotees are not in material Nature, but foolish persons think that They are.

Chaitanya Charitamrita means that the spirit soul is immortal, and that activities in the Spiritual World are also immortal. The *Mayavadis*, those who hold to the view that the Absolute is impersonal and formless, say that a realized soul has no more need to talk. The *Vaishnava* says, "No, talking begins at that stage. Our previous talk was nonsense and had no value; now let us begin real talk: talks of Krishna."

The *Mayavadis* use the example of the water pot: when the pot is not filled with water, it makes a sound; but when the pot is filled it makes no sound. But am I a water pot? Can I be compared to a water pot? Logically, an analogy points out similarities, and the greatest number of similarities between the two objects makes the best analogy. A water pot is not an active living force. A pot can't move. So ever-silent meditation is inadequate. Why? *Because we have so much to say about Krishna that we don't have time to finish when there are only twenty-four hours in a day.* The fool, however, is celebrated as long as he doesn't speak. When he breaks his silence his lack of knowledge is exposed. *Chaitanya Charitamrita* shows that there are so many things to discover, simply for glorifying the Supreme.

Krishna Das Kaviraj Goswami writes: "I offer my respects to my Spiritual Masters." He uses the plural to express the disciplic succession. Not that *my* Spiritual Master only is offered obeisances, but the whole *Parampara*, the chain of disciplic succession. The *Guru* is addressed in the plural to show the highest respect. After offering respect to the disciplic succession, it is offered to devotees, other Godbrothers, the Spiritual Master, expansions of Godhead, and His first manifestation of energy. Krishna Chaitanya appears in all together: God, Guru, devotee, expansion. As His associate Nityananda, He is a manifestation; as Adwaita, He is an incarnation; as Gadadhar, He is the internal potency; and as Srivas, He is the marginal living entity. Krishna is not thought of alone, but is conceived all at once, as is described by Ramanujacharya: In Suddha Adwaita philosophy energy, expansion, and incarnation are *Oneness in diversity*. Everything together is God.

Chaitanya Charitamrita is thus the post-graduate study of spiritual knowledge. One advances from the *Bhagavad Gita*, through *Srimad Bhagwatam*, to *Chaitanya Charitamrita*. Although all are on the same Absolute level, yet by comparative study, *Chaitanya Charitamrita* is on this higher platform, and every verse is perfectly composed. The process of offering obeisances is to directly offer respects to Chaitanya and Nityananda—these two Personalities are compared to the Sun and the Moon, who dissipate darkness. Both the Sun and the Moon have risen together in this case: Chaitanya is so kind that to dissipate the darkness They both appear together.

Who is Krishna Chaitanya? In the *Upanishads*, the Supreme Absolute Truth is described in an impersonal way, but the Personal view is also given in the *Isha Upanishad*, at the end, after a description of the All-pervading: "My dear Lord, You are hidden by the Cover of *Brahmajyoti*. Let me penetrate that *Brahmajyoti* to approach the Supreme Personality of Godhead." Those who have no such power stop at the effulgence; but at the end of the *Upanishad* there is a hymn to the *Personality* of Godhead. The impersonal *Brahman* is described there. That *Brahman* is the glaring effulgence of the body of Chaitanya. The *Paramatma* is the partial representation of Chaitanya. He is that Supreme Personality of Godhead, full with six opulences: wealth, fame, strength, beauty, knowledge, and renunciation. You should know that He is Krishna, and nothing is equal to, or greater than, Him. There is no superior conception. He is the Supreme Person.

There is a nice verse by Rupa Goswami, who, as a confidential devotee, was taught for more than ten days continuously by Lord Chaitanya. He has written about Lord Chaitanya: "There were many incarnations of Krishna, but He excels all others. He is giving something that was never given by an incarnation before, not even by Krishna Himself."

Chaitanya begins from the surrendering point, and He is completely spiritual. He begins at the end of material existence, when one gives up all material attachment. In the *Bhagavad Gita*, Krishna began by distinguishing the soul from matter, and ended at the point of the soul surrendered in devotion. But there is no stoppage of talk there, as the *Mayavadis* would have it. The real talk only begins. As is stated in the *Vedanta Sutra*, "Now talking begins. Now we can inquire into the Supreme Absolute Truth." Rupa Goswami writes: "Your incarnation is greater than all. What You have given! It is the highest form of devotional service."

One who accepts the existence of God is in devotional service. To acknowledge, "God is great" is something—but not much. Chaitanya preached like an *Acharya*, a great teacher, up to the point of friendship. In the *Gita*, Krishna showed Arjuna His Universal Form because he was a dear friend; but Arjuna asked forgiveness for this friendship on seeing Krishna as the Lord of the Universes. Through Lord Chaitanya you can become a friend of Krishna, where there is no limit. You can become a friend, not in adoration, but in complete freedom. You can also be related to God as His father. This is *Srimad Bhagwatam* philosophy. There is no other literature in the world where God is treated as the devotee's son. Usually He is the Father Who supplies the demands of the son. Chaitanya is the first to treat God as a son. How? *By service.* The son demands, and the father supplies. You don't take the supply, you give. Krishna's mother, Yasoda, said to the Lord: "Here—eat or You'll die. Eat nicely." Krishna will depend on your mercy. This is such a uniquely high level of friendship. And you can believe that you are His father.

And, above all, you can treat Krishna as your Lover, as if He's so much attached to you that He expresses His inability to reciprocate. "I cannot repay your love. I have no more assets to return." Krishna was thus so obliged to the Gopis, that He felt His inability to return their love. Devotional service is such an excellent platform—and this was given by Chaitanya. It was never given by any previous incarnation or Acharya.

"Devotional service itself is the highest platform—the glorious platform which You have contributed. You are Krishna, yellowish, *Sachinandan*, son of Sachi. *Chaitanya Charitamrita* hearers may keep You in their hearts. Then it will be easy to understand Krishna through Chaitanya." Chaitanya came to deliver Krishna. Rupa Goswami writes: "You are the most charitable Personality. You are delivering Krishna *Prema*, unalloyed love for Krishna. And so I offer You my respects."

We have heard the phrase, "Love of Godhead." How far this love of Godhead can actually be developed we can learn from the *Vaishnava* philosophy. Simply theoretical knowledge of love of God you can find in many places and many Scriptures; but what that love of Godhead actually is, and how it is developed—that can be found in the *Vaishnava* literature. It is the unique and the highest development of love of God that is given by Chaitanya Mahaprabhu.

Now we have a little sense of love. Why? It is due to love of Godhead. Anything which we find within our experience, even in this conditional life, is situated in the Supreme Lord, Who is the ultimate Source of Everything. In our original relationship with the Supreme Lord there is real love. That love is reflected through material conditions, but reflected pervertedly, and not exactly. Real love means that which is continuous, and without a break, but because that love is reflected pervertedly in this material world, love lacks continuity and is inebriating. If we want real, transcendental love, then we have to transfer our love to the Supreme Lovable Object—Krishna the Supreme Personality of Godhead. This is the whole basic principle of Krishna Consciousness.

In material consciousness we are trying to love that which is not at all lovable. We are giving our love to dogs, to cats—with the risk that if we love cats and dogs too much, at the time of our death we may be fixed in thinking of them, and therefore take our next birth in a family of cats or dogs. Everything without love of Krishna leads downward. In the Hindu Scripture, the chastity of woman is very much recommended. Why? Because if a woman becomes much addicted in love of her husband, at the time of death she will remember him, and in the next life she is promoted to a man's body. Man's life is better than woman's, because a man has better facility for understanding spiritual science.

But Krishna Consciousness is so nice that it makes no distinction between man and woman. In the *Bhagavad Gita* you will find: "If somebody, even if he is born in a low family, even a woman or a *Sudra* or a *Vaishya*—anyone who takes shelter of Me is sure to achieve My association." That is guaranteed. And Krishna says that if these people can achieve the highest perfection of life, then why not the real *Brahmins*, devotees, and saintly kings? They are sure to achieve the highest perfection.

Chaitanya Mahaprabhu gave us information: First of all you must know that in every country or every Scripture there is some hint of love of Godhead, but nobody knows what love of Godhead actually is. That is the distinction between other Scriptures and the Vedic Scriptures. The others have some idea of love of God—but regarding *how* to love Godhead, and *what* is Godhead, they have no idea. They promote official love of Godhead. But here Chaitanya Mahaprabhu gives a practical demonstration of how to love God in a conjugal relationship. Chaitanya Mahaprabhu takes the part of Radharani and tries to love Krishna as Radharani loved Him. Krishna could not understand, "How does Radharani give Me such pleasure?" So in order to study Radharani, Krishna lived Her role and tried to understand Himself. This is the secret of Lord Chaitanya's incarnation. That is explained in the next verse.

This verse says, "I offer my respectful obeisances unto the Supreme Lord, Who is absorbed in the modes of Radharani's thought." He is Krishna, but He has taken the mode of Radharani to show how to love Krishna. And what is Radha Krishna? Radha Krishna is the exchange of love. And what is that love? This is not ordinary love. Krishna has immense potencies, of which three are principal: internal, external, and marginal potency. In the internal potency there are three divisions: *Sambit, Alahadini* and *Sandhini*.

The Alahadini potency is the pleasure potency. We must always know that we also have this pleasure-seeking potency. We are all trying to have pleasure; this is the nature of the living entity. We are now trying to enjoy our pleasure potency in this material condition, with this body, by bodily contact. But do you think that Krishna, Who is always Spiritual, will also seek pleasure on this material plane? What nonsense this is! Krishna describes this place as non-permanent and full of miseries. Do you think Krishna is going to seek pleasure in this material form? How is it possible? He is the Supersoul, He is the Supreme Spirit; how can He seek pleasure in matter?

Therefore, to learn how Krishna's pleasure can be obtained, you have to study the first Nine Cantos of *Srimad Bhagwatam*. In the Tenth Canto, Krishna's pleasure potency is displayed as He plays with Radharani, and as He plays with the damsels of Vraja. Unfortunately, people of less intelligence turn at once to the pleasure potency sports of Krishna in the *Dasama Skanda*, the Tenth Canto. These pictures of Krishna embracing Radharani, or of the *Rasa* Dance, are unfortunately not understood by ordinary men, because they do not understand Krishna. They will falsely understand that Krishna is like us, and just as we want to embrace a young girl, so He embraces the Gopis. These people write books because they think that this is a kind of religion where we can indulge in sex and become religionists. This is called *Prakrita Sahajia*—materialistic lust.

One should understand what Radha Krishna is. Radha and Krishna display the pleasure potency of the internal energy of Krishna. That pleasure potency of Krishna's internal energy is a most difficult subject matter, unless one understands what Krishna is. Krishna cannot see any pleasure in this material world. But He has got that pleasure potency. Because we are part and parcel of Krishna, therefore that pleasure potency is within us also. But we are trying to exhibit that pleasure potency in matter, while Krishna does not. The object of His pleasure potency is Radharani. That means Krishna exhibits His potency or His energy as Radharani, and then exchanges loving affairs with Her. Krishna cannot take pleasure in this external energy. This is very difficult to understand—but just try: Krishna exhibits His internal energy, His pleasure potency, as Radharani. That means that Krishna manifests Himself. As He has so many extensions, so many expansions, so many incarnations; so Radharani is the manifestation of His internal pleasure potency.

Radharani is also Krishna. There is no difference between the energy and the energetic. Without energy there is no meaning to energetic, and without the energetic there is no meaning to energy. Similarly, without Radha there is no meaning to Krishna, and without Krishna there is no meaning to Radha. Therefore the *Vaishnava* philosophy first of all worships the internal pleasure potency of the Supreme Lord. It is always said, "Radha Krishna." Although the author is going to explain the intricacies of this pleasure potency, he first of all utters the name of Radha. Similarly, those who worship the Name of Narayan first of all utter the name of Lakshmi; those who are worshippers of Lord Rama first of all utter the name of Sita. Sita Rama, Radha Krishna, Lakshmi Narayan—the potency always first.

Radha and Krishna are One. When Krishna desires to enjoy pleasure He manifests Himself. The spiritual exchange of love affair is the display of the internal potency or pleasure potency of Krishna. We say "when" Krishna desires, although just when He did desire, we cannot say. But we speak in this way because in conditional life we take it that everything has some beginning. In the Absolute, or spiritual life, there is no beginning; there is no end. But in order to understand that Radha and Krishna are One, and that They become divided, that question "When?" automatically comes to be asked. When Krishna desired to enjoy His pleasure potency, He manifested Himself in the separate Form of Radharani. Again, when Krishna wanted to understand Himself through the agency of Radha, They became united—and that unification is called Lord Chaitanya.

Why has Krishna assumed that Form? That will be explained. "What is the glory of Radha's love?" Krishna asks. "Why is She so much in love with Me? What is the special qualification in Me that Radharani is attracted to, and what is Radharani's process of loving Me?" He is the Supreme—why should He be attracted by anyone's love? He is full in Himself. We search after the love of a woman because we are imperfect. The love of woman, that potency, that pleasure, is absent in me, and therefore I want a woman. But Krishna is surprised: "Why am I attracted by Radharani? And what is the special significance in Me that Radharani is so much attached to? Now, when Radharani feels My love, what is Her feeling?" In order to taste the flavor or the quality, the essence of that loving affair, Krishna appeared as the Moon appears in the sea. Just as the Moon was produced by the churning of the sea, so by churning the spiritual love affairs, the Moon appeared as Chaitanya Mahaprabhu, whose complexion was just like the Moon. This is figurative language, but it is the purport of why Chaitanya Mahaprabhu has appeared. The full significance will be explained in later chapters.

The author of *Chaitanya Charitamrita* is describing the manifestation of the Supreme. After offering His respects to Lord Chaitanya, he next offers them to Nityananda. Who is Nityananda? He now explains. First of all, Nityananda is manifested as Samkarshan. Samkarshan is the origin of Maha Vishnu, a form of God. This first manifestation of Krishna is Valara n, and then Samkarshan; from Samkarshan to Pradyumna: in this way the expansion takes place. It works in the same way as one candle is the origin, and another candle is lit from that original and from that another and another—this is explained in *Brahma Samhita*: The Supreme Lord Govinda is the Original Candle, and from that Original Candle many thousands of candles, one after another, are expanded, and they are called Vishnu. Just as one candle after another makes a very nice exhibition of light, similarly, Krishna has expanded Himself into so many lights, and we are also lights. We are smaller lights, while Vishnu is the bigger light. But they are all Krishna, all expansions.

That Vishnu, when there is a need of material creation, expands Himself as Maha Vishnu, Who lies down on the Causal Ocean. From His nostrils all the Universes are breathed out. From that Causal Ocean all the Universes have sprung up, and this Universe also is floating in that Causal Ocean. Outside is water. You have seen the picture of Vamanadev when He expanded His leg up to the covering of the sky of this Universe. There was a hole there, and through that hole Karana water leaked in; and a little drop is flowing as the river Ganges. Therefore the Ganges is accepted as the most sacred water of Vishnu, and is worshipped by all Hindus, from the Himalayas down to the Bay of Bengal. The Maha Vishnu, lying on the Causal Ocean, is a plenary expansion of Rama. This Rama, when we say *HARE KRISHNA, HARE RAMA*—this Rama means the Samkarshan, Nityananda.

The author of *Chaitanya Charitamrita* describes what is "beyond this material expansion." The cosmic material expansion is called Maya because it has no eternal existence. It is sometimes manifested and sometimes not manifested. Therefore it is called Maya. Krishna Das now says, "beyond this manifestation." In the *Bhagavad Gita* Eighth Chapter, it is explained that there is another Nature which is eternal, and which is beyond *Bakta* and *Abakta*. *Bakta* means manifested, and *Abakta* means unmanifested. This material world has a manifested aspect and a potential state, which is called non-manifested. Beyond both the potential non-manifested stage and the manifested stage there is another, spiritual Nature. We can understand this superior Nature as the living force. That is described in the *Bhagavad Gita*. The living force is manifest in this body: this body is of the inferior Nature, matter. The superior Nature is the spirit that is moving the world. The symptom of that superior Nature is consciousness. Similarly, beyond this material Nature there is another, superior, Nature which is conscious. There everything is conscious. We cannot imagine that. Here the objects are not conscious. But in the Spiritual World the table is conscious, the land is conscious, the tree is conscious—everything is conscious.

Now, you cannot imagine how far this material manifestation is extended. You have no measurement. Everything is calculated by imagination or by some imperfect method. But here we are getting information of what lies beyond this. Those who believe in experimental knowledge may inquire how it is possible: We cannot calculate how far this Universe is extended, and we cannot reach even the nearest planet; so how is it that we can obtain information beyond this material Nature? That which is beyond your conceivable power is called *Achintya*, inconceivable. What is inconceivable, don't argue about. It is useless. How can you? It is inconceivable.

That which is inconceivable to your limited energy, limited sense perception—how can you reach that plane by argumentative logic? Don't argue. Then, how is it known? Accept it. The *Bhagavad Gita* says: "It has to be understood by the disciplic succession." Just as Brahma, the original creature, was given lessons by Krishna, Brahma imparted those lessons to his disciple Narada, and Narada imparted that knowledge to his disciple, Vyasdeva. Vyasdeva imparted that knowledge to his disciple, Madhvacharya; Madhvacharya on down to Madhavendra Puri, who imparted the same lesson to Ishwara Puri. And Ishwara Puri imparted the same lesson to Chaitanya Mahaprabhu.

People may ask that, if Chaitanya Mahaprabhu is Krishna Himself, then why did He need a Spiritual Master? Of course, He did not need any Spiritual Master, but just because He was playing *Acharya* (teaching how to behave in spiritual life), He accepted a Spiritual Master. Even Krishna accepted a

Spiritual Master. That is the system. If you want to know that which is inconceivable, you must accept the disciplic succession. Because the knowledge is coming down from the Supreme, down, down, down—it is perfect. Suppose a hundred generations before, there was something confidential that your forefather told his son, which has finally been passed down to you. Although you are not in touch with the direct personality, yet because it is coming through disciplic succession, the same truth is expressed.

How was Brahma informed of this sort of knowledge? That is also stated in the *Srimad Bhagwatam:* The original learned scholar is Brahma; and Krishna, the Supreme Absolute Truth, the Personality of Godhead, impressed transcendental knowledge into the heart of Brahma. *By the heart.* So two processes of knowledge exist: One process depends upon the Supreme Personality of Godhead as the Supersoul seated within you. He informs you. And *He also expands Himself as the Spiritual Master.* The Guru also informs you.

So in both ways, from within and from without, the information is transmitted. We simply have to receive it. If we receive knowledge in this way, it doesn't matter that it is inconceivable. In the *Bhagwatam*, you will find much information about the *Vaikuntha* planetary systems, which are beyond the material Universe. Just as with *Chaitanya Charitamrita*, the knowledge is there, and you simply have to take it. But you have to receive it by the *Parampara* system. You cannot approach the Truth, which is inconceivable to your experimental knowledge. It is not possible. We want to know everything by experimental knowledge. That is foolishness. It is not possible. According to the Vedic way, sound is evidence. Sound is very important in Vedic understanding. Sound is evidence, if the sound is pure. In the material world, also, you understand things thousands of miles away simply by sound vibration. As soon as you call by telephone or radio, there is sound. In San Francisco, 3000 miles away, as soon as you receive the sound—"Mr. Such-and-Such speaking"—you understand. The evidence is sound. Where is the informant, is he standing there before you? No—but as soon as you hear the sound you know. Sound is the most authoritative evidence. These things are received by sound vibration.

We have the information that beyond this cosmic manifestation there are the very extensive *Vaikunthas*. This material manifestation is only one-fourth of the manifestation. There is not only this Universe, but there are innumerable Universes. Just as there are innumerable planets within this Universe, so this is only one Cosmos; there are innumerable Universes, and, all combined together they are one-fourth of the manifestation of the Creation. The other three-fourths of the manifestation is *Vaikuntha Loka*, the Spiritual World. In that Vaikuntha Loka every Narayan has His four expansions: Samkarshan, Pradyumna, Aniruddha and Vasudeva. (That Samkarshan is Nityananda.) These Universes surround the body of the Supreme; and Vishnu is Master of this material Nature.

As the husband and wife combine together to create, so Maya is the wife and the Supreme Maha Vishnu is her Husband. This is also confirmed in the *Bhagavad Gita*: "This expansive material Nature is My wife, and all the living entities are born of Me." How is Vishnu contacting Maya? That contact is also described in the *Bhagavad Gita*: Simply by a glance: "He glanced over the material Nature and it became impregnated." This is Spiritual. *We* must impregnate by a particular part of our body, but the Supreme Lord, Krishna or Vishnu, can impregnate any part by any part. Simply by glancing He can cause conception. The reason *why* is found in the *Brahma Samhita*: the spiritual body of the Supreme Lord is so powerful that any part can perform the duty of any other part. We can only touch with the hand, but Krishna can touch you by glancing. We can only see with the eyes, we cannot touch or smell with our eyes; but Krishna can smell and can also eat with His eyes.

When we offer *Prasadam*, foodstuffs, to Krishna, we don't see that He is eating; but, simply by glancing at the food, He can eat. Simply by seeing. We have the idea, because we have this mouth, that unless we devour the whole thing, we cannot eat. But that *everything is spiritual*—that we cannot imagine. We *see* that we are offering to Krishna, and He is not eating. Is it by our imagination that He is accepting *Prasadam?* No, it is not like that. Actually, He is eating, but His eating is different from our eating. Our eating process will be similar to His when we are completely on the spiritual platform. There, every part of the body can act for the other parts of the body.

You have seen that picture where Brahma is born from the navel of Vishnu, Who is lying down. And Vishnu's energy, Lakshmi, the Goddess of Fortune, is serving Him, sitting by the side of His leg. Vishnu does not require Lakshmi to give birth to Brahma. How then can you expect that there is sex life in the Spiritual World? Sex life here in this material world is required to produce children, but in the Spiritual World you can produce children, as many as you like, without any help from a wife. So there is no sex life there. Vishnu produces Brahma from His navel without the help of His wife. There are many such instances. This is the inconceivable spiritual energy. Because we do not experience spiritual energy, we think these are fictional stories. No. You think that way because you have no conception of spiritual energy: it is so powerful that it can do anything and everything. It has full independence.

From each pore of the body of Maha Vishnu these Universes emanate, seedlike, and then they develop. They are exhaled when He breathes also. Just as when a man is diseased the infection is carried by perspiration, by breathing and by touching: that is a scientific fact. If a man is infected with smallpox bacteria, you can simply touch his perspiration and become infected. This occurs even in this material world. So this is all possible. It is not impossible. It simply requires some intellectual capacity to understand. From Maha Vishnu's Spiritual Body so many Universes emanate. When He exhales they come out, and when He inhales the whole thing is gone. This is the material Universe. Just imagine: the existence of each and every Universe is contained in one breath of Vishnu. That is stated in the *Brahma Samhita*. We have calculated the age of Brahma, but actually you cannot conceivably calculate even one day of Maha Vishnu. 4,200,000,000 years is only twelve hours of Brahma. And the whole life of Brahma is just within the period of one breath of Maha Vishnu. Just consider what is the breathing power of the Supreme Lord. That Maha Vishnu is the plenary partial representation of Krishna.

Next comes the Garbodakshayee Vishnu, from Whom Brahma is born. Within that lotus stem from this Vishnu's navel there are so many Universes. And just as the mother increases the family members, similarly Brahma was first created by Garbodakshayee Vishnu, and Brahma created the whole human society, animal society—everything. Maha Vishnu's plenary expansion is Garbodakshayee Vishnu, and His plenary expansion is Kshirodakshayee Vishnu. In this way, in each and every Universe, there is one Garbodakshayee Vishnu and one Kshirodakshayee Vishnu. That Kshirodakshayee Vishnu lies on the milk ocean, within this Universe, and He is the Controller and the Maintainer of the Universe. Brahma is the Creator, Vishnu is Maintainer, and when it will be required to annihilate the Universe, then Shiva will come and finish everything.

So far, Krishna Das Kaviraj has discussed Lord Chaitanya and Lord Nityananda, and now he describes Adwaita Acharya. In our morning prayers we sing the Names of Lord Chaitanya and His Associates:

Sri Krishna Chaitanya, Prabhu Nityananda, Sri Adwaita, Gadadhar, Srivas adi Gour bhaktavrinda.

They are all expansions of the same One. So Adwaita Acharya is an expansion of Maha Vishnu. You have seen the picture of Maha Vishnu lying on the Causal Ocean and breathing out innumerable universes. That Maha Vishnu is incarnated as Adwaita. This Adwaita Acharya is the incarnation of that Maha Vishnu, Who creates this material world through the agency of the material energy. Therefore Adwaita Acharya is also the Lord, or an expansion of the Lord. Why is He called Adwaita? *Adwaita* means nondual. His name is such because He is non-different from the Supreme Lord. And He is called Acharya, teacher, because He disseminated Krishna Consciousness. In this He is just like Chaitanya Mahaprabhu—although He is Sri Krishna Himself, He appeared as a devotee to teach how to love Krishna. So Adwaita Acharya appeared just to distribute the knowledge of Krishna Consciousness. He is also the incarnation of a devotee.

Krishna is manifested in five different expansions, and Himself and all of His other Associates appear as devotees of the Supreme Lord. Some of them are like Adwaita Acharya—He is an incarnation of Maha Vishnu. And one is known as Bhakta Nityananda Prabhu, Who also appeared as a devotee. So Chaitanya Mahaprabhu is the Source of energy for all devotees. If we take shelter of Chaitanya Mahaprabhu for Krishna Consciousness, it becomes very easy. There is a very nice song: "My dear Lord Chaitanya, please have mercy upon me, because there is no one who is such a merciful Lord as You are. You have descended to deliver all fallen souls, but You will not find a more fallen soul than me; therefore, my claim to be delivered is most urgent. Because Your mission is to deliver the fallen souls, and nobody is more fallen than me, I have my priority."

Now the author begins his obeisances to Krishna. The author, Krishna Das, was an inhabitant of Vrindaban. Some incidents from his life will be described in the Fifth Chapter of the *Chaitanya Charitamrita*. He was a great devotee. He had been living in Katwa, a small subdivisional city in the district of Bardwan in Bengal, with his family who also worshipped Radha Krishna, when there was some misunderstanding—not on family matters, but about devotional service. In the midst of this misunderstanding, Nityananda Prabhu advised him in a dream to leave his home and go to Vrindaban. Although he was very old, he started out that very night, and came to live at Vrindaban. He met some of the Goswamis there. His tomb remains in the temple where I live in Vrindaban. This is Krishna Das Kaviraj Goswami, the author of *Chaitanya Charitamrita*. This *Chaitanya Charitamrita* was requested by the devotees of Vrindaban. He began at a very old age, but by the grace of Lord Chaitanya he finished this nice, most authoritative book on Chaitanya's philosophy and life: *The Character and Activities of the Eternal Living Force*.

Because he lived in Vrindaban, there are three temples that are very important: One temple is Madanmohan, another is Govinda, and the third is Gopinath. These temples are the ones visited by all pilgrims. About 300 or 400 years after the construction of these temples, with the development of Vrindaban city, many other temples were built, but when Krishna Das Goswami was living, there were not so many. The only principle temples were these three—Madanmohan, Govinda, and Gopinath. Because he was a resident of Vrindaban, he must offer his respects to the deities. And his first offering is respect. He considers himself as a layman and very slow to make progress. He asks God's favor: "My progress in spiritual life is very slow, so I am asking Your help."

He is offering his obeisances first to Vigraha. Vigraha, according to devotional service, is the deity Who can help us in dovetailing ourselves with Krishna Consciousness. Our first business is to know Krishna, and to know our relationship with Krishna. To know Krishna is to know oneself, and to know oneself means to know one's relationship with Krishna. What is our relationship with Krishna? That is learned by worshipping Madanmohan Vigraha. Therefore, Krishna Das Goswami first establishes his relationship with Madanmohan Vigraha. When one is established in relationship with Krishna, then he begins his function. The functional deity is Govinda.

He offers his obeisances to Govinda, Who resides in Vrindaban. Vrindaban is the place where there are desire trees. Actually, in the Spiritual World of Vrindaban, it is explained, that the land is of touchstone and the trees are desire trees. *Desire tree* means whatever you want you can have. And the Lord is herding spiritual cows, known as *Surabhi* cows. And He is worshipped by hundreds and thousands of Gopis, who are all Goddesses of Fortune. When Krishna descends, this same Vrindaban descends. Just as when a Governor or a President goes to someplace, all his entourage and paraphernalia, secretary, military—everything goes there with him. Similarly, when Krishna comes, His land also comes. Therefore Vrindaban is considered to be not in the material world. And therefore devotees take shelter in Vrindaban. Vrindaban in India is considered the replica of the original Vrindaban; and so one should accept the trees of Vrindaban as being the same *Kalpa briksha*, desire trees. Now, one may say of the Vrindaban trees, "Oh, we can ask anything?" But first of all you should become a devotee. You simply cannot go and test them to see whether these trees are desire trees. Actually, when the Goswamis were there, the *Kalpa briksha* was there. The Goswamis were each under one tree for one night, and all their wants were satisfied. So how could they live that way unless the trees were so nice as desire trees? For the common man it seems very wonderful that the Goswamis could simply live underneath one tree one night, and the next tree another night, and have everything they needed. But it is all possible. As we make progress in our devotional service, we can realize this.

There is another devotee, an Acharya, who describes Vrindaban: "When my mind becomes cleansed of all dirty hankering for material enjoyment, then I shall be able to see Vrindaban!" So Vrindaban is actually experienced by persons who have finished with material enjoyment. Everything is spiritual. This becomes revealed. We cannot challenge it. As you become more Krishna conscious, as you become more advanced, everything is revealed to you.

Actually, Vrindaban is as good as the Spiritual Vrindaban, and therefore Krishna Das Kaviraj Goswami says that underneath one of the desire trees of Vrindaban there is a nice throne decorated with valuable jewels on which Radharani and Krishna are seated. And His dear friends and the Gopis are all serving Them: somebody is singing, and somebody is dancing, somebody is offering betel nuts and refreshment, somebody is decorating with flowers. In this way there are 108 Gopis who are the constant companions of Sri Radha and Krishna. That scene is described in *Chaitanya Charitamrita*.

In India it is still a fashion of recreation to sit on a swinging throne, and, if it is moving, it is very refreshing. In each and every home they have a hanging throne, and when a man comes home from the office, if it is practical, it is moved for some time and he becomes refreshed. So, similarly, the same system prevails, especially in the month of *Sravam*, July, when there is the function called *Julun*. During *Julun*, in all the houses—not only of Vrindaban but all over India—the people hang thrones. In every house and village they place Krishna and Radha and decorate them with flowers and move the throne and offer dancing and *Kirtan*. If you like you can introduce that system here. *Julun* goes on for one month, the temples are decorated and thousands of visitors come as spectators. Generally, people go to Vrindaban at that time. Krishna and Radha are seated on the throne, surrounded by His friends.

"I offer my respects to Radha and Krishna," Krishna Das says. This Radha and Krishna deity shows us *how to serve Radha and Krishna*. Madanmohan is simply to establish that "I am Your eternal servant." Now, in Govinda, there is actually acceptance of service. Therefore it is the functional deity.

The next deity is Gopinath. The author offers blessings here to the audience in the Name of Gopinath, the Master or Proprietor of the Gopis, Who attracted all the Gopis by the sound of His flute, because He wanted to dance with them. In the Tenth Canto of *Srimad Bhagwatam* this is described: Some of the Gopis are sleeping somewhere with their husbands, some are taking milk, some are caring for their children—they were all busy young girls. But as soon as they heard Krishna's flute, they at once left their places.

All these Gopis were childhood friends. In India the girls are married by the age of twelve years, and the boys are married at not less than eighteen years. Krishna was not married at that time as He was a Boy fifteen or sixteen years old. So, He called these girlfriends from their homes, although they were married, and they used to come and dance together. That is called the *Rasa* Dance. Hearing the transcendental sound of the flute, as soon as He would sound the vibration, all the Gopis would come and join Him at a particular place, which was called *Bonsibat*. If you go to Vrindaban you will find that *Bonsibat* still exists. It is a very sanctified place, and pilgrims go there and offer their respects. Believe it or not, it is said that there are the same trees that were there at the time of Krishna. That is not so astonishing, however, because I saw some redwood trees in Muir Forest in San Francisco which were said to be 7000 years old. So it is not impossible.

Krishna advented 5000 years ago, and if some of the trees are still standing, it is not unprecedented, because here also there are very old trees. The particular tree under which Krishna used to call the Gopis to come and dance the *Rasa* Dance at night with Him—that tree is still there. That is described in *Chaitanya Charitamrita*.

"May that Gopinath, the Master of the Gopis, Krishna, bless you. May you become blessed by Gopinath." Gopinath is called for blessing because He used to attract the Gopis. As He attracted the Gopis by the sweet sound of His flute, so the author desires that He may also attract your mind by that transcendental vibration.

TEACHINGS OF LORD CHAITANYA

PART I

Rupa Goswami and His Younger Brother Anupam (Ballava) Meeting
Lord Chaitanya at Prayag (Allahabad)

CHAPTER ONE

Teachings to Rupa Goswami

Srila Rupa Goswami, the younger brother of Sanatan Goswami, went to Prayag, the modern Allahabad, with his younger brother Ballabha, and when they heard that Lord Sri Chaitanya Mahaprabhu was staying there, both of them became very much pleased. They went to see Lord Chaitanya and saw that the Lord was going to visit the temple of Bindumadhava. While the Lord was going, chanting and dancing, thousands of people were following Him and some of them were crying, some were laughing, some were dancing, and some singing. Some of them were fallen on the ground, offering obeisances to the Lord. And all of them were roaring with the Holy Name of *Krishna, Krishna.* Prayag is situated on the confluence of the Rivers Ganges and Yamuna. And it is said that in spite of its being at the junction of two rivers, it remained without being overflooded until the appearance of Lord Chaitanya, when the city was overflooded by the tide of love of Krishna.

The two brothers, Rupa Goswami and Ballabha, saw the great crowd and the wonderful scene, staying aloof in an uncrowded place. The Lord was

21

dancing, raising His two hands, and roaring with the words, *Hari Bol! Hari Bol!* All the people assembled there were astonished, struck with wonder at the Lord's activity, and it is very difficult to describe the actual situation. The Lord was acquainted with one Deccanist Brahmin, and the Lord came back to the Brahmin's house to accept prasadam. While Lord Chaitanya was sitting at the house of this Deccanist Brahmin, the two brothers, Rupa Goswami and Ballabha, arrived there. From a distant place they fell down on the ground to offer obeisances, and were chanting many Sanskrit verses from Scriptures. The Lord saw Rupa Goswami in front of Him, thus offering obeisances. He was very much pleased, and asked him: "My dear Rupa, please get up." The Lord informed Rupa Goswami about the causeless mercy of Krishna on him, because Krishna had delivered him from the materialistic way of life which is based simply on pound-shilling-pence.

The Lord accepted the two brothers as His own devotees, and cited one verse from the Scriptures which states that a Brahmin who has studied the four Vedas may not be His devotee, but a pure devotee coming from a very low family may be accepted by Him. The Lord then embraced the two brothers, and by His causeless mercy He touched His Lotus Feet on their heads. When they were so blessed both the brothers came to offer their prayers to the Lord in their own words. The prayers said that Lord Sri Krishna Chaitanya Mahaprabhu, Who is Krishna Himself, has assumed the Form of fair complexion, *Gouranga*, and is the most munificent Incarnation of Krishna, because He is distributing love of Krishna. Srila Rupa Goswami also quoted one verse which was later on found in the book, *Govinda Lilamrita*. The verse says as follows: "Let me be surrendered unto the Lotus Feet of Sri Krishna Chaitanya Mahaprabhu, Who is the greatest, most merciful Personality of Godhead, and Who delivers those merged in ignorance, and offers them the highest gift of love of Krishna, and thus makes them mad after Krishna Consciousness."

After this incident the Lord was invited by Ballabha Bhatta to the other side of the Ganges, and He went there. But wherever He used to go, Rupa Goswami would follow Him, and was staying with Him. The Lord felt inconvenience in crowded places, and therefore He asked Rupa Goswami to accompany Him to the bank of the Ganges known as Dasaswamedhaghat. And for ten days He instructed Rupa Goswami about the Truth of Krishna, the principles of devotional service, and the transcendental mellows. All was described in full detail, so that in future he could distribute the science of Krishna in his book, *Bhakti Rasamrita Sindhu*. Srila Rupa Goswami has described this incident in the first verse of *Bhakti Rasamrita Sindhu* which speaks about the causeless mercy of the Lord upon him. The Supreme Personality of Godhead is cognizant, All-Powerful, and, by His causeless mercy, He empowers a living entity to receive His mercy. People in general, being under the spell of conditional life, are averse to devotional service and Krishna Consciousness. They are unaware of the principles of Krishna Consciousness: namely, one's eternal relationship with the Supreme Personality of Godhead; the ultimate goal of life, which is to return back to Home, back to Godhead; and the process of returning to the spiritual world. These things are unknown to the conditioned soul. Lord Chaitanya, out of His causeless mercy, instructed Rupa Goswami on the principles of devotional service, and later on Rupa Goswami distributed to the people in general the science of devotional service.

Srila Rupa Goswami has described Lord Chaitanya in the Prologue to *Bhakti Rasamrita Sindhu* as follows: "I am offering my respectful obeisances unto the Lotus Feet of the Personality of Godhead, known as Lord Chaitanyadeva because, inspired by Him, I am feeling it within my heart to write something about devotional service. Therefore, I am engaged in writing this great book on the science of devotion, known as Bhakti Rasamrita Sindhu."

Lord Sri Chaitanya Mahaprabhu instructed Rupa Goswami continually for ten days, and He began His teaching as follows: "My Dear Rupa, the science of devotional service is just like a great ocean, and it is not possible to show you all the length and breadth of the great ocean. But I shall simply try to explain about the nature of the ocean by just taking a drop out of it; and you can thus taste it and understand what is that ocean of devotional service."

Within this *Brahmanda*, or Universe, there are innumerable living entities, and according to their own fruitive activities they are transmigrating from one species of life to another, and from one planet to another. In this way their encagement in material existence is being continued since time immemorial. The living entities are atomic parts and parcels of the Supreme Spirit. There is, however, a measurement for the length and breadth of the atomic spiritual spark. It is said in the *Srimad Bhagwatam*, Tenth Canto, Eighty-seventh Chapter, 36th verse, that if you divide the tip of a hair into 100 parts, and again if you divide one part of that into another 100 parts, such 1/10,000th part of the tip of a hair is the length and breadth of the individual soul. This is also confirmed in the Vedas, in the *Svetasvataro Upanishad*.

This atomic magnitude of the individual living entity is again described in the *Srimad Bhagwatam*, Eleventh Canto, Sixteenth Chapter, 11th verse, as follows: (This is a speech given by one of the four Kumaras, known as Sananda, on the occasion of performing a great sacrifice;) He said, O Supreme Truth! if the living entities were not infinitesimal living sparks of the Supreme Spirit, then each minute spark would have been all-pervading, and there would be no necessity of its being controlled by superior power. But if the constitution of the living entity is accepted as being the minute part and parcel of the Supreme Lord, then automatically he becomes a controlled living entity under supreme energy or power. This is his constitutional position. Therefore, if he remains as he is created in that natural position, he can attain full freedom. As such, if somebody by mistake calculates that his constitutional position is equal to the constitutional position of the Supreme Personality of Godhead, then he becomes contaminated by the doctrine of non-duality and his efforts in transcendental life are without any effect.

The Lord continues His teaching, saying that there are two kinds of living entities: one is called eternally liberated, and the other is called eternally conditioned. Out of the eternally conditioned living entities, again they are divided into two classes, namely, the moving and the non-moving entities. Those who cannot move, who, like trees, for example, are standing in one place, are called non-moving entities. And those who are moving, such as birds and beasts, are called *Jangam*, or moving entities. These moving entities are also divided into three: there are the *tiryak*, or the birds: some of them can fly in the sky, and swim on the water, as well as walk on the land. Besides this *tiryak*, there are aquatics; and there are animals and human beings, who are moving on the land. Out of the many millions and trillions of living entities on the land, the species of human beings are very few. Out of that small quantity of human beings there are many who are actually without any advancement in spiritual science, and are without cleanliness in their habits, without any faith in the existence of the Supreme Personality of Godhead, and are simply like animals. They may be deducted from the human society or from the civilized society of human beings.

We shall hardly find a few human beings who believe in the Scriptures or in the existence of God, or in good behavior for the human being. Such believers are known as *Aryans*, or those who believe in advancing in spiritual life. Out of such persons believing in the Scriptures and in the advancement of human civilization, there are two classes of men, who are known as the right-eous and the unrighteous. Of those who are righteous, most execute fruitive activities. That means they prefer to perform righteous activities in order to derive some good result from them for sense gratification. Out of many,

many such persons who are engaged in good righteous activities for sense gratification some of them come to know about the Absolute Truth, and they are called *Jnanins*, meaning persons who are seeking after the Absolute Truth, or philosophers—empiric philosophers. Out of many hundreds and thousands of such empiric philosophers some actually become liberated. This liberation means that theoretically one can understand that a living entity is not made of any of the material elements; that he is spirit soul, different from matter. Simply by understanding this doctrine, even theoretically, one may be called *mukta*, or liberated; but actually a *mukta*, or liberated soul, is he who understands his constitutional position as part and parcel eternal servitor of the Lord. Such liberated souls, if they are engaged with faith and devotion in the service of the Lord, are called *Krishna-bhaktas*, or Krishna conscious persons.

These Krishna conscious persons are free from all material desires. Those who are liberated theoretically simply know that the living entity is not made of any material element. Although they may be classified amongst the liberated souls, they have desire. They have the desire to become one with the Supreme Personality of Godhead. Such persons are very much attached to the ritual performance of the Vedic injunctions, and to righteous activities, in order to enjoy material welfare. And even when some of them are out of material enjoyment, they want enjoyment in the spiritual world, to merge into the existence of the Supreme Lord. And some of them are also desirous of getting the perfection of mystic powers, known as the Yoga principles. So long as all these desires are within the heart of a person, he cannot understand the nature of pure devotional service, and on account of being agitated by such desires, he is not peaceful. So long as there is any desire for material perfection, he cannot be at peace. The devotees of Lord Krishna are not desirous of material achievement, and as such they are the only peaceful persons within this material world. This is confirmed in the *Srimad Bhagwatam*, Sixth Canto, Fourteenth Chapter, 4th verse: It is said there as follows: "O great sage, out of many millions of liberated persons, and persons who have achieved success in mystic Yoga powers, one who is completely devoted to the Supreme Personality of Godhead and is therefore very peaceful is very rarely to be found."

The Lord continued to explain that in this way many thousands and millions of living entities are wandering within this material world, and some of them, by the grace of Lord Krishna and the Spiritual Master, can get the seed of devotional service. The pious or religious man is generally inclined to worship the deities in various temples and if by chance he offers obeisances and worshipful respects to Lord Vishnu, even without his knowledge, and he receives the favor of a Vaishnava, a devotee of the Lord, at that time he accumulates some asset in the matter of approaching the Supreme Personality of Godhead. This is very plainly understood from the *Srimad Bhagwatam* in the matter of the life of the great sage Narada. Narada got the chance of serving the Vaishnavas in his previous life, and thus he was favored by the devotees of the Lord, with the result that he became a great sage, as he is known— Narada Muni.

The Vaishnavas or devotees are generally very compassionate toward the conditioned souls, and even being uninvited by any conditioned soul, a devotee goes from door to door to enlighten people from the darkness of nescience, and to inject in them knowledge in various ways about their constitutional position of being engaged in devotional service, or Krishna Consciousness. Such persons are devotees empowered by the Lord, and they are especially empowered to distribute devotional consciousness, or Krishna Consciousness, to the people in general. They are known as authorized Spiritual Masters. It is just by the mercy of such an authorized Spiritual Master that a conditioned soul gets the seed of devotional service. The causeless mercy of the Supreme Personality of Godhead is first appreciated when one is in touch with a bona fide Spiritual Master who can enlighten the conditioned soul to the highest position of devotional life. Therefore, Lord Chaitanya said that by the mercy of the Spiritual Master, one can achieve the causeless mercy of the Lord; and by the mercy of the Supreme Personality of Godhead, one can get the mercy of the bona fide Spiritual Master.

By such mercy from the Spiritual Master and Krishna one receives the seed of devotional service, and one has to sow the seed in the field of his heart just as a gardener sows the seed of a valuable tree. After sowing the seed one has to pour water in the form of chanting and hearing the Holy Name of the Supreme Lord, or by taking part in the discussion of the science of devotional service in the society of pure devotees. When the plant of devotional service sprouts up from the seed of devotion, it begins to grow freely, and when it is full grown it then surpasses the length and breadth of this Universe and enters into the transcendental position of the spiritual world, where everything is effulgent in the *Brahmajyoti*, and the plant penetrates even the Brahmajyoti, and then gradually enters into the planet known as *Goloka Vrindaban*, and there the plant takes shelter at the Lotus Feet of Krishna. That is the ultimate goal of devotional service. After attaining such a position, the plant produces fruit which is known as the fruit of love of Godhead. The devotee or the transcendental gardener has, however, to pour water on the plant daily, in regulation, by the process of chanting and hearing. Without chanting and hearing, or without pouring water on the root of the plant, there is every chance of the plant becoming dried up.

The Lord continued to say that there is another source of danger while pouring water on the root of the plant. When the plant of devotional service grows, some animal may come and eat the whole thing or destroy the plant, just like an ordinary plant is also destroyed by the animal. And when the green leaves of the plant are taken away by some animal, the plant generally dries up. So one has to take precaution about the plant of devotional service not being disturbed by other animals. An animal is used to refer to offenses unto the pure devotee of the Lord, which is called *Vaishnava Aparadh*. This offense unto the pure devotee is compared to a mad elephant: As a mad elephant, if it enters into the garden, causes tremendous loss to the plants and trees, so in the devotional discharge, if there is any offense unto the feet of the pure devotee, it creates havoc in the matter of advancing in devotional service. Therefore, one has to defend the plant by fencing it properly; one has to take care, while discharging devotional service, not to commit any offense to the pure devotees. If one is cautious in the matter of not committing offenses unto the pure devotees, then the plant of devotional service is properly protected.

Offenses are of ten kinds, and they are also known as offenses unto the Holy Name: The first offense is to blaspheme great devotees who have tried to spread the Glories of the Holy Name all over the world. If one is unnecessarily envious of a devotee who is trying to spread the Holy Name all over the world, in execution of the order of his Spiritual Master, such a rascal is the greatest offender at the Feet of the Holy Name. The Holy Name of Krishna is non-different from Krishna, and Lord Krishna cannot tolerate such offenses as to decry a pure devotee who is spreading His Holy Name all over the world. The second offense is to deny that Lord Vishnu is the Absolute Truth; There is no difference between His Name, Quality, Form, Pastimes, and Activities; but one who sees a difference in these different functions of the Supreme Lord is also an offender. In the same way, the Lord being supreme, nobody is equal to or greater than the Supreme Lord. Therefore, if anybody thinks that the Lord or His Name are equal to the personality of some demigod, he is also an offender. Such a conception of equality between the Supreme Lord and the demigods is not very congenial to the performance of devotional service.

The third offense is to consider the bona fide Spiritual Master as one of the common men. The fourth offense is to blaspheme Vedic literature and the corollaries of Vedic literature, the Puranas. The fifth offense is to consider the Glories of the Holy Name as an exaggeration. The sixth offense is to imagine a perverted meaning of the Holy Name. The seventh offense is to commit sinful activities on the strength of chanting the Holy Name. It is understood that by chanting the Holy Name one gets freed from sinful reactions, but that does not mean that one should perversely act sinfully on the strength of his chanting the Holy Name of the Lord. That is the greatest offense. The eighth offense is to consider that religious ritualistic performances, austerity or renunciation or the performance of sacrifices are on an equal level with chanting the Holy Name. Chanting of the Holy Name is as good as the Supreme Personality of Godhead, and other pious activities may be a means to approach the Supreme Personality of Godhead, but when they are employed for some material achievement they are called offensive. The ninth offense is that the Glories of the Holy Name of God may not be preached to a faithless person, and to speak about the Glories of the Holy Name unto such persons is also another offense. The tenth and last offense is to maintain material attachment even after hearing and chanting the Holy Name of God. The idea is that by chanting the Holy Name without any offense, one may be elevated to the liberated condition. And the liberated condition means that one gets freedom from all kinds of material attachment: so if it is found that a chanter of the Holy Name still has material attachment, then that is called an offense.

When the plant of devotional service is growing, there is still another chance of disturbance. Along with the growth of the plant of devotional service there are other plants also growing. They are material desires. When one is advanced in devotional service, it is natural that many persons will come to the devotee for becoming his disciples, and will offer him some material gains. So if a person becomes attracted by the increased number of disciples and the material conveniences offered by the disciples, and forgets his duty as a bona fide Spiritual Master, that is another disturbance in the growth of the plant of devotional service. It may be that, by taking advantage of material convenience, one becomes addicted to enjoy the material comforts of life.

Another disadvantage is to desire liberation. Another disadvantage is to be neglectful of the restrictions or prohibitions. The prohibitions are mentioned in the authorized Scriptures: one should not indulge in the association of woman or illicit sex life, one should not indulge in intoxication, one should not eat anything other than Krishna *prasadam* (food offered to Krishna), and one should not take part in gambling. These are the restrictions for devotional service, and if one does not follow these principles strictly then there may be a severe disturbance in the discharge of devotional service.

Another disturbing element is to aspire after material name and fame by discharging devotional service. If one is not particularly careful, then by the process of watering the plant of devotional service, other unnecessary plants, as described above, may grow, and that may hamper the progress of devotional service. The idea is that, by the watering process, these unnecessary plants grow very luxuriantly and the gardener does not see the impediments offered to the main plant of devotional service. It is the duty of the neophyte devotee to cut out all the unnecessary plants grown by the watering process. In other words, if one is careful against the growth of unnecessary plants, then the main plant grows luxuriantly and reaches the ultimate goal, the planet known as Goloka Vrindaban. To reach the ultimate goal, the Goloka Vrindaban planet, is the real result of devotional service, the real fruit grown of the plant of devotional service. When the living entity engaged in such devotional service relishes that fruit of love of Godhead, then he forgets all other ritualistic activities, religiousness for improvements in economic conditions, satisfaction of the senses, and the desire to become one with the Supreme Lord by merging into His effulgence.

There are many phases of spiritual knowledge and transcendental bliss, such as performance of the ritualistic sacrifices recommended in the Vedas, the execution of austerities and pious duties, and the practice of mystic Yoga. They have their different respective results to be enjoyed by the performer, but all these results may appear to be very glittering only so long as one is not elevated to the transcendental loving service of the Lord. There is a nice comparison in this connection: that a person bitten by a serpent remains unconscious so long as there is no smelling of the particular type of medicine recommended. As soon as the bitten person smells that particular type of medicine, however, he at once becomes conscious, and no longer can he remain unconscious by the poisonous effects.

Love of Godhead can be awakened from the dormant position by executing pure devotional service. And what is that devotional service? What are its symptoms? These were all described by Lord Chaitanya to Rupa Goswami:

In the matter of pure devotional service, there cannot be any other desire than to become advanced in Krishna Consciousness. In Krishna Consciousness there is no scope for worshipping any demigods, or any other Form of Krishna, or to indulge in speculative empiric philosophy, or to be engaged in fruitive activities. One should be freed from all these contaminations. One should accept only favorable things for keeping the body and soul together, not for increasing the demands of the body. Only the bare necessities of the body should be accepted, and putting the bodily necessities second, one should primarily cultivate Krishna Consciousness by chanting the Holy Name of God. Pure devotional service means to engage all the senses that we have in the service of the Lord. At the present moment our senses are all designated because the body is designated. So we think that this body belongs to a particular society or a particular country or a particular family: that is the designative understanding of the body; and similarly the senses belong to the body, and if the senses act under such a designative concept of life, family-wise, society-wise, or nation-wise, then one cannot cultivate Krishna Consciousness. The senses must be purified. One should purely understand that he belongs to Krishna, his life belongs to Krishna, his identity is eternal servitorship to Krishna—and in this way if one engages his senses in the service of the Lord, that is called pure devotional service.

A pure devotee accepts transcendental loving service to the Supreme Personality of Godhead, but does not accept any kinds of liberation for his personal sense gratification. It is stated in the *Srimad Bhagwatam*, Third Canto, Twenty-ninth Chapter, verses 10-12, as follows: Lord Kapiladeva explains in those verses about the pure nature of devotional service: that as soon as a pure devotee hears the Glories and transcendental Qualities of the Supreme Personality of Godhead, Who is seated in everyone's heart, at once his mind flows towards the Lord, as the water of the Ganges flows down towards the sea. Such spontaneous attraction of the devotee's mind to the service of the Supreme Personality of Godhead is the significance of pure devotional service. Devotional service, engagement in the service of the Supreme Personality of Godhead without any cause, and without being hampered by any material impediment, is called pure devotion. The pure devotee does not desire to live in the same planet with the Personality of Godhead, he does not desire the same opulence as the Supreme Personality of Godhead, and he does not desire to have the same form as the Supreme Personality of Godhead. He does not desire to live along with Him side by side, neither does he desire at any time to merge into the existence of the Supreme Person, even if these things are offered by God to the devotee. The thing is that a devotee is so much absorbed in the transcendental loving service of the Lord that he has no time to think of any other benefit beyond his engagement. Just as an ordinary materialistic businessman, when he is absorbed in his business, does not think of any other thing, so a pure devotee, when he is engaged in the pure devotional service of the Lord, does not think of anything beyond that engagement.

By these symptoms alone one can be understood to be elevated to the topmost position of devotional service. And it is with such transcendental loving service alone that one can surpass the influence of *Maya*, and can relish pure love of Godhead. So long as one has the desire for material benefit, or for liberation, which are called the two witches of allurement, one cannot relish the taste of transcendental loving service to the Supreme Lord.

There are three stages of devotional service: the first stage is called the beginner's cultivation stage, and the second is called the realization of the service, and the third, the supreme stage, is called attainment of love of Godhead. There are nine different methods for cultivating devotional service, such as hearing, chanting, remembering, etc. All these processes are employed in the neophyte stage of cultivation. If one is engaged in the matter of chanting and hearing with devotion and faith, then gradually his material misgivings become vanquished. Gradually his faith in devotional service increases more and more, and such stages assure him a higher perfectional position. Thus, one becomes firmly fixed, increases the taste for it, becomes attached to it, and feels an ecstasy which is called the preliminary stage of love of Godhead. Attainment of ecstasy is produced by execution of the cultivation of devotional service. Such attainment, when still more developed by that same process of hearing and chanting, gradually becomes thickened, and it assumes the name of love of Godhead.

In the stage of transcendental love of God, there are further developments, which are known as transcendental affection, emotion, ecstasy, and extreme, intense attachment. These are technically known as *raga, anuraga, bhava, mahabhava*. These are technical terms. The process is exemplified by the gradual thickness of sugarcandy juice. Sugarcandy juice in the first stage is liquid; and when by evaporation it becomes thicker and thicker, it becomes molasses, then granules, then sugar, then rock candy, and so on. These are different stages of the liquid sugar juice, and similarly there are different stages of the development of transcendental love for the Supreme Personality of Godhead.

When one is situated on the transcendental platform, that stage is called steady. Unless one is situated on the transcendental platform, the practice or love of Godhead may not be steady. One may fall down. But when one is situated on the transcendental platform he becomes steady, and there is no fear of falling down. This stage of understanding is technically called *sthaibhava*.

There are still further developments stepping forward from the position of sthaibhava, and these are called *vibhava, anubhava, satwik*, and *byabhibhachary;* and when these four ingredients are added to the steadfast position of pure transcendental life, that is called exchange of *rasa* or transcendental flavor. This exchange of loving reciprocation between the lover and the beloved is generally called *Krishna-bhakti-rasa,* the transcendental taste of exchanging loving sentiments between the devotee and the Supreme Personality of Godhead. But we must know that this development of the transcendental loving exchange of flavors, stands on the steadfast position of *sthaibhava,* as explained before. The basic principle of *vibhava* is *sthaibhava,* and the other activities are auxilliary assistants for the development of transcendental love.

The ecstasy of transcendental love has two components, the context, and the cause of the excitement. The context is also divided into two parts: the subject and the object: The exchange of devotional service is the subject, and Krishna is the Object. And the transcendental Qualities of Krishna are the causes of excitement. That means that a devotee becomes excited to serve the Supreme Personality of Godhead Krishna, being enamoured by the transcendental Qualities of Krishna. The *Mayavadi* philosophers say that the Absolute Truth is without specific qualities, and the Vaishnava philosophers say that being without qualities, (nirguna) means that the Absolute Truth has *no material qualities, but that the spiritual qualities are so great and so enchanting that even liberated persons become attracted by the Supreme Lord.* This fact is very nicely explained in the *atmarama* verse of *Srimad Bhagwatam:* those who are already situated in self-realization are also attracted by the transcendental Qualities of Krishna. That means Krishna's Qualities are not material—they are pure and simple transcendental qualities.

The highest stage of ecstasy can be divided into thirteen transcendental activities, which are as follows: 1. dancing, 2. rolling on the floor, 3. singing, 4. clapping, 5. bristling of the body, 6. thundering, 7. yawning 8. breathing, 9. forgetting social conventions, 10. throwing down saliva, 11. laughing 12. headache, 13. coughing. All these thirteen symptoms do not awake simultaneously or at one time, but they act according to the exchange of transcendental flavor. Sometimes one symptom is prominent and at other times the other symptom is prominent. Transcendental flavor is also divided into five. Principally, the initial stage is called *santa rati,* appreciation of the greatness of the Supreme Personality of Godhead by persons who are liberated from the material contamination, but not exactly engaged in transcendental loving service. They are on the appreciative neutral stage.

The second stage is when a person appreciates that he is everlastingly subordinate to the Supreme Personality of Godhead, and he is everlastingly dependant on the causeless mercy of the Supreme Person. At that time there is an awakening of natural affection, as a grownup son becomes attracted with the father's benediction. At that stage a living entity wants to serve the Supreme Personality of Godhead instead of being engaged in the service of *Maya*, Illusion. This stage is called *dasya rati*.

The next developed stage of transcendental love is called *sakhya rati*. Here one associates with the Supreme on an equal level with love and respect. That stage is further developed in the matter of joking and in exchange of different relaxations, by laughing, and so forth. This is called fraternity with the Personality of Godhead without any bondage. Practically, at that stage one forgets his inferior position as a living entity, although he has the greatest respect for the Supreme Person.

When the transcendental flavor or taste of fraternity is further developed, it is called *vatsalya rati*, filial affection. At that time the living entity tries to be the parent of God. Instead of the Lord being worshipped, the living entity as a parent of the Supreme Person becomes the object of worship for the Supreme Person. Then the Lord depends on the mercy of such pure devotees. This is called *vatsalya rati*. The Lord puts Himself under the control of the devotee for being brought up nicely. Such a devotee attains to the position of embracing the Supreme Personality of Godhead or kissing His Head. These are developments of parental filial affection for the Supreme Lord.

The next developed stage is called *madhurya rati*, or the transcendental exchange of tastes between the lover and the beloved in conjugal love. At this stage of loving affairs the damsels of Braja and Krishna glanced over one another in conjugal love. In that stage of transcendental loving service there is an exchange of glancing and a movement of the eyebrows and an exchange of nice pleasing words and attractive smiling between one another. Besides the five primary reciprocations of flavor there are seven secondary reciprocations, consisting of laughing, wonderful vision, chivalry, pitiableness, anger, ghastliness, and devastation. Bhisma, for example exchanged with Krishna in the transcendental flavor of chivalry. Hiranya Kasipu experienced an exchange of the ghastly and devastating Feature of the Supreme Lord.

The five primary *rasas*, or flavors, constantly remain within the heart of the pure devotee, and the other seven, which are secondary, sometimes appear and disappear, and enrich the existing flavors and tastes. After enriching the primary flavors, they disappear. The example of *Santa Bhaktas* or santa devotees are the nine yogis named Kavi, Havi, Antariksha, Prabuddha, Pippalayana,

Havirhotra, Dravid or Drumil, Chamass, and Karabhajan. The four Kumaras, great sages, are: Sanaka, Sanandan, Sanatkumar and Sanatana. Examples of devotees in the transcendental mode of servitorship are, in the Gokula, Raktak, Chitrik, Patrak; these are all servants of Krishna. In Dwarka there are Daruka, and in the Vaikuntha planets, there is Hanuman, and other persons. Devotees in friendship are like Sridam in Vrindaban, and Bhima and Arjuna in Dwarka or on the Battlefield of Kurukshetra. So far as those in paternal love with Krishna are concerned, the devotees are his mother, father, uncle, and similar relatives. In conjugal love, the devotees are first the damsels of Braja, Vrindaban, and the Queens and Goddesses of Fortune in Dwarka. No one can count how many they are.

Attachment for Krishna is also of two kinds: One kind of attachment is with awe and veneration. There is a lack of freedom in such attachments, which are exhibited in Mathura and the Vaikuntha planets. In such Abodes of the Lord, the flavor of transcendental loving service is restricted. But in the Gokula, Vrindaban, the exchange of loving is freely done, and the cowherd boys and the damsels of Vrindaban, although they know that Krishna is the Supreme Personality of Godhead, do not show awe and veneration on account of their thick and thin relationship in great intimacy with Him. Out of these five principal transcendental tastes, awe and veneration are sometimes impediments to perceiving the Lord's greatness, or in the matter of service to the Lord. But in the matter of friendship and paternal affection, and in conjugal love, such awe and veneration is reduced. For example, when Krishna appeared as the Son of Vasudeva and Devaki they prayed to the Lord with awe and veneration, because they understood that the Supreme Lord Krishna or Vishnu had appeared before them as their little child. This is confirmed in the *Srimad Bhagwatam*, Tenth Canto, Fourty-fourth Chapter, 51st verse: Devaki and Vasudeva, after knowing the Supreme Personality of Godhead, began to pray to Him, although He was present as their Child. Similarly, when Arjuna saw the Universal Form of the Lord, he was also afraid, and he begged pardon because in his dealings with Krishna as an intimate friend, he had engaged in much unceremonious behaviour with Him.

This is stated in the *Bhagavad Gita*, that Arjuna prayed, "My Dear Krishna, I have sometimes insulted You, calling You my dear Friend Krishna, without knowing the greatness of Your inconceivable power. Therefore, please forgive me, because I was mad to address You like a common friend or a common man." Similarly, when Lord Krishna was playing jokes on Rukmini, she thought Krishna might leave her, and therefore she was very much afraid, and became perturbed. At that time Rukmini was fanning Krishna, and as soon as she was afraid that Krishna would leave, the fan fell down from her hand and the hairs on her head became scattered. As a plantain tree falls by a blast of windy air, so she became almost unconscious and fell down. But so far as Yasoda, Krishna's mother in Vrindaban is concerned, it is stated in the *Srimad Bhagwatam*, Tenth Canto, Eighth Chapter, 36th verse, that the Personality of Godhead, Who is worshipped by all the Vedas and Upanishads, and the Samkhya system of philosophy, and all such authorized Scriptures—that Personality of Godhead was accepted as if born in her belly. In the same *Srimad Bhagwatam*, Tenth Canto, Ninth Chapter, 12th verse, it is stated that mother Yasoda bound the Boy Krishna with a rope as if He was the Son born of her body, and appeared just like an ordinary child with a material body. Similarly, the description of Krishna's being treated as an ordinary man is given in the *Srimad Bhagwatam*, Tenth Canto, Eighteenth Chapter, 24th verse: When He was defeated by His friends, the cowherd boys, Krishna carried Sridam on His shoulders.

Similarly, regarding the Gopis' dealings with Sri Krishna at Vrindaban, it is described in the *Srimad Bhagwatam*, Tenth Canto, Thirtieth Chapter, verses 36–38, as follows: When Sri Krishna took away Srimati Radhika alone from the group of the Rasa Dance, at that time Srimati Radhika thought that Krishna had left all the other Gopis. Although they are equally beautiful, He satisfied Her in this way. With pride, She began to say, "My Dear Lord Krishna has left the beautiful Gopis, and He is satisfied with Me alone." She thought like that and felt pride. Addressing Krishna in the forest She said, "My Dear Krishna, I am unable to move anymore. Now if You like You can take Me anywhere as You desire." When Radhika requested Krishna in such a way, Krishna replied, "You'd better come to My shoulder," and as soon as He said this, He disappeared from the scene, on which Srimati Radhika repented very much.

When Krishna disappeared from the scene of the Rasa Dancing, all the Gopis began to repent, saying, "My Dear Krishna! We have come here, leaving aside our husbands, sons, relatives, brothers, and friends! Neglecting their advice we have come to You, and You know better what is the reason for our coming here. You know that we are captivated by the sweet sound of Your flute, and therefore we have come. O, You are so cunning that at this dead of night You have left girls and women like us! It is not very good for You."

The word *sama* means controlling the mind from being diverted in various ways, and fixing it up in the Supreme Personality of Godhead. And one who is so fixed up in the Supreme Personality of Godhead is situated on the *sama* platform. On that platform the devotee understands that Krishna is the basic principle of everything that be within our experience. The same thing is explained in the *Bhagavad Gita*: after many, many births in the cultivation of knowledge, one surrenders unto Vasudeva because he can understand that Krishna is present in everything, that He is distributed all over the cosmic manifestation. Everything is under the control of the Supreme Lord, and everything, being situated in His energy, is different from Krishna in His Personal Form. The same thing is explained in the *Bhakti Rasamrita Sindhu*, in which it is said that when intelligence is fixed on Krishna, that is called the quality of *sama*. This is spoken by the Supreme Personality of Godhead: *Samo mannisthata buddhee:* that without being elevated to the platform of *santa rati*, nobody can be fixed in knowing the greatness of Krishna, the diffusion of His different energies which are the cause of all manifestation. The same thing is further explained in the *Srimad Bhagwatam*, Eleventh Canto, Nineteenth Chapter, 33rd verse: equilibrium of the mind can be achieved by one who has fixed his conclusion on the Supreme Personality of Godhead as the Original Source of everything, and when one can control his senses, that is called *sama*. When one is ready to tolerate all kinds of suffering for controlling the senses and to keep the mind in equilibrium, that is called *titiksha*, or tolerance. And when one can control the urges of the tongue and the genital, that is called *dhriti*. From *dhriti* one becomes *dhira*, the pacified. A pacified person is never disturbed by the urges of the tongue and genital.

If one can fix up his mind in Krishna without any deviation, such a steadfast position in Krishna Consciousness is called *santa rasa*. In *santa rasa* two things are visible—unflinching faith in Krishna, and cessation from all material desires. The specific qualities of *santa rasa*, unflinching faith in Krishna and withdrawal from all kinds of desires which are not in connection with Krishna, are common factors in all the other *rasas* as well. Just like sound vibration is generally present in all other elements, namely air, fire, water, and earth: sound vibration is produced from the sky, so this sound is present in all other elements. Similarly, the qualities of *santa rasa*, unflinching faith in Krishna and desirelessness toward anything which is not Krishna—these two qualities are present in other transcendental relationships, such as *dasya*, servitorship, *sakhya*, fraternity, *vatsalya*, paternal affection, and the *madhurya rasa*, conjugal love.

When we speak of non-Krishna it does not mean that anything exists without Krishna. There cannot be anything non-Krishna because everything is a product of the energy of Krishna. And Krishna and His energies being identical, indirectly, everything is Krishna. As an example: consciousness is common to every living entity, but consciousness when it is purely centered on Krishna, when it is called Krishna Consciousness, is pure. And consciousness when it is other than Krishna Consciousness, or consciousness directed at sense gratification, is called non-Krishna. So in the polluted state the conception of non-Krishna comes. But in the pure state there is nothing but Krishna Consciousness. The active interest in Krishna—that Krishna is mine or I am Krishna's, and therefore my business is to satisfy the senses of Krishna—is a higher status than the *santa rasa*. Simply to understand the greatness of Krishna is to achieve that status of *santa rasa*, in which the worshipable object is the impersonal Brahman or Paramatman. This activity of worship of the impersonal Brahman and the Paramatman is the field of activities in empiric philosophical speculation and mystic Yoga practice. But when one develops still further in Krishna Consciousness or spiritual understanding, one appreciates that that Paramatman, the Supersoul, is the eternal worshipable object, and he surrenders unto Him: *Bohunam Janmanamante:* after many, many births. After many, many births in worship of the Brahman and Paramatman, when one surrenders unto Vasudeva Paramatman as the Supreme Master, and accepts oneself as eternally the servant of Vasudeva, he becomes a great transcendental realized soul. And at that time, on account of thick and thin relationship with the Supreme Absolute Truth, one begins to render some sort of transcendental loving service unto the Supreme Personality of Godhead. And therefore the status of *santa rasa,* neutrality, transforms into servitorship. It is then called *dasya rasa.*

In the *dasya rasa* status, the conception of the Supreme Lord is exhibited in the greatest quantity of awe and veneration. The greatness of the Supreme Lord is appreciated in *dasya rasa* also. It is marked here that in the status of *santa rasa* there is no spiritual activity of service, but in the status of *dasya rasa,* that service begins. Therefore, in the *dasya rasa* two qualities are there: this means the quality of the *santa rasa,* and the consciousness of the transcendental taste of fraternity.

The existence of the transcendental qualities of *santa rasa* and *dasya rasa* is certainly there, but beyond that there is another quality, confidential attachment, which is pure transcendental love. This confidence in the Supreme Personality is technically known as *visrambha.* In that status of *visrambha,* fraternity, there is no sense of awe or veneration toward the Supreme Personality of Godhead. As such, in the transcendental relationship of *sakhya rasa* there are three transcendental qualities: the sense of greatness, the sense of kinship, and the sense of intimacy without any impression of awe or veneration. Therefore, in the relationship of fraternity, one transcendental quality is further increased.

Similarly, in the status of paternal affection there are four qualities: above the three qualities already mentioned there is another sense of the devotee, that the Supreme Lord is dependent on the mercy of the devotee. As parent of the Supreme Personality of Godhead, the devotee also sometimes chastises the Supreme Personality of Godhead, and considers Him as maintained by such devotee. This transcendental sense of being the maintainer of the Supreme Maintainer is very much pleasing both to the devotee and the Supreme Personality of Godhead.

The Lord instructed Srila Rupa Goswami to write the transcendental literature named *Bhakti Rasamrita Sindhu*, the Science of Devotional Service, indicating therein the substance of the five transcendental relationships. It is explained there how the transcendental quality of *santa rasa* in the shape of unflinching faith in Krishna, is further developed to the form of *dasya rasa* with the spirit of service, and then to *sakhya rasa* for undeterred fraternity, and can be still more developed in the transcendental flavor of paternal love, with the sense of maintaining the Lord. All culminates in the highest platform of conjugal love, wherein all the different transcendental relationships exist simultaneously.

CHAPTER TWO

Sanatan Goswami

I offer my respectful obeisances unto Lord Chaitanya Mahaprabhu, by whose mercy even a person in the lowest status of life can find direction in transcendental devotional service to the Lord.

After Lord Chaitanya Mahaprabhu accepted the renounced order of life, *Sannyasa*, He travelled all over India. During this period, He went to Maldaha, a district in Bengal, and in that portion of the land there was a village by the name of Ramkeli. Two government ministers of the Nawab Hussain Shah's regime lived there, namely Dabir Khas and Shakar Mallik, later renamed Sanatan Goswami and Rupa Goswami. They had a chance to meet Lord Chaitanya, and after meeting Him they decided that they would retire from the government service and join His Samkirtan movement. The two brothers at once took steps to leave their material engagements, and appointed two learned *Brahmins* to perform certain Vedic religious rituals in order to achieve complete freedom for the devotional service of Krishna.

These preliminary activities are known as *Purascharya*. The ritual function of this process is that three times a day one has to worship and offer respects to one's forefathers, offer oblation to the fire, and respectfully offer foodstuffs to a learned Brahmin. Five items; the time, the worship, the offering of respect, the offering of oblation into the fire, and the offering of foodstuffs to a Brahmin; comprise *Purascharya*. In the *Hari Bhakti Vilas*, the directional authoritative book, these rituals are mentioned.

After performance of these religious rituals, the younger brother Shakar Mallik (Rupa Goswami), returned to his home with an immense amount of money which he had acquired during his government service. The silver and gold coins he brought back filled a large boat. After arriving home he divided the accumulated wealth first into two, and distributed one part to the Brahmins and Vaishnavas. Thus, for the satisfaction of the Supreme Personality of Godhead, he distributed fifty per cent of his accumulated wealth to persons engaged in the Supreme Lord's transcendental loving service. The Brahmins are meant to understand the Absolute Truth; and thereafter, when one is actually engaged in the loving service of the Lord, he is called a Vaishnava. Both the Brahmins and the Vaishnavas are supposed to be fully engaged in transcendental service, and Rupa Goswami, considering their important transcendental position, gave them fifty per cent of his wealth. The balance was again divided into two: one part he distributed to his relatives or dependent family members, and the other he kept against personal emergency.

This distribution of personal wealth is very instructive for all who desire to be elevated to the advancement of spiritual knowledge. Generally, a person bequeaths all his accumulated wealth to the family members, and then retires from family activities for progress in spiritual knowledge. But here we find the exemplary behavior of Rupa Goswami: he gave fifty per cent of his wealth for spiritual purposes. This should be the example for every one of us. The twenty-five per cent of his accumulated wealth which he kept against personal emergency he deposited with a good business firm, since in those days there were no banks. Another ten thousand coins were deposited for expenditures by his elder brother, Sanatan Goswami.

Rupa Goswami at this time received information that Lord Chaitanya Mahaprabhu was preparing to proceed toward Vrindaban from Jagannath Puri. He sent two messengers to receive actual information of the Lord's itinerary, and he made his own plans to go to Mathura to meet the Lord there. It appears that Rupa Goswami got permission to join Lord Chaitanya, but Sanatan Goswami did not. Therefore, Sanatan Goswami entrusted his respon-

Sanatan Goswami's Resignation from the Government Service
of Nawab Hussin Shah of Bengal (15th century)

sibility in the government service to his immediate assistants, and he remained at home to study *Srimad Bhagwatam*.

He engaged some ten or twenty learned Brahmins, and began an intensive study of *Srimad Bhagwatam* in their company. While he was thus engaged, he submitted sick reports to the Nawab, but the ruler was very anxious for his advice in government matters, and therefore he suddenly appeared one day at Sanatan Goswami's house. The Nawab entered the assembly of Sanatan Goswami and the Brahmins, and out of respect all of them stood up to receive him and they offered him a place to sit. The Nawab said:

"You have submitted sick reports, but I sent my physician to see you, and he reported that you have no illness. I did not know why you were submitting sick reports and not attending to your service, so I have personally come to see you. And I'm much perturbed by your behavior. As you know, I completely depend on you and your responsible work in governing. I was therefore free to act in other matters because I was depending on you, but if you do not join me, your past devotion will be spoiled. Now, what is your intention? Please tell me."

On hearing this, Sanatan Goswami replied that he was unable to work anymore and it would be very kind of the Nawab if he appointed somebody else to execute the work that was entrusted to him. The Nawab became very angry at this and said, "Your elder brother lives like a hunter, and if you also retire from the administration then everything will be finished." It is said that the Nawab used to treat Sanatan Goswami as a younger brother. The Nawab was engaged in conquering different parts of the country, and he was also engaged in hunting, and therefore he depended more or less on Sanatan Goswami for administration; and so he pleaded with him: "If you also retire from the government service, how will the administration be run?" Sanatan Goswami replied very gravely: "You are the governor of Gouda, and you punish different kinds of criminals in different ways. So you are at liberty to punish anyone according to his activity." The purpose of his reply was that the governor was engaged in hunting animals and killing men to expand his kingdom; so let both of them suffer according to the acts they were performing.

The Nawab was intelligent, and he understood Sanatan Goswami's purpose and left the place in an angry mood. Shortly afterward, he went off to conquer Orissa, and ordered the arrest of Sanatan Goswami until he returned.

Rupa Goswami then learned that his elder brother Sanatan had been arrested by the Nawab. He sent information by messenger that the ten thousand coins in Gouda (Bengal) in custody of the Grocer, could be used to release him from the Nawab's detention. Rupa Goswami, with his younger brother whose name was Sri Ballabha, then started for Vrindaban to meet Chaitanya Mahaprabhu. Sanatan offered five thousand coins to the keeper of the jail in which he was being kept in custody. He advised the jailkeeper to gladly accept the five thousand coins from him and let him go, because by accepting such money he would be materially benefitted, and at the same time he would be acting very righteously in freeing Sanatan for spiritual activities.

The custodian replied, "Of course I can let you go, because you have done many services for me and you are in government service. I know that, but I am afraid of the Nawab when he hears that you are free. I'll have to explain. How can I accept such a proposal?" Sanatan gave a story which the custodian might submit to the Nawab—as to how he had escaped—and he then raised his offer to ten thousand coins. The custodian then agreed to the proposition, as he was very anxious to get the ten thousand coins. And so he let him go.

Sanatan then proceeded to Lord Chaitanya Mahaprabhu. He did not go on the open road but travelled instead through the jungles until he arrived at a place in Bihar called Pabda, and rested there in the hotel. The hotel keeper, meanwhile, was informed by an astrologer employed at the hotel that Sanatan Goswami had some gold coins with him, and he wanted to take them from him. And so he spoke with superficial respect: "You just take your rest tonight, and in the morning I shall arrange for you to get out of this jungle trap." Sanatan, however, was suspicious of the behavior of the hotel keeper, and he inquired from his accompanying servant Isan whether he had some money. Isan told him that he had seven gold coins with him. Sanatan did not like the idea of the servant carrying such money. He was angry with him and said, "Why do you carry this death knell on the road?"

Sanatan at once took the seven gold coins and offered them to the hotel keeper; he then requested the hotel keeper to help him through the jungle. He informed him that he was on a special journey for the government and could not travel on the open road, and therefore it would be very kind if the hotel keeper would help him to get over the jungle mountain. The hotel keeper replied, "I understood that you had eight coins with you and I was thinking of killing you to take them. But you are very good, I can understand, and so you don't have to offer me the money. I'll get you out of the hill-tract."

Sanatan replied, "If you don't accept these coins then somebody else will take them from me. Somebody will kill me for them, so better you take them. I offer them to you." The hotel keeper then gave him full assistance and that very night he helped him to get past the hills.

When Sanatan emerged, he requested his servant to go home with the one coin that he had still with him, and he would go on alone. After the departure of his servant, Sanatan felt completely free. With torn clothing and with a water-pot in his hand he began to proceed toward Lord Chaitanya Mahaprabhu. On the way he met his rich brother-in-law who was also in the service of the government, and who offered him an excellent blanket, which Sanatan accepted at his special request. Then he parted from him and went on alone to see Chaitanya Mahaprabhu at Benares.

When he reached Benares, he understood that the Lord was there and he was very glad. He was informed by people that Lord Chaitanya Mahaprabhu was staying at the house of Chandra Sekhar Acharya, and he went there. Chaitanya Mahaprabhu was inside the house and He could understand that Sanatan had arrived at the door. He asked Chandra Sekhar to call the man who was sitting at His door, "He is a Vaishnava, a great devotee of the Lord." Chandra Sekhar went out to see the man but he saw no Vaishnava at the door; he saw only a man who appeared to be a mendicant. The Lord then asked to see the mendicant. When Sanatan entered the courtyard of the house, Lord Chaitanya hurriedly came to receive him and embraced him. When the Lord embraced him, Sanatan became overwhelmed with spiritual ecstasy, and he began to say, "My dear Lord, please do not touch me." But both of them embraced each other and began to cry. Seeing Sanatan and Lord Chaitanya acting thus, Chandra Sekhar was struck with wonder. Lord Chaitanya received Sanatan in this way, and asked him to sit down with Him on a bench.

He was touching the body of Sanatan with his hand and Sanatan asked Him, "My dear Lord, please do not touch me." The Lord replied, "I am touching you just for My purification, because you are a great devotee. By your devotional service you can deliver the whole universe for going back to Godhead."

In this connection the Lord quoted a nice verse from *Srimad Bhagwatam*. The purport of the verse is that a person who is a devotee of Lord Krishna, one hundred per cent engaged in devotional service, is far better than a Brahmin who is learned in all the Vedic literature, but who is not engaged in the devotional service of the Lord. The devotee can purify every place and every thing because he is carrying the Supreme Lord within his heart.

In the Vedic literature it is also stated that the Supreme Personality of Godhead does not recognize even a person who is very learned in all the divisions of the Vedas; but, rather, He likes a person even if born of a low family, provided that person is a devotee. Instead of offering charities to some Brahmin who is not a devotee, if something is offered to a devotee, that offering is accepted by the Lord. In other words, anything offered to the Lord may be given to His devotees. Chaitanya Mahaprabhu also quoted from *Srimad Bhagwatam* that, if a Brahmin, although qualified with the twelve different qualities of a Brahmin, is not a devotee of the Supreme Lord, then he is lower than the lowest of the low—even though born in a high family. A devotee, although born in a *Chandala* (dogeater) family, can purify his whole family for 100 generations past and future by devotional service, whereas a proud Brahmin cannot even purify himself. It is said in the *Hari Bhakti Sudodaya*, "O devotee of the Lord, to see you is the perfection of the eyes, to touch your body is the perfection of bodily activities, to glorify your qualities is the perfection of the tongue—because it is very rare to find a pure devotee like you."

The Lord next said to Sanatan that Krishna is very merciful, and is the Deliverer of the fallen soul. "He has saved you from *Maharauraba*." This *Maharauraba*, hell, is described in *Srimad Bhagwatam*. It is for persons who are engaged in killing animals. It is stated there that butchers or animal-eaters go to that hell. Sanatan replied, "I do not know the mercy of Krishna, but I can understand that Your mercy is causeless upon me. You have delivered me from the entanglement of material life."

Then the Lord inquired: "How did you get free from your custody? I understood that you were arrested." Sanatan narrated the whole story of how he was released. Lord Chaitanya then informed him, "I have seen your two brothers, and I have advised them to proceed toward Vrindaban."

Lord Chaitanya now introduced Chandra Sekhar to Sanatan, and there was a pleasant invitation made for Sanatan to dine with him. The Lord requested Chandra Sekhar to take Sanatan to the barber and make him gentle, because Sanatan had grown a long beard which Sri Chaitanya Mahaprabhu did not like. He therefore asked Chandra Sekhar to take Sanatan to a bath and get him clean-shaved. He asked him to change his clothes also.

After taking a bath and cleansing himself, Sanatan requested Chandra Sekhar to give him some good cloth. When Lord Chaitanya was informed that Sanatan did not accept new garments, but accepted only some used garments from Chandra Sekhar, He was very glad. The Lord sat down for lunch and asked Chandra Sekhar to keep food for Sanatan. Chandra Sekhar did not offer him food immediately, however, but after the Lord finished His eating there were some remnants of His foodstuff, and that was offered to Sanatan while the Lord went for His rest.

After this, Lord Chaitanya introduced one Maharastrian Brahmin, His devotee, to Sanatan; and that Maharastrian Brahmin invited Sanatan to accept lunch daily at his place, as long as he remained at Benares. Sanatan said, "So long as I remain at Benares, I will beg from door to door; and the Lord will be so good as to accept from you this invitation for daily lunch at the Brahmin's house."

By this behavior of Sanatan Lord Chaitanya was very much pleased; but He noticed the valuable blanket that was given to Sanatan by his brother-in-law while on route to Benares. Although Lord Chaitanya was overlooking the blanket, Sanatan understood that Lord Chaitanya Mahaprabhu did not approve of such a valuable garment on his body, and he planned to get rid of it. He immediately went to the bank of the Ganges and there saw a mendicant washing an old quilt. Sanatan asked him to trade the old quilt for the valuable blanket. The poor medicant thought that Sanatan was joking with him, so he said, "How is that? You appeared to be a very nice gentleman, but you are mocking me in this unmannerly way."

Sanatan informed him, "I am not joking with you. I am very serious. Will you kindly exchange that torn quilt for this blanket?" Then Sanatan exchanged his blanket for the torn quilt, and he came before the Lord.

The Lord inquired, "Where is your valuable blanket?"

Sanatan informed Him about the exchange at the Ganges of the blanket for the torn quilt. The Lord then loved him for this and He thanked Sanatan: "You are intelligent enough and you have now finished all your attraction for material wealth." In other words, the Lord accepts a person for devotional service only when he is completely free from all materialistic possessions. The Lord said to Sanatan, "It would not look well to become a mendicant and go begging from door to door while at the same time you have such a valuable blanket on your body; it is contradictory, and people would look at it with abhorrence." Sanatan replied to the Lord, "Whatever I am doing to become free from material attachment, it is all Your mercy." The Lord was very much pleased with him, and both of Them discussed spiritual advancement.

Previous to this meeting of Sanatan and Lord Chaitanya, Lord Chaitanya met the householder-devotee, Ramananda Roy. In that meeting, which is discussed in a different chapter, Lord Chaitanya asked Ramananda Roy questions and Ramananda replied as if he were the teacher of the Lord. But in this case Sanatan will put questions to the Lord and the Lord will answer them.

The instruction and teachings of Lord Chaitanya are very important for people in general. He teaches the process of devotional service, which is the constitutional position of every living entity; it is every man's duty to advance in spiritual science. All these things are very nicely discussed in the talks between Lord Chaitanya and Sanatan Goswami. At the mercy of Lord Chaitanya Sanatan was able to put questions before Him, and these are replied to properly.

The meeting of Sanatan and Lord Chaitanya teaches us that in order to understand spiritual subject matters, one must approach a Spiritual Master like Lord Chaitanya Mahaprabhu and make submissive enquiries. This is also confirmed in the instruction of the *Bhagavad Gita:* that one should approach a man of authority, and learn from him about spiritual science.

CHAPTER THREE

Teachings to Sanatan Goswami

In the instructions of Lord Chaitanya to Sanatan Goswami we can understand the science of God in the matter of His transcendental Form, His opulences, and His devotional service—for everything is being described to Sanatan Goswami by the Lord Himself. At that time Sanatan fell at the feet of the Lord and with great humility asked about his own real identity. He spoke as follows:

"I am born of a lower family, my associations are all abominable, and I am fallen, the most wretched of Mankind. I was suffering in the dark well of material enjoyment, and I never knew the actual goal of my life. I do not know what is beneficial to me. Although in the mundane sphere I am what is known as a great learned man, I am in fact so much of a fool that I even accept that I am learned. You have accepted me as Your servant, and You have delivered me from the entanglement of material life. Now You can tell me what my duty is in this liberated state of life."

In other words, as we see by this plea, liberation is not the final word in perfection. There must be activities in liberation. Sanatan clearly asks: "You have saved me from the entanglement of material existence. Now, after liberation, *what is my duty?* Kindly explain it to me." Sanatan further inquired, "Who am I? Why are the three-fold miseries always giving me trouble? And, finally, tell me how I will be relieved from this material entanglement? I do not know how to question You about the advancement of spiritual life, but I beg that You kindly, mercifully, let me know everything that I should know."

This is the process of acceptance of a spiritual master by the disciple: One should approach a spiritual master and humbly submit to him, and then inquire from him about one's spiritual progress.

The Lord was pleased by Sanatan's submissive behavior, and He replied as follows: "You have already received benediction from Lord Krishna, and therefore you know everything, and you are free from all the miseries of material existence." The Lord further replied that, because Sanatan was in Krishna Consciousness, naturally, by the grace of Krishna, he was already conversant with everything, but "Because you are a humble devotee, you are asking me to confirm what is already realized by you. This is very nice." These are the characteristics of a true devotee. In the *Narada Bhakti Sutra* it is said that one who is very serious about developing his Krishna Consciousness, by the grace of the Lord, has his desire for understanding Krishna fulfilled very soon. The Lord said, "You are a suitable person for protecting the devotional service of the Lord. Therefore it is My duty to instruct you in the science of God, and I will explain to you everything step by step."

It is the duty of a disciple approaching a spiritual master to enquire about his constitutional position. In conformity to that spiritual process, Sanatan has already asked, "What am I, and why am I suffering from the three-fold miseries?" The three-fold miseries are called *adhyatmic, adhibhautic,* and *adhidaivic. Adhyatmic* means caused by the body and mind: sometimes the living entity suffers bodily, and sometimes he is distressed mentally—both are *adhyatmic* miseries. We experience these miseries even in the womb of our mother. There are many forms of misery that take advantage of our delicate body and give us pain.

Miseries inflicted by other living entities are called *adhibhautic.* There are many living entities, such as bugs born of eggs, that cause us miseries while we are sleeping in bed. There are many living entities, like cockroaches, that sometimes give us pain, and there are other living entities born on different kinds of planets, and they also cause us miseries.

So far as *adhidaivic* miseries are concerned, they originate with the demigods from the higher planets. For instance, sometimes we suffer from serious cold weather, sometimes we suffer from the thunderbolt, sometimes from earthquakes, tornadoes, droughts and other natural disasters. So we are always suffering one or another of these three kinds of miseries.

Sanatan's enquiry was: "What is the position of the living entities? Why are they always undergoing these three kinds of miseries?" Sanatan has admitted his weakness: although he was known by the mass of people as a greatly learned man (and actually he was a highly learned Sanskrit scholar)— and although he accepted the designation of a very learned man given him by the mass of people, yet he did not actually know what his constitutional position was, and why he was subjected to the threefold miseries.

The necessity of approaching a spiritual master is not a fashion, but is for he who is seriously conscious of the material miseries, and who wants to be free of them. It is the duty of such a person to approach the spiritual master. We find similar circumstances in the *Bhagavad Gita:* When Arjuna was perplexed by so many problems involving whether to fight or not, he accepted Lord Krishna as his Spiritual Master. There also it was a case of the Supreme Spiritual Master instructing Arjuna about the constitutional position of the living entity.

In the *Bhagavad Gita* we are informed that the constitutional nature of the individual entity is spirit soul: he is not matter. Therefore, as spirit soul, he is part and parcel of the Supreme Soul, the Absolute Truth, the Personality of Godhead. We also learn that it is the duty of the spirit soul to surrender; for only then can he be happy. The last instruction of the *Bhagavad Gita* is that the spirit soul is to surrender completely unto the Supreme Soul, Krishna, and in that way realize happiness.

Here, also, Lord Chaitanya, in answering the questions of Sanatan, repeats the same truth; but without giving him information about the spirit soul which is already described in the *Gita*. He begins from the point where Krishna ended His instruction. It is accepted by great devotees that Lord Chaitanya is Krishna Himself. And from the point where He ended His instruction in the *Gita*, He now begins His instruction again, to Sanatan. The Lord said to Sanatan:

"Your constitutional position is that you are pure living soul. This material body is not the identity of your real self, neither is your mind your real identity, nor your intelligence, nor is false ego the real identity of the self. Your identity is that you are the eternal servitor of the Supreme Lord, Krishna. Your position is that you are transcendental. The superior energy of Krishna is spiritual in constitution, and the inferior external energy is material. You are between the material energy and the spiritual energy, and therefore your position is marginal. In other words, you belong to the marginal potency of Krishna. You are simultaneously one with, and different from, Krishna. Because you are spirit, therefore you are not different from Krishna. But because you are only a minute particle of Krishna, you are therefore different from Him."

This simultaneous oneness and difference always exists in the relationship between the living entities and the Supreme Lord. From the marginal position of the living entities, this "simultaneously one and different" concept is understood. The living entity is just like a molecular part of the sunshine, whereas Krishna is compared to the blazing, shining sun. Lord Chaitanya compared the living entities to the blazing sparks from the fire, and the Supreme Lord to the blazing fire of the sun. The Lord cites in this connection a verse from *Vishnu Purana*, in which it is stated that everything that is manifested within this cosmic world is but an energy of the Supreme Lord. For example, as the fire emanating from one place exhibits its illumination and heat all around, so the Lord, although situated in one place in the spiritual world, manifests His different energies everywhere. And the whole world of cosmic representation is but different manifestations of His energy.

The energy of the Supreme Lord is transcendental and spiritual, and the living entities are part and parcel of that energy. But there is another energy called material energy, which is covered by the cloud of ignorance, and thereby divided into the three modes, or *gunas*, of material Nature. Lord Chaitanya quoted from *Vishnu Purana* that all inconceivable energies reside in the Supreme Personality of the Lord, and the whole cosmic manifestation acts due to the same inconceivable energy of the Supreme Lord.

The Lord says that the living entities are also known as *Kshetrajna*, or "Knower of the field of activities." In the Thirteenth Chapter of the *Gita*, the body is described as the field of activities, and the living entity as *Kshetrajna*, the knower of that field. Although the living entity is constitutionally conversant with spiritual energy, or has the potency to understand, he is covered by the material energy, and he consequently believes this body to be himself. This is called false ego. In material existence, deluded by this false ego, the bewildered living entity changes his different bodies and suffers various kinds of miseries. The knowledge of his true position is present to different extents in different varieties of living entities.

In other words, it is to be understood that the living entity is part and parcel of the spiritual energy of the Supreme Lord. The material energy is inferior energy, and therefore man has the potency to become uncovered from this material energy and utilize the spiritual energy. It is stated in the *Bhagavad Gita* that the superior energy is covered by the inferior energy. Due to this covering, the living entity is subjected to the miseries of the material world, and, in proportion to the different degrees of obscureness, he suffers material miseries. Those who are a little enlightened suffer less, but, on the whole, everyone is subjected to material miseries, due to being covered by the material energy.

The Lord also quoted from the *Gita*, Seventh Chapter, in which it is stated that earth, water, fire, air, ether, mind, intelligence, and ego all combine together to form the inferior energy of the Supreme Lord. But the Superior Energy is the real identity of the living being. Because of that energy the whole material world functions. The cosmic manifestation, made of material elements, has no power to act unless it is moved by the superior energy, the living entity. So, actually, the conditional life of the living entity is forgetfulness of his relationship with the Supreme Lord in the superior energy. When that relationship is forgotten, conditional life is the result. Only when man revives his real identity, that of eternal servitor to the Lord, does he become liberated.

CHAPTER FOUR

The Wise Man

Nobody can trace the history of the living entity's entanglement in material energy. Therefore the Lord says that it is beginningless. Beginningless means that conditional life exists prior to the Creation—it is simply manifested with, and after, the creation. Due to forgetfulness of his nature, the living entity, although spirit, suffers all kinds of miseries in material existence. It is to be understood here that there are also other living entities who are not entangled in this material energy. Such living entities are situated in the Spiritual World, and they are called liberated souls. They are always engaged in Krishna Consciousness, in devotional service.

The activities of those who are conditioned by material Nature are taken into account, and in their next life, according to these activities, they are offered different grades of material bodies. In the material world the spiritual soul in conditional life is subjected to different rewards and punishments. When he is rewarded, he is elevated to the higher planets, due to his righteous activities. And there he becomes one of the many demigods. And when he is punished for his abominable activities, he is thrown into different kinds of hellish planets, and there he suffers the miseries of material existence more acutely. The Lord gives a very nice example of this punishment: Formerly a king used to punish a criminal by dunking him in the river, and then raising him again for a breath, and then again dunking him once more in the water. Material Nature punishes and rewards the individual entity in just the same way. When he is punished he is dunked into the water of material miseries, and when he is rewarded he is taken out of it for some time. Elevation of the living entity to higher planets or to a higher status of life is never permanent. He has to come down again to be submerged in the water. All this goes on in this material existence. Sometimes one is elevated to the higher planetary system, and sometimes one is thrown into the hellish condition of material life.

In this connection the Lord recites a nice verse from *Srimad Bhagwatam*, taken from the instruction of Narada Muni to Vasudeva, the father of Krishna. In this quotation from the nine sages who were instructing Maharaj Nemi, it is stated that forgetfulness of the relationship with Krishna is called *Maya*. Actually, Maya means "that which is not." It has no existence. Therefore, that the living entity has no connection with the Supreme Lord is a false conception. He may not believe in the existence of God, or he may think he has no relationship with God, but these are all "illusions," or Maya. Due to his absorption in this false conception of life, man is always fearful and full of anxieties. In other words, a Godless concept of life is Maya; and, therefore, one who is actually learned in the Vedic literature surrenders unto the Supreme Lord with great devotion, and accepts Him as the Supreme Goal. When a living entity becomes forgetful of the constitutional nature of his relationship with God, then he is at once overwhelmed by the external energy, and this is the cause of his false ego, identifying his body as himself. His whole conception of the material Universe is due to this false conception of the body. He becomes attached to this body, and to the by-products of this body. To escape this entanglement he has simply to perform his duty—to surrender unto the Supreme Lord with intelligence, with devotion, and with sincere Krishna Consciousness.

A conditioned soul falsely thinks himself happy in the material world, but if he is favored by an unalloyed devotee—by hearing instruction from the unalloyed devotee—he gives up the desire for material enjoyment and becomes enlightened in Krishna Consciousness. As soon as one enters into Krishna Consciousness, his desire for material enjoyment at once is vanquished, and gradually he becomes free from material entanglement. For example, because there is no question of darkness where there is light, Krishna Consciousness is like the light that dispels the darkness of material sense enjoyment.

A Krishna conscious person is never under the false conception that he is One with God. He does not think that he would be happy by working for himself. He engages all his energy in the service of the Supreme Lord, and thereby becomes released from the clutches of illusory material energy. In this connection the Lord quotes a verse from the *Bhagavad Gita*, Seventh Chapter, to the effect that the material energy containing the three modes of material Nature is very strong. It is very difficult to escape the process of material energy, but one who surrenders unto Krishna easily becomes free from the clutches of Maya.

The Lord went on to teach that the conditioned soul, for each and every moment in which he is engaged in some fruitive activity, is forgetting his real identity. Sometimes when he is fatigued, when he is tired of material activities, he wants liberation and wants to become one with the Supreme, but at other times he thinks that by working hard for his sense gratification he will be happy. In both cases he is covered by material energy. For the enlightenment of such bewildered conditioned souls, who are working under false identification, the Lord has presented us with so much Vedic literature, such as the *Vedas*, the *Puranas*, and the *Vedanta Sutra*—all intended to guide the human being back to Godhead. The Lord has presented further instructions, advising that when a conditioned soul is accepted by the mercy of the spiritual master, and when he is guided by the Supersoul, he takes advantage of the various Vedic Scriptures, becomes enlightened, and makes progress in his spiritual realization. It is understood that Lord Krishna is always merciful to His devotees, and therefore He has presented all this Vedic literature, by which one can understand his relationship with Krishna, and can act in that relationship—with the result that he is gifted with the ultimate goal of life.

Actually every living entity is destined to reach the Supreme Lord, and everyone can understand his relationship with the Supreme Lord. The execution of duties to attain perfection is known as devotional service, and in maturity such devotional service becomes Love of God, the factual goal of life for every living being. The living entity is not intended to achieve success in religious perfection or economic development or sense enjoyment. Religiousness, economic development, sense enjoyment, and liberation should not actually be desired by the living entity. The real desire of the entity should be to achieve the stage of loving transcendental service to the Lord.

The All-attractive features of Lord Krishna help one in attaining Krishna Consciousness, and when one is engaged in Krishna Consciousness he can realize the relationship between Krishna and himself.

In this connection the Lord quotes one story from the commentary of *Madhva* which occurs in *Srimad Bhagwatam*, Fifth Canto. The story involves the instruction of Sarvajna to a poor man who came to him to have his future told. When Sarvajna saw the horoscope of the poor man, he was at once astonished that the man was so poor, and he said to him, "Oh, why are you so unhappy? I see from your horoscope that you have some hidden treasure left to you by your father. The horoscope, however, states that your father could not disclose this to you because he died in a foreign place. But now you can search out the hidden treasure left by your father and be happy." This story is cited because the living entity is suffering due to his ignorance of the hidden treasure of his Father. The hidden treasure of the Father, Krishna, is *Love of Godhead*. In every Vedic Scripture the conditioned soul is advised to *find that hidden treasure*, which is known as Love of God. As is stated in the *Bhagavad Gita*, a conditioned soul, although he is the son of the Wealthiest— the Personality of Godhead—does not realize it; therefore the Vedic literature is given to him to help him search out his Father and his paternal property.

Sarvajna further advised the poor man: "Don't try to dig on the southern side of your house to find the hidden treasure. If you do so, you'll be attacked by a poisonous wasp and you will be baffled in finding the treasure. The search should be to the eastern side where there is actual light—which is called devotional service, or Krishna Consciousness. On the southern side there is ritualistic performance of the Vedic Scripture, and on the western side there is speculative empiric knowledge, and on the northern side there is the Yoga system, or the meditational process for self realization."

If somebody searches for his ultimate goal by the ritualistic process, he will be baffled. Such a process involves the performance of rituals under the guidance of the priest who takes money in exchange for service. A man thinks he will be happy by such performances, but actually they will not make him happy. Even if he does gain some result therefrom, it is only temporary, and his material distresses will continue. So he will never become truly happy by such a ritualistic process. Instead, his material pangs increase more and more.

Similarly, digging for the hidden treasure on the northern side is compared with one's self-realization by dint of the meditational process. By the meditational process perfection is to think oneself One with the Supreme Lord. This merging into the Supreme by the living entity is something like the great serpent swallowing up the smaller serpent. From practical experience we see sometimes that a big serpent swallows up a smaller one, and the merging into the spiritual existence of the Supreme is analogous. The small serpent is, therefore, searching after perfection, and he is swallowed by the big serpent.

Digging on the western side is compared to the hidden treasure protected by *Yakasa*, the evil spirit that protects it. The idea is that hidden treasure can never be delivered by one who asks the favor of the Yakasa for attaining it. The result is that he will simply be killed. The Yogins who practice meditation are analogous to the small serpents. The speculative process of self-realization, or *Jnana*, is also suicidal in this case.

Actually, one has to dig for the hidden treasure from the eastern side, which is called devotional service in full Krishna Consciousness. That is the perpetual hidden treasure, and when one attains to that achievement, he becomes perpetually rich. One who is poor in devotional service and Krishna Consciousness is always in need of material gain. Sometimes he suffers the bites of poisonous things, and sometimes he is baffled; sometimes he follows the philosophy of monism and therefore loses his identity, and sometimes he is swallowed by the big serpent. By giving up all these things and becoming fixed in Krishna Consciousness, or devotional service to the Lord, he achieves the perfection of life.

CHAPTER FIVE

How to Approach God

Actually, all Vedic literature directs the human being toward the perfect stage of devotion. The paths of fruitive activities, speculative knowledge and meditation do not lead one to the perfectional stage, but the Lord actually becomes approachable by the process of devotional service. Therefore, one is recommended throughout the Vedic literature to accept the process of devotional service. Lord Chaitanya quoted in this connection a verse from the *Srimad Bhagwatam*, Eleventh Canto, Fourteenth Chapter, in which the Lord says, "My dear Uddhava, neither philosophical speculation nor Yoga achievements nor penances can give Me such pleasure as can devotional service practiced by the living entities." He can only be achieved by devotional service, as He is dear only to the devotees. If a person born in the lowest family of humanity is a devotee, then he becomes freed from all contamination. Devotional service is the only path by which to achieve the Supreme Personality of God.

This is the only perfection accepted in all Vedic literature. As a poor man upon receiving some treasure becomes at once happy, so, when one attains to devotional service, automatically the pains of material existence are vanquished. As one advances in devotional service, one attains love of Godhead, and as he advances in the love for the Supreme he becomes free from all material bondage. The disappearance of poverty and liberation from bondage are not, however, the end results of love of Krishna. Actually, the love of Krishna, love of God, exists in relishing the reciprocation of loving service. In all Vedic literature one will find that attainment of this loving relationship between the Supreme Lord and the living entities is the function of devotional service. Our actual function is devotional service, and our ultimate goal of achievement is love of Godhead. Therefore, in all Vedic literature Krishna is the ultimate center. By knowledge of Krishna all problems of life are solved.

The Lord said that, according to *Padma Purana*, there are different *Puranas* for worshipping different types of demigods; but such indications for worship only bewilder persons into thinking that the demigods are supreme. And yet, if the *Puranas* are scrutinized and studied it will be found that Krishna, the Supreme Personality of Godhead, is the only Object of worship. For example, in the *Markandio Purana* there is mention of Devi worship, worship of the goddess Durga or Kali. But in that same *Chandika* it is also stated that all these demigods—even in the shape of Durga or Kali—are different energies of Vishnu. Therefore, even the study of the *Puranas* will reveal Vishnu, the Supreme Personality of Godhead, to be the only Object of worship.

The conclusion is that, directly or indirectly, all types of worship are more or less indicating a worship of the Supreme Personality of Godhead, Krishna. In the *Bhagavad Gita* it is confirmed that anyone who worships the demigods is in fact only worshipping Krishna, because the demigods are different parts of the Body of Vishnu, or Krishna. That such worship of demigods is really irregular is also clearly stated in the *Bhagavad Gita*.

Srimad Bhagwatam confirms this by the question: What is the object of worshipping the different types of demigods? In Vedic literature there are various divisions of ritualistic activities. One is called *Karmakanda*, or purely ritualistic activities; another is called *Upasana-kanda*, or speculating on the Supreme Absolute Truth. What then is the purpose of the ritualistic sections of Vedic literature, and what is the purpose of different mantras or hymns indicating the worship of different types of demigods? And what is the purpose of philosophical speculation on the subject of the Absolute Truth? The *Srimad Bhagwatam* replies that all these different methods defined in Vedic literature indicate the worship of the Supreme Lord, Vishnu. They are all indirect ways of worshipping the Supreme Personality of Godhead. Sacrifices contained in the ritualistic portion of the literature are to satisfy the Supreme Lord Vishnu, because *Yajna*, sacrifice, is specifically meant to satisfy Vishnu. Vishnu's Name is also *Yajneshwara*, or Lord of the Sacrifices.

The neophytes are not all on the transcendental level, and therefore, according to their situations in the different modes of material Nature, they are advised to worship different types of demigods so that, gradually, they may rise to the transcendental plane and be engaged in the devotional service of Vishnu, the Supreme Personality of Godhead. For example, it may be said that some of the neophytes are attached to flesh-eating; and for them the *Puranas* prescribe that they can eat flesh after offering it to the deity Kali.

The philosophical sections of the Vedic hymns are meant to enable one to distinguish the Supreme Personality of Godhead from Maya. After indicating the position of Maya, the Supreme Personality of Godhead is approached in pure devotional service. That is the purpose of philosophical speculation. This is confirmed in the *Bhagavad Gita* in the Seventh Chapter: *Bahunam janmanam ante:* "The philosophical speculators and empiric philosophers, after speculating for many, many births, ultimately come unto the Supreme Lord Krishna, and accept that Vasudeva (Krishna) is everything." Therefore, all Vedic rituals and different types of worship or philosophical speculation ultimately aim at Krishna.

The Lord then told Sanatan Goswami about Krishna's multiforms and His unlimited opulence. He also described the nature of the spiritual manifestation, the material manifestation, and the manifestation of the living entity. He also informed Sanatan Goswami that the planets in the Spiritual Sky, known as *Vaikunthas*, and the Universes of the material manifestation, are to be known as different types of manifestations; for they are creative manifestations of the two different types of energies—namely, the material energy and the spiritual energy. Therefore, as far as Krishna Himself is concerned, He is directly situated in His spiritual energy, or specifically in His internal potency.

To help us understand the difference between the manifestation of the spiritual energy and the material energy, there is clear analysis of the two in the Second Canto of *Srimad Bhagwatam*. Also, Sukadeva Goswami, by commenting on Verse One of the Tenth Canto, makes a similar clear, analytical study. Lord Chaitanya accepts Sukadeva Goswami as an authorized commentator on the *Srimad Bhagwatam*. Therefore He quotes his writing in this connection; and He explains that in the Tenth Canto of the *Bhagwatam* the life and activities of Krishna are described because Krishna is the Shelter of all other manifestations. Therefore Sukadeva Goswami worshipped and offered his obeisances unto Krishna, the Shelter of everything.

This purport maintains that in this world there are two different principles: the one principle is the origin, or the shelter of everything, and the other principle is the deduction from the original principle. The Supreme Truth is the shelter of all manifestations. That Supreme Truth is called *Asraya*. All other principles, which remain under the control of the *Asraya-tattwa*, or the Absolute Truth, are called *Asrita*, or subordinate corollaries and reactions. The purpose of the material manifestation is to give the conditioned soul a chance to become liberated and return to the *Asraya-tattwa*, or the Absolute Truth.

So everything that is in the cosmic Creation is dependent on the *Asraya-tattwa*, the Supreme Absolute Truth. As such, the creative manifestation, or Vishnu manifestation, the different types of demigods and manifestations of energy, the living entities, the material elements—everything is dependent on Krishna, the Supreme Truth. *Srimad Bhagwatam* indicates that everything, directly and indirectly, has Krishna as the Supreme Shelter. Therefore the analytical study of Krishna is the perfect knowledge, as is confirmed in the *Bhagavad Gita*.

Lord Chaitanya described the different features of Lord Krishna in the following manner, and asked Sanatan Goswami to hear attentively: He said that Krishna originally is the Son of Nanda Maharaj, and He is the Absolute Supreme Truth. He is the Cause of all causes, and He is the Origin of all emanations and all incarnations, yet there in Vraja or Goloka Vrindaban He is just like a young boy. His Form is eternal, full of bliss and full of knowledge absolute. He is the Shelter of everything, and He is the Proprietor or Master of everything.

In this connection Lord Chaitanya gives evidence from *Brahma Samhita*, Fifth Chapter, 1st verse, which states that Krishna is the Supreme Personality of Godhead and His Body is full of knowledge, eternal and blissful. He is the Original Person, known as Govinda, and He is the Cause of all causes. Therefore, Krishna is the Original Personality of Godhead; He is full of all six opulences, and His Abode is known as Goloka Vrindaban, the highest planetary system in the Spiritual Sky.

Lord Chaitanya also quotes a verse from the *Srimad Bhagwatam*, First Canto, Third Chapter, in which it is stated clearly that all the incarnations described in that particular verse are either direct expansions of Krishna, or are, indirectly, expansions of the expansions of Krishna. But the Krishna Name mentioned there is the Original Personality of Godhead, and He appears on this Earth, in this Universe or in any other Universe, when there is a disturbance created by the demons, who are always trying to disrupt the administration of the demigods.

To understand Krishna there are three different processes: the process of empiric philosophical speculation, the process of meditation in the mystic *Yoga* system, and the process of Krishna Consciousness, or devotional service. Accordingly, in these different processes: 1) by empiric philosophical speculation, the impersonal *Brahman* feature of Krishna is understood; 2) by the process of meditation or *Yoga* mysticism, the feature of the Supersoul, the All-pervading expansion of Krishna, is understood; and 3) by devotional service in full Krishna Consciousness, the Original Personality of Godhead, Krishna is realized.

In this connection Lord Chaitanya quotes first from the *Srimad Bhagwatam*, First Canto, Second Chapter, which states that those who are knowers of the Absolute Truth describe the Absolute Truth in three features: some describe the Absolute as impersonal *Brahman*, and some describe the Absolute Truth as the localized All-pervading Supersoul, and some know that the Absolute Truth is the Supreme Personality of Godhead, Krishna. In other words, *Brahman*, the impersonal manifestation, and *Paramatma*, the localized manifestation, and the Supreme Personality of Godhead, are One and the same; but, according to the different processes adopted, He is realized in different features—*Brahman*, *Paramatma* and *Bhagavan*.

Impersonal *Brahman* realization is simple realization of the effulgence emanating from the transcendental Body of Krishna. We compare this effulgence of the transcendental Body of Krishna to the sunshine: just as the sun disc is there, the sun planet is there, and the Sungod is there, and the sunshine is the shining effulgence of that original Sungod. Similarly, *Brahmajyoti*, the spiritual effulgence, impersonal Brahman, is nothing but the Personal effulgence of Krishna.

To support this analysis Lord Chaitanya quotes one important verse from *Brahma Samhita*, where Lord Brahma says: "I worship the Supreme Personality of Godhead, Govinda, by Whose Personal effulgence there is the unlimited manifestation of the *Brahmajyoti*, and in that *Brahmajyoti* (the impersonal manifestation of Krishna's Bodily effulgence) there are innumerable Universes, each full of innumerable planets."

Lord Chaitanya further says that the Paramatma, the All-pervading feature situated in everyone's body, is but a partial manifestation or expansion of Krishna. But because Krishna is the Soul of the soul, there He is called Paramatma, Supreme Self. Lord Chaitanya now quoted a verse from *Srimad Bhagwatam* concerning the talks of Maharaj Parikshit and Sukadeva Goswami. In that verse it is understood that Maharaj Parikshit, while hearing about the transcendental Pastimes of Krishna in Vrindaban, inquired from his Spiritual Master, Sukadeva Goswami, as to why the inhabitants of Vrindaban were so much attached to Krishna. To this question Sukadeva Goswami answered that Krishna should be known as the Soul of all souls. He is the Soul of all individual souls, and He is also the soul of the localized *Paramatma*. He was acting just like a human being to attract persons to Him and to show that He is not formless.

He is as good as other living beings, but He is the Supreme and other living beings are all subordinate to Him. All living beings therefore can enjoy spiritual bliss, eternal life and full knowledge in His association. Lord Chaitanya also quotes a verse from *Bhagavad Gita*, in which the Supreme Lord speaks to Arjuna about His different kinds of opulences, saying that He Himself enters into this Universe by one of His plenary portions, Garbodakshayee Vishnu, and He also enters into each Universe as the Kshirodakshayee Vishnu, and then expands Himself as Supersoul in everyone's heart. Therefore, He says, if anyone wants to understand the Supreme Absolute Truth in perfection, he must take to the process of devotional service in full Krishna Consciousness. Then it will be possible for him to understand the last word of the Absolute Truth.

CHAPTER SIX

His Forms are One and the Same

By devotional service one can understand that Krishna first of all manifests Himself as *Svayamrupa*, His Personal Form, then as *Tadekatmarupa*, and then as *Avesharupa*. In these three features He manifests Himself in His transcendental Form. The feature of *Svayamrupa* is the Form in which Krishna can be understood by one who may not understand His other features. In other words, the Form in which Krishna is directly understood is called *Svayamrupa*, or His Personal Form. The *Tadekatmarupa* is that Form which most resembles the *Svayamrupa*, but has some differences of bodily features. This *Tadekatmarupa* is divided into two manifestations, called the Personal expansion and the Pastime expansion. As far as *Avesharupa* is concerned, sometimes Krishna empowers some suitable living entity to represent Him. When a living entity acts as a representative of the Supreme Lord, he is called *Avesharupa*, or *Shaktavesha Avatara*.

His Personal Form is again divided into two: *Svayamrupa* and *Svayaprakash*. As far as His *Svayamrupa* (or Pastime Form) is concerned, it is in that Form that He remains always in Vrindaban with all the inhabitants of Vrindaban. That Personal Form is again divided into two, known categorically as the *Prabhava* and *Baibhava* Forms. For example, Krishna expanded Himself in multiple Forms in the *Rasa* Dance. When He danced with the Gopis, He expanded Himself in multiple Forms to dance with each and every Gopi who took part in that dance. Similarly, He expanded Himself into 16,108 Forms at Dwarka when He married 16,108 wives.

There are some instances of great mystics also expanding their bodily features in a different way, but that sort of expansion by the Yoga process is not applicable to Krishna. In the Vedic history, for example, Saubhary Rishi, a sage, expanded himself into eight forms by the Yoga process, but that expansion was simply a manifestation, for Saubhary remained one. But as far as Krishna is concerned, when He manifested Himself in different Forms, each and every one of them was a separate individual. When Narada Muni visited Krishna at different palaces at Dwarka, he was astonished at this, and yet Narada is never astonished to see the expansion of the body of a Yogi since he knows the trick himself. Yet, in a verse in the *Srimad Bhagwatam*, it states that Narada was astonished to see the expansions of Krishna. He wonders how the Lord was present in each and every house of the 16,108 palaces with His queens.

Krishna Himself was in a different Form with each queen, and He was acting in different ways. For example, in one Form He was talking with His wife, in another Form He was engaged with His children, and in yet another Form He was performing some household work. These different activities are called actions in the Lord's different emotions, and when He is in these "emotional" Forms, the expansions are known as *Vaibhavaprakash*. Similarly, there are other unlimited expansions of the Forms of Krishna, but even when they are divided or expanded without limit, they are still one and the same. There is no difference between one Form and another; that is the Absolute nature of the Personality of Godhead.

In the *Srimad Bhagwatam* it is stated, in the Tenth Canto, Fortieth Chapter, that at the time when Akrura was carrying both Krishna and Valaram from Gokula to Mathura, he entered into the water of the Yamuna River and could see in the waters all the spiritual planets in the Spiritual Sky. He saw there the Lord in His Vishnu Form, along with Narada and the four Kumaras, and he saw how they were worshipping. This is described in the *Srimad Bhagwatam* as "Form." It is stated in the *Bhagavat Purana* that there are many worshippers who are purified by different processes of worship, such as the *Vaishnava*, or the Aryans, who also worship the Supreme Lord according to their convictions and their spiritual understanding. Each process of worship involves the understanding of different Forms of the Lord, as mentioned in the Scriptures, but the ultimate idea is to worship the Supreme Lord Himself.

In the feature of His *Vaibhavaprakash* the Lord manifests Himself as Valaram. The feature of Valaram is as good as Krishna; the difference is that Krishna is blackish and Valaram is whitish. The *Vaibhavaprakash* Form was also displayed when Krishna appeared in the four-handed Form of Narayana before Devaki when He entered this world, and then at the request of His parents He transformed Himself into a two-handed Form. Therefore, sometimes He becomes four-handed and sometimes He becomes two-handed. When He is in a Form of two hands, that is actually *Vaibhavaprakash*, and when He is four-handed, that is *Vrabhavavilasa*. In His Personal Form He is just like a cowherd boy, and He thinks Himself that; but when He is in the Vasudeva Form He thinks Himself the son of a Kshatriya, and He feels Himself also to be a Kshatriya, a princely administrator.

Form, Opulence, Beauty, Wealth, Attractiveness and Pastimes are fully exhibited in His Form as the Son of Nanda. In some of the *Vaishnava* literature it is found that sometimes, in His Form as Vasudeva, He becomes attracted to the Form of Govinda in Vrindaban. Sometimes, as Vasudeva, He desires to enjoy as Govinda does, although the Govinda Form and the Vasudeva Form are one and the same. There is a passage in the *Laleeta Madhava*, Fourth Chapter, in which Krishna addresses Uddhava as follows: "My dear friend, this Govinda Form as a cowherd boy attracts Me. I wish to be like the damsels of Vraja, attracted by this Govinda Form." Similarly, in the Eighth Chapter, Krishna says: "O how wonderful It is! Who is this Personality? After seeing Him I am attracted by Him, so that now I am desiring to embrace Him just like Radhika." When this Form of Krishna becomes a little differentiated, it is called *Tadekatma*.

In this *Tadekatmarupa* Form there are two divisions also: One is called *Svamsa*. Both in the *Vilasa* and *Svamsa* Forms there are again many differential features, which are also divided into *Prabhava* and *Baibhava*. As far as the *Vilasa* Forms are concerned, there are innumerable *Prabhava Vilasas*: Krishna expands Himself as Vasudeva, Samkarshan, Pradyumna, Aniruddha. Sometimes the Lord thinks Himself a cowherd boy, and sometimes He thinks Himself the son of Vasudeva, a Kshatriya—and this "thinking" of Krishna is called "Pastimes."

In His *Prabhava Prakasa* and *Prabhava Vilasa* He is in the same Form, but appears differently as Krishna and Valadeva. His expansion as Vasudeva, Samkarshan, Pradyumna and Aniruddha, mentioned above, is in the Original *Chaturvuha*, or four-armed Forms.

There are innumerable four-armed manifestations in different planets and different places. For instance, these four-armed manifestations are both in Dwarka and Mathura eternally. And from these four Forms originally there are the principle twenty-four Forms, named differently in terms of the different adjustments of the symbols held in the hands—and they are called *Baibhava Vilasa*. The same four Formal manifestations of Krishna are on each planet of the Spiritual Sky, called the Narayan *Loka* or *Vaikuntha Loka*. In the *Vaikuntha Loka* He is manifested in a four-handed Form, called Narayan. And from each Narayan there is a manifestation of the four Forms mentioned above (Vasudeva, Samkarshan, Pradyumna and Aniruddha). Therefore, Narayan is in the center, and the four Forms surround the Narayan Form.

Each of the four Forms again expands into three, and they all have their different Names, beginning from Kesava. They are twelve in all. Such Forms are known by different Names according to the different placements of the symbols in the hands of Narayan.

As far as the Vasudeva Form is concerned, the three expansions are Kesava, Narayana, and Madhava. The three Forms of Govinda are known as Govinda, Vishnu, and Sri Madhusudan. It should be noted, however, that this Govinda Form is not the same Govinda Form as manifested in Vrindaban (as the Son of Nanda). Similarly, Pradyumna is also divided into three Forms known as Trivikrama, Vamana, and Sridhar; and, similarly, there are three Forms of Aniruddha, known as Hrishikesha, Padmanava and Damodara.

CHAPTER SEVEN

Unlimited Forms of Godhead

These twelve different Vaikuntha Forms of Lord Krishna are known as the predominating deities for the twelve months. According to the *Vaishnava* almanac, the months are called by the different Names of Krishna. This calendar begins from the month of Margasirsa, equivalent to late October-November. The month of November is known by the Vaishnavas as Kesava. December is called Narayan. January is called Madhab, and February is Govinda. March is Vishnu, April Vasudeva, May Trivikram and June Vamana. July is called Sridhar; August Hrishikesha, September is called Padmanava and October is Damodar.

This Damodar is different from the Damodar in Vraja. The Name Damodar was given when Krishna was bound by ropes by His mother—but the Damodar Form in the month of October is a different manifestation. Similarly, the Vaishnava community marks different parts of the body and each mark is known by one of these twelve different Names of the Supreme Lord. The mark on the forehead is called Kesava, and on the belly, the breast and on the arms there are different Names, the same as those of the months.

The four Forms, Vasudeva, Samkarshan, Pradyumna and Aniruddha, are also expanded in the *Vilasa Murti*. These are eight in number, and their Names are Purushottam, Achyuta, Nrishingha, Janardana, Hari, Krishna, Adhoksaja and Upendra. Out of these eight Names, two Names, Adhoksaja and Purushottam, are the *Vilasa* or Forms of Vasudeva. Similarly, Upendra and Achyuta are the Forms of Samkarshan; Nrishingha and Janardana are the Vilasa Forms of Pradyumna; and Hari and Krishna are the two Vilasa Forms of Aniruddha. This Krishna is different from the original Krishna.

These twenty-four Forms are known as the *Vilasa* manifestation of the *Pravhav* (four-handed) Form, and they are differently named according to the different position of the symbolic representations, that is, the mace, the disc, the lotus flower and the conch shell. Out of these twenty-four Forms, there is also a division of *Vilasa* and *Baibhava*. Names mentioned herein, such as Pradyumna, Trivikram, Vamana, Hari and Krishna are also different in features. Then, coming to the *Prahava Vilasa* of Krishna, which is Vasudeva, Samkarshan, Pradyumna and Aniruddha; there are a total of twenty further variations. All of them have *Vaikuntha* planets in the Spiritual Sky, which are situated in eight different directions. And, although each of them is eternally in the Spiritual Sky, still, some of them manifest in the material world also.

In the Spiritual Sky all the planets dominated by the feature of Narayan are eternal. And the topmost planet in the Spiritual Sky is called Krishna Loka. That Krishna Loka is divided into three different portions: Gokula, Mathura, and Dwarka. In the Mathura portion the Form of Kesava is always situated. He is also represented on this earthly planet. In India there is a place called Mathura where *Kesava Murti* is worshipped and, similarly, there is a Purushottam Form in Jagannath Puri in Orissa. In Anandaranya there is the Form of Vishnu, and in Mayapur, the birthplace of Lord Chaitanya, there is the Form of Hari. Many other Forms are situated elsewhere on this earthly planet.

Not only in this Universe, but in all the other Universes such Forms are distributed everywhere. On this earthly planet also it is indicated that all the world is divided into seven islands, and it is understood that on each and every island there are similar Forms. But at the present moment they are found only in India. They are indicated to be in other parts of the world, but at present there is no information telling where they are situated. But from Vedic literature we can understand that there are Forms in other parts of the world.

These different Forms of Krishna are distributed all over the world and the Universes to give pleasure to the devotees. Not that the devotees are only born in India. Actually, in all parts of the world, there are devotees who have simply forgotten their identity. Such Forms-incarnate come not only to give pleasure to the devotee but to re-establish devotional service, and to perform other activities which vitally concern the Supreme Personality of Godhead. Some of them are incarnations as mentioned in the Scriptures, such as the Vishnu incarnation, Trivikram incarnation, Nrishingha incarnation and Vamana incarnation.

In the *Siddhartha Samhita* there is a description of the twentyfour Forms of Vishnu, named differently in terms of the different symbolic representations in the four hands. When describing the different positions of paraphernalia in the hands of *Vishnu Murti*, the counting should begin first with the lower right hand, then to the upper right hand, next to the upper left hand and, lastly, to the lower left hand. In this way Vasudeva is represented by club, conch shell, wheel and lotus flower. Samkarshan is represented by club, conch shell, lotus flower and wheel. Similarly, Pradyumna is represented by wheel, conch shell, club and lotus flower. Aniruddha is represented by wheel, club, conch shell and lotus flower.

In the Spiritual Sky the representations of Narayan, twenty in number, are calculated as follows: Hrishikesha is represented by conch shell, wheel, flower and club. Narayan is represented by conch shell, lotus flower, club and wheel. Sri Madhava is represented by club, wheel, conch shell and lotus flower. Sri Govinda is represented by wheel, club, lotus flower and conch shell. Vishnu Murti is represented by club, lotus flower, conch shell and wheel. Madhusudan is represented by wheel, conch shell, lotus flower and club. Trivikram is represented by lotus flower, club, wheel and lotus flower. Sridhar is represented by lotus flower, wheel, club and conch shell. Padmanava is represented by conch shell, lotus flower, wheel and club. Damodar is represented by lotus flower, wheel, club and conch shell. Purushottam is represented by wheel, lotus flower, conch shell, and club. Sri Achyuta is represented by club, lotus flower, wheel and conch shell. Sri Nrishingha is represented by wheel, lotus flower, club and conch shell. Janardan is represented by lotus flower, wheel, conch shell and club. Sri Hari is represented by conch shell, wheel, lotus flower and club. Sri Krishna is represented by conch shell, club, lotus flower and wheel. Adhoksaja is represented by lotus flower, club, conch shell and wheel. Upendra is represented by conch shell, club, wheel and lotus flower.

According to *Hayasirsha Pancharatra* there are sixteen Forms, and they are all different in Name, in terms of the wheel and club being differently situated.

The conclusion is that the Supreme Original Personality of Godhead is Krishna—He is called *Leela* Purushottam, and He is principally in Vrindaban as the Son of Nanda. It is also learned from the *Hayasirsha Pancharacha* that nine forms are protecting two *Puris*, known as the Mathura Puri and the Dwarka Puri: the four Forms of Vasudeva, Samkarshan, Pradyumna, and Aniruddha, and besides these four Forms, there are Narayan Forms, Nrishingha Forms, Hayagriva Forms, Varaha Forms and Brahma. The above descriptions are different manifestations of the *Prakasa* and *Vilasa* Forms of Lord Krishna.

Now Lord Chaitanya informs Sanatan Goswami that there are different Forms of the *Svamsa* also: *Svamsa* Forms are divided into the Samkarshan division and the incarnation division. From the Samkarshan division come the three Purusha Avatars: the Karanodakshayee Vishnu, Garbhodakshayee Vishnu and Kshirodakshayee Vishnu. The other division is called *Leela* avatars, such as the Lord's incarnation as a Fish, as a Tortoise, etc.

There are six kinds of incarnations: 1. the *Purusha* Avatar incarnations, 2. the *Leela* Avatar incarnation, 3. the *Guna* Avatar, 4. the *Manu* Avatar, 5. the *Yuga* Avatar, and 6. the *Saktavesh* Avatar. Out of six kinds of Vilasa manifestations of Krishna there are two divisions based on His age. They are called Balya and Pauganda. The original Form of Krishna as the Son of Nanda enjoys in two Forms of childhood, namely *Balya* and *Pauganda*.

The conclusion is that there is no end to the expansions and incarnations of Krishna. Here Lord Chaitanya describes some of them to Sanatan just to give him an idea of how the Lord is expanding and how He is enjoying. This is confirmed in the *Srimad Bhagwatam*, in the First Canto, Third Chapter. It is said there that there is no limit to the emanations of incarnations of the Supreme Lord, just as there is no limit to the waves of the ocean.

Krishna's first incarnation is as the three Purusa Avatars, namely the Maha Vishnu (or Karanodakshayee) Avatar, Garbhodakshayee Avatar and Kshirodakshayee Avatar. This is confirmed in the *Sasvata, Tantra*.

Krishna's energies are also divisible into three: His energy of thinking, His energy of feeling, and His energy of acting. In His energy of thinking He is the Supreme Lord, in His energy of feeling He is Lord Vasudeva, and in His energy of acting He is Samkarshan Valaram. Without thinking, feeling, and acting there could be no possibility of the Creation. Although there is no creation of the Spiritual World, yet there is the creation of this material world. But both the Spiritual World and the material world are manifestations of the energy of acting—in the Form of Samkarshan and Valaram—of Krishna.

The Spiritual World, the Vaikuntha planets and Krishna Loka, is situated in His energy of thinking. Although there is no creation of the eternal Spiritual World, still it is to be understood that they depend on the thinking energy of the Supreme Lord. This thinking energy is described in the *Brahma Samhita*, Fifth Chapter, second verse. It is said there that the Supreme Abode, known as Goloka, is manifested just like a lotus flower with hundreds of petals. Everything is manifested by the Ananta or Valaram or Samkarshan Form. The material cosmic manifestation and the different Universes are manifest through the Maya, or material energy. The material Nature or material energy is not the cause of all this cosmic manifestation. It is caused by the Supreme Lord, by His different expansions through the material Nature; and without the superintendence of the Supreme Lord there is no possibility of any creation.

The Form by which the energy of the material Nature works to bring about creation is called Samkarshan. It is understood that under the superintendent energy of the Supreme Lord this cosmic manifestation is created. The example is given: iron becomes hot in contact with fire, and when it is red hot, it is just like fire.

In the *Srimad Bhagwatam*, Tenth Canto, Forty-sixth Chapter, it is said that Rama and Krishna are the Origin of all living entities. These two Personalities enter into everything. A list of the incarnations occurs in the *Srimad Bhagwatam*, First Canto, Third Chapter, as follows: 1. Kumaras, 2. Narada, 3. Varaha, 4. Matsya, 5. Yajna, 6. Naranarayan, 7. Kardemikapeel, 8. Duttatreya, 9. Hayasirsha, 10. Hansa, 11. Dhruvapriya Prishni Garva, 12. Rishava, 13. Prithu, 14. Nrishingha, 15. Kurma, 16. Dhanvantari, 17. Mohini, 18. Vamana, 19. Bhargava, 20. Raghavendra, 21. Vyas, 22. Pralambari Valarama, 23. Krishna, 24. Buddha, 25. Kalki. Almost all of these twenty-five *Leela* Avatars appear in one day of Brahma, which is called a *Kalpa*, and sometimes they are called Kalpa Avatars. Out of these, the incarnation of Hansa Mohini is not permanent; but Kapila, Dattatreya, Rishava, Dhanvantari and Vyas are five eternal Forms, and they are more celebrated. The incarnations of the Tortoise, the Fish, Naranarayan, Baraha, Hayagriva, Prisnigarbha, and Valadeva are considered as incarnations of *Vaibhava*. Similarly, there are three incarnations of the qualitative modes of Nature. They are called Brahma, Vishnu and Shiva.

Of the *Manvantara* Avatars, there are fourteen: 1. Yajna, 2. Bibhu, 3. Satyasen, 4. Hari, 5. Vaikuntha, 6. Arjita, 7. Vaman, 8. Sarbabhouma, 9. Rishava, 10. Viswaksen, 11. Dharmasetu, 12. Sudhama, 13. Yogeswar, 14. Vrihatbhanu. Out of these fourteen Manvatar incarnations, Yajna and Vamana are also Leela Avatars. The balance are Pastime Manvantar Avatars. These fourteen Manvantar

Avatars are also known as *Bhaiva* Avatars.

The four *Yuga* Avatars are also described in the *Bhagwatam:* in the *Satya Yuga* the incarnation of God is white, in the *Treta Yuga* the incarnation of God is red, in the *Dvarpara Yuga* the incarnation of God is blackish; and the incarnation in the *Kali Yuga* is also blackish, but sometimes in a special *Kali Yuga* the color is yellowish. So far as the *Saktavesh* Avatars are concerned, they include Kapila and Rishava, the *Saktavesh* Avatar, Ananta, Brahma (sometimes the Lord Himself becomes Brahma), Satyasen as the incarnation of knowledge, Narada as the incarnation of devotional service, King Prithu as the incarnation of administrative power and Rishava as the incarnation of subduing evil principles.

CHAPTER EIGHT

The Avataras

Lord Chaitanya continued: The expansions of Lord Krishna Who come to the material Creation are called *Avataras* or incarnations. *Avatara* means one who descends from the higher Spiritual Sky. In the Spiritual Sky there are innumerable Vaikuntha planets, and from such a planet the expansion of the Supreme Personality of Godhead comes into this Universe, and therefore He is called *Avatara. Avataran* means to descend.

The first descent of the Supreme Personality of Godhead from the expansion of Samkarshan is the *Purusha* incarnation. This is confirmed in the *Srimad Bhagwatam*, both in the First Canto, Third Chapter, as well as in the Sixth Chapter. It is said there that the Supreme Personality of Godhead descends as the first *Purusha* incarnation for the material Creation, and He immediately manifests sixteen elementary energies. He is known as Maha Vishnu, lying on the Causal Ocean, and He is the Original incarnation in the material world. He is the Lord of time, Nature, cause and effect, mind, ego, and the five elements, the three modes of nature, the senses, and the Universal Form. He is independent, and the Master of all objects movable and immovable in the material world.

The influence of material Nature cannot reach beyond the *Viroja*, or Causal Ocean, and this is confirmed in the *Srimad Bhagwatam*, Second Canto, Ninth Chapter. On the Vaikuntha planets there is no influence of the modes of material Nature. There is no mixture of the modes of goodness, passion, and ignorance, and neither is there any influence of material time. On those planets the liberated associates of Krishna live eternally, and they are worshipped both by the demigods and the demons.

The material Nature acts in two capacities, as *Maya* and *Pradhana*. Maya is the direct cause and Pradhana means the elements of material manifestation. The first Purusha Avatara, Maha Vishnu, glances over the material Nature and thereby the material Nature becomes agitated, and the Purusha Avatara thus impregnates matter with the living entities. By this glancing, consciousness is created, and consciousness is known as *Maha Tattwa*. The predominating deity of *Maha Tattwa* is Vasudeva. Consciousness is then divided into three departmental activities, under the three gunas, or modes of material Nature. Consciousness in the mode of goodness is described in the *Srimad Bhagwatam* Eleventh Canto, and the predominating deity is called Aniruddha. Consciousness in the mode of material passion produces intelligence, and the predominating deity is called Pradyumna. He is the Master of the senses. Consciousness in the mode of ignorance is the cause of production of the ether, the sky, and the cause of production of the hearing instrument, the ear. The cosmic manifestation is the combination of all these, and thereby innumerable Universes are created. Nobody can count how many Universes there are.

These innumerable Universes are being produced from the pores on the body of Maha Vishnu. It is also said that, as innumerable atoms are coming and going through the holes in a window, so from the pores of the body of Maha Vishnu innumerable Universes emanate. From His breathing also innumerable Universes are being produced and annihilated. All His energies are spiritual—they have nothing to do with the material energy. In the *Brahma Samhita* this fact is stated also. In the fifth Chapter, 54th verse, it is said that the predominating deity of each Universe, Brahma, lives only during one breath of Maha Vishnu. Maha Vishnu again is the original Supersoul of all the Universes, and He is also the Master of all the Universes. That is the description of the first incarnation, known as Maha Vishnu.

The second Vishnu incarnation enters into each and every Universe. In each and every Universe He spreads water from His body, and on that water He lies down. From His navel the stem of a lotus flower grows, and on that lotus flower the first creature, Brahma, is born. Within the stem of that lotus flower there are fourteen divisions of planetary systems, which are created by Brahma.

In each Universe the Lord as Vishnu maintains the Universe, tending to its needs, and although He is within the Universe, the influence of material energy cannot touch Him. The same Vishnu, when it is required, takes the Form of Lord Shiva and annihilates the cosmic creation. These three secondary incarnations; namely, Brahma, Vishnu and Shiva, are the predominating deities of the three modes of material Nature. The second incarnation of Vishnu, known as Garbhodakshayee, is worshipped as the Hiranygarbha Supersoul, Who has thousands of heads, as described in the Vedic hymns. This second incarnation, Garbhodakshayee Vishnu, is the Master of the Universe, and in each Universe there is a manifestation of the Garbhodakshayee Vishnu. Although He is within the material Nature, still He is not touched by it.

The third incarnation of Vishnu is also an incarnation of the mode of goodness. As the Kshirodhakshayee Vishnu, He is also the Supersoul of all living entities, and He resides on the ocean of milk within the Universe. Thus Lord Chaitanya described the Purusha Avatars.

He then described the *Leela* Avatars: He said that there is no limit or counting for the *Leela*, or "Pastime," Avatars, but some of them are described by the Lord, for example: Matsya, Kurma, Raghunath, Nrishingha, Vamana and Baraha.

A description of the qualitative incarnations of Vishnu, or Guna Avatars, is as follows: Brahma is one of the living entities, but he is very powerful on account of his devotional service. Such a primal living entity, by the influence of the mode of material passion, is situated as Brahma. He is made powerful by Garbhodakshayee Vishnu directly, and therefore Brahma has power to create innumerable living entities. A description of Brahma is given in the *Brahma Samhita*, Fifth Chapter, 50th Verse. Brahma is likened to the valuable stones influenced by the rays of the Sun, and the Sun is likened to the Supreme Lord Garbhodakshayee Vishnu. If in some Kalpa there is no suitable living entity who can act in the position of Brahma, then Garbhodakshayee Vishnu Himself manifests as Brahma and acts in that way.

Similarly, by expanding Himself as Lord Shiva, He is engaged when there is a necessity to annihilate the *Bramhanda*. Lord Shiva, in association with

Maya, has many Forms; generally, they are numbered at eleven. Lord Shiva is not one of the living entities—he is more-or-less Krishna Himself. The example is given of the distinction between milk and yogurt. Yogurt is a preparation of milk, but still yogurt cannot be used as milk. Similarly, Lord Shiva is an expansion of Krishna, but he cannot act as Krishna, nor can we derive the spiritual restoration from Lord Shiva that we can derive from Krishna. The essential difference is that Lord Shiva has a connection with the material Nature, but Vishnu has nothing to do with the material Nature. In *Srimad Bhagwatam*, Tenth Canto, Eighteenth Chapter, it is said that Lord Shiva is a combination of the three kinds of transformed consciousness, known as *Baikrik*, *Taijsa* and *Tamasa*.

The Vishnu incarnation, although Master of the modes of goodness within each Universe, is in no way in touch with the influence of material Nature. Everything of Vishnu is equal to Krishna, but still Krishna is the original Source. Vishnu is partial, and Krishna is whole. This is the version of the Vedic literature. In the *Brahma Samhita* there is the example of an original lamp which lights a second lamp; although both the lamps are of equal candle power, still one is accepted as the original, and the other is said to be kindled by the original lamp. The Vishnu expansion is like that. He is Vishnu, He is equally powerful, but the original Vishnu is Krishna. Brahma and Lord Shiva are obedient servants of the Supreme Lord and the Supreme Lord as Vishnu is an expansion of Krishna.

After describing the Leela Avatara and Guna Avatara, Lord Chaitanya then explained to Sanatan Goswami about the *Manvantara Avatara*. He states that there is no counting of the *Manvantara Avatara*. The Manus are fourteen in one *Kalpa*, or one day of Brahma. One day of Brahma is calculated at 432 million years, and during that period of time there are fourteen Manus. Brahma lives for 100 years on this scale. Therefore, during the lifetime of Brahma, if fourteen Manus appear in one day, then there are 420 Manus during the month of Brahma, and during the year of Brahma there are 5,040 Manus. Brahma lives for 100 years, and it is calculated that there are five hundred four thousand Manus in one Brahma's duration of life. There are innumerable Universes, and one can just imagine how many Manvantara incarnations there are in the total.

The Universes are being produced by the breathing out of Maha Vishnu, and no one can calculate how many Manus there are at one time. Each Manu is called by a different name. The first Manu is called Svayambhuba. He is the son of Brahma personally. The second Manu is called Swarochis; he is the son of the predominating deity of fire. The third Manu is called Uttam; and he is the son of King Priyabratha. The fourth Manu is called Tamasa; and he is the brother of Uttama. The fifth Manu is called Raivata. He is the brother of Tamasa. The sixth Manu is also the brother of Tamasa. The sixth Manu is called Chaksus; and he is the son of Chaksu. The seventh Manu is called Baivasvata. He is the son of the Sungod, born of a different wife, whose name is Chakya. The ninth Manu is called Daksasavarni. He is the son of Baruna. The tenth Manu is called Brahmasavarni, and he is the son of Upsloka. Four other Manus are known as Rudrasavarni, Dharmasavarni, Indrasavarni, and Raichya. All are sons of Lord Shiva.

After finishing the description of the Manu incarnations, the Lord described to Sanatan Goswami the *Yuga* Avatars. He said that there are four Yugas, or millennia. The first Yuga is called Satya, the second is called Treta, the third is called Dvapara, and the fourth is called Kali. In each millennium the Lord takes different colors in different incarnations. In the Satya Yuga the color of the principal incarnation is white. In the Treta Yuga the color of the principal incarnation is red, and in the Dvapara Yuga the color of the principal incarnation is blackish—Krishna. And, in the Kali Yuga, the color of the principal incarnation is yellow. This is confirmed in the *Srimad Bhagwatam*, Tenth Canto, Eighth Chapter, as spoken by Gargamuni while calculating the horoscope of Krishna in the house of Nanda Maharaj.

In the Satya Yuga the process of self-realization is meditation, and this process of meditation was taught by the incarnation of God in the color of whiteness. This incarnation gave benediction to the sage Kardum for obtaining, as his son, an incarnation of the Personality of Godhead. In the Satya Yuga everyone meditates on Krishna, and each and every living entity is in full knowledge. Other meditations, which are not recommended in this present age, are still being attempted as meditational processes by people who are not in full knowledge.

The process for self-realization in the Treta millennium is performance of different sacrifices, and this is taught by the incarnation of God in His red color. In the Dvapara millennium, Krishna is Personally present, and He is worshipped by everyone, and that is the process of self-realization for that age. Krishna is blackish in color, He is the incarnation Himself, and He induces people to worship Him, as is stated in the Bhagavad Gita. The *Srimad Bhagwatam* also, in the Eleventh Canto, Fifth Chapter, states that the worship of Krishna is made by the hymn: "Let me offer my obeisances unto the Supreme Personality of Godhead, Vasudeva." This is the hymn generally practiced by the people to worship the Supreme Lord Krishna in the Dvapara millennium.

The next millennium is Kali Yuga, in which we are now. In this age the

Lord incarnates to preach chanting of the Holy Name of Krishna. The Lord appears in this age in yellowish color, and He teaches people love of God by chanting the Name of Krishna. The process of teaching is done Personally by Krishna, and He exhibits His love of Godhead by chanting, singing, and dancing with thousands of people following Him. This particular incarnation of the Supreme Personality of Godhead is foretold in the *Srimad Bhagwatam*, Eleventh Canto, Fifth Chapter; in which it is stated that the Lord incarnates in the Age of Kali as a devotee, always chanting *Hare Krishna, Hare Krishna, Krishna Krishna, Hare Hare/Hare Rama, Hare Rama, Rama Rama, Hare Hare.*

But, it is stated there, His complexion is not like the Krishna of the Dvapara Yuga. He is always engaged in preaching love of Godhead through the *Sam-kirtan* movement, and those who are intelligent adopt this process of self-realization. It is also stated in the *Srimad Bhagwatam*, Twelfth Canto, Third Chapter, that the self-realization which could be achieved in the Satya millennium by meditation, in the Treta millennium by the performance of different sacrifices, and in the Dvapara millennium by worshipping the Lord Krishna, could be achieved in the Age of Kali simply by chanting these Holy Names: *Hare Krishna*. In the *Vishnu Purana* also the same thing is confirmed: that for this age there is no use of meditation or the performance of sacrifices or temple worship. Simply by chanting the Holy Name of Krishna—*Hare Krishna, Hare Krishna, Krishna Krishna, Hare Hare/Hare Rama, Hare Rama, Rama Rama, Hare Hare*—one can achieve perfect self-realization.

When Lord Chaitanya was describing the incarnation in this Age of Kali, Sanatan Goswami, who had been a government minister and was perfectly capable of drawing a conclusion, indirectly asked Lord Chaitanya, "How can one understand the advent of an incarnation?" He could understand that Lord Chaitanya was the incarnation of Krishna, corroborating the description of the incarnation of the Kali millennium; and he also could understand that, in the future, there would be many imitation incarnations following the incarnation of Lord Chaitanya, because Lord Chaitanya played as an ordinary Brahmin boy, though His devotees accepted Him as an incarnation. Sanatan knew there would be many pretenders, and so he inquired from Lord Chaitanya: "How can one understand the symptoms of an incarnation?"

The Lord replied to the inquiry of Sanatan Goswami: "As one can understand different incarnation of different millenniums with reference to the context of the Vedic literature, similarly, one can understand who is actually the incarnation of Godhead in this Age of Kali."

Specially stressed is the reference to authoritative Scriptures: one should try to understand the characteristics of an incarnation with reference to the Scripture, not whimsically. An incarnation of the Supreme Lord never declares Himself to be an incarnation. But His followers, with reference to the context of the authoritative Scriptures, must ascertain who is an incarnation and who is a pretender.

The real incarnation is described with reference to two features: the principal feature is called Personality, and the other is called the marginal feature. Any intelligent person can understand the characteristics of an Avatara, or incarnation, by these two features. There is a description of the characteristics of the body and of the activities. The description of the body is the principal feature for identifying an incarnation, and the activities are the marginal feature. This is confirmed in the beginning of *Srimad Bhagwatam*, where the features are very nicely described in the 1st verse of the First Canto. In that verse there are two terms, *Param* and *Satyam*. Lord Chaitanya indicated that the words *Param* and *Satyam* show Krishna in His principal feature. The other, marginal features are that He taught Vedic knowledge to Brahma, and that He incarnates as the Purusha Avatar to create the cosmic manifestation. These are occasional features for some special purposes.

One should try to understand and distinguish the principal feature and the marginal feature of an Avatar. Nobody can declare himself an incarnation without these two features, and therefore, any intelligent man will study the principal features and marginal features before accepting a pretender. Sanatan Goswami tried to confirm Lord Chaitanya's Personal characteristics as those of the incarnation of this age, and Lord Chaitanya confirmed it—though not directly. He simply said: "Leave aside all this discussion, let us go on about the description of the *Saktavesh Avatar*."

The Lord then said that there is no limit or counting of *Saktavesh Avatars*, but some of them can be mentioned as examples. The *Saktavesh* incarnation are of two kinds: one direct, and the other indirect. When the Lord Himself comes, He is called *Shakshat*, or direct Saktavesh Avatar, and when He empowers some living entity to represent Him, that one is called indirect, or *Avesa*, incarnation.

Examples of indirect Avatars are the four Kumaras, Narada, Prithu, and Parsuram. They are actually living entities, but there is specific power given to them by the Supreme Personality of God. Examples of direct, or Shakshat, Avatar are the Shesha incarnation or Ananta incarnation.

When a specific opulence of the Supreme Lord is invested in some specific entities, they are called Avesa Avatars. The four Kumaras represent the specific opulence of knowledge of the Supreme Lord. Narada specifically represents the devotional service of the Supreme Lord. The devotional service of the Lord is there also in Lord Chaitanya, Who is considered to be the full representation of devotional service. In Brahma the opulence of creative power is invested. In Ananta the power of the sustenance of all the planets is invested. In the Shesha incarnation the power is in serving the Supreme Lord. And in King Prithu is the power of maintaining the living entities. Similarly, in Parsuram the power of killing the evil elements is invested. So far as *Vibhuti*, or the special favor of the Supreme Personality of Godhead, is concerned, there is a description in the *Bhagavad Gita*, Tenth Chapter. It is said there that any living entity who appears to be especially powerful or beautiful should be known as specifically favored by the Supreme Lord.

The Lord, after finishing the description of the Saktavesh incarnation, began to speak about the age of the Supreme Lord. He said that the Supreme Lord Krishna is always like a 16-year-old boy, and when He desires to descend to this Universe, He first of all sends His father and mother, who are His devotees, and then He advents Himself as the incarnation, or comes Personally. All His activities, beginning from the killing of the Putana demon, are being displayed in innumerable Universes, and there is no limit to them. At every moment, at every second, His manifestations of different Pastimes are seen in the different *Brahmandas*, or Universes. Therefore, His Pastime activities are just like the waves of the Ganges River: as there is no limit to the flowing of the waves of the Ganges, similarly, there is no cessation of the manifestations of the different features of Lord Krishna's incarnation in different Universes. He displays from childhood many Pastime functions, and ultimately He exhibits the *Rasa* Dance.

It is said that all the Pastime functions of Krishna are eternal, and that is confirmed in every Scripture. People in general cannot understand how Pastimes are being performed by Krishna, but Lord Chaitanya gave a comparable instance in the orbit of the Sun. According to Vedic astrological calculation, the twenty-four hours of a day and night are divided into 60 *Dandas*. The days are again divided into three thousand six hundred *Palaas*. So the Sun disc can be perceived in every 60 *Palaas*, and the time constitutes a *Danda*. Eight Dandas make one *Parahara*, and the Sun rises and sets within four *Paraharas*. Similarly, four *Paraharas* constitute the duration of night, and after that the Sun is again seen as risen. Similarly, all the Pastimes of Krishna can be seen in any of the *Brahmandas*, just like the Sun can be seen in its movement through three thousand six hundred *Palaas*.

Lord Krishna remains in this Universe for 125 years only, but all the Pastimes of that period are exhibited in each and every Universe, including His Appearance, His Boyhood Pastimes, His Youth, and His manifestation of later Pastimes—until the last at Dwarka. All those Pastimes are present in one or another of the myriad *Brahmandas*, at any given time. Therefore the Pastimes are called eternal. In other words, as the Sun is eternally existing and we can see it rise and set due to our different planetary position, similarly, the Lord's Pastimes are going on, but only at certain intervals can we see the Pastimes of Krishna in this particular Universe. As described above, His Abode is the Supreme Planet known as *Goloka Vrindaban* and, being Absolute, His Name, Fame, everything is equal to Krishna. And, by the will of Krishna, the same *Goloka Vrindaban* is manifested in this Universe and other Universes also.

Therefore, although the Lord is always in His Supreme Abode, *Goloka Vrindaban*, by His Supreme will the activities there are also manifested in the innumerable Universes; and when He appears, He appears in those particular places. And in every manifestation of Krishna the six opulences are displayed.

CHAPTER NINE

The Opulences of Krishna

Lord Chaitanya is especially merciful to the innocent, unsophisticated person. His name is Patitpavan, the Deliverer of the most fallen conditioned soul. A conditioned soul may be fallen to the lowest position, but that does not prevent him from advancing in spiritual science, provided he is innocent. Sanatan Goswami was considered to be fallen in the social status because he was in the service of the Mohammedan government, and had been excommunicated from the Brahmin society. But because he was a sincere soul Lord Chaitanya showed him special favor by granting him a wealth of information in the matter of spiritual science.

The Lord next explained to Sanatan Goswami about the situation of different spiritual planets in the Spiritual Sky. The spiritual planets are known as *Vaikuntha* planets. The Universes of the material Creation have a limited length and breadth; but so far as the Vaikuntha planets are concerned, because they are spiritual, there is no limitation to their dimensions. Lord Chaitanya informed Sanatan Goswami that the length and breadth of each and every

Vaikuntha planet is hundreds and thousands of millions and billions of miles. Nobody can measure billions of miles or measure the actual extent of such Vaikuntha planets. Each of them is unlimitedly expanded, and in each and every one of them there are residents who are full with all six opulences-- wealth, strength, knowledge, beauty, fame, and renunciation. And the Supreme Personality of Godhead is present in each. In each and every Vaikuntha planet a different expansion of Krishna has His eternal Abode. And Krishna has His original eternal Abode on the planet called Krishna Loka, or Goloka Vrindaban.

We have experience in this Universe that even the largest planet is lying in only one corner of outer space. For example the Sun is supposed to be some million times bigger than the Earth, and still it lies in one corner of outer space. Similarly each of the Vaikuntha planets, although unlimited in length and breadth, lies in some corner of the Spiritual Sky, known as *Brahmajyoti*. In the *Brahma Samhita* this *Brahmajyoti* is described as *Niskla ananta Asesa*, or undivided and unlimited, without any trace of the material modes of Nature. All the Vaikunthas are like the petals of a lotus flower, and the principal part of that lotus is the center of all the Vaikunthas, and that is called Krishna Loka, or Goloka Vrindaban.

Therefore, the expansions of Krishna in various forms as described herein, as well as His different Abodes on the Spiritual Planets in the Spiritual Sky, are unlimited. Even demigods like Brahma and Shiva cannot see or even estimate how many planets there are or how vast is their extension. This is confirmed in the *Srimad Bhagwatam*, Tenth Canto, Fourteenth Chapter: "No one can estimate the length and breadth of all the Vaikuntha planets." It is said there that not only the demigods like Brahma and Shiva are unable to make such an estimate, but also Ananta, Who is an incarnation of the Lord in His opulence of strength, cannot describe any limitation to the Lord's potency, or to the area of the different Vaikuntha planets.

In this connection the prayers of Brahma, mentioned in the *Srimad Bhagwatam*, Tenth Canto, Fourteenth Chapter, are very convincing. Lord Brahma says, "O my dear Lord, O Supreme Personality of Godhead, O Supersoul, O Master of all Mystic Powers—nobody can know or explain Your potential expansion through Your *Yogamaya* energy, which extends all over the three worlds. The scientist and the learned man cannot even estimate the atomic constitution of any single planet. They may be able to count the molecules of snow in the sky, or they may even count the number of stars in the sky, but no one can estimate how You descend on this Earth or in this Universe,

with Your innumerable transcendental potencies and energies and qualities."
Lord Brahma informed Narada that, of all the great sages who were born
before Narada, including he himself, none can understand the potential
strength and energy of the Supreme Lord. So he admitted that if even Ananta,
who has thousands of tongues, tries to estimate the Lord's potential energy,
he will fail.

Brahma prayed, therefore: "My Lord, You are unlimited, and no one
has estimated the limit to Your potencies. I think that even Your Lordship
does not know the range of Your potential energies. An unlimited number of
planets float in the sky just like atoms, and great Vedantists who are engaged
in research to find You find everything different from You, and at last they
decide that You are everything."

When Lord Krishna was within this Universe, Brahma played a trick
on Him in order to confirm that the cowherd boy in Vrindaban was actually
Krishna. By his power he stole all the cows and calves, and the friends of
Krishna, who were engaged in herding the animals. But when he returned
from hiding them to see the result, he saw that Krishna was playing with the
same cows and calves and cowherd boys; because by His *Vaikuntha* potency
He had expanded all the stolen cows, calves and friends. He saw millions and
billions of them, and he also saw millions and billions of tons of cane and
fruit, and lotus flowers and horns. And all the cowherd boys were decorated
with different clothes and ornaments, and nobody could count their vast
number. Brahma saw that each of the cowherd boys had become a four-
handed Narayan, like the predominating deity of each *Brahmanda*, and he
saw that innumerable Brahmas also were engaged in offering obeisances to the
Lord. He also saw that all of them were emanating from the body of Krishna,
and after a second they were also entering into the body of Krishna. Brahma
became struck with wonder by this extraordinary feat of Krishna, and in his
prayer he admitted that anybody and everybody could say that he knows
about Krishna—but so far as he was concerned, he did not know anything
about Krishna. "My dear Lord," he said, "the potencies and opulences which
You have exhibited just now are beyond the capacity of my mind and understanding."

Lord Chaitanya then explained that not only Krishna Loka, but even
Krishna's Abode on this planet, known as Vrindaban, cannot be estimated
in potency. Vrindaban is estimated as thirty-two Scriptural miles, but even
though Vrindaban in India is thirty-two miles, yet in some part of Vrindaban
all the Vaikunthas exist. The area of the present Vrindaban consists of twelve

forests and is about eighty-four *croses*, or one hundred sixty-eight miles in area. But Vrindaban City is estimated at about sixteen *croses*, or thirty-two miles.

The Lord again said that the potencies and opulences of Krishna are unlimited. Whatever He told to Sanatan Goswami was only a partial presentation, but by such a partial presentation one can at least imagine the whole. While Lord Chaitanya was speaking to Sanatan Goswami about the opulences of Krishna, He was deep in ecstasy, and in that transcendental state He began to cite a verse from the *Srimad Bhagwatam*, Third Canto, Second Chapter, which runs as follows: After the disappearance of Krishna, Uddhava, when he met Vidura, spoke as follows: "Krishna is the Master of all demigods, including Lord Brahma, Lord Shiva and the expansion of Vishnu within this Universe. Therefore, no one is equal to or greater than Him, and He is full in all six opulences. All the demigods engaged in the administration of each *Brahmanda* offer their respectful obeisances, and therefore the helmets on their heads are beautiful, being decorated with designs of the Lotus Feet of the Supreme Lord."

Therefore, as is stated in the *Brahma Samhita*, Fifth Chapter, 1st Verse, Krishna is the Supreme Personality of Godhead, and no one can be equal to or greater than Him. That is the conclusion. The rulers of this Universe, known as Brahma, Shiva and Vishnu, although being masters of each and every Universe, are also servants of the Supreme Lord Krishna.

Lord Krishna is the Cause of all causes. He is also the Cause of the Maha Vishnu, or the first incarnation controlling this material Creation. From Maha Vishnu there is Garbhodakshayee Vishnu and Kshirodakshayee Vishnu. Krishna is the Master of the Garbhodakshayee Vishnu, the Kshirodakshayee Vishnu, and He is also the Supersoul within every living entity and every Universe. The Maha Vishnu is described in the *Brahma Samhita*: Through His breathing innumerable Universes are produced, and in each Universe there are innumerable Vishnu *Tattwas*. But Lord Krishna is the Master of Them all; or They are partial plenary expansions of Krishna.

From revealed Scriptures it is understood that Krishna lives in three transcendental places: The most confidential residence of Krishna is Goloka Vrindaban. There He stays with His father, mother, and friends; and He exhibits His transcendental relationships and His Mercy amongst His eternal entourage. There the *Yogamaya* acts as a maidservant in the matter of His dancing of *Rasa Leela*. The residents of the Vrajabhumi think, "The Lord is glorified by particles of His transcendental mercy and affection, and we, the residents of Vrindaban, have not the slightest anxiety on account of His merciful existence."

It is stated in the *Brahma Samhita*, Fifth Chapter, 49th verse: all the Vaikuntha planets in the Spiritual Sky are below the planet known as Krishna Loka. The other planets are known as Vishnu Loka. In that Krishna Loka the Lord enjoys His transcendental bliss in multiple forms; and all the opulences of the Vaikunthas are fully displayed in the one Krishna planet. The associates of Krishna are also full with six opulences. In the *Padmollar Khand*, Two hundred twenty-fifth Chapter, 57th verse, it is stated that the material energy and the spiritual energy are separated by water which is called the Viroja River. That river is flowing from the perspiration of the first incarnation of Purusha. On the other bank of the Viroja is the eternal Nature, unlimited and all-blissful, called the Spiritual Sky; which is the Spiritual Kingdom, or the Kingdom of God.

The Spiritual Planets are called "Vaikuntha" because there is no lamentation there, no fear, and everything is eternal. The Spiritual World is calculated to be three-fourths the energies of the Supreme Lord, and the material world is one-fourth of His energy. No one can understand this three-fourths, since even this material world, which is only one-fourth of His energy, cannot be described. Lord Chaitanya now tried to convey to Sanatan Goswami something about the extent of the one-fourth display of Krishna's energy. In this connection He cited an incident from *Srimad Bhagwatam* when Brahma, the Lord of the Universe, came to see Krishna at Dwarka:

When Brahma, the first creature of this Universe, approached Krishna, the doorman informed Krishna that Brahma had arrived to see Him. On hearing this Krishna inquired as to *which* Brahma had come? The doorman again came to Brahma and asked him, "Which Brahma are you? Krishna has asked."

Brahma was struck with wonder. Why was this question asked by Krishna? He informed the doorman, "Please tell Him that Brahma who is the father of the four Kumaras and who has four heads has come to see Him."

The doorman informed Krishna, and then asked Brahma to come inside. Brahma offered his obeisances unto the Lotus Feet of Krishna, and Krishna received him with all honor, and then asked him why he had come, what his purpose was.

Brahma replied, "I shall speak about my purpose in coming here, but first I have a doubt. Will You kindly remove it? You have asked through Your doorman *which* Brahma has come to see You. So may I inquire if there are any other Brahmas besides me?"

On hearing this Krishna smiled, and He at once called for many Brahmas from many other Universes. The four-headed Brahma then saw many Brahmas coming to see Krishna, and to offer their respects. Some of them had ten heads, some of them had twenty, some of them one hundred heads, and some of them a million heads. This four-headed Brahma could not even count the Brahmas coming to see Krishna to offer their obeisances. Krishna then called many demigods from other Universes, and all came to offer their respects to the Lord.

Seeing this wonderful exhibition by Krishna, the four-headed Brahma became nervous, and he began to think that he was just like a mosquito in the midst of many elephants. All of them came and offered their respectful obeisances unto the Lotus Feet of Krishna, and therefore Brahma thought that nobody can estimate the unlimited potency of Krishna.

All the helmets of the different demigods and Brahmas shone as they assembled there, and when combined together there was a great sound of all of them praying to the Lord. They began to say, "My dear Lord, it is a great mercy upon us that You have called us to see You. Is there any particular order? If there is any order, we will carry it out at once."

Lord Krishna replied, "There is nothing especially required of you, but I wanted to see you so I called you all together at one time. I offer My blessings upon you. Don't be afraid of the demons."

All of them replied that by His mercy, "Everything is all right. There are no disturbances at the present moment. By Your incarnation everything inauspicious is vanquished." As each of the Brahmas saw Krishna, every one thought Krishna was only within his Universe. After this incident He wished all the Brahmas farewell, and after offering their respects, they returned to their respective Universes.

On seeing this, the four-headed Brahma who had come to see Krishna at once fell down at the Feet of Krishna and said, "What I thought about You before is all nonsense. Let everyone say that they may know You in perfection, but as far as I am concerned, I cannot even conceive how great You are. You are beyond my conception, beyond my understanding."

Krishna then informed the four-headed Brahma; "This particular Universe is only four thousand million miles broad, but there are many other millions and billions of Universes which are far, far greater than this one. Some of them are millions and billions and trillions of miles broad. All these Universes require similar strong Brahmas; not only four-headed."

Krishna also informed Brahma, "This is only the one-quarter part of My creative potency. The three-quarters part of My creative potency is in the Spiritual Kingdom."

The four-headed Brahma then parted from Krishna, after offering his obeisances; and he could understand what the meaning of the Lord of the three-quarters energy was.

The Lord is known therefore as Tradhiesa. This name stands for His principle Abodes; namely, Gokula, Mathura, and Dwarka. These three places are full of opulences, and Lord Krishna is the Master of them all. Krishna is therefore situated in His transcendental potency. He is the Master of all transcendental energies, and He is full with six opulences. Because He is the Master of all opulences, all the Vedic literature acclaims Krishna as the Supreme Personality of Godhead.

Lord Chaitanya then sang before Sanatan Goswami a very nice song about the opulences of Krishna:

"All the Pastimes of Krishna are exactly like the activities of a human being. Therefore it is to be understood that His Form is like that of a human being. A human being is an imitation of His Form. His dress is just like a cowherd boy's, with a flute in His hand, and He seems to be just like a newly grown youth, always playful, playing just like an ordinary boy."

The Lord wanted to explain to Sanatan Goswami about the beautiful aspects of Krishna. He said that if anyone can understand these beautiful qualities of Krishna, he is dipped into the ocean of nectar. One of Krishna's potencies is called *Yogamaya*, which is transcendental and beyond the material energy, but He exhibits His transcendental potency even within this material world just to satisfy His confidential devotees. His appearance in this material world is meant for His devotees. His qualities are so attractive that Krishna Himself becomes eager to understand Himself. He is fully decorated and stands with His body curved in three ways, and His eyebrows are always moving and His eyes are so attractive that all the Gopis become enchanted. His special Abode is on top of the Spiritual Sky, and He resides there with His similar associates, the Gopis, and all the Goddesses of Fortune. He is known there as Madanmohan.

There are many different Pastimes of Krishna such as His Pastime in the Forms of Vasudeva and Samkarshan. In the material sky His Pastimes are as the first incarnation of the Purusha, or the Creator of the material world. There are also Pastimes as the incarnation of the Fish or Tortoise, as manifestations of His incarnation of energies. There are His Pastimes in the Form of Lord Brahma and Lord Shiva, as the incarnation of the material qualities;

His Pastimes as King Prithu as an empowered incarnation; His Pastimes as the Supersoul in everyone's heart; and His Pastimes as the impersonal *Brahman*.

He has innumerable Pastimes, but the most important Pastimes of Krishna are His human-like activities, in which He frolics in Vrindaban, dances with the Gopis, plays with the Pandavas on the Battlefield of Kurukshetra, and plays in Mathura and Dwarka. The most important part of His exhibition of Pastimes is in the human Form, especially as a cowherd Boy with flute in hand and appearing just like a newly grown youth. A partial manifestation of His Pastimes in Goloka Mathura and Dvaravati, or Dwarka, can overflood the whole Universe with love of Godhead. Everyone can become attracted by the beautiful qualities of Krishna.

The manifestation of His internal potency is not even exhibited in the Kingdom of God, or on the planets of Vaikuntha. But He exhibits that internal potency within the Universe, by descending from His Personal Abode, through His inconceivable mercy. Krishna is so wonderful and attractive that He Himself becomes attracted by His beauty, and that is proof that He is full of all inconceivable potencies. So far as Krishna's ornaments are concerned, when they decorate His body it appears that the ornament does not beautify Krishna, but that the ornament itself becomes beautiful since it is on His body. He appears always curved in three ways, and He attracts all the living entities and all the demigods. He attracts even the Narayan Form in each and every *Vaikuntha* planet.

CHAPTER TEN

The Beauty of Krishna

Krishna is known as Madanmohan because He conquers the mind of Cupid. He is Madanmohan by His favors to the damsels of Vraja, and by accepting their devotional service. The Lord is engaged there in the Rasa Dance as the new Cupid, after conquering Cupid's pride. He is Madanmohan by His capacity to conquer the minds of women with His five arrows called Form, Taste, Smell, Sound and Touch. The pearls of the necklace which is hanging on the neck of Krishna are as white as ducks; and the feather of the peacock which is decorating the head of Krishna is colored just like the rainbow. His yellow garment is like lightning in the sky. Krishna is like the newly arrived clouds; and the Gopis are just like footbells on His feet. When the cloud pours rain on the grains in the field it appears that Krishna is nourishing the hearts of the Gopis by calling down His Pastime rain of mercy. The ducks fly in the sky in the rainy season, and the rainbow is also seen in the sky at that time. Krishna freely moves with His friends as a cowherd boy in Vrindaban; and when He plays His flute all the living creatures, mobile and immobile, become overwhelmed with ecstasy, and they quiver and tears flow in their eyes.

His conjugal love is the summit of His various opulences. The Lord is the Master of all riches, all strength, all fame, all beauty, all knowledge, and all renunciation. Out of these, His perfect beauty is His conjugal attraction. The Form of Krishna, the conjugal beauty, is eternally existent in Krishna alone, whereas His other opulences are present in His Narayan Form.

When Lord Chaitanya was describing the superexcellence of Krishna's conjugal attraction, He felt a transcendental ecstasy, and caught up the hands of Sanatan Goswami and began to say how fortunate the damsels of Braja were. He recited in this connection a verse from *Srimad Bhagwatam*, Tenth Canto, Twenty-fourth Chapter: "How much penance and austerities the damsels of Vrindaban must have undergone, for they are able to drink the nectar of Krishna, Who is All Beauty, All Strength, All Riches, All Fame, and Who is the center of all the beauties of bodily luster."

The Body of Krishna, the ocean of the eternal beauty of youth, can be seen as moving in waves of beauty. And there is a whirlwind at the sound of His flute. Those waves and that whirlwind make the hearts of the Gopis flutter like dry leaves on the trees, and when the leaves fall down to Krishna's Lotus Feet, they can never rise up again from there. There is no comparison with that beauty, because no one has beauty greater than, or equal to, Krishna. He is the Origin of all incarnations, including the Form of Narayan. Otherwise, how could the Goddess of Fortune, who is a constant companion of Narayan, give up the association of Narayan, and engage herself in penance for gaining the association of Krishna? This is the superexcellent beauty of Krishna, the everlasting mine of all beauty. And from that beauty all other beautiful things emanate.

The attitude of the Gopis is just like a mirror on which the reflection of Krishna's beauty develops at every moment. Both Krishna and the Gopis increase their transcendental beauty at every moment, and there is always transcendental competition between them. Nobody can appreciate the beauty of Krishna by proper discharge of his occupational duty, or by austerities, or by mystic Yoga, or by cultivation of knowledge, or by offering different kinds of prayer. Only those who are on the transcendental platform of love of God—who only out of love are engaged in devotional service—can appreciate the transcendental beauty of Krishna. Such beauty of Krishna is the essence of all opulences, and His characteristics in that connection are only appreciable in Goloka Vrindaban and not anywhere else. In the Form of

Narayan the beauties of mercy, reputation, etc. are all established by Krishna. But His gentleness and magnanimity cannot be possible in Narayan. They are found only in Krishna.

Lord Chaitanya very much relished all these verses from *Srimad Bhagwatam* which He explained to Sanatan. In particular He explained the verse from the Ninth Canto, Ninth Chapter, 24th verse, as follows: "The Gopis used to relish the beauty of Krishna as a ceremony of perpetual enjoyment. They enjoyed the beautiful Face of Krishna, His beautiful Ears with earrings, His broad Forehead, and His Smile; and while enjoying the sight of Krishna's beauty they used to criticise the defect of the creator, Brahma, for the separation from their vision of Krishna by the momentary blinking of their eyelids."

The Vedic hymn which is known as *Kamagayatri* describes the Face of Krishna as the king of all moons. In metaphorical language there are many different moons, and they are all one in Krishna—the moon of the mouth, the moon of the cheeks, the moon-spots of sandalwood pulp, the beauty moon of the fingertips of His hand, and the tip of His toes—in this way there are twenty-four and a half moons, and Krishna is the central figure of all these different kinds of moons.

The dancing movement of Krishna's earrings, eyes, and eyebrows are very attractive to the damsels of Vraja. Activities in devotional service increase the sense of devotional service. What else is there for two eyes to see beyond the face of Krishna? One cannot sufficiently see Krishna with only two eyes; and one feels incapable and thus becomes bereaved. Such bereavement is slightly reduced when one criticizes the creative power of the creator. The unsatiated seer of the face of Krishna then laments as follows:

"I do not have thousands of eyes; I have only two eyes and even these two eyes are disturbed by the movements of the eyelids. So it is to be understood that the creator of this body is not very intelligent. He is not conversant in the art of ecstasy. He is simply a prosaic creator. He does not know how to fix things in different positions for only seeing Krishna."

The Gopi's minds are always engaged in relishing the sweetness of Krishna's Body. He is the Ocean of beauty, and His beautiful Face, His beautiful Smile, and the luster of His Body are always attractive to the Gopi's mind. In the *Krishna Karnamrita* these three things have been described as sweet, sweeter, and sweetest. When there are three kinds of contamination in the constitutional body, it is called convulsion. So, similarly, a perfect devotee of Krishna attains a stage of convulsion when he is so overwhelmed by seeing the beauty of Krishna's Body, His Face, and the beauty of Krishna's Smile. This ocean of transcendental convulsion before Krishna's beauty sometimes continues without any treatment, just as with ordinary convulsions a physician does not allow one to drink water for relief.

The devotee increasingly feels *the absence of Krishna*, because without Him one cannot drink the nectar of His beauty. When there is the transcendental sound of Krishna's flute, the devotee's anxiety to hear that flute penetrates the covering of this material world and enters into the Spiritual Sky, and the transcendental sound of the flute enters into the ears of the followers of the Gopis. The sound of Krishna's flute always resides within the ear of the Gopis, and increases their ecstasy. At the time when it is heard no other sound can enter into the ear, and in their family activities they are not able to reply properly because all these beautiful sounds are vibrating.

Thus Lord Chaitanya explained the transcendental constitution of Krishna, His expansions, His bodily luster, and everything connected with Him. In short, Lord Chaitanya explained Krishna as He is. And, Krishna being the essence of everything, He began to explain the process by which one can approach Krishna. He said that devotional service to Krishna is the only process. This is the verdict of all Vedic literature. The sages have declared as follows: "If somebody inquires into the Vedic literature as to what is the process of transcendental realization, or if somebody consults the *Puranas* (which are considered the sister literature)—in all of them the conclusion is that the Supreme Personality of Godhead, Krishna, is the Object of worship."

Krishna is the Absolute Truth, the Supreme Personality of Godhead, and He is situated in His internal potency, which is known as *Swarupshakti* or *Atmashakti*, as described in the *Bhagavad Gita*. He expands Himself in various multiple Forms. Some of them are known as Personal Forms, and some of them are known as separated Forms. Thus He is enjoying in all the spiritual planets as well as in the material Universes.

The expansions of His separated Forms are called living entities, and they are classified according to the energies of the Lord. Such living entities are divided into two classes: one is eternally liberated, and the other is eternally conditioned. Eternally liberated living entities never come into contact with the material Nature, and they do not have any experience of material life. They are eternally engaged in Krishna Consciousness, or devotional service to the Lord, and they are counted as associates of Krishna. Their pleasure, the only enjoyment of their life, is derived by rendering transcendental loving service to Krishna.

Those who are eternally conditioned, on the other hand, are ever divorced from the transcendental loving service of Krishna, and thus they are subjected to the three-fold miseries of material existence. On account of the conditioned soul's eternally existing attitude of divorce from Krishna, the spell of material energy awards him two kinds of bodily existence: one is the gross body, consisting of the five elements, and the other is the subtle body, consisting of mind, intelligence, and ego. Because he is covered by these two kinds of bodies, the conditioned soul is eternally suffering the pangs of material existence, known as the three-fold miseries. We are subjected to six kinds of enemies, such as lust and anger, etc., and that is the everlasting disease of the conditioned soul.

Diseased and conditioned, the living entity is transmigrating all over the Universe. Sometimes he is situated in the upper planetary system, and sometimes he is travelling in the lower planetary system. That becomes his normal conditioned life. This disease can be cured only when the expert physician, the bona fide Spiritual Master, is met and followed. When the conditioned soul faithfully follows the instructions of such a bona fide Spiritual Master, the material disease is cured and the living entity is promoted to the liberated stage, and again attains to the devotional service of Krishna, and goes back Home, back to Krishna.

A conditioned living entity should come to the consciousness of his real position. He should pray to the Lord: how long and how much will I be under the rule of the different bodily functions, such as lust and anger? As masters of the conditioned soul, lust and anger are never merciful; and there is no cessation of the conditioned soul's service to such bad masters. When he comes to his real consciousness, or Krishna Consciousness, he gives up serving those bad masters and approaches Krishna with a frank and open heart to achieve His shelter. Then he prays to Krishna to be engaged in His transcendental loving service.

In the Vedic literature fruitive activities have sometimes been highly praised, and sometimes the mystic process of Yoga is praised; and, sometimes, the speculative search for knowledge is praised. They are each considered as a different way to self-realization. But in spite of praise for the different paths of self-realization, in every writing the path of devotional service has been accepted as the foremost. In other words, devotional service to Lord Krishna is the highest perfectional path of self-realization, recommended to be performed directly. The effects of fruitive activities, mystic meditation, and the cultivation of speculative knowledge are not direct methods of self-realization. They are indirect methods because without the addition of devotional service none of these recommended paths can lead to the highest perfection of self-realization. Therefore, such paths to self-realization are ultimately dependent on the path of devotional service.

CHAPTER ELEVEN

Service to the Lord

Any recommended path for self-realization can be successful only when it is mixed with devotional service. This was explained by Narada Muni, the Spiritual Master of Vyasadeva, when Vyasadeva was not satisfied even after compiling heaps of books of Vedic knowledge. Vyasadeva was sitting in a state of depression by the banks of the River Saraswati when Narada Muni arrived. Upon seeing Vyasa so dejected, he explained the deficiency in the compilation of his various books. He said as follows:

"Even pure knowledge without being completed by transcendental devotional service does not look well. What to speak of fruitive activities when they are not in devotional service? How can they be of any benefit to the performer?"

There are many sages who are expert in performing austerities; there are many men who give much in charity; there are many famous men, scholars and thinkers; and those who are very expert in the Vedic hymns. All such achievements are certainly very auspicious, but unless they are utilized for attaining devotional service to the Lord, they are unable to award the desired results. Therefore, in *Srimad Bhagwatam*, Sukadeva Goswami offered his respectful obeisances to the Supreme Lord, Who is the only One Who can award such success.

It is accepted by all classes of philosophers and transcendentalists that no one who lacks knowledge can be liberated from the material entanglement. Still, knowledge without being mixed with devotional service holds no possibility of awarding liberation. In other words, when *Jnana*, or the cultivation of knowledge, opens the path of devotional service, then alone can it give one liberation, and not otherwise.

In the *Srimad Bhagwatam* this is also stated by Brahma: "My dear Lord, devotional service unto You is the best path for self-realization. If somebody gives up that path and becomes engaged in the cultivation of knowledge, or in speculation, he will undergo a troublesome process, without achieving any desired results. Just as a person who beats the empty husk of the wheat cannot get the grain, so those who are engaged simply in speculative knowledge cannot achieve the desired result of self-realization. Their only gain is trouble."

The *Bhagavad Gita* says, in the Seventh Chapter, 14th verse, that this material Nature is very strong, and not surmountable by an ordinary living entity. Only those who surrender unto the Lotus Feet of Krishna can cross over the ocean of material existence. The self-forgetfulness of the living entity —forgetting that he is eternally the servitor of Krishna—is the cause of his bondage in conditional life, and the cause of his being attracted by the material energy. That attraction is the shackle of material energy. It is very difficult for a person to become free as long as he desires to lord it over the material Nature. It is recommended, therefore, that one should approach a Spiritual Master who can train him in devotional service, and thus he can get out of the clutches of material Nature, and achieve the Lotus Feet of Krishna.

There are divisions of human society, like the *Brahmins*, or intellectuals; the *Kshatriyas*, administrators; the *Vaishyas*, businessmen; and the *Sudras*, or laborers; and there is the *Brahmachary*, or student, the *Grihastha* or householder, the *Vanaprasthas*, retired; and the *Sannyasis*, renounced life. And, in every case, if the individuals lack engagement in devotional service, Krishna Consciousness, even though engaged in their prescribed duty, they cannot get release because of their material consciousness. On the contrary, even by discharging their prescribed duties, they glide down to hell. Therefore, all persons engaged in their prescribed occupational duties must cultivate Krishna Consciousness in devotional service, if they want liberation from the material clutches.

In this connection, Lord Chaitanya cited a verse from the *Srimad Bhagwatam* which was delivered by Narada as the path of Bhagavat cultivation. He said that the four divisions of human social life, as well as the four different orders of life, are born out of the gigantic Form of the Lord: the *Brahmins* are born out of the mouth of the Universal Form of the Lord, the *Kshatriyas* are born out of the arms of His Personality, the *Vaishyas* are born out of His waist, and the *Sudras* are born from the legs of that Personality. As such, they are qualified in different modes of material Nature, within the Form of *Virata Purusha*. Out of these four orders of life, or social divisions, if anyone is not engaged in the devotional service of the Lord, then in spite of his being in his prescribed occupational, functional duty, he falls from his position.

Lord Chaitanya says that those of the *Mayavadi*, or impersonalist, school may artificially think themselves as one with God, or liberated, but according to Him and to *Srimad Bhagwatam*, they are not actually liberated. In this connection, He quoted a verse from the *Srimad Bhagwatam*, Tenth Canto, Second Chapter, in which it is said: "Those who think that they are liberated in the Mayavadi philosophical way, but who do not take to the devotional service of the Lord, even after undergoing the severest type of penance or austerity, and even after sometimes approaching the Supreme post, still, for want of devotional service, fall."

The Lord explained that Krishna is just like the Sun, and Maya, or the illusory material energy, is just like darkness. Therefore, one who is constantly in the sunshine of Krishna does not have any chance of being deluded by the darkness of material energy. This is very nicely explained in the four prime verses of *Srimad Bhagwatam*, and is also confirmed in the Second Canto of *Srimad Bhagwatam*, Fifth Chapter, which states: "The illusory energy, or Maya, is ashamed to stand before the Lord."

But the living entities are constantly being bewildered by the same illusory energy. The living entity in his conditioned state discovers many kinds of word-jugglery for getting apparent liberation from the clutches of Maya; but actually a person who sincerely surrenders unto Krishna even by saying only once, "My dear Lord Krishna, from this day, I am yours," at once gets out of the clutches of the material energy.

This is confirmed in the *Ramayan, Lankakanda*. There the Lord says, "It is My duty and vow that if somebody surrenders unto Me without any reservation, then I give him all protection." Somebody may develop the idea of enjoying fruitive activities, or liberation, or *Jnana*, or perfection in the Yoga system, but if such a person by chance becomes very intelligent, then he will give up all those paths and engage himself in sincere devotional service to the Lord. The *Bhagwatam* also confirms, in the Second Canto, Third Chapter, that a person—whatever he may be, either full with all desires for material enjoyment or desirous of liberation—if he is actually intelligent, should engage himself in perfect devotional service.

Persons who are ambitious for deriving material benefit from devotional service are not pure devotees, but because they are engaged in devotional service they are considered fortunate. They do not know that the result of devotional service is not material benediction; but, because they engage themselves in devotional service of the Supreme Lord, ultimately they will come to the understanding that material enjoyment is not the result of engagement in His devotional service. Krishna says that such persons, engaged in His devotional service, are certainly foolish for wanting some material benefit in exchange. Such persons are foolish because, instead of achieving the stage of love of Godhead, they try to accept something which is poisonous for them. Although such persons want material benefit from Krishna, Krishna being All-powerful considers the person's position and gradually liberates him from such an ambitious life, and engages him in devotional service. And when he is actually in devotional service he forgets his past ambitions and desires for material benefits.

In the *Srimad Bhagwatam*, Fifth Canto, Nineteenth Chapter, this is confirmed as follows: "Lord Krishna certainly fulfills the desire of His devotees who come to Him in devotional service. But He does not fulfill such desires as would again cause miseries. In spite of being materially ambitious, because they are engaged in the transcendental service of the Lord, such devotees are gradually purified of desire for material enjoyment, and come to desire the pleasure of devotional service."

Generally people come to the association of devotees for mitigating some material wants. But the influence of a pure devotee frees a man from all material desires, and he relishes the taste of devotional service. Devotional service is so nice and pure that it purifies the devotee, and he forgets all material ambitions as he engages fully in the transcendental loving service of Krishna. A practical example is Druva Maharaj, who wanted something from Krishna, and for that reason engaged in devotional service. But when the Lord appeared as four-handed Vishnu before Druva, he said, "My dear Lord, I engaged myself in Your devotional service with great austerity and penances, and thus I am now seeing You. It is always very difficult to see You, even for the great demigods and great sages, and I am now pleased and all my desires are satisfied.

I do not want anything further. While I was searching for some broken glass, I have found a great and valuable gem." Druva Maharaj stated his full satisfaction, and he refused to ask anything from the Lord.

The living entity who is transmigrating through the 8,400,000 species of life is sometimes likened to a log which is gliding downstream on the waves of the river. Sometimes, by chance, the log comes to the shore and it is saved from being forced to drift further downstream. There is a nice verse in the *Srimad Bhagwatam* in which every conditioned soul is encouraged: "Nobody should be depressed, thinking that he will never be out of the clutches of matter; because there is the possibility of being rescued exactly like the log which floats on the river for some time, and then comes to rest on the bank." This fortunate opportunity is also discussed here by the Lord.

Such fortunate incidents are considered the beginning of the decline of one's conditional life. They occur if there is the association of pure devotees of the Lord. By association of pure devotees of the Lord, one actually develops his attraction for Krishna. There are different types of rituals and activities: some of them develop into material enjoyment, and some of them develop into material liberation. If a living entity takes to ritualistic activities which develop into his pure devotional service to the Lord, in the association of pure devotees, then he naturally develops devotional service in his mind.

There is a nice verse in the *Srimad Bhagwatam*, Tenth Canto, Fifty-first Chapter, where it is stated by Muchakunda: "My dear Lord, a living entity, while travelling in this material world through different species of life, may develop towards liberation. By chance he may come in contact with pure devotees. Only at that time is he liberated from the clutches of the material energy, and he becomes a devotee of Yourself, the Personality of Godhead."

When a conditioned soul becomes a devotee of Krishna, Krishna by His causeless Mercy trains him in two ways: He trains him by the Spiritual Master from the outside, and He trains him from the inside by the Supersoul. In this connection there is a very nice verse in the *Srimad Bhagwatam*, Eleventh Canto, Twenty-ninth Chapter, in which it is said: "O my dear Lord, if somebody should get a duration of life like Brahma's, still he would be unable to express his gratitude to You for the benefits derived from remembering You; because, out of Your causeless mercy, You drive away all inauspicious conditions for a devotee, expressing Yourself from outside as the Spiritual Master, and from inside as the Supersoul."

Somehow or other, if somebody gets in touch with a pure devotee and thus develops a desire for devotional service to Krishna, he gradually rises up to the platform of love of Godhead, and thus he is freed from the clutches of the material energy. This is explained in the *Srimad Bhagwatam*, Eleventh Canto, Twentieth Chapter, where the Lord says: "For one who becomes attracted by the topics of My Activities out of his own accord—being neither lured nor repelled by material activities—the path of devotional service, leading to the perfection of love of God, becomes possible."

It is not possible, however, to achieve such a stage of perfection without being favored by a pure devotee, or a *Mahatma*, a great soul. Without the mercy of a great soul no one can even be liberated from the material clutches, what to speak of rising to the platform of love of Godhead? This is confirmed in the *Srimad Bhagwatam*, Fifth Canto, Eleventh Chapter, spoken in connection with the meeting of the King Rohugana of the Sind province in Siberia with King Bharata. The King expressed surprise at seeing Bharata's great stage of spiritual perfection in life.

Bharata replied: "My dear Rohugana, no one can attain the perfected stage of devotional service without being favored by a great soul, or pure devotee. No one can attain such perfectional stages simply by following the regulative principles of Scriptures, nor by acceptance of the renounced order of life, nor by prosecuting the prescribed duties of householder life, nor by becoming a great student of spiritual science, nor by accepting severe austerity and penances performed for realization."

Similarly, in the same *Bhagwatam*, Seventh Canto, Fifth Chapter, in connection with the conversation of Prahlad Maharaj with his father, Hiranyakasipu, the following statement appears: "When the atheist father Hiranyakasipu inquired from his son where he got such an attitude of devotional service, the boy replied: 'So long as one is not favored by the dust of the feet of pure devotees, then he cannot even touch the path of devotional service, which is the solution of all the varieties of problems of material life.'"

Lord Chaitanya said to Sanatan Goswami that all the Scriptures stress association with pure devotees of Godhead. The opportunity to associate with a pure devotee of the Supreme Lord is the beginning of one's complete perfection. This statement is also confirmed in the *Srimad Bhagwatam*, First Canto, Eighteenth Chapter. It is said there that the facility and benediction achieved by the association of a pure devotee cannot be compared with anything: neither elevation to the heavenly kingdom, nor liberation from this material energy.

Lord Krishna, also, while giving instruction to Arjuna, in the *Srimad Bhagavad Gita*, confirmed this as the most confidential instruction, in the

Eighteenth Chapter, 65th verse. The Lord said there: "My dear Arjuna, you are My affectionate friend and relative, and therefore, for your benefit, I am giving you the most confidential knowledge: Just become always mindful of Me, become always a devotee of Mine, become a constant worshipper of Me, and just become a soul surrendered to Me. That is the only way by which you can achieve My Abode. Because you are My very dear friend, My most confidential knowledge is disclosed herewith to you."

Such a direct instruction of Krishna to Arjuna is more important than any Vedic injunctions or regulative service. There are certainly many Vedic injunctions, such as ritualistic performances, sacrificial performances, regulative duties, meditation, and the speculative process of knowledge; but Krishna's direct order—"You just give up everything and become My devotee, My worshipper"—should be taken as the final order of the Lord, and one should follow that principle.

If one is convinced by this direct order of the Lord in the *Bhagavad Gita*, and becomes attached to His devotional service and gives up all other engagements, then he undoubtedly becomes successful. *Srimad Bhagwatam* also says, to confirm this statement, that one should be engaged in other paths of self-realization only so long as one is not convinced by the direct order of the Lord, Sri Krishna. As stated in *Srimad Bhagwatam* and *Bhagavad Gita*, the direct order of the Lord is to give up everything and be engaged in devotional service.

This firm conviction is known as faith. Faith means that one is firmly convinced that, simply by devotional service to Lord Krishna, everything else is performed—including the regulative principles of ritualistic duties, sacrifices, performance of Yoga, and the speculative pursuit of knowledge. Everything else is performed if one is convinced that devotional service to the Lord includes everything. This is also found in the *Srimad Bhagwatam*, Fourth Canto, Thirty-first Chapter. It is said there: "As by watering the root of the tree the branches, the twigs, the leaves, and the fruits become nourished; and as in supplying foodstuffs to the stomach all the senses become satisfied— similarly, simply by devotional service to Krishna, all other worship and all other processes are completed." Such a faithful and firmly convinced person is eligible to be elevated as a pure devotee.

Now, amongst the devotees there are three classes, according to the degree of conviction: The first class devotee is one who is conversant with all kinds of Vedic literature, and at the same time has the firm conviction mentioned above. He is a first class devotee, and he can deliver all others from the pangs of material miseries. The second class devotee is firmly convinced and of strong faith, but has no power to cite evidence from revealed Scriptures. The third class devotee is one whose faith is not very strong but is eligible to be promoted to the position of second class devotee or first class devotee by the gradual cultivation of devotional service.

It is said in *Srimad Bhagwatam*, Eleventh Canto, Second Chapter, that the first class devotee always sees the Supreme Lord as the Soul of all living entities. Therefore, in seeing all living entities, he sees Krishna and nothing but Krishna. A devotee who places his full faith in the Supreme Personality of Godhead, who makes friendship with the pure devotees, who shows favor to the innocent person, and who avoids those who are atheistic or are against devotional service—such a devotee is called a second class pure devotee. And a person who is engaged in the devotional service of the Lord according to the direction of the Spiritual Master, or by family tradition, and worships the diety of the Lord, but has not much cultivation of knowledge in devotional service, and does not know who is a devotee and who is a non-devotee—such a person is called a third class pure devotee. The last-mentioned are not actually pure devotees. They are almost in the devotional line, but their position is not very secure.

The purport is that, when a person shows his love for God and his friendship for the devotees and his mercy for the innocent and his reluctance to the non-devotees, he becomes in the category of a pure devotee. Such a person, by developing devotional service, can perceive that every living entity is part and parcel of the Supreme. In each and every living entity he can see the Supreme Person, and therefore he becomes highly developed in Krishna Consciousness. At this stage he does not make any distinction as to who is a devotee and who is a non-devotee. He sees everyone in the service of the Lord. A pure devotee, however, continues to develop all great qualities in his body, while engaged in Krishna Consciousness and devotional service. It is stated in *Srimad Bhagwatam*, Fifth Canto, Chapter Eighteen, that anyone who has attained pure unalloyed devotional service to the Supreme Lord develops all the good qualities of the demigods; whereas a person who hasn't developed pure devotional service to the Lord, in spite of his being materially qualified, is sure to go astray as he hovers on the mental plane. Therefore, his material qualification is valueless.

CHAPTER TWELVE

The Devotee

A person in Krishna Consciousness, fully devoted in the transcendental loving service of the Lord, develops many good qualities, or godly qualities— pertaining to the demigods. There are many such qualities, but Lord Chaitanya described only some of them to Sanatan Goswami: A devotee of the Lord is always kind to everyone. He does not pick a quarrel with anyone. He takes the essence of life, spiritual life. He is equal to everyone. Nobody can find fault in a devotee. His magnanimous mind is always fresh and clean and without any material obsessions. He is a benefactor to all living entities. He is peaceful and always surrendered to Krishna. He has no material desire. He is very humble and is fixed in his direction. He is victorious over the six material qualities such as lust and anger. He does not eat more than what he needs. He is always sane. He is respectful to others; but for himself he does not require any respect. He is grave. He is merciful. He is friendly. He is a poet. He is an expert. And he is silent.

In the *Srimad Bhagwatam*, Third Canto, Twenty-fifth Chapter, the person in Krishna Consciousness, devoted to the loving service of the Lord, is also described: Such a devotee or person in Krishna Consciousness is always tolerant and merciful. He is a friend to all living entities. He has no enemies. He is peaceful, and he is decorated with all good qualities. These are the symptoms of the person in Krishna Consciousness.

It is also said in the *Bhagwatam* that if one gets the opportunity to serve a great soul—a Mahatma—then his path to liberation is open. Those who are, however, attached to persons in the materialistic conception of life are on the path of darkness. Those who are actually holy are transcendentalists, equipoised, very peaceful, without any anger, and friendly to all living entities. Therefore becoming Krishna conscious, or a devotee of the Lord, is caused simply by association with such holy men. And to develop love of Godhead, the association of holy devotees is also needed. For anyone who comes in contact with a holy man, as mentioned above, the path of advancement in spiritual life is now opening. And, by following that path, he is sure to develop Krishna Consciousness in full devotional service.

In the *Srimad Bhagwatam*, Eleventh Canto, Second Chapter, Vasudeva, the father of Krishna, asks Narada Muni about the welfare of life. In reply, Narada Muni quotes a passage from the discussion of the nine sages with King Nimi: "O holy sages, I am just trying to ask what the paths of well-being for every living entity are. And, a moment of association with holy men is the most valuable thing in life. That moment will open the path of advancement in spiritual life." This is also confirmed in the *Srimad Bhagwatam*, Third Canto, Twenty-fifth Chapter.

Association with holy persons and the discussion of transcendental subject matters with them convinces one about the purposeful course. Very soon, hearing of Krishna becomes pleasing to the ear, and satisfactory to one's heart. After reception of such messages from holy persons or pure devotees, if one tries to apply them in his own life, then naturally the path of Krishna Consciousness becomes developed in faith, attachment, and devotional service—one after another.

The Lord then informed Sanatan Goswami about the behavior of a devotee. The sum and substance of such behavior enunciated by the Lord is that one should always be aloof from unholy association. That is the sum and substance of the behavior of a devotee. And what is unholy association? It is association with one who is too attached to women, and one who is not a devotee of Lord Krishna. These are unholy persons. The purport is that, as one is advised to associate with holy devotees of the Lord, so one has to be careful to avoid the association of unholy non-devotees of the Lord. Those who are pure devotees of Krishna are very careful to keep aloof from these two kinds of unholy non-devotees.

The result of unholy association with non-devotees is described in the *Srimad Bhagwatam*, Third Canto, Thirty-first Chapter. It is said there that one should simply give up association with a person who is a playmate for women; because, in association with such an unholy person, one becomes bereft of all good qualities, such as truthfulness, cleanliness, mercifulness, gravity, intelligence, shyness, beauty, fame, forgiveness, control of the mind, control of the senses, and all opulences that are automatically achieved by the devotee. A man is never so degraded as when he is degraded by association with persons who are too attached to women.

Regarding this matter of disassociation from unholy persons, Lord Chaitanya quoted a verse from *Katyayani Samhita*: "One should rather tolerate the miseries of being locked in a cage full of fire than tolerate the miseries of associating with those who are not devotees of the Lord." It is also advised that one should not see the faces of persons who are irreligious, or without any devotion for the Supreme Personality of Godhead. It is recommended by the Lord that one should scrupulously renounce the association of unwanted persons, and completely take shelter of the Supreme Lord Krishna. The same instruction is also given to Arjuna by Krishna in the last pages of *Bhagavad Gita*: "You give up everything and just surrender unto Me, and I shall take care of you, and protect you from all the reactions to sinful activities."

The Lord is very kind to His devotees. He is very grateful. He is able and magnanimous. Therefore, it is our duty to believe in the words of the Supreme Personality of Godhead. And if we are intelligent enough and educated enough, we shall follow this principle without any hesitation. As said by Aukrur in addressing Krishna, in the *Srimad Bhagwatam*, Tenth Canto, Eighty-fourth Chapter: "Who can become a surrendered soul to any other than Yourself? Who is so dear, Who is so truthful, Who is so friendly, and Who is so grateful? You are so perfect and complete that even though You give Yourself to Your devotee, still You are full and perfect. You can therefore satisfy all the desires of the devotee, even to delivering Yourself to Your devotee."

A person who is intelligent and able to understand the philosophy of Krishna Consciousness, therefore, naturally gives up everything and takes to the shelter of Krishna only. In this connection, Lord Chaitanya recited a verse spoken by Uddhava in the *Srimad Bhagwatam*, Third Canto, Second Chapter:

"How can one take shelter of anyone else but Krishna, Who is so kind? Even though Bakasur's sister planned to kill Him when He was an infant, by applying poison to her breast and offering it to Him to suck and thus to die—still that heinous woman received salvation, and was elevated to the same post as His own mother." The verse refers to the time Putana planned to kill Krishna when He was a child, by poisoning her breast and offering it to Him to suck. Krishna accepted it and sucked the milk from the breast of that demoniac woman, and at the same time sucked out her life also. But the result was that Putana was raised to the same post as His own mother.

There is no essential difference between a fully surrendered soul and a man in the renounced order of life. The only difference is that a fully surrendered soul has the distinguishing symptom of being completely dependent upon Krishna. This surrendering process can be characterized by six different qualities: The first quality is that one should accept everything that is favorable to the discharge of Krishna duties or devotional service. One should be determined to accept the process. The second is that he should give up everything which is unfavorable to the discharge of devotional service; and one should be so determined to give it all up. Thirdly, one should be convinced that nobody else can protect him except Krishna, and therefore he has full faith that he will be protected by the Lord. It should be mentioned here that the impersonalists think that being One with Krishna, or One with the Supreme Lord, is their actual identity. A devotee, however, does not destroy his identity, but he lives with full faith that Krishna will kindly protect him in every respect.

Fourthly, a devotee should always accept Krishna as his Maintainer. Fruitive performers generally expect protection from demigods; but a devotee does not expect any protection from any demigod. He is fully convinced that Krishna will protect him from all kinds of unfavorable conditions. Fifth, a devotee is always conscious that his desires are not independent. Unless Krishna fulfills them, his desires cannot be fulfilled. Lastly, one should always think of himself as the most fallen, so that Krishna may take care of him.

Such a surrendered soul should take shelter in a holy place like Vrindaban, Mathura, Dwarka, Mayapur, and should surrender himself to the Lord, saying, "My Lord, from today I am Yours. You can protect me or kill me as You like." The devotee takes shelter of Krishna in such a way. Krishna is grateful and accepts him and gives him all kinds of protection. This is confirmed in the *Srimad Bhagwatam*, Eleventh Canto, Twenty-ninth Chapter. It is said there that if a person who is about to die takes full shelter of the Supreme

Personality of Godhead and offers himself fully under His care, he actually attains immortality at that time, and is eligible to become in association with the Supreme Lord, and to enjoy transcendental bliss.

The Lord then explained to Sanatan Goswami about the various types and symptoms of practical devotional service. When devotional service becomes practical—to be performed with our present senses—at that time it is called practical devotional service. Actually, devotional service is the eternal life of the living entity, and is lying dormant in everyone's heart. The practice which invokes that dormant devotional service is called practical devotional service. The purport is that a living entity is constitutionally part and parcel of the Supreme Lord. The Lord is compared to the Sun, and the living entities are compared to the molecules of sunshine. Under the spell of illusory energy, that spiritual spark is almost extinct. But, by practical devotional service, one is again revived to his natural constitutional position. When one is practicing such devotional service, it means that he is going back to his original normal position of liberation. Such devotional service can be practiced with one's senses, under the direction of a bona fide Spiritual Master.

The beginning of such spiritual activities for making advancement in Krishna Consciousness, or devotional service, is to hear. Hearing is the most important subject matter for advancement in Krishna Consciousness. One should be very eager to hear favorably about Krishna. One should give up speculative knowledge or fruitive activities, and simply worship and desire to achieve love of Godhead. That love of Godhead is eternally existent within oneself. One has to simply practice the process of hearing. Hearing and chanting are the principal processes of devotional service.

Such devotional service may be regulative or affectionate. One who has not developed transcendental affection for Krishna should conduct his life under the direction of Scriptural injunction, and the guidance of the Spiritual Master. In the *Srimad Bhagwatam*, Second Canto, First Chapter, Sukadeva Goswami advises Maharaj Parikshit as follows:

"O best amongst the Bharatas, it is the prime duty of persons who want to become fearless to hear about the Supreme Personality of Godhead, Hari, and to chant about Him, and always remember Him. Lord Vishnu is always to be remembered, and not to be forgotten for even a moment. He is the sum and substance of all regulative principles."

The purport is that there are so many rules and regulations in the revealed Scriptures: so many recommended activities, and so many prohibited activities—but when all of them are taken together, it appears that remembrance of the Supreme Lord is always the essence of everything. Remembrance of the Supreme Personality of Godhead always within one's heart is the practical action of devotional service. In that performance of devotional service there is no regulative principle. There are no do's and don't's.

Generally, in devotional service, one should accept the following principles: 1. One is to take shelter of a bona fide spiritual master. 2. It is necessary to be initiated by the spiritual master; 3. to serve the spiritual master; 4. to inquire and to learn love from the Spiritual Master; 5. to follow in the footsteps of holy persons devoted to the transcendental loving service of the Lord. 6. For the satisfaction of Krishna one should be prepared to give up all kinds of enjoyment and miseries. 7. One should live in a place where Krishna had His Pastimes. 8. One should be satisfied with whatever is sent by Krishna for maintenance of his body and should not be anxious to receive more than that. 9. One should observe fasting on *Ekadasee* day, the eleventh day after the full moon and the eleventh day after the new moon, when no grains, cereals or beans are eaten. Simple vegetables and milk are taken in moderate amounts, and chanting of *Hare Krishna*, reading Scripture, etc. is increased. 10. One should show respect to devotees, the cow and trees such as the banyan tree.

These ten items are essential for a neophyte devotee who is beginning to follow the path of devotional service. The next stage is as follows: 11. One should try to avoid offenses in the service to the Lord, and in chanting the Holy Names of the Lord. There are ten kinds of offenses in chanting the Holy Name and they should be avoided. The offenses are: 1. Blaspheming a devotee of the Lord; 2. Considering the Lord and the demigods on the same level, or to think that there are many Gods; 3. To neglect the orders of the spiritual master; 4. To minimize the authority of Scriptures (the Vedas); 5. To interpret the Holy Names of God; 6. To commit sin on the strength of chanting; 7. To instruct the Glories of the Lord's Name to the unfaithful; 8. To compare the Holy Name with material piety; 9. To be inattentive while chanting the Holy Name; 10. To remain attached to material things in spite of chanting the Holy Names. 12. One should avoid the association of unholy non-devotees. 13. One should not attempt to have many disciples. 14. One should not take the trouble of understanding various books or to understand partially any particular book, and one should avoid discussing different doctrines. 15. One should be equipoised both in gain and loss. 16. One should not be subject to any kind of lamentation. 17. One should not disrespect demigods, or other Scriptures. 18. One should not tolerate blaspheming the Supreme

Lord and His devotees. 19. One should avoid ordinary topics of novels and fiction, but there is no injunction that one should avoid hearing ordinary news. 20. One should not give any trouble to any living creature, including a small bug.

The first ten items are affirmative, and the second ten are prohibitive. In the *Bhakti Rasamrita Sindhu* complied by Sri Rupa Goswami, it is said that one should be very liberal in behavior and should avoid any undesirable behavior. Out of the twenty regulations mentioned above, the most important are to accept the shelter of a bona fide Spiritual Master, to be initiated by him, and to serve him.

The process of devotional service can be analyzed as follows: 1. Hearing, 2. Chanting, 3. Remembering, 4. Worshipping, 5. Praying, 6. Serving, 7. Engaging as a servitor, 8. Being friendly, 9. Offering everything, 10. Dancing before the deity, 11. Singing, 12. Informing, 13. Offering obeisances, 14. Standing up to show respect to the devotees, 15. When a devotee goes, following him up to the door, 16. Entering into the temple of the Lord, 17. Circumambulating the temple, 18. Reading prayers, 19. Vibrating hymns, 20. Performing *Samkirtan*, or congregational chanting, 21. Smelling the incense and the flowers offered to the deity, 22. Accepting the *Prasadam* (food offered to Krishna), 23. Seeing *Aritrik* or ceremonial performance of receiving the Lord, 24. Seeing the deity, 25. Offering to the Lord His own palatable foodstuff, 26. Meditating, 27. Offering water to the tulsi tree, 28. Offering respect to the *Vaishnavas*, or advanced devotees, 29. Living in Mathura or Vrindaban, 30. Understanding *Srimad Bhagwatam*, 31. Trying for Krishna to one's utmost, 32. Expecting the mercy of Krishna, 33. Performing the ceremonial functions of Krishna with devotees, 34. Surrendering in all respects, 35. Observing different ceremonial functions.

To these thirty-five items another four are to be added: 1. Marking the body with sandalwood pulp to show that he is a *Vaishnava*, 2. Painting the body with the Holy Names of the Lord, 3. Covering the body with the remnants of the cover of the deity, 4. Accepting *Charanamrita*, or the water washed of the Lord. Adding these four items to the above thirty-five, we have thirty-nine items for devotional service. Out of them, 1. To associate with devotees, 2. To chant the Holy Name of the Lord, 3. To hear *Srimad Bhagwatam*, 4. To live in a holy place such as Mathura or Vrindaban, 5. With great devotion, to serve the deity—these five items are very important. They are especially mentioned by Rupa Goswami in his book *Bhakti Rasamrita Sindhu*.

The thirty-nine items above, added with these five items, become forty-four. Add to that 20 preliminary occupations, and the total is sixty-four different items for conducting devotional service. One can adopt these sixty-four items by his body, mind and senses, so that gradually his devotional service becomes pure. Some of the items are completely separate, and some are identical, and others appear to be mixed.

Srila Rupa Goswami has recommended that one should live in association of those of the same mentality. Therefore, it is necessary to form some association of Krishna Consciousness and live together for the cultivation of Krishna knowledge and devotional service. The most important item for living in that association is to understand *Srimad Bhagavad Gita* and *Srimad Bhagwatam* mutually. When faith and devotion are developed, they become transformed into the worship of the deity and chanting of the Holy Name, and living in a place like Mathura and Vrindaban.

These five items, mentioned after the thirty-nine, are very important and essential. If one can simply discharge the last mentioned five items, even if they are not done sufficiently, one can be elevated to the highest perfectional stage. One may be able to perform one item or many items, according to one's capacity, but the principle factor of one's complete attachment to devotional service makes him advance on the path. There are many devotees in history who attained the perfection of devotional service simply by discharging the duties in one item. And there are many other devotees, like Maharaj Amburish, who executed all the different items.

Some individual devotees who attained perfection in devotional service by executing only one item are: Maharaj Parikshit, who was liberated in full perfection simply by hearing. Sukadeva Goswami who became liberated and perfect in devotional service simply by chanting. Lakshmi, simply by serving the Lotus Feet of the Lord. King Prithu attained perfection simply by worshipping; Akrura simply by praying; Hanuman only by becoming the servant of Lord Rama. Arjuna attained perfection simply by becoming a friend to Krishna, and Bali Maharaj simply by offering whatever he had in his possession.

So far as Maharaj Amburish is concerned, he practically performed all the items of devotional service: he first of all engaged his mind on the Lotus Feet of Krishna. He engaged his words, his power of speaking, in describing the transcendental qualities of the Supreme Personality of Godhead. He engaged his hands in washing the temple of the deity, his ears in hearing the words of Krishna, and he engaged his eyes in beholding the deity of Krishna. He engaged his touch for rendering service to the devotees, and he engaged his sense of smell to accept the fragrance of the flowers offered to Krishna. He engaged his tongue in tasting the tulsi leaves offered to the Lotus Feet of Krishna, his legs in going into the temple of Krishna, and he engaged his head in offering obeisances unto the deity of Krishna. All his desires and ambitions were engaged in the devotional service of the Lord. Therefore, he is the leader in discharging all kinds of devotional service in different ways.

Anyone who engages in the devotional service of the Lord in full Krishna Consciousness becomes freed of all debts to the sages and demigods and forefathers, to whom we are generally indebted. In the *Srimad Bhagwatam* this is confirmed: "Anyone who fully engages himself in the service of the Lord, without discharging any other duty, O King, is no longer indebted or servant to the demigods, to the sages, to other living entities, to his relatives, to any man, or to the forefathers." The purport is that every man, just after his birth, becomes at once indebted to all the above personalities, and one is expected to discharge many kinds of ritualistic functions because of this indebtedness. But for a person who is fully surrendered unto Krishna, there is no obligation. In spite of not discharging such obligations, he is free from all debt to such persons.

It should be carefully noted, however, that when a person gives up all other duties and simply takes to the transcendental service of Krishna, he has no desire, and he is not subjected to, or apt to be performing, sinful activities. If, however, he performs any sinful activities—not wilfully, but by chance—then Krishna gives him all protection. He does not require to purify himself by any other method. This is confirmed in the *Srimad Bhagwatam*, Eleventh Canto, Fifth Chapter: "A devotee who is fully engaged in the transcendental loving service of the Lord is protected by the Supreme Person. But in case such a devotee unintentionally commits some sinful activity, or may be obliged to act in some sinful activity under certain circumstances, God gives him all protection, being situated within his heart."

The processes of speculative knowledge and renunciation are not practically the chief items for acquiring a higher standard of devotional service. One doesnot have to take to the principles of nonviolence and sense control, although there are rules and regulations for acquiring these qualities in other processes. Without being engaged in the practice of such processes, a devotee develops such high qualities simply by discharging devotional service to the Lord. In *Srimad Bhagwatam*, Eleventh Canto, the Lord says that for those who are actually engaged in the devotional service of the Lord there is no necessity for cultivating speculative knowledge or renunciation.

CHAPTER THIRTEEN

Devotional Service in Attachment

Out of sheer misunderstanding some transcendentalists think that knowledge and renunciation are some of the items necessary for rising to the standard of devotional service. This is not so. The cultivation of knowledge and the renunciation of fruitive activities may be necessary to understand one's spiritual existence in relation to the material conception of life, but they are not part and parcel of the devotional service. The results of knowledge and fruitive activities are liberation and material sense gratification, respectively. Therefore, they cannot be part and parcel of devotional service. Rather, they have no intrinsic value in the discharge of devotional service. When one is freed from the resultant action of knowledge and fruitive activities, then one can be situated in devotional service. A devotee of Lord Krishna is by nature nonviolent and self-controlled, both in the mind and the senses. Therefore, he does not have to try separately to acquire the qualifications which result from cultivating knowledge and from fruitive activities.

When Sri Uddhava was asking Krishna about the rules and regulations, and the subjects of restriction as they are stated in the Vedic language, he asked, "Why is it that from the Vedic hymns one is enlivened in the matter of material enjoyment, while, from the instruction of Vedas, one also is freed from all illusion and is encouraged to have liberation?" The rules are supposed to be ordained by the Supreme Personality of Godhead, but apparently there are contradictions, and so Uddhava inquired about how to be free from these contradictory statements of the Vedas.

In reply to this, Lord Krishna informed him about the superexcellence of devotional service: "For persons who are already engaged in devotional service to Me, and who are fixed in their minds about Me, endeavoring for the cultivation of knowledge and renunciation are not practical or necessary."

The purport is that devotional service is by itself independent of any other process. The processes of cultivating knowledge and renunciation, or meditation, may be a little helpful in the beginning, but they cannot be considered paraphernalia for discharging devotional service. In other words, devotional service can be discharged independently of the cultivation of knowledge and renunciation. In this connection, there is a verse from *Skanda Purana*, in which Parbut Muni said to a hunter tribesman: "O hunter, the qualifications which you have now acquired, such as nonviolence and others, are not astonishing, because one who is engaged in devotional service to the Supreme Lord cannot be the source of any trouble for anyone under any circumstances."

The Lord next said to Sanatan Goswami: "So far I have explained devotional service under regulative principles. Now I shall explain devotional service to you in terms of transcendental attachment."

The inhabitants of Vrindaban, Vrajabhumi, are practical living examples of devotional service. Theirs is ideal devotional service with attachment. Such devotion cannot be found anywhere else except in Vrajabhumi, Vrindaban. If one develops devotional service and attachment by following in the footsteps of the inhabitants of Vrajabhumi, that is called *Raga Marga Bhakti*, or devotional service in pursuance of attachment for the Lord. There is a statement in the *Bhakti Rasamrita Sindhu* about this: "Devotional service with ecstatic attachment for that service, which becomes a natural factor for the devotee, is called *Raga*, or transcendental attachment." The devotional service discharged in that standard of Raga is called *Ragatmika*, devotion. Deep attachment and complete absorption in the object of love is called *Raga atmika*, devotion. Examples can be seen in the activities of the residents of Vrajabhumi, and one who becomes attracted to Krishna by hearing of such attachment is certainly very fortunate. When he becomes deeply affected by such devotional service as that of the residents of Vrajabhumi, and tries to follow in their footsteps, he does not care for the restrictions or regulations of the revealed Scriptures. That is the characteristic of discharging *Raga Bhakti.*

Devotional service with attachment is a natural inclination. One who has been attracted by such a natural inclination does not accept any argument against his conviction, even though such arguments are presented according to Scriptural injunction. This natural inclination is also based on Scriptural injunction, and so a person who has attachment for that particular type of devotional service toward the Supreme Lord is not required to change it simply on the strength of Scriptural argument. In this connection we should note that the class of so-called devotees known as *Prakrita-sahajia* follow their own concocted ideas and represent themselves as Krishna and Radha, and indulge in debauchery. This kind of devotional service and attachment is false. They are actually gliding down the hellish path. This is not the standard of *Ragatmika,* or devotion. This *Prakrita sahajia* community is actually cheated and very unfortunate.

Devotional service with attachment can be executed in two ways: externally and internally. Externally, the devotee strictly follows the regulative principles, beginning with chanting and hearing and other regulations, while internally he always thinks of the attachment which attracts him to serve the Supreme Lord. He always thinks of his special devotional service and attachment. Such a real devotee's attachment does not violate the regulative principles of devotional service, but he adheres to them strictly; and yet, within his mind, he always thinks of his particular attachment.

All the inhabitants of Vrajabhumi, Vrindaban, are very dear to Krishna. A devotee in attachment selects one of the inhabitants and follows in his footsteps in order to be successful in his own devotional service. A pure devotee in attachment always follows such a personality of Vrajabhumi within himself. It is advised in *Bhakti Rasamrita Sindhu* that a pure devotee in devotional service with attachment, should always remember the activities of a particular inhabitant of Vraja, even though he is not able to live directly in Vrajabhumi or Vrindaban. Thus he may always think of Vrajabhumi and Vrindaban.

Such confidential devotees in attachment are divided into several categories: some of them are servants, some of them are friends, some of them are parents and some of them are conjugal lovers. In devotional service with attachment one has to follow a particular type of devotee of Vrajabhumi.

In the *Srimad Bhagwatam,* Third Canto, Twenty-fifth Chapter, it is stated: "The word *Matpara* is used only for persons who are satisfied with the idea of becoming an adherent of Me alone. They consider that I am their Soul, I am their Freind, I am their Son, I am their Master, I am their Well-wisher, I am their God, and I am their Supreme Goal. My dear Mother, there is no action of time upon such devotees." In the *Bhakti Rasamrita Sindhu*, the author offers his respectful obeisances to such persons who always think of Krishna as He is, as when He is Son, Well-wisher, Brother, Father, Friend, or any such relationship. Anyone following the principles of devotional service with attachment, and in terms of a particular devotee in Vrajabhumi certainly achieves the highest perfectional love of Godhead in that spirit.

There are two developmental characteristics for such seeds of love of Godhead. They are known as *Rati*, or attachment, and *Bhava*, the condition immediately preceding love of Godhead. By these two characteristics the Supreme Lord Sri Krishna is conquered by such devotees. These two characteristics are there before any symptoms of love of Godhead. This was explained by Lord Chaitanya to Sanatan Goswami. Lord Chaitanya said that there is really no end to describing the system of devotional service with attachment, and He is simply trying to offer a sampling of such devotional service.

Lord Chaitanya then said to Sanatan Goswami that He would describe the ultimate goal of devotional service, that which is meant for such a person who wants to attain perfection. When one's attachment for Krishna becomes very deep, this condition is called love of Godhead. Such a state of being is called the permanent situation of the devotee. Kaviraj Goswami has offered in this connection his respectful obeisances unto Lord Chaitanya for His sublime teachings of love of Godhead. It is stated in the *Chaitanya Charitamrita*: "O You Supreme Personality of Godhead, whoever awarded such pure devotional service to anyone else? O most magnanimous Incarnation of the Personality of Godhead, for my part I offer my respectful obeisances to this Incarnation, known as Gaura Krishna."

In the *Bhakti Rasamrita Sindhu* the state of being in love of Godhead is compared to the sunshine emanating from the Sun of love for Godhead; and this shining makes the devotee's heart more and more lovely. The heart of such a devotee is situated in a transcendental position, beyond the modes of goodness of material Nature. And the process of making the heart further and further sterilized by the sunshine of love is called *Bhava*. This description of *Bhava* is given by Rupa Goswami. *Bhava* is called the permanent characteristic; and the crucial point of progress for *Bhava* is called the marginal state of love of Godhead. When the *Bhava* state becomes deeper and deeper, the learned devotees call that state of being love of Godhead. In the *Narada Pan-*

charatra there is a verse in which it is stated: "When one is firmly convinced that Vishnu is the only Object of love and worship, and there is no one else and no demigod for his devotional service, it is accepted that he is feeling intimacy in love of Godhead, as is approved by such personalities as Bhisma, Prahlad, Uddhava and Narada."

If someone, on account of some righteous activities which provoke devotional service, is influenced by such an attitude of service, and takes shelter of the good association of the pure devotees, then he develops an attachment for chanting and hearing. In such a state of mind the development of chanting and hearing makes him advance further and further in the matter of regulative devotional service to the Supreme Lord. And, as he advances in the regulative service of the Supreme Lord, so, proportionately, his misgivings for the material world diminish. Beginning with faith, and advancing in the process of hearing and chanting, the devotee becomes more and more firmly fixed in that faith. That faith gradually develops into taste, and that taste gradually develops into attachment. When the attachment becomes purer, then it is exhibited in two characteristics, which are called *Bhava* and *Rati*. When this principle of *Rati* becomes deeper, it is called love of Godhead. Love of Godhead is the ultimate goal of human life.

This process is summarized in the *Bhakti Rasamrita Sindhu* by Rupa Goswami: "The first thing required is faith, and from faith one associates with pure devotees, and, by such association, one develops devotional service. And when he develops devotional service, his misgivings are diminished. Then he is situated in firm conviction, and from that conviction he develops a taste and advances up to the attachment stage of life, known as the regulated principles of devotional service. And, after that stage, when he still further makes progress, it is called *Bhava*, or a permanent situation. Such love of God can go further and deeper and deeper, and then is called the highest stage of love of Godhead."

In Sanskrit, this highest stage is called *Prema*. The word *Prema* can be explained as love of God without any exchange or return. Actually, the words *Prema* and *love* are not synonymous, but still one can say that *Prema* is the highest stage of love. One who has attained this stage of *Prema* is the most perfect human being. *Srimad Bhagwatam* also confirms this statement in the Third Canto, Twenty-fifth Chapter: Only by the association of pure devotees can one develop a taste for Krishna Consciousness; and when he tries to apply such developed Krishna Consciousness in his life, one can achieve all other things up to the stages of *Bhava* and *Prema*.

Lord Chaitanya next described the symptoms of a person who has developed from faith to the stage of *Bhava*. He is characterized as follows: he is never agitated even if there are causes for agitation. The next characteristic is that he does not waste his time for a moment. He is always anxious to do something for Krishna Consciousness. Even if he has no engagement, he'll find some work to do for Krishna's satisfaction. The next characteristic is that he does not like anything which is not connected with Krishna. He never hankers after personal respect. Although he is in the best position, still he does not hanker after being honored by others. And he is confident in his task. He is never under the impression that he is not making progress or achieving the Supreme goal of life or going back to Godhead, going back to Home. He is fully convinced that he is making progress toward that site. As such, with more and more confidence, he is always very busy to achieve that highest goal of life. He is very much attached to the gratification of the Lord, or chanting, or hearing about the Lord. At all times he is always attached to describing the transcendental qualities of the Lord. He wants to live in such places as Mathura, Vrindaban, or Dwarka. These symptoms are all visible in a person who has developed to the stage of *Bhava*.

This state of *Bhava* is described in connection with King Parikshit, when he was sitting on the bank of the Ganges to meet his death because of being cursed by a Brahmin boy. He spoke as follows: "All the Brahmins present here, as well as Mother Ganges, may know that I am a soul completely surrendered to Krishna. I do not mind even if I am immediately bitten by the snake sent by the Brahmin boy. Let the snake bite me as it likes, but I shall be pleased if all of you present here go on chanting the message of Krishna." Such a devotee is always anxious to see that his time is not wasted in anything which is not connected with Krishna. As such, desires derived from fruitive activities, or from yogic meditation, or by the cultivation of knowledge are not liked by him. He is simply attached to favorable words in relation with Krishna. Such pure devotees of the Lord always go on praying to the Supreme Lord with tears in their eyes, and their minds are always engaged in recollecting the activities of the Lord, and with their bodies they offer obeisances. Thus they are satisfied. Any devotee who is acting in such devotional service dedicates his life and body for that purpose.

King Bharata was also a pure devotee, and under his name India is called *Bharatvarsa*. He left his household life and kingdom at an early age. He left his devoted, beautiful wife, his son and friends and kingdom and everything just as if they were stool. Such are the symptoms of persons who have developed *Bhava* in their devotional service. Such a person in devotional service always thinks of himself as the most wretched, and he is only satisfied that someday or other Krishna will be kind enough to favor him by engaging him in devotional service. In the *Padma Purana* another instance of the pure devotee is found, where the king, although the best of all human beings, was begging from door to door and was even praying to the lowest of human society, the *Chandala*.

Sri Sanatan Goswami later composed the following verse: "I am low in love of Godhead, and I haven't any asset for hearing about devotional service. Neither do I have any understanding of the science of devotional service, nor do I have any cultivation of knowledge, nor any righteous activities behind me; nor am I born of high family. But, O Darling of the damsels of Braja, still I maintain a hope for achieving You, and that hope is disturbing me." So a devotee, being touched deeply by such strong desire, always chants *Hare Krishna, Hare Krishna, Krishna Krishna, Hare Hare/Hare Rama, Hare Rama, Rama Rama, Hare Hare.*

In this connection a nice verse by Bilvamongal appears in *Krishna Karnamrita:* "O Player of the nice flute, Krishna, the beauty of Your boyhood activities is very wonderful in this world. You know the agitation of my mind, and I know what You are. Nobody knows how confidential our relationship is. Now my eyes are anxious to see You and Your face, but I cannot see You. Please—let me know what I shall do." A similar passage appears in *Bhakti Rasamrita Sindhu,* by Rupa Goswami, which states: "O Govinda! this young girl with tears in her eyes is crying in a sweet voice, chanting Your Glories." Such pure devotees are always anxious to describe the Glories of Krishna, and to live in a place where Krishna exhibited His Pastimes.

A similar verse appears again in *Krishna Karnamrita:* "This Body of Krishna is so nice, His Face is so nice—everything about Him is only sweet and fragrant." A similar passage also appears in the *Bhakti Rasamrita Sindhu:* "O Lotus-eyed One, when shall I be able to always chant Your Holy Name, and being agitated in that chanting, when shall I be able to dance on the bank of the Yamuna?"

All the above descriptions made by Lord Chaitanya to Sanatan Goswami are called symptoms of the *Bhava* stage of devotional service. Next He proceeds to describe the symptoms of actual love for Krishna. He says that nobody can understand a person who has developed love of Krishna—neither his words, his activities, nor his symptoms. Even if one is very learned, it is very difficult for him to understand a pure devotee in love of Godhead. This is confirmed in *Bhakti Rasamrita Sindhu* also.

A person engaged in devotional service becomes slackened in his heart when singing the glorification of the Supreme Lord. Because the Lord is very dear to him, in glorifying the Lord's Name, Fame, etc., he becomes almost like an insane man, and in such a condition of life sometimes he laughs, sometimes he cries, sometimes he dances—and without any consideration of the situation, he continues in such activities. And, by gradual development of his love of Godhead he increases his affection, his emotion, his ecstasy. Such attachment, *Mahabhava*, is the highest stage of devotional love. It can be found like molasses or sugar, which are different stages of the same thing. But the highest stage is called sugar candy. In different stages of the same juice, sugar candy becomes more and more palatable. Similarly, in love of Godhead, by a gradual process of development, transcendental pleasure is increased to the highest stage for the real devotee.

CHAPTER FOURTEEN

The Ecstacy of the Lord and
His Devotees

The symptoms of highly developed devotional service exhibited by the
pure devotees sometimes are imitated by persons who are not actually pure
devotees of Krishna. This is described in the *Bhakti Rasamrita Sindhu*. Such
symptoms without devotional service to Krishna are purposeful, they are not
actual. Sometimes those who are not conversant with this science of devotional
service are captivated by the exhibition of such symptoms, but those who
are in knowledge of the science of devotional service do not accept such
symptoms. They are simply imitation, or only the beginning. That is accepted
by the learned devotees.

According to the different divisions and grades of devotees, the permanent
situations of the devotional attitude are divided into five categories: 1. peacefulness, 2. servitude toward Krishna, 3. friendship with Krishna, 4. parental
affection toward Krishna, and 5. conjugal love for Krishna. There is a different
taste and relish in each of the different divisions of love of Godhead, and a
devotee situated in a particular type of devotional service is happy in that

121

position. The characteristic symptoms of a pure devotee are laughing and crying; when emotions are favorable, they laugh; and when the emotion is not favorable, they cry.

But above these two emotions there is the permanent situation of love which is called *Sthaaibhava*. In other words, the attachment to Krishna is called a permanent situation. That permanent loving attitude is sometimes mixed with different kinds of tastes, and they are named *Bibhava*, *Anubhava*, *Byabhichary*. *Bibhava* is a particular taste for attachment to Krishna, and is divided into two further categories, namely *Alambana* and *Uddipana*. The cause that increases one's love of Krishna is said to be *Bibhava*, in the *Agni Purana* and other authoritative Scriptures. Such taste is increased as *Alambana*, when Krishna is the Objective. When Krishna's transcendental qualities include a devotional emotion, by His Activities, His beautiful smiling Face and flavor of Body, the sound of His flute, His sound of the Nopur, or conch shell, the marks of His sole, His dwelling place, His paraphernalia of devotional service: such as tulsi leaves, devotees, and the performance of ceremonies, and *Ekadasee*—this devotional emotion so induced is called *Alambana*, or *Uddipana*. When feeling and emotions within oneself are exhibited, that is called *Anubhava*. In the *Anubhava* attitude, one dances and sometimes falls down, sometimes sings loudly, sometimes shows convulsions, sometimes yearns, sometimes breathes very heavily—all without any concern for the situation.

Those external features exhibited on the body of the devotees are called *Udbhasvar*. The *Byabhichary* symptoms are thirty-three in number. Such symptoms principally comprise the matter of words and different features of the body. These different features of the body, such as dancing and trembling and laughing, etc., when mixed with the *Byabhichary* symptoms are called *Samchary*. And, when *Bhava*, *Anubhava* and *Byabhichary* symptoms are mixed together they make the devotee dive into the ocean of immortality. That is called the *Bhakti Rasamrita Sindhu*, The Ocean of the Pure Nectar of Devotional Service; and one who is merged into that ocean is always concentratedly in transcendental pleasure on the waves and sound of that particular ocean.

The particular flavors, or tastes of the devotees who merge into that ocean of *Bhakti Rasamrita* are known as neutrality, servitude, friendship, parenthood and conjugal love. The conjugal love taste, however, with symptoms of decorating the body for attracting Krishna, is very prominent. The flavor of servitude increases up to affection, anger, fraternity and attachment. The relish of friendship increases up to affection, anger, fraternity, attachment and devotion. In the relish of parenthood, the attachment increases up to affection,

Lord Chaitanya Fainting in the Temple of Lord Jagannath

anger, fraternity and devotion. There are special flavors of friendship with the Supreme Lord, as manifested in friends such as Subal. There the devotion increases up to *Bhava*.

The different flavors are also divided into two kinds of ecstasy, called *Yoga* and *Biyoga*, or meeting and separation. In the relish of friendship and parenthood, the feelings of meeting and separation are various.

The situations known as *Rudha* and *Adhirudha* are possible in the flavor or conjugal love. Conjugal love, as exhibited by the queens at Dwarka, is called *Rudha*, and the conjugal love exhibited at Vrindaban by the damsels of Vraja is called *Adhirudha*. The highest perfections of *Adhirudha* affection in conjugal love can be divided into two: when they are actually getting together it is called *Madana*, and when they are separated it is called *Mohana*. In the ecstasy of *Madana* there are symptoms of kissing one another, and in the ecstasy of *Mohana* there are two kinds of symptoms: *Udghurna* and *Chitrajalpa*. There are altogether ten divisions in the *Chitrajalpa* platform. In the *Srimad Bhagwatam* there is a portion known as *Bhramorgita*, and different kinds of *Chitrajalpa* are mentioned there. *Udghurna* is a symptom of separation, and there is also the symptom called transcendental insanity. In that transcendental insanity one thinks that he himself has become the Supreme Personality of Godhead. In such an ecstasy he imitates the symptoms of Krishna in different ways.

There are two kinds of dresses in conjugal love. They are called *Sambhoga* and *Bipralambha*. On the *Sambhoga* platform the dresses are unlimited, and on the *Bipralambha* platform they are four in number.

The ecstasy exhibited before the meeting of the love and the beloved, and the ecstasy between them after meeting, and the state of mind of not meeting the beloved is called *Bipralambha*, and that *Bipralambha* or previous state of love is a nourishing element for meeting afterwards. When the lover and beloved meet all of a sudden and embrace one another, feeling an ecstasy of happiness, that state of mind is called *Sambhoga*. *Sambhoga* ecstasy is also known, in different situations, by four names: 1. *Samksipta*, 2. *Samkirna*, 3. *Sampanna*, 4. *Samriddhiman*. Such symptoms are also visible during dreams.

The state of being before actually meeting one another is called *Purvaraga*. The obstacles to the meeting of the lover and the beloved are called *mana*, or anger. When the lover and beloved are separated in different places, that sense is called *Pravas*. And the feelings of separation which are present even during the meeting, under certain conditions, are called love anxieties. This anxiety of love is exhibited in the *Srimad Bhagwatam*, Tenth Canto, Ninetieth

Chapter, when the princesses were keeping awake nights watching Krishna sleeping. They were afraid of Krishna's separation, and were talking amongst themselves of how they had been affected by the beautiful Eyes and Smiling of Krishna.

The Supreme Lover is Krishna, and He is situated in Vrindaban. The Supreme Beloved is Radharani. As Krishna is the Supreme Lover, there are 64 important qualifications of Krishna, on hearing which, the devotee takes transcendental pleasure. The characteristics of Krishna are explained in the *Bhakti Rasamrita Sindhu* as follows: 1. His body is well-constructed. 2. It is full of auspicious symptoms; 3. beautiful; 4. very glorious; 5. strong; 6. always looking like a boy of sixteen; 7. well-versed in different languages; 8. truthful; 9. decorated with pleasing words; 10. expert in speaking; 11. very learned; 12. intelligent; 13. influential; 14. joyful; 15. cunning; 16. expert; 17. grateful; 18. firmly convinced. 19. He knows how to deal with different circumstances; 20. is always conversant with Scriptural injunctions; 21. clean; 22. controlled by devotees; 23. steady; 24. self-controlled; 25. forgiving; 26. grave; 27. speculative; 28. fairdealing; 29. magnanimous; 30. religious; 31. a great hero; 32. merciful; 33. respectful; 34. competent; 35. gentle; 36. modest; 37. Protector of the surrendered soul; 38. Deliverer; 39. Friend of the devotees; 40. submissive to love; 41. all auspicious; 42. most Powerful; 43. famous; 44. devoted to all living entities; 45. worshipable by everyone; 48. full with opulence; 49. Supreme; 50. full with riches.

All the above-mentioned 50 qualities are fragmentally present in every living entity. When they are completely spiritually free and situated in their original condition, all the above-mentioned 50 qualities can be perceived in human life—but in minute quantity. There are five other transcendental qualities, as mentioned below, which can be seen in Vishnu, the Supreme Lord, and partially in Lord Shiva also—but they are not visible in the living entities. They are as follows: 1. always situated in His original condition; 2. omniscient; 3. evergreen or always fresh; 4. eternally blissful; 5. conversant, the master of all perfection.

Besides the above-mentioned five transcendental qualities, there are five other qualities which can be seen in the Spiritual Sky, especially in the Vaikuntha planets where Narayana is the predominating deity. They are: 1. inconceivable potencies; 2. able to sustain innumerable Universes; 3. the Seed of all incarnations; 4. to give the highest perfection to enemies who are killed by Narayana; and 5. the most attractive of the self-realized persons. The above-mentioned 60 qualities are visible up to Narayana. And Krishna has four other special qualities which are: 1. able to manifest wonderful Pastimes, 2. His transcendental flute-playing; 3. eternal youth; 4. His Personal Beauty.

As Krishna has 64 transcendental qualities, described above, so Srimati Radharani has 25 transcendental qualities by creation, material and spiritual. But Radharani can control even Krishna by Her transcendental qualities. Such transcendental qualities are described as follows: 1. She is sweetness personified. 2. She is a fresh young girl. 3. Her eyes are always moving. 4. She is always brightly smiling. 5. She has all the signs of fortunate lines in Her body. 6. By the flavor of Her person even Krishna becomes agitated. 7. She is expert in the art of singing. 8. She can speak very nicely and sweetly. 9. She is expert in presenting Herself by feminine attraction. 10. She is modest and gentle. 11. She is always very merciful. 12. She is transcendentally cunning. 13. She knows how to dress nicely. 14. She is always shy. 15. She is always respectful. 16. She is always patient. 17. She is very grave. 18. She is enjoyable by Krishna. 19. She is always situated on the highest devotional platform. 20. She can give shelter to all kinds of devotees. 22. She is always affectionate to superior and inferior. 23. She is always obliged by the dealings of Her associates. 24. She is the greatest among all the girlfriends of Krishna. 25. She always keeps Krishna under Her control.

So Krishna and Radharani are both transcendentally qualified, and both are attractive for each other. But still, in that transcendental attractiveness, Radharani is better than Krishna. This attractiveness of Radharani is the transcendental taste in conjugal love. Similarly, there are transcendental tastes in the flavors of servitude, friendship, and other relationships with Krishna. They can be described as follows, with reference to the context of *Bhakti Rasamrita Sindhu.*

Persons who have been thoroughly cleansed by devotional service and are always joyful and full of elevated consciousness, who are very much attached to the studies of *Srimad Bhagwatam*, always cheerful in the association of devotees, and who have accepted the Lotus Feet of Krishna as the ultimate shelter of their lives; who are pleased to perform all details of devotional service—have in their pure hearts the transcendental ecstasy of attachment, developed out of old and new reformatory performance. That state of being, enriched with love of Krishna and transcendental experience, becomes gradually developed into the mature oneness of spiritual life. Such a spiritual taste of life cannot be possible for those who are not in Krishna Consciousness and in devotional service.

This fact is further corroborated in the *Bhakti Rasamrita Sindhu*, where it is said: "For the non-devotee it is very difficult to understand the taste of devotional service. Only one who has completely taken shelter of the Lotus Feet of Krishna, and whose life is merged in the ocean of devotional service, can understand this transcendental relish."

Lord Chaitanya thus explained briefly about the transcendental situation or spiritual relish of life, and He said that this is the fifth stage of perfection. The first stage of perfection is to become a religious man in the ordinary sense in the material world. The second stage of perfection is to become materially rich. The third stage of material perfection is complete sense enjoyment; and the fourth stage of material existence is knowledge of liberation. But above liberation are those who are already liberated: they can stand on the fifth stage of perfection, which is called Krishna Consciousness, or devotional service to the Lord. The highest perfection of such devotional service in Krishna Consciousness is described as the taste of the ecstasy of spiritual relish.

The Lord then related to Sanatan Goswami that, before teaching him, He had already taught his younger brother, Rupa Goswami, at Prayag Allahabad. He assured Sanatan Goswami that Rupa Goswami had been empowered by Him to spread the knowledge which He had given him. Similarly, He ordered Sanatan Goswami to write books on the transcendental loving service of the Lord, and authorized him to re-excavate the different sites of Krishna's Pastimes in the district of Mathura. He was also advised to construct temples at Vrindaban, and to write books on the principles of Vaishnavism, as authorized by Sri Chaitanya Mahaprabhu. Sanatan Goswami executed all His desires; he constructed the temple of Madanmohan at Vrindaban, and he wrote books on the principles of devotional service such as *Hari Bhakti Vilasa.*

Lord Chaitanya taught Sanatan Goswami how to live in the material world in complete relationship with Krishna, and He taught him also that there is no necessity of dry renunciation. The purport is that, in the present day, there are many persons who accept the renounced order of life without any spiritual advancement. Lord Chaitanya did not approve of such acceptance of *Sannyasa* without perfect knowledge in Krishna Consciousness. Actually we find that there are many so called *Sannyasis* who are acting like less than ordinary men, yet are passing themselves off as the renounced order of life. Lord Chaitanya Mahaprabhu did not accept such hypocrisy, and He taught Sanatan Goswami to write elaborately on the subject matter in his different books.

This perfectional stage of spiritual life, even while being in the material world, is described in the Twelfth Chapter of the *Bhagavad Gita* as follows: "Such a devotee, who is not envious of any living entity, who is friendly, who is merciful, who is detached from material possessions, who is situated in pure identification without any false conception of the body, who is equipoised both in happiness and distress, who is forgiving, always satisfied and always engaged in devotional service, always being surrendered with body and mind unto the Supreme Lord—he is very dear to Me." Such a devotee, who never gives trouble to any living entity either by the body or by the mind, who is never affected by material distress and happiness, is never angry or pleased with anything material, who is freed from all kinds of material affection, is very dear to the Supreme Lord. Such a devotee is never dependent on anyone in this world. He who is a soul completely surrendered to the Supreme Lord, who is purified, expert, neutral, painless, and aloof from any material endeavor which requires too much attention—such a devotee is also very dear to Lord Krishna.

A person who is never subjected to material happiness, material hatred, lamentation and ambition, and who is aloof from all auspicious and inauspicious activities of the material world and fully devoted in Krishna Consciousness—he is very dear to Lord Krishna. A devotee who treats equally a so-called enemy, and a so-called friend in the material world, and who is not disturbed by any warmth or coolness due to the affection of his skin, and who is without any attachment and equally situated when he is respected or when insulted, always grave, satisfied in any condition of life, without any fixed house for residence and always fixed in Krishna Consciousness—is very dear to Lord Krishna. Even if one is not situated in some transcendental position, still, if and when one approves of such transcendental life he also becomes very dear to Krishna.

In the *Srimad Bhagwatam*, Second Canto, Second Chapter, there is a very nice verse in which it is said that a devotee should always remain dependent on the mercy of the Supreme Lord. As far as his material necessities are concerned, he should be satisfied with whatever is obtained without any endeavor. Sukdeva Goswami advised in that connection: that a devotee should never approach a materialistic person for any kind of help. So far as his bodily necessities are concerned, he may pick up a torn cloth thrown in the street, he can take fruits offered by the tree, he can drink water which is flowing in the river, and he can live in the cave constructed by Nature herself, in the hill and mountain regions. Above all, if he is unable to do all these things, he should completely depend on the Supreme Lord, understanding that the Supreme

Lord provides everyone with food and shelter, and therefore He will never fail to care for His devotees who have fully surrendered unto Him. In both ways the devotee is always protected, and therefore he should not be at all anxious for his maintenance of life. Sanatan Goswami thus inquired into all phases of devotional service, and Lord Chaitanya taught him most confidentially from authoritative Scriptures like *Srimad Bhagwatam* in the matter of devotional service and Krishna Consciousness.

He then referred to the Vedic literature known as *Harivansa*, about the situation of the transcendental Abode of Krishna. This information was disclosed by Indra when he offered his prayer after his defeat in challenging the potency of Krishna. In the *Harivansa* it is stated that above the Earth there is sky, where the birds can fly, and those who are expert in operating airplanes can fly; but the birds and those flying airplanes are unable to reach the higher planetary systems. The first higher planetary system begins from the Sun planet. The Sun planet is situated in the middle of the Universe, and above the Sun planet there are other planetary systems where persons elevated by great austerities and penances are situated.

The whole material Universe is called *Devidham*, and above the *Devidham*, there is *Shivadham*, where Lord Shiva with his wife Parvati eternally reside. In that planetary system is the Spiritual Sky, where innumerable Spiritual Planets, known as Vaikunthas, are situated. And, above Them, there is Krishna's Planet known as *Goloka*. *Goloka* means the planet of the cows. Krishna is very fond of cows, and therefore His Abode is known as Goloka. Goloka is bigger than all the material and spiritual planets put together.

In that prayer of *Harivansa*, Indra admitted that he could not understand the situation of *Goloka* even by asking Brahma. Those who are devotees of Narayana, another expansion of Krishna, become situated in the *Vaikuntha* Planets; but it is very difficult to reach the *Goloka* Planet. That can be reached only by persons who are devotees of Lord Chaitanya or Lord Sri Krishna. Indra then admitted that, "You have descended from that Goloka Planet in the Spiritual World, and the disturbance which I have created was due to my foolishness"—and he therefore begged excuse from Lord Krishna.

The last phase of the Pastimes of Lord Krishna is described in the *Srimad Bhagwatam* as *Mousala Leela*, including the mystery of Krishna's disappearance from this material world. He played a Pastime that He was killed by a hunter. There are many disruptive explanations of the last portions of Lord Krishna's Pastimes, such as the description of the incarnation of His hair, and Lord Chaitanya described them in their right interpretation.

As far as the incarnation of King Kansa is concerned, this is mentioned in *Srimad Bhagwatam*, in the *Vishnu Purana*, and in *Mahabharata*. It is stated there that the Lord snatched from His Head two kinds of hair: a grey hair and a black hair, and the separate hairs entered into the wombs of two queens of the Yadu dynasty, namely Rohini and Devaki. It is stated there that Lord Krishna descends to this material world for vanquishing all the demons; but some say that Krishna is the incarnation of Vishnu, Who is lying on the ocean of milk within this Universe. Srila Rupa Goswami and his commentator, Sri Valadev Vidya Bihshan, have discussed this point fully, and have established the exact truth. Sri Jiva Goswami also discussed this point in the *Krishna Sandarbha*.

When Lord Chaitanya finished his instruction to Sri Sanatan Goswami, Sanatan, being empowered and enlightened, was so transcendentally pleased that he at once fell at the Feet of Lord Chaitanya, and began to speak:

"I am born of a very low family and I have always been in association with lowly people, and therefore I am the lowest of the sinful persons. But You are so kind that You have taught me lessons which are not even understandable by the greatest being, Brahma. And by Your grace I have appreciated the conclusions which You have taught me. But I am so low that I cannot touch even a drop of the ocean of Your instruction. If You therefore want me, who am nothing but a lame man, to dance—then kindly give me Your benediction, by placing Your Feet on my head."

He prayed for the Lord's confirmation that the teachings might be actually evolved in his heart, by the grace of the Lord—otherwise there was no possibility of them being described by him. The purport is that *Acharyas*, or spiritual masters, are authorized by higher authorities. Instruction alone cannot make one an expert. Unless one is blessed by the spiritual master, or the *Acharya*, such teaching cannot become fully manifested. Therefore, one should seek the mercy of the spiritual master, so that the instruction of the spiritual master may develop within himself. After the prayer of Sanatan Goswami, Lord Chaitanya placed His Feet over the head of Sanatan, and gave him benediction, that all the instruction He had given him would develop in him fully.

That was the description of the ultimate stage of love of Godhead. Lord Chaitanya said that such a description cannot be made very elaborately, but He had informed him as far as possible.

CONCLUSION: Anyone who attentively hears these discussions and instructions of Lord Chaitanya to Sanatan Goswami very soon becomes

130 of Teachings of Lord Chaitanya

situated in Krishna Consciousness, and can be engaged in devotional service to the Lord.

CHAPTER FIFTEEN

Explanation of the *Atmarama*
Verse in *Srimad Bhagwatam*

Lord Chaitanya next explained a verse, appearing in *Srimad Bhagwatam*, which is very famous and known as the *Atmarama* verse: It runs as follows: *Atmaramas cha munayanirg rantha apiurukrame, Kurvanti ahaituki bhaktim ittlhvambhuta guna harih.* The general meaning is that those who are liberated souls and fully satisfied within themselves will later become devotees of the Lord. This is especially meant for the impersonalist class, because the impersonalist souls have no information of the Supreme Personality of Godhead. They try to be satisfied in the impersonal Brahman, but Krishna is so attractive and so strong that He attracts even the minds of such impersonalists. That is the purport of the verse.

This verse had been explained previously to a great Vedantist, known as Sarvabhouma Bhattacharya. Sanatan Goswami, after taking his lessons from Lord Chaitanya, referred the incident to the Lord and prayed again for His explanation of the *Atmarama* verse. The author of *Chaitanya Charitamrita*, appreciating this explanation of the *Atmarama* verse, has glorified Lord Chaitanya by his prayer. Sanatan Goswami fell flat at the Feet of Lord Chaitanya, and requested Him to explain the *Atmarama* verse as He formerly had explained it to Sarvabhouma Bhattacharya. He explained his eagerness to hear the same explanation again, so that he might be enlightened.

When the Lord was thus requested by Sanatan Goswami He replied: "I do not understand why Sarvabhouma Bhattacharya has so much appreciated my explanation. As far as I am concerned I don't remember what I said to him. But because you are asking, I shall try to explain whatever I can remember, by your association." The speaker and the audience are very intimately connected; the speaker is enlightened by the presence of the audience. In transcendental subject matters the speaker or the Master can speak very nicely in relationship with the understanding of the audience. Therefore, Lord Chaitanya said, "Generally I do not know how to explain a Sanskrit verse, but I shall try to explain whatever I can by your association only."

He then said that there are 11 different items in the *Atmarama* vers... They are as follows: 1. *Atmarama*, 2. *Cha*, 3. *Munayah*, 4. *Nirgrantha*, 5. *Api*, 6. *Urukrame*, 7. *Kurvanti*, 8. *Ahaituki*, 9. *Bhaktim*, 10. *Itthvambhuta*, 11. *Harih*. The Lord then began to explain each and every items as mentioned above:

So far as *Atmarama* is concerned, He said that the word *Atma* is used to mean: 1. the Supreme Absolute Truth, 2. the body, 3. the mind, 4. endeavor, 5. intelligence, 6. conviction, and 7. nature. Therefore, anyone who takes pleasure in the cultivation of the knowledge of these items, is called *Atmarama*. (The Lord explained hereinafter about the different kinds of *Atmarama*, or transcendentalists).

The next item is *Muni*. Persons who are very great thinkers are called *Muni*. Sometimes this *Muni* is also used for persons who are very grave. *Muni* is also used for great sages, great austere persons, great mystics and learned scholars.

The fourth item, *Nirgrantha*, means freed from the bondage of illusion. Another meaning of *Nirgrantha* is "one who has no connection with spiritual injunctions." *Grantha* means revealed Scriptures. There are many instructions for spiritual realization, but persons who have no connection with such Scriptural injunctions are also known as *Nirgrantha*. *Nir* is an affix which is used with three meanings: it is used to mean no connection, and to mean constructing, and also prohibiting. There are many persons who are foolish, low-born and misbehaved, and they have no entrance into the revealed Scriptures and injunctions. Therefore, they are also called *Nirgrantha*. Because *Grantha* is also used for the purpose of riches, and for the purpose of collection, therefore

Nirgrantha, in other words, means one who is after collecting riches and who is bereft of all riches.

The word *Urukrama* is used in the sense of a highly powerful person. *Krama* is also used in the sense of stepping: one who can step very far forward is also called *Urukrama.* The greatest stepping forward was shown by Lord Vamanadev: by stepping forward with His Foot, He covered the whole Universe. Therefore, *Urukrama* means the Supreme Lord Vamanadev. This extraordinary feature of Lord Vamanadev is explained in the *Srimad Bhagwatam* as follows: "Nobody can estimate the inconceivable potencies of Lord Vishnu. Even if one can count the number of the atomic combinations of this material world, still he is not able to count the different energies of the Supreme Lord. The Lord, Vamanadev, was so powerful that by stepping forward with His foot He covered the whole Universe, beginning from the Brahmaloka down to the Patalaloka."

The inconceivable energies of the Lord are spread all over the Creation of the Supreme Lord. He is All-pervading, and by His energy He sustains all planetary systems. And, by His display of pleasure potency, He is situated in His personal Abode, known as Goloka. By His expansion of opulence He is situated all over the *Vaikuntha* Planets as Narayan. By expanding His material energy, He has created innumerable Universes with innumerable planets within them. Therefore, no one can estimate the wonderful activities of the Supreme Lord. As such, the Supreme Lord is known as *Urukrama,* or the wonderful Actor.

In the Visvaprakash Dictionary, the meaning of the word *Krama* is described as an expert display of energies, as well as stepping forward very quickly, and the word *Kurvanti* is used for working for others. There is another word similar to this, used when the activities are done for one's personal sense gratification. But the word *Kurvanti* is used when activities are performed for the satisfaction of the Supreme. Therefore this word can be used only for the purpose of rendering transcendental service to the Lord.

The word *Hetu* is used as the reason, or the cause. People are engaged generally in transcendental activities for three causes: namely, some of them want material happiness, some of them want mystic perfection, and some of them want liberation from this material bondage. So far as material enjoyment is concerned, there are varieties; nobody can ennumerate how many kinds of material enjoyments there are. So far as perfections in mystic powers are concerned, there are eighteen. So far as kinds of liberation from the material bondage are concerned, there are five. The state of being where all these different kinds of enjoyment are conspicuous by their absence is called *Ahaituki*. The qualification *Ahaituki* is especially mentioned because by *Ahaituki* service of the Lord one can achieve the favor of the Lord.

The word *Bhakti* is taken in ten different ways. Out of the ten, one is called *Sadhan Bhakti*, occupational devotional service. The other nine are called *Prema Bhakti*, love of Godhead. Those who are situated in the neutral position attain the development of perfection up to love of Godhead. Similarly, those who are situated in the relationship of master and servant attain love of Godhead up to the stage of attachment. Those who are in the relationship of friends attain their love of Godhead up to the point of fraternity. Those who are in love of Godhead as parents are elevated up to the point of emotion. But only those who are in conjugal love with the Supreme have ecstasy elevated to the highest of ecstasies. These are the different meanings of the term *Bhakti*.

The Lord then explained the different meanings of *itthambhutagunah*. He also explained the word *Guna* in its different meanings. *Ittham bhuta* means full transcendental, before which even the transcendental pleasure known as *Brahmananda* becomes like straw. In the *Hari Bhakti Sudhodaya* it is said by the devotee: "My Lord, O Supreme, simply by understanding You or seeing You, the pleasure which we derive is so great that the pleasure in *Brahmananda* becomes insignificant." In other words, the pleasure derived by understanding Krishna as He is, the All-attractive Reservoir of all pleasures, and the Reservoir of all pleasure-giving tastes, with all transcendental qualifications, attracts one to become His devotee. By such attraction one can give up fruitive activities, endeavoring for liberation, or the intense desire to achieve success in Yoga mystic power. The attractive power of Krishna is so intense, that without any respect for any other means of self-realization, one surrenders unto the Supreme Personality of Godhead—simply by that attraction.

Guna means the unlimited transcendental qualities of Krishna, primarily His *Sat-Chit-Ananda* Form. In His transcendental blissful knowledge and eternity He is fully perfect; and, therefore, such perfection becomes more manifest when He becomes controlled by the attention of the devotee. God is so kind and merciful that He can give Himself in exchange for the devotional service of a devotee. His transcendental qualities are such that His perfection in His beauty, His perfect reciprocation of love between Himself and His devotees, and His flavor of all transcendental qualities attract different kinds of transcendentalists and liberated souls, by different manifestations of these qualities.

For example, He attracted the mind of one of the Kumaras, Sanaka, simply by the flavor of the flowers offered to Him. And the mind of

Sukadeva Goswami was attracted by the transcendental Pastimes of Lord Krishna. He attracted by His Personal Beauty the minds of the damsels of Vrindaban, and He attracted the attention of Rukmini by His bodily feature and transcendental qualities. He attracts the mind of the Goddess of Fortune by playing the flute and by different other features of transcendental attraction. He attracts the minds of all young girls; He attracts the minds of elderly ladies by His childlike activities; and He attracts the minds of His friends by His friendly activities. When He appeared in Vrindaban, He attracted even the birds and beasts and the trees and the plants. Everyone became attracted in love and affection for Krishna.

The word *Hari* has different meanings, of which two are principals. *Hari* means that He takes away all inauspicious things from the devotee's life, and that He attracts the mind of the devotee by awarding him transcendental love of Godhead. He is so attractive that anybody remembering Krishna in some way or other becomes free from the four kinds of material miseries. With special attention for His devotee, the Lord banishes the devotee's different forms of sinful activities, which are a stumbling block for the advancement of devotional service. This is called routing the influence of ignorance. And, by hearing alone, one develops love for Him. That is the gift of the Lord. On one side He takes away our inauspicious things, and on the other side He awards the most auspicious things. That is the meaning of *Hari*.

When a person becomes developed in love of Godhead, then by His attractive power of transcendental qualities, He attracts the devotees body, mind and everything for the Lord. Such are the merciful activities of Krishna and such are His transcendental qualities. He is so attractive that, out of transcendental attachment for Him, a devotee will give up all the four principles of spiritual life: namely religiousness, economic development, regulation of sense gratification, and salvation. The words *Api* and *Cha* are adverbs. They can be utilized for virtually any purpose, but still the purpose of *Cha*, or "and," means that the whole construction may have seven different readings.

The Lord established the import of eleven items in the verse of *Atma rama*. Then He began to explain the imports of each item as follows: the word *Brahman* means the greatest in all respects. He is the greatest in all opulences. Nobody can excel over His richness, nobody can excel over His strength, nobody can excel over His fame, nobody can excel over His beauty, nobody can excel over His knowledge, and nobody can excel over His renunciation. Therefore, the real meaning of *Brahman* is the Supreme Personality of Godhead, Krishna.

In the *Vishnu Purana* the meaning of *Brahman* is given: He is the greatest and there is no limit to His expanding as the greatest. One may conceive of *Brahman's* greatness, yet it is growing in such a way that nobody can estimate how far or how great He actually is.

That Supreme Personality of Godhead is realized in three aspects, but they are all one and the same. The Absolute Truth, the Supreme Personality, Krishna, is everlasting. In the *Srimad Bhagwatam* it is said that He exists before the manifestation of this cosmic world, and He exists during its continuance, and He will continue to exist after the annihilation of this cosmic manifestation. Therefore, He is the Soul of everything great. He is All-pervading, He is All-witnessing, and He is the Supreme Form of everything.

To understand and achieve that Supreme perfection of the Absolute Truth, there are three different kinds of transcendental processes mentioned in the Vedic literature. They are called: the process of knowledge, the process of mystic *Yoga*, and the process of devotional service. The followers of different processes realize the Supreme Truth in different aspects; namely, those who are following the process of knowledge realize Him as impersonal *Brahman;* those who are following the process of *Yoga* realize Him as the localized Supersoul; and those who are following the process of devotional service realize Him as the Supreme Personality of Godhead, Sri Krishna. In other words, although *Brahman* means Krishna and nothing else, still, according to the process followed by different transcendentalists, He is realized in three different aspects.

So far as devotional service is concerned, it is divided into two processes. In the beginning, it is called *Bidhibhakti*, or devotional service with regulated principles. And in the highest stage it is called *Raga bhakti*, or devotional service in pure love.

The Supreme Personality of Godhead is the Absolute Truth, but He is manifested by expansions of different energies also. Those who are following the principles of devotional service in regulative forms ultimately achieve the *Vaikunthas* in the Spiritual World. Whereas one who is following the principles of love in devotional service reaches to the Supreme Abode, Krishna Loka or Goloka.

The transcendentalists can also be divided into three: namely the *Akama*, or one who does not have any material desires; the *Moksa kama*, or persons who seek liberation from the material miseries; and *Sarva kama*, or persons who have material desires to enjoy. The most intelligent transcendentalist gives up all other processes and engages himself in the devotional service of the Lord, even though he may have many desires. Not by any kind of transcendental activities, either in fruitive action or the cultivation of knowledge, nor by mystic yogic cultivation, can a person achieve the highest perfection, without adding a tinge of devotional service to them.

Except for devotional service, all other forms of transcendental processes are just like nipples on the neck of a goat. There are some nipples hanging on the neck of a goat, but they do not supply milk. If one is to derive, therefore, the actual perfection of his process he must take to the devotional service of Krishna.

In *Bhagavad Gita* it is stated, in the Seventh Chapter, 16th verse, that there are four kinds of beginners in devotional service whose backgrounds are very righteous. They are the distressed, the inquisitive, the seeker of material profit, and the *Jnani*, or the wise man. These four kinds of people, when they are coated by previous righteous activities, come to the devotional service of the Lord. Out of these four, those who are distressed and those who are in need of material possessions are called *devotees with desires*, whereas the other two, the inquisitive and the wise, are under the heading of *seeking liberation*. But, because they worship Krishna, they are considered to be very fortunate. In due course of time, if they give up all their desires and become pure devotees of the Supreme Lord, they are called *the most fortunate*.

Such fortunate beginners can develop only in the association of pure devotees of Lord Krishna. When one is associated with such pure devotees, one becomes a pure devotee himself. This is confirmed in the *Srimad Bhagwatam* in the First Canto, Tenth Chapter, as follows: "A person who is actually intelligent is able, by association with pure devotees, to hear about Lord Krishna and His activities." These activities are very attractive, and he does not give up such association with the Lord.

Except for the association of pure devotees, any association is called *Kaitava*, or cheating. This is also confirmed in *Srimad Bhagwatam*, First Canto; where it is stated that any cheating process which obstructs transcendental realization is to be thrown off. By the *Srimad Bhagwatam* one can understand reality as it is, and that becomes auspicious in helping one to transcend the three kinds of material miseries. *Srimad Bhagwatam* is compiled by the greatest sage, Vyasadeva, as a work of his mature experience; and therefore, by understanding *Srimad Bhagwatam*, one can immediately capture the Supreme Lord within his heart, by devotional service.

Lord Chaitanya then explained that the word *Projjhitta* means desire for liberation, which is explained by one great commentator as the most obstructive stumbling block for realization of the Supreme Lord. But, somehow or other, if somebody comes to Krishna and begins to hear about Him, Krishna is so kind that He awards him His Lotus Feet as a center for the devotee. Such a devotee or transcendentalist forgets everything and engages himself in the devotional service of the Lord.

For anyone who comes to the Lord in devotional service, or in full Krishna Consciousness, the reward is the Supreme. Once engaged for the Supreme, he will no longer ask for anything, as does the distressed man and he who desires material possessions. The method of devotional service, the service itself, association with pure devotees in the causeless mercy of the Lord—these three things can act so wonderfully that, whether the devotee is a distressed soul or in want of material possessions or inquisitive—or even if he is a wise man cultivating knowledge—he can give up all activities, and his mind becomes absorbed in Krishna.

The summary is that, henceforward, whatever meaning would apply for all the words in the *Atmarama* verse will be meant only for Krishna.

So far, Lord Chaitanya has spoken only of the introduction to the *Atmarama* verse. Now he will explain its real position:

In the cultivation of knowledge there are two kinds of transcendentalists. One of them is the worshipper of the impersonal *Brahman*, and the other is the desirer of liberation. Monists worship the impersonal feature of *Brahman*, and therefore they are called the worshippers of *Brahman*. The worshippers of *Brahman* are divided into three further stages: the neophyte practitioner, one who is absorbed in *Brahman* realization, and one who has actually realized himself as *Brahman*. If devotional service is added, the knower of *Brahman* can then become liberated. Otherwise, there is no possibility.

Anyone who is fully engaged in devotional service in Krishna Consciousness is understood to be already a soul realized in *Brahman*. Devotional service is so strong that one is attracted to Krishna even from the process of *Brahman* worship. The Lord awards such a devotee the perfection of a spiritual body, and he is eternally engaged in the transcendental quality of Krishna. When he understands and becomes attracted by transcendental qualities, he wholeheartedly becomes engaged in devotional service. For example, the four Kumaras and Sukadeva Goswami were liberated souls from the very beginning, and still, later in life, they became attracted to the Pastimes of Krishna—and they became devotees. Devotees like the four Kumaras—one of whom, Sanaka Kumara, was attracted by the flavor of the flowers offered to Krishna—were all attracted by the transcendental qualities of the Lord, and thus became engaged in His devotional service. The nine mystics mentioned in the Eleventh Canto of *Srimad Bhagwatam* are understood to have been transcendentalists from birth by hearing the transcendental qualities of Krishna from Brahma and Lord Shiva and Narada.

Sometimes one becomes attracted to Krishna and His transcendental qualities simply by looking upon the beautiful features of His transcendental Body, and in that case also one gives up the desire for liberation and becomes engaged in the devotional service of the Lord. The devotee repents his loss of time in the so-called cultivation of knowledge, and becomes a pure devotee of the Lord.

There are two kinds of liberated souls even in this material body: the soul liberated by devotional service, and the soul liberated by the cultivation of knowledge. The difference is that the liberated soul in devotional service becomes more and more elevated, being attracted by the transcendental qualities of Krishna, whereas the dry speculators who simply cultivate knowledge without any connection with devotional service become fallen on account of their many offences.

This is confirmed in the *Srimad Bhagwatam*, Tenth Canto, Second Chapter. It is said there, "O my Lord, the intelligence of those who think themselves liberated without a touch of devotional service is not pure, because, even though they rise to the highest point of liberation by severe penances and austerity, still, with no center at Your Lotus Feet, they are sure to fall down again into this material existence." *Bhagavad Gita* also confirms this, in the Eighteenth Chapter, 54th verse—one who is actually situated in the *Brahman* realization has nothing to lament for and nothing to desire. He is equipoised toward everyone, and thus is eligible for being situated in devotional service.

This same thing is accepted by Bilvamongal Thakur. In his later life, he lamented that, "I was situated as a monist, to become One with the Supreme Lord, but somehow or other, I contacted a Naughty Boy, and I became His eternal servitor." In other words, those who become self-realized souls by executing devotional service can achieve a transcendental body, and by being attracted to the transcendental qualities of Krishna, they become engaged fully in pure devotional service.

Anyone who is not attracted to Krishna is understood to be still under the spell of Maya. Therefore, one who is trying to be liberated by devotional service is actually liberated from the spell of Maya. In the Eleventh Canto of *Srimad Bhagwatam* there are many instances of devotees who became liberated in this life simply by their engagement in devotional service.

CHAPTER SIXTEEN

Conclusion of Teachings to Sanatan Goswami

Persons who desire liberation by the cultivation of knowledge are of three kinds: the desirers for liberation; the liberated in this material existence; and the actually self-realized. As for desiring to become liberated, there are many such persons in this world, and sometimes they engage themselves in devotional service for this purpose. It is corroborated also in *Srimad Bhagwatam*, in the First Canto, Second Chapter, that those who actually desire liberation give up all kinds of worship of the demigods, and, without being envious of them concentrate their minds in the worship of Narayan, the Supreme Personality of Godhead. Such persons are engaged in the service of the Supreme Personality of Godhead, Narayan; and when they are in contact with pure devotees, they become engaged in the devotional service of Krishna, and give up the idea of liberation. In the *Hari Bhakti Sudhodaya*, there is a nice verse in which it is stated: "O great soul, although there are many faults within this miserable life, yet there is one glory—the association of pure devotees. Cultivate such association. By such association our desire for liberation diminishes."

In the *Srimad Bhagwatam*, Eleventh Canto, Second Chapter, verse 35, it is stated that man's fearfulness is due to his material conception of life and to his forgetting his eternal relationship with the Supreme Lord. Therefore, he finds himself having only perverted memories. Such things have happened due to the spell of material energy. Therefore, a person with enough intelligence will engage himself in full devotional service with the Supreme Lord as his Spiritual Master and worshippable God. The purport is that nobody can attain a revolution without being engaged in devotional service to the Lord. When, however, he is free from this material contamination, he can fully engage himself in Krishna Consciousness.

In the *Srimad Bhagwatam*, Tenth Canto, Fourteenth Chapter, it is clearly said that, for a person who is engaged in devotional service to understand things as they are, but who lacks any intention of being engaged in Krishna Consciousness, the trouble undergone for his understanding is his only achievement. There is no substance to his life. Every living entity is part and parcel of the Supreme Lord, and therefore it is the duty of every living entity to serve that Supreme Whole. Without doing that the living entity falls into material contamination, and his service is lost.

Lord Chaitanya then concluded that these six kinds of *Atmarama* engage themselves in some kind of devotional service to Krishna. In other words, all the transcendentalists at different times ultimately come to the understanding of rendering devotional service to Krishna, and become fully Krishna conscious. Even when one is very learned, or if one is very extravangant, still, he can be engaged in the devotional service of the Lord.

The six kinds of transcendentalists are the neophyte transcendentalist, the absorbed transcendentalist, one actually situated in transcendence, a person caring for liberation, persons actually liberated, and persons who are actually engaged in their constitutional position. All of them are called *Atmarama*. When a person becomes *Atmarama*, or a great thinker in Krishna Consciousness, he is fully engaged in devotional service. There are many *Atmaramas* according to the grammatical rules, but one word, *Atmarama*, is sufficient to represent all other *Atmaramas*. In the collective sense all the *Atmaramas* are inclined to worship the Supreme Lord Krishna.

The mystic who worships the Supersoul within himself is also called *Atmarama*. Such Atmarama yogis are of two kinds: the one is called *Sagarbha*, the other is called *Nigarbha*. In *Srimad Bhagwatam* it is stated, in the Second Canto, Second Chapter: "Some of the yogis meditate within the heart on the localized situation of Vishnu, Who is four-handed with four symbols: the conch shell, the wheel, the club and the lotus." The yogi who thinks of the four-handed Vishnu becomes developed in devotional ecstasy, and attains the different symptoms of that position. Sometimes he cries, sometimes he feels separation. In this way he becomes merged in transcendental bliss. So, as a result of such transcendental bliss, he is practically entrapped like a fish.

Such *Sagarbha* and *Nigarbha* yogis can be divided into three: the beginner, the person who is already on the ascendent, and he who has already achieved a perfection. In the *Bhagavad Gita* they have been described in the Sixth Chapter as follows: Persons who are trying to ascend on the path of the mystic Yoga system are called *Aruruksha*. In *Aruruksha* Yoga there are different kinds of sitting postures and there is concentration of the mind. For one who is already ascended on the path of Yoga, meditation and detachment are the causes. And when one has no attachment for working in the matter of sense gratification, then gradually he becomes free, and becomes situated in ecstasy and is called Yoga *Rudha*. Such mystic yogis, if they in some way or other come in contact with a saintly person, also are converted to become devotees of Krishna.

So far as the word *Urukrama* is concerned, it is already explained: *Urukrama* means the Supreme Lord, and all these *Atmaramas* are engaged in devotional service to *Urukrama*. Before engaging themselves in devotional service, such transcendentalists are called *Shantas*, or they are called pacified devotees.

Atma, self, is also known as the mind. Sometimes there are mental speculationists who present philosophical thoughts in different ways, but when they come into contact with saintly persons engaged in devotional service, they also become devotees.

Concerning the two classes of yogis, *Sagarbha* and *Nigarbha*, the *Srimad Bhagwatam*, in the Tenth Canto, Eighty-seventh Chapter, describes them as follows: "The yogis begin their practice by worshipping the abdomen, and try to concentrate their attention on their intestines. Then gradually they rise to the heart, and concentrate the mind on the heart. Then gradually they rise to the top of the head. One who can rise to that portion is understood to have become perfect, and is no longer subjected to birth and death." Even such yogis, if they come in contact with pure devotees, will also render causeless devotional service to the Lord.

Another meaning of *Atma* is to endeavor. In every practice there is endeavor, and the ultimate endeavor is to reach the highest perfectional stage of devotional service. In the *Srimad Bhagwatam*, First Canto, Fifth Chapter, 18th verse, it is stated that one should try for the highest achievement, which cannot be attained even in the highest planetary system—nor in the lowest. The idea is that material happiness and miseries are available, in the course of time, in any of the planetary systems; but the highest achievement, devotional service, cannot be achieved anywhere without endeavor. Therefore, in the *Narada Purana*, it is said that one who is serious about understanding the highest perfectional stage of devotional service, simply by his endeavor, can become successful in everything.

One cannot, therefore, achieve the highest perfectional stage of devotional service without personal endeavor. And, as is stated in the *Bhagavad Gita*, Tenth Chapter: "For he who is constantly engaged in such devotional service, the Supreme Lord, Who is situated in everyone's heart, gives the intelligence by which he can make undeterred progress in devotional activities."

The word *Atma* is also meant for patience and perseverance. By patience and perseverance one can achieve the highest stage of devotional service.

Another meaning for *Muni* is "the bird and large black bee." Another meaning of *Nirgrantha* is "the foolish person." Even the birds, even the black bee, and even the foolish engage themselves in the service of the Supreme Lord, when they are favored by the pure devotee. For example, it is stated in the *Srimad Bhagwatam* that the birds are devoted to the service of the Supreme Lord. In the Tenth Canto, Fifteenth Chapter, there is a statement that the black bees are following Krishna and Valarama. Taking that incident, Lord Valarama described the devotional service of the wasps unto the Supreme Personality of Godhead. He said, "O Supremely Virtuous One, the Original Personality of Godhead, just see how these bees and wasps are following You, glorifying Your transcendental Fame, and thus worshipping You. Actually, these wasps are not as they appear, but they are great sages, and are taking the opportunity to worship the Supreme Soul now. Although You are not knowable by ordinary persons, still they know You and they are following You and glorifying You."

Similarly, there is another verse in *Srimad Bhagwatam*, Tenth Canto, Fifteenth Chapter, in which the peacocks were receiving Valarama and Krishna, and it is said in this connection: "O Worshippable One, just see how the peacocks who are returning to their nests are receiving You in full pleasure. The peacocks are just like the damsels of Vraja. And the cuckoos on the branches of the trees are also receiving You in their own way. The residents of Vrindaban are so glorious that everyone is prepared to render their respective devotional service to the Lord."

Similarly, there is another verse in the *Srimad Bhagwatam*, Tenth Canto,

Thirty-fifth Chapter, 11th verse, in which it is stated. "O just see how the cranes and swans on the water are singing the glories of the Lord! And they are meditating, standing in the water, worshipping the Supreme Lord." There is another verse in *Srimad Bhagwatam*, Second Canto, Fourth Chapter, in which it is stated: "Even the aborigines and uncivilized human beings like Kiratas, Huns, Andhra, Pulinda, Pukksa, Abhira, Kank, Yuvana and Khasa, and many other human beings in the lower species of life—all can be purified simply by taking center of the pure devotees." So Sukadeva Goswami offered his respectful obeisances unto the Lord, Vishnu, Whose devotees can work so wonderfully.

Another meaning of *Driti* is to realize oneself as elevated. In that position one feels himself free from all miseries, and is elevated to the highest standard of life. Therefore, all devotees of Krishna in full Krishna Consciousness are free from all kinds of material pleasures. They are full with the service of the Lord, and they are always jolly, being engaged in such transcendental service. They are experienced men of happiness. They are so happy that they do not even desire to be promoted to the spiritual planets, because they are happy in every sphere of life. Being fully in the transcendental service of the Lord, they do not desire any material things or material sense pleasures. There is another verse spoken by the Goswamis in which it is stated, "Persons who have fixed up their moving senses in the service of the Supreme Lord can be called peaceful."

And so, *Atmarama* means that even the birds, even the beasts, even the fools—everyone—becomes attracted by the transcendental qualities of Krishna, and they engage in His service, and therefore become liberated.

Still another meaning of *Atma* is "intelligence." One who has special intelligence is also called *Atmarama*. Such *Atmaramas* with special intelligence are of two kinds: One is the learned sage, and another is the fool, one without book knowledge. But both of them may have the opportunity of associating with the pure devotee. The foolish *Atmaramas* can also give up everything, and in pure devotional service engage themselves in Krishna Consciousness. In the *Srimad Bhagwatam*, it is said that the Lord is the Origin of everything, and that everything emanates from Him. Anyone who is actually intelligent can understand the Supreme Lord Krishna as the Source of everything, and thus engages himself in His service. There is another verse in *Srimad Bhagwatam*, Second Canto, Seventh Chapter, 45th verse: "What to speak of persons who are intelligent enough by study of the *Vedas*—even less intelligent persons, like the woman, the laborer class and the *Huna savarapi*, the birds, the beasts—*everyone* can achieve the highest perfectional stage of life." It is stated in the *Bhagavad Gita*, Tenth Chapter, 10th verse, that when a person becomes highly intelligent and engages himself in Krishna Consciousness, then Krishna in reciprocation gives him the intelligence by which he can be promoted to the Abode of the Supreme Lord.

The Lord said to Sanatan Goswami that the association of good devotees, engagement in the transcendental service of the Lord, understanding *Srimad Bhagwatam*, and chanting the Holy Name of the Lord, as well as residing in a place like Vrindaban or Mathura—these five things are very important for elevating oneself to the transcendental plane. Not to speak of attaining all the five—if one becomes expert in one of them, then he also is, without fail, elevated to the stage of love of Godhead. But anyone who is actually intelligent should give up all other desires and engage himself in the transcendental service of Krishna. The influence of devotional service is such that a person so engaged gives up all material desires and becomes fully attached to taking center unto Krishna, being moved by the transcendental qualities of the Lord. That is the beauty of the Lord to His devotee.

Another meaning of *Atma* is "nature." *Atmarama* means that everyone is enjoying the particular nature he has acquired. But the ultimate nature, or the perpetual, eternal nature of the living entity is to serve the Supreme Lord. Anyone who attains to the perfection of understanding his real nature— of eternally being the servitor of the Lord—gives up his designative (material, or bodily) conception of life. That is real knowledge. Those who are in pursuit of knowledge and get the opportunity of associating with a pure devotee also become engaged in devotional service of the Lord. Sages like the four Kumaras, as well as the fools and the birds, can be engaged in the transcendental service of the Lord. Being favored by Krishna's causeless mercy, everyone can be elevated to the standard of Krishna Consciousness.

One becomes attracted by the transcendental qualities of Krishna and begins his devotional service. It is stated in the *Srimad Bhagwatam*, Tenth Canto, Fifteenth Chapter, in glorifying the land of Vrindaban: "This land, Vrajab-humi, is glorified by the touching of Your Sole. By the touching of Your Fingers, the creepers also glorify You. By Your looking on the hills and the rivers and the lower animals, they are all glorified. And, so far as the Gopis are concerned, they, being embraced by Your transcendental Arms, are also glorified." The Gopis glorified Vrindaban in the following words: "My dear friends, all these inhabitants of our Vrajabhumi, including the birds, beasts and trees, everyone, while seeing Lord Krishna going to the pasturing ground with His friends, accompanied by Valadeva and singing on Their flutes—all are glorified."

The Lord said that *Atma* also means "this body." The yogis who practice bodily exercises, considering the body as the self, also are elevated to the transcendental service of the Lord if they are associated with pure devotees. There are many persons who have the concept of this body being the self. They are engaged in many kinds of fruitive activities, including bathing rituals and ordinary worldly activities. But when they come in contact with a pure devotee, they also engage themselves in the transcendental service of the Lord.

In the *Srimad Bhagwatam*, First Canto, Eighteenth Chapter, it is stated: "O my dear Suta Goswami, you have given us the nectar of Krishna's Lotus Feet, although we have become darkened by the sacrificial smoke of these fruitive activities." The *Srimad Bhagwatam*, Fourth Canto, Twenty-first Chapter, states: "The Ganges water is flowing from the tip of the Lotus Feet of Krishna, and by bathing in that Ganges water, everyone—including the fruitive actors and all the sages—is washing the dirty things from within the mind."

Those who are in the concept of the body as the self, or those who are full of material desires, are also called, in a sense, *Atmarama*. When they are associated with the pure devotees of the Lord, they give up their material desires and become perfect in the service of the Lord. The best example of this is found in the *Hari Bhakti Sudhodaya*, in connection with the character of Druva. In the Seventh Chapter, 28th verse, it is stated by Maharaj Druva: "My dear Lord, I came to worship You desirous of having some land on this Earth; but, fortunately, I have You, Who are beyond the perception of great sages and saintly persons. I came to search out some particles of colored glass, but I've found instead a very valuable gem like You. I am satisfied. I have no desire to ask You anything."

There is another meaning to the word *Nirgrantha*—"foolish hunter," or "wretched poor man." Such a hunter also got salvation and engaged himself in the devotional service of the Lord by association of the pure devotee Narada. The following story is about this hunter's meeting with Narada:

There was a hunter in the forest of Prayag, who was fortunate enough to meet Narada while he was coming back from Vaikuntha after visiting Lord Narayan. Narada came to Prayag to bathe in the confluence of the Ganges and the Yamuna. While passing through the forest, he saw a bird lying on the ground, half-killed, and pierced by an arrow. It was chirping piteously. At another place he saw a deer flapping in agony. In another place he saw that a boar was suffering and, in another place, he saw a rabbit flapping in pain. All this made him very compassionate, and he bagan to think, "Who is the foolish man that has committed such sinful activities?" A devotee of the Lord is generally compassionate for the miseries of the living entities, and so what to speak of great Narada? He became very aggrieved by this scene, and after proceeding a few steps, he saw the hunter engaged in hunting with his bow and arrows. The hunter's complexion was very black, and his eyes were red, and it was dangerous even to see him standing there with his bow and arrows, just like an associate of Yamaraja—Death. Seeing him in that position, Narada Muni entered deeper into the forest and approached him. And, while Narada Muni was passing through the forest, all the animals who were caught in the hunter's traps fled away. The hunter became very angry over this, and he was just going to call Narada vile names but, by the influence of Narada, who was such a saintly person, the hunter could not utter ill names.

Rather, with gentle behavior, he inquired from Narada: "My dear sir, why have you come before me while I am hunting? Are you astray from the general path? By your coming here all the animals assembled in my traps have now fled away."

Narada replied, "Yes, I'm sorry. I have come to you to find my own path, just to inquire from you. But I have seen that there are many boars and deer and rabbits on the path, and they are lying on the forest floor flapping before death, half-dead. Who has committed these sinful acts?"

The hunter replied, "What you have seen is all right; it is done by me."

Then Narada said, "If you are hunting all these poor animals, why don't you kill them at once? You half-kill them, and they are flapping in death-pains. This is a great sin. If you want to kill any animal, why don't you kill it completely? Why do you leave it half-killed, and allow the animal to die flapping?"

The hunter replied, "My dear Lord, my name is Mrigari, the enemy of the animals. According to the teachings of my father, I have been raised to half-kill the animals by leaving them flapping. When a half-dead animal flaps, I take great pleasure in that."

Narada then implored the hunter; "I beg one thing from you, and please accept it."

The hunter replied, "Oh, yes sir, I shall give you whatever you like. If you want some animal skins, come to my home. I have so many skins of animals, tigers, and deer. Whatever you like I shall give you."

Narada replied, "I do not want such things. But I want something else. If you kindly grant it to me, then I shall tell you. Please, henceforth from tomorrow, whenever you kill an animal, please kill it completely, and don't leave it half-dead."

The hunter replied, "Oh, my dear sir, what are you asking of me? Why are you asking this? What is the difference between half-killing and killing completely?"

Narada replied, "If you half-kill the animals, then they suffer too much pain, and if you give too much pain to other living entities, it is a great sin. When you kill an animal completely, there is much offense, but it is not so great as that accrued by half-killing an animal. In other words, pain which you give to the half-dead animals will have to be accepted by you also in some of the future births awaiting you."

Although the hunter was very sinful, yet in association of a great devotee like Narada, his mind became softened, and he was afraid of the sins. Those who are grossly sinful are not afraid at all of committing sins; but here we can see that because his purification began in the association of a great devotee like Narada, he was afraid of his sinful activities.

The hunter therefore said, "My dear sir, from my childhood I have been taught to kill animals like that. So would you kindly tell me how can I get rid of all the offenses and sinful activities which I have committed? I am surrendering unto your feet. Please save me from all the reactions of my sinful activities in the past, and just direct me in the proper path so that I can be free."

Narada replied, "If you actually want to follow my direction, then I can tell you the real path of being freed from these sinful reactions."

The hunter agreed, and told Narada Muni, "Whatever you direct, I shall follow without any hesitation."

Narada then asked him to first break his bow, and then he would disclose the path of liberation.

The hunter replied, "You are asking me to break my bow, but if I break it then what will be the means of my living?"

Narada replied, "Don't worry for your living. I shall send you sufficient grains so that you can live."

Thereupon, the hunter broke his bow and fell down at the feet of Narada. Narada got him to stand up, and instructed him: "Just go to your home and whatever money and valuables you have there, distribute amongst the devotees and Brahmins, and just come out with me, wearing only one cloth. Construct a small thatched house on the bank of the river, and sow the tulsi plant by the house. Just circumambulate the tulsi tree, and every day taste one fallen leaf, and always chant *Hare Krishna, Hare Krishna, Krishna Krishna, Hare Hare/Hare Rama, Hare Rama, Rama Rama, Hare Hare*. So far as your living is concerned, I shall send you the required grains. But you will only accept as much grain as you require for yourself and your wife."

Narada then relieved the half-dead animals and, after getting free from that dreadful condition, they fled away. By seeing the miracle executed by Narada, the black hunter was struck with wonder, and after taking him to his home, he again bowed down at his feet.

Narada returned to his place, and the hunter, after returning to his home, began to execute the instructions which Narada had given him. In the meantime, the news spread among all the villages that the hunter had become a devotee, and therefore the residents of the villages came to see the new *Vaishnava*. It is the custom of persons following the Vedic way of life to bring some grains or some fruits whenever they go to see some saintly person. All the villagers saw that the hunter now had turned into a great devotee, and they began to bring eatables. So every day he was offered grains and fruit, so much that no less than ten to twenty people might eat there. But, according to Narada's instruction, he did not accept anything more than what he required to live on, for both himself and his wife.

After some days had passed, Narada said to his friend Parbut Muni: "I have a disciple. Let us go and see him, and see if he is doing well."

When the two great sages, Narada and Parbut, came to the place of the hunter, and the hunter saw his Spiritual Master coming from the distance, he began to go to him with great respect. But while he was going to receive the great sages, there were ants on the field, and it was a hindrance to his passing. When he reached the sages, he wanted to bow down before them, but he saw there were many ants and he slowly cleared away the ants with his cloth. When Narada saw that the hunter was trying to save the lives of the ants in such a way, it reminded him of a verse from the *Skanda Purana*. That verse states: "Is it not wonderful for a devotee of the Lord, that he is not inclined to give any sort of pain, even to the ant?"

The purport is that, formerly, the hunter took pleasure by half-killing animals, but now that he had become a great devotee of the Lord, he was not prepared to give pain even to an ant.

The hunter received the two great sages at his house, and he offered them a sitting place, and brought water and washed their feet, and took water to them for drinking, and both the husband and wife touched the water on their heads. After this they began to feel ecstasy, and began to dance, singing *Hare Krishna, Hare Krishna, Krishna Krishna, Hare Hare/Hare Rama, Hare Rama, Rama Rama, Hare Hare*—raising their hands and dancing with their clothing flying.

When the two great sages saw the ecstasy of love of Godhead in the body of the hunter, Parbut Muni addressed Narada: "You are a touchstone, and so by your association even a great hunter has turned into a great devotee."

There is a nice verse in the *Skanda Purana* which says: "My dear Devarsi (Narada), you are glorious, and by your mercy even the lowest creature, such as a hunter, also became elevated to such a state of devotion, and attained transcendental attachment for Krishna."

Narada then enquired of the hunter-devotee: "Are you getting your foodstuff regularly?"

The hunter replied, "You send so many people, and they bring so much eatables that we both cannot eat so much."

Narada replied, "That's all right. Whatever you are getting, it is all right. Now continue your devotional service in that way." And after saying that, both Narada and Parbut Muni disappeared from that place.

This recitation of the story of the hunter is offered by Lord Chaitanya to show that even a hunter can be engaged in the devotional service of Krishna by the influence of pure devotees.

He then said that another meaning of *Atma* is: all varieties of the Personality of Godhead. Generally, the Personality of Godhead Himself, Krishna, and His different expansions, are all known as the Personality of Godhead. So anyone who is engaged in the devotional service of any Form or extension of the Supreme Personality of Godhead is also called *Atmarama*, and all such devotees engage themselves either in the regulative principles of devotional service, or in devotional service in transcendental love.

These two kinds of devotees also are divided into three categories: the associates, those in the perfection of devotional service, and those newly-engaged in devotional service. Newly engaged devotees can be divided into two: ones who have already attained an attachment for the Lord, and others who have not attained such attachment for the Lord. And, according to the two divisions of devotional service, namely the regulative principles and attachment by transcendental love, all these four classes of devotees become eight in number. By following the regulative principles of devotion, the perfect associates of the Lord are divided further into four classes: the servants, the friends, the parental superiors, and the fiancees.

Just as devotees are sometimes perfected by devotional service, so some of them are eternally perfect. In the regulative principle of devotional service, according to the advanced standard and the beginner's standard, there are sixteen kinds of devotees in transcendental loving service of the Lord. Therefore, such *Atmaramas* can be considered to exist in 32 divisions. If you apply the words *Muni, Nirgrantha, Cha* and *Api* in the 32 classes, then it becomes a description of 58 different types of devotees. All these devotees can be sheltered by one word: *Atmarama*. Just as in the forest, there may be different kinds of trees, but only by saying that there are trees there, the meaning is understood.

Thus the Lord completed 60 different meanings of the word *Atmarama*. And then He again said that *Atma* means "the living entity, beginning from the first living creature, Brahma, down to the ant." He cited a verse from *Vishnu Purana*, Sixth Chapter, in which it is stated that the energies of the Lord are all spiritual. Of them, the energy which is known as the source of the living entity is also spiritual, but the other energy, which is full of ignorance and is manifested in material activities, is called material Nature. The living entities are innumerable, even in the material creation, and if by chance one of them or some of them can get the association of a pure devotee, then they can be engaged in the pure devotional service of Krishna. The Lord said, "Formerly I thought of 60 different meanings for the word *Atmarama*, but here another meaning came to My mind by your association."

Sanatan Goswami, after hearing from the Lord about different meanings of the word *Atmarama*, was struck with wonder and fell down in devotion at the feet of Lord Chaitanya. He said, "I understand that You are Personally the Supreme Personality of Godhead, Krishna, and with Your breathing there are many manifestations of the Vedic literature. You are the Teacher of *Srimad Bhagwatam*, so You know best the meanings of the verses of *Srimad Bhagwatam*. It is not possible for others to understand the confidential meanings of *Srimad Bhagwatam* without Your mercy."

The Lord then replied to Sanatan Goswami, "Do not try to eulogize Me in that way. Just try to understand the real nature of *Srimad Bhagwatam*: *Srimad Bhagwatam* is the sound representation of the Supreme Lord Krishna: therefore, *Srimad Bhagwatam* is not different from Krishna. So, as Krishna is unlimited, similarly, in each word and each letter of *Srimad Bhagwatam*, there are unlimited meanings, and one can understand them by association of devotees. Don't, then, say that *Bhagwatam* is a collection of answers to questions."

There were six questions put by the sages of Nayamisharanya to Sukadeva Goswami, and Sukadeva Goswami explained or answered the six questions in the *Srimad Bhagwatam*. There is a verse in the Vedic literature in which Lord Shiva says, "So far as *Bhagwatam* is concerned, I may know or Sukadeva may know or Vyasadeva may know It or not know It—but actually *Bhagwatam* is to be understood by devotional service, and from a devotee, and not by one's own intelligence or by learned comments."

The sages of Nayamisharanya asked, "My dear sir, kindly tell us now, after the departure of the Lord for His own Abode, if the principles of religion have gone with Him. How can we find such principles after His departure?" The reply was as follows: "After the departure of Krishna to His Abode with all religious principles, His representation, the *Srimad Bhagwatam*, the *Maha Purana*, stands as the blazing, illuminating sun."

The Lord then said, "I am just like a madman, to describe this verse of *Atmarama* in so many ways; so you must not mind if I have said something mad. But if somebody becomes a madman like Me, he can understand the real meaning of *Srimad Bhagwatam* as I have explained it."

Then Sanatan Goswami, with folded hands, fell down at the feet of Lord Chaitanya and prayed as follows: "My dear Lord, You have asked me to prepare the regulative principles of devotional service, but I belong to the lowest caste. I have no knowledge. I do not know how such an important task can be finished my me. If You will kindly give me some hints about the preparation of such a book on devotional service, then it may be that I shall be qualified to write such a book."

The Lord then blessed him, saying, "Whatever you write, by the grace of Krishna, everything will come out of your heart to be accepted as you have asked. I'll give you some notes that you can take down: The first and foremost thing is that one should accept a bona fide Spiritual Master. That is the beginning of spiritual life."

After indicating that one should begin by accepting a Spiritual Master, He requested Sanatan Goswami to write the symptoms of a true *Guru*, and the symptoms of a true devotee. The symptoms of a devotee are described in the *Padma Purana*: A person who is a qualified Brahmin, and at the same time qualified with all the symptoms of a devotee, can become the Spiritual Master of all classes of men, and such a devotee and Spiritual Master must be respected as God Himself. But a person, even though he may be born of a very respectful Brahmin family, cannot become a bona fide Spiritual Master if he is not a devotee of the Lord. One should not, therefore, be misguided to think that a bona fide Spiritual Master is required to be born of a so-called Brahmin family. The idea is that a Spiritual Master must be a qualified Brahmin—*by the symptoms of his activities.*

This is confirmed in the *Srimad Bhagwatam* when Narada speaks of the different symptoms of the different divisions of social life, and when he summarizes that Brahmins and Kshatriyas and Sudras should be selected by their particular individual qualificational symptoms. And Sridhar Swami has noted, in his comment, that birth in the family of a Brahmin does not mean that one is a Brahmin—he must be qualified with the symptoms of a Brahmin, as they are described in the Shastras. Practically, also, we have experience that there are many devotees in the disciplic succession of the *Gaudiya Vishnu Sampradaya*, such as the two great acharyas Thakur Narottam and Shyamananda Goswami, who were not born in Brahmin families, but were accepted as Spiritual Masters by many Brahmins of fame, such as Ganganarayana Ramakrishna.

In this way, there are symptoms of the prospective devotee; and both the disciple and the Spiritual Master must each see whether the other is eligible to become a bona fide Spiritual Master or a bona fide student of the Spiritual Master. Then one should know that the worshippable object is the Supreme Personality of Godhead, and all kinds of different Mantras, sacred songs, should be understood.

The Lord also instructed that Sanatan should describe the symptoms of persons who are eligible to accept the Mantra, and how the Mantras should be understood and perfected by ritualistic performances. Then He described initiation, morning duties, and duties of cleanliness—washing the face, washing the teeth—working, and prayers both in the morning and in the evening; how to worship the Spiritual Master, how to mark the body with *Gopichandan*, how to collect the tulsi leaves, how to wash the room and the temple of the Lord, and how to awaken Krishna from His sleeping. He described different methods for worshipping the Lord, which is called the method of fivefold paraphernalia and fifty-fold paraphernalia. How to worship the Lord by five times offering worship and *Aruti;* how to offer foodstuff to Krishna, how to lay Him down on the bed. There are different symptoms of the Form of the Lord and *Salagram Seela,* such as the effect of going to holy places where there are different temples of the Lord, and seeing the Form of God in the temples. There is the glorifying of the transcendental Name of the Lord, and the different offences in the matter of worshipping. When worshipping the Lord there are other things: paraphernalia such as the conch shell, water, and fragrant flowers; prayers and hymns, circumambulation, offering obeisances, regulative principles of *Puroscharam*, and accepting Krishna *Prasadam*, rejecting foodstuff which is not offered to Krishna, and not indulging in defaming a devotee who has the actual symptoms of a devotee.

There are also symptoms of a holy man, the process of satisfying the sage, and rejecting the society of undesirable persons; and hearing *Srimad Bhagwatam* constantly. Also to be followed are duties of the day, duties of the fortnight, and observing fasting on *Ekadasee* day; the duties of the month, observing ceremonies like the birthday of the Lord, the three specific dates of fasting,

Ekadasee, Janmastami, Vamanadvadasi, Sri Ramanavami and Nrishingha Chaturdasi. And, in observing such fasting days, there is the consideration of *Beeddhaa*, or overlapping of fasting days with other situations of the month, and how they are helpful in the advancement of devotional service. Lord Chaitanya instructed Sanatan Goswami that in every step he should give documentary evidence from the *Puranas*. Also mentioned is how to establish the temples of the Lord, and the general behavior and symptoms of a Vaishnava, and the duties and occupation of the Vaishnava. Thus the Lord in summary explained all the details of writing books on Vaishnava regulative principles.

Sanatan Goswami was a great devotee of the Lord, and was directly instructed to spread the cult of *Bhakti* by writing many books. There is a description of him in *Chaitanya Chandrodaya*, where it is said that Sanatan Goswami was one of the ministers of the Nawab Hussein government; in fact, he was the most important personality in the government. His brother, Rupa Goswami, was also a minister in the government, and both of them gave up the lucrative government service and became mendicants to serve the Supreme Lord. Within their hearts they are full of transcendental loving service, but externally they are just like ordinary mendicants, with a great liking for the cowherd boy of Vrindaban. Sanatan Goswami was very dear to all pure devotees of his time.

TEACHINGS OF LORD CHAITANYA

PART II

CHAPTER SEVENTEEN

Lord Chaitanya, The Original Personality of Godhead

Following in the footsteps of Kaviraj Krishnadas Goswami, we may offer our respectful obeisances unto the Lotus Feet of Lord Chaitanya.

He is described as follows: Lord Chaitanya is the only shelter for the forlorn, or the most fallen, and He is the only hope for persons who are completely devoid of spiritual knowledge. Let us try to discuss His great contribution of devotional service.

The Supremely Powerful Lord Krishna becomes manifest in five different potentialities. Although He is One without any second, still, for serving five different specific spiritual purposes, He is manifested in five. Such diversity is eternal and blissful, as opposed to the conception of montonous oneness. From the version of Vedic literature, we can understand that the Absolute Truth, the Supreme Personality of Godhead, eternally exists with His diverse energies. Lord Chaitanya appeared with full diverse energies, and they are five in number; and, therefore, He is said to be Krishna with diverse energies, presented as Lord Chaitanya.

As there is no difference between the energy and the energetic, so it is in the Lord's appearance as Sri Chaitanya Mahaprabhu and His four Associates, Nityananda Prabhu, Adwaita Prabhu, Gadadhara, and Srivas. Among these five diverse manifestations of the Supreme Lord as incarnation, expansion and energies there is no spiritual difference. They are five in One Absolute Truth. For relishing transcendental flavors in the Absolute Truth they are five diverse manifestations, and they are called the Form of a devotee, the identity of a devotee, and pure devotional service personified.

Out of these five diversities of the Absolute Truth, the Form of Lord Chaitanya is the Original Personality of Godhead, Krishna. The identity of Krishna as Lord Nityananda is as the manifestation of the first expansion of the Supreme Lord. And, similarly, Adwaita Prabhu is an incarnation of the Supreme Lord. All these three belong to the category of Vishnu Tattwa, or the Supreme Absolute Truth. Srivas is the representation of a pure devotee, and Gadadhara is the representation of the internal energy of the Lord for advancement in the cause of pure devotion. Therefore Gadadhara and Srivas, although within the category of Vishnu, are diverse energies of the Supreme Lord. In other words, they are not different from the energetic, but, still, for relishing transcendental relationships, they are manifested diversely. The whole process of devotional service is transcendental reciprocation of the flavors of relationship between the worshipped and the worshipper. Without such a diverse exchange of transcendental flavors, devotional service has no meaning.

In the Vedic literature (*Katho Upanishad*) there is a verse which says that the Supreme Lord is the Supreme Living Entity amongst all living entities. There are innumerable living entities, but there is One Living Entity Who is the Supreme Absolute Godhead. The difference between that Singular Living Entity and the plural number of living entities is that the Singular Living Entity is the Lord of all. Lord Chaitanya is that Supreme Living Entity, Who descended Himself for claiming the fallen innumerable living entities. In other words, the specific purpose of Lord Chaitanya's advent in recent ages was to establish the Vedic fact that there is One Supreme Personality of Godhead predominating over, or maintaining, the numerous personalities of living entities. The *Mayavadi*, impersonalist, philosophers cannot understand this, and therefore Lord Chaitanya advented Himself, to convince the people in general about the real nature of the relationship between the Supreme and the many entities.

In the *Bhagavad Gita*, the last instruction of Lord Krishna is that everyone should give up all other engagements and should engage in the devotional service of the Lord. But after His disappearance, persons with less intelligence misunderstood Him. They became contaminated with the *Mayavadi* philosophy, which produced so many mental speculators that people became misled about the actual position of the Absolute Truth and the living entity. Lord Chaitanya, therefore, although the Supreme Lord Krishna Himself, again appeared to teach the fallen souls of this material world how to approach Lord Krishna. The philosophy of *Bhagavad Gita* is that one should give up everything and be done with this world of material attachment. A pure devotee of Lord Krishna and one who follows the philosophy of Lord Chaitanya are the same. Chaitanya's philosophy is: one should give up everything and worship God, Krishna. The difference is that Krishna, as the Supreme Lord, the personality of Godhead, spoke the same words indicating Himself, and the *Mayavadi* philosophers misunderstood Him. Therefore, Lord Chaitanya indicated the same thing: one should not declare himself to be as good as Krishna, but should worship Krishna as the Supreme Lord.

It is a great mistake if we accept Lord Chaitanya as one of the conditioned souls; He is to be understood as the Supreme Absolute Truth, the Personality of Godhead, Sri Krishna Himself, In the *Chaitanya Charitamrita*, therefore, it is said of Lord Chaitanya: "Krishna is now present in His five diverse manifestations," as is being explained here. Unless one is in uncontaminated goodness, it is very difficult to understand Lord Chaitanya as the Supreme Personality of Godhead Himself. Therefore, to understand Lord Chaitanya one has to follow the direct disciples of Lord Chaitanya, the six Goswamis, and especially the path chalked out by Srila Jiva Goswami.

The most astonishing factor is that Lord Chaitanya, although the Supreme Personality of Godhead, Krishna, never exhibited Himself as Krishna. Rather, whenever He was detected by intelligent devotees as Lord Krishna, and addressed as Lord Krishna, He denied it, and sometimes He closed His ears, protesting that one should not be addressed as the Supreme Lord. This was His indirect teaching to the *Mayavadi* philosophers: that one should never pose oneself as the Supreme Lord falsely, and thereby misdirect the followers. The followers also should not be foolish enough to accept anyone and everyone as the Supreme Personality of Godhead, without testing with the Scriptures and by activities. One should not, however, mistake Lord Chaitanya with His five diverse manifestations as ordinary human beings. He is the Supreme Personality of Godhead, Krishna Himself. The beauty of Lord Chaitanya is that, although He is the Supreme Personality of Godhead Himself, He Himself as a great devotee is teaching all the conditioned souls how devotional service should be conducted. The conditioned souls who are interested in devotional service should follow, therefore in the exemplary footsteps of Lord Chaitanya, to learn how Krishna can be achieved by devotional service. In other words, the Supreme Lord Himself teaches the conditioned soul how He should be approached by devotional service.

By analytical study of the five diverse manifestations of the Supreme Lord we can know that Lord Sri Chaitanya Mahaprabhu is the Supreme Absolute, and that Lord Nityananda is an immediate expansion of the Supreme Absolute Truth. We can understand that Adwaita Prabhu is also in the category of the Supreme Personality of Godhead, but he is the subordinate to Lord Chaitanya and Nityananda Prabhu. The Supreme Personality of Godhead and His immediate subordinate expansions are all worshippable by the other two, namely, the internal potential representation, and the marginal potential representation.

The internal potential representation, Gadadhara, represents the pure devotee, and the marginal potential representation is a confidential devotee. Both these categories are worshippers of the other three categories, but all of them—the two worshippable categories and the two in the worshipper category—are engaged in the transcendental loving service of the Supreme Personality of Godhead, Sri Chaitanya Mahaprabhu.

There is a specific difference between the pure devotee and the confidential devotee. Different potencies of the Lord are engaged in serving the Supreme Lord in different transcendental relationships. They are situated in conjugal love, in parental affection, in friendly affinity and in obedient servitude. By impartial judgement, it is found that the internal potencies of the Supreme Lord, engaged in conjugal love with Him, are the best of all devotees. As such, both internal devotees and confidential devotees are attracted by the conjugal love of the Supreme Absolute Truth, and are the most confidential devotees of Lord Chaitanya. Other pure devotees, who are more or less attached to Sri Nityananda Prabhu and to Adwaita Prabhu, are attracted by other transcendental relationships, such as parental affection, friendly affinity and obedient servitude. When such devotees are very much attached to the activities of Lord Chaitanya, at once they become confidential devotees in conjugal love with the Supreme Lord.

There is a very nice song sung by a great devotee and *Acharya* in the disciplic succession from Lord Chaitanya. His name is Sri Thakur Narottamdas. Sri Thakur says as follows: "When will there be a transcendental vibration all over my body simply by attending to the Name of Gauranga? When will there be incessant flowing of my tears simply by uttering *Harer Nama* of the Lord? When will Lord Nityananda be merciful upon me, and all my desires for material enjoyment become insignificant? When shall I be purified by giving up all contaminations of material enjoyment; and when shall I be able to see the transcendental Abode, Vrindaban? When shall I be eager to accept the six Goswamis as my prime guidance? And when shall I be able to understand the conjugal love of Krishna?" In other words, nobody should be eager to understand the conjugal love of Krishna without undergoing disciplinary training under the six Goswamis of Vrindaban.

The *Samkirtan* movement inaugurated by Lord Chaitanya is a transcendental Pastime of the Lord: "So that I may live simultaneously to preach and popularize this movement in the material world." And in that Samkirtan movement of Lord Chaitanya, Nityananda and Adwaita are His expansions, and Gadadhara and Srivas are His internal and marginal potencies.

The living entities are called marginal potency because they have, potentially, both attitudes, namely the tendency to surrender unto Krishna, and the tendency for becoming independent of the Supreme Lord, and being contaminated by the material world through the propensity for material enjoyment. When a living entity is predominated over by the desire for material enjoyment and becomes entangled in material contamination, at that time he is subjected to the three-fold miseries of material existence. There is a very nice example in this connection. It is just like a seed sewn in the earth. If it is overpowered by too much water, there is no possibility of the seed being fructified. Similarly, even if a man is captivated by material enjoyment, and even if the seed of such enjoyment is within the heart of the conditioned soul but he is overwhelmed, over powered by a flood of transcendental activities in love of God, then his potential seed cannot fructify into a conditional life of material existence. The conditional living entities in the material world, especially at the present age of Kali, are being overpowered by the flood of love of God inaugurated by Lord Chaitanya and His Associates.

There is a nice verse in this connection, written by His Holiness Prabodhananda Saraswati in his book *Sri Chaitanya Chandramrita*. In that verse it is stated that materialistic persons are very enthusiastic in the matter of maintaining their family members, wife and children; and there are many mystic speculators who are engaged in speculating on being liberated from the miseries of material life, and therefore they undergo various kinds of austerities and penances. But persons who have discovered the greatest transcendental flavor, in the movement of Lord Chaitanya Mahaprabhu, no longer have any taste for all those activities.

Persons who are under the impression that, in the Form of the Supreme Personality of Godhead, and in the matter of His devotional service, there is material contamination, are called *Mayavadi*. According to their imperfect speculation, the impersonal Brahman is considered the only existence of the cosmic manifestation. As soon as there is a conception of the Supreme Personality of Godhead, they consider that it is in contact with Maya, or the external material energy. Similarly, such persons consider all incarnations of the Supreme Lord to be contaminated by this material Nature. According to them, this material body of the living entity, and the action of matter on all the different kinds of identifications of the living entity, are called material manifestation. According to them, liberation means that there is no longer any individual identification, or pure living entity. In other words, a living entity, when he is liberated, becomes One with the Supreme Impersonal Brahman.

According to Mayavadi philosophy it is understood that, in the Personality of Godhead, in the Abode of the Supreme Personality of Godhead, and in the matter of devotional service, the emotional devotees are all under the spell of Maya, and are therefore subjected to the material condition. Persons who forget the transcendental nature of the Supreme Personality of Godhead, His transcendental Abode and devotional service, as well as the devotee, consider that these are different examples of material activity. Such persons are called *Karmis*, or actors in fruitive activities. When one thinks that there is a possibility of arguing about transcendence, he is called agnostic. And when one thinks that there is the possibility to criticize transcendence, he is called atheist. Lord Chaitanya wanted to accept all these different kinds of agnostics, atheists, skeptics, and unfaithfuls, and swallow them in the flood of love of God. Therefore, He accepted the four orders of life—and He accepted the renounced order of life, in order to attract all these forces.

Lord Chaitanya remained a householder until twenty-four only, and in the twenty-fifth year of His life, He accepted the renounced order. After accepting the renounced order, He attracted many other renounced order Sannyasis. During the time that He had been executing the Samkirtan movement in His family, many Mayavadi Sannyasis did not take His movement very seriously. Similarly, the speculative students, atheists, and those who are attached to fruitive activities and unnecessary criticism were also delivered by the Lord after He accepted the Sannyasi order of life. The Lord was so kind that He accepted all of them, and delivered to them the most important factor of life: love of God.

To fulfill the mission of the Lord, bestowing love of God upon the conditioned souls, He devised many methods to accept all those disinterested in the matter of love of God. After He accepted the renounced order, all agnostics and critics, atheists and mental speculators became the students and followers of Lord Chaitanya. Even many of those who were not Hindus or the followers of the Vedic principles of life also accepted Lord Chaitanya as the Supreme Teacher.

Those Sannyasis who were known as the Mayavadi philosophers of Benares were the only persons who avoided the mercy of Sri Chaitanya Mahaprabhu. The plight of the Mayavadi philosophers is described as follows by Sri Bhaktisiddhanta Saraswati Goswami: "The Mayavadi philosophers of Benares are less intelligent because they want to measure everything by direct perception. But everything they have is a calculation of material perception. The Absolute Truth is transcendence, but according to them there is no variegatedness in transcendence, because they say that anything which is full of variegatedness is Maya."

During Chaitanya Mahaprabhu's time there were other philosophers, known as the Mayavadi philosophers of Sarnatha. Sarnatha is a place near Benares where Buddhist philosophers were residing, and even today there are many Stupas of the Buddhist Mayavadi. The Mayavadi philosophers of Sarnatha are different from the impersonalists who believe in the impersonal manifestation of Brahman. According to the Sarnatha philosophers there is no spiritual existence. Spiritually, both the Mayavadi philosophers of Benares and the philosophers of Sarnatha are entrapped by the material Nature. None of them actually knows the nature of the Absolute Transcendence. The philosophers of Benares, although accepting the Vedic principles superficially and accepting themselves as transcendentalists, do not agree to accept spiritual variegatedness. They have no information about devotional service, and therefore they are called "non-devotees," or against the devotional service of Lord Krishna.

The impersonalists speculate on the Supreme Personality of Godhead and His devotees, subjected to the direct perception of knowledge. The Lord and His devotee and His devotional service, however, are not subject to direct perception. In other words, spiritual variegatedness is unknown to the Mayavadi philosophy, and therefore all the Mayavadi philosophers and Sannyasis began to criticize Him because He was conducting the Samkirtan movement. They were surprised to see Lord Chaitanya, because He belonged to the Mayavadi sect of Sannyasis, having accepted His Sannyasa order from Keshav Bharati, who belonged to the Mayavadi school. They were surprised to see Him engaged in chanting and dancing, and not engaged in the matter of hearing or reading Vedanta, as is the custom. The Mayavadi philosophers are very fond of Vedanta, and misinterpret it in their own way. The Mayavadi Sannyasis, instead of understanding their own position, began to critize Lord Chaitanya as an unauthorized Sannyasi. They criticized that He was sentimental and not actually a bona fide Sannyasi. All these criticisms were carried to Lord Chaitanya when He was at Benares, and He was not at all surprised. He smiled when the news was carried to Him. He, however, did not associate with the Mayavadi Sannyasis, but used to remain alone and execute His own mission. And after staying for some days in Benares, He started for Mathura.

CHAPTER EIGHTEEN

The Conversations With Prakasananda

According to the principles of the Mayavadi Sannyasis, singing, dancing, and playing on musical instruments are strictly prohibited; they are called three kinds of sinful activities. The Mayavadi Sannyasi is supposed to engage his valuable time simply in the matter of Vedanta study. When the Mayavadi Sannyasis in Benares saw that Lord Chaitanya was indulging in singing, dancing and playing musical instruments, and was always chanting *Hare Krishna, Hare Krishna, Krishna Krishna, Hare Hare/Hare Rama, Hare Rama, Rama Rama, Hare Hare*, they concluded that this Sannyasi was not educated, and, out of sentiment, He was misleading some of the followers. Sankaracharya has said that a Sannyasi should always be engaged in studying Vedanta, and should be satisfied simply having one cloth and nothing more. Lord Chaitanya was neither studying Vedanta in formality, nor did He cease from singing and dancing, and so He was criticized by all the Sannyasis at Benares, as well as by their householder followers.

Lord Chaitanya got this news from His students and disciples, and when

He heard that they were all criticizing Him, He simply smiled and started for Mathura and Vrindaban. But He came back again to Benares on His way to Jagannath Puri from Mathura. When He came back to Benares, He stayed at the house of Chandra Sekhar, who was considered a *Sudra* because he was a clerk. In spite of Sekhar being a Sudra, Lord Chaitanya Mahaprabhu made His residential quarter at his place. Lord Chaitanya made no such distinction between Brahmin or Sudra—anyone devoted, He accepted. Customarily, a Sannyasi is supposed to take shelter in the house of a Brahmin, or eat at the house of a Brahmin, but Chaitanya Mahaprabhu, as the independent Supreme Personality of Godhead, had His own discretion, and He decided to stay at Chandra Sekhar's house.

In those days, by misuse of the Brahminical hereditary principle, the Brahmins made it a law that anyone who was not born of a Brahmin family was a Sudra. So even the Kshatriyas and the Vaidyas were also called Sudras. Vaidyas are supposed to be descendents of Brahmin fathers and Sudra wives, and therefore they are sometimes called Sudras. So Chandra Sekhar Acharya, although born of a Vaidya family, was called, at Benares, a Sudra. As long as Lord Chaitanya stayed at Benares, He stayed at Chandra Sekhar's apartment, and He used to take His food at the place of Tapan Mishra.

When Sanatan Goswami met Lord Chaitanya at Benares he learned from Lord Chaitanya the process and principles of devotional service during two months of continuous teaching. The instructions of Lord Chaitanya to Sanatan Goswami have been described in our First Part of Lord Chaitanya's teachings. After that teaching, Sanatan Goswami was authorized to propagate the principles of devotional service and the *Srimad Bhagwatam*. But, during this time, both Tapan Mishra and Chandra Sekhar Acharya were feeling very sorry about strong criticism against Lord Chaitanya Mahaprabhu, and they came together and prayed for the Lord to meet the Mayavadi Sannyasis.

They informed Lord Chaitanya: "We have been mortified by hearing unfavorable criticism from the Mayavadi Sannyasis against You. It has become intolerable for us." They requested He do something so that these criticisms would be stopped.

While they were thus discussing the criticism of the Mayavadi Sannyasis, a Brahmin came to Lord Chaitanya and invited Him, as he had invited all the other Sannyasis, to his place. Only Chaitanya had not been invited, and so he now had come to invite Him. He knew that Chaitanya Mahaprabhu did not mix with the Mayavadi Sannyasis, and therefore he fell down at Chaitanya Mahaprabhu's feet and implored Him: "Although I know that You do not

Lord Chaitanya Meets Prakasananda Saraswati at Benares

accept invitations, still, it is my request—please come and take *Prasadam* at my place with the other Sannyasis. If You accept this invitation it will be considered a special favor to me."

The Lord took this opportunity and accepted the invitation of the Brahmin, in order to meet the Mayavadi Sannyasis. It was, practically, an arrangement made by the Lord Himself. The Brahmin who invited Him knew that Lord Chaitanya did not accept any invitations, but still he was very eager to invite Him.

The next day Lord Chaitanya went to the house of the Brahmin. He saw that all the Mayavadi Sannyasis were sitting there. He offered His respects to all the Sannyasis, as was usual, and then He went to wash His Feet. After washing His Feet, He sat down at that spot, not amongst the Mayavadi Sannyasis, but in a place where water was kept for washing the feet. While He was sitting there, the other Sannyasis saw a glaring effulgence emanating from His body. All the Mayavadi Sannyasis were attracted by this glaring effulgence, and they stood up and showed Him respects. Amongst them there was one Sannyasi whose name was Prakasananda Saraswati. He was the chief amongst all the impersonalist Sannyasis, and he addressed Lord Chaitanya with great humility, and asked Him to come and sit amongst them.

He said, "My dear sir, why are You sitting in that filthy place? Please come and sit with us."

Lord Chaitanya replied: "Oh, I belong to an inferior sect of Sannyasis. Therefore I think I should not sit with you. Let Me sit down here."

Prakasananda Saraswati was surprised to hear such a thing from such a learned man, and he actually took His hand and requested Him to please come and sit down with him. Lord Chaitanya was seated, and Prakasananda Saraswati enquired, "I think Your name is Sri Krishna Chaitanya, and I understand that You belong to our Mayavadi sect because You have taken Your Sannyasa from Keshav Bharati, who belongs to the Sankara Sampradaya."

According to the Sankara sect, there are ten different names for Sannyasi. Out of them, the three names, Tirtha, Asram and Saraswati, are considered to be the most enlightened and cultured among the Sannyasis. Lord Chaitanya was a Vaishnava, and therefore naturally He was humble and meek, and He wanted to give the better place to Prakasananda, who belonged to the Saraswati Sampradaya. According to Sankara principles, a disciple of the Bharatic school is called *Chaitanya*. But Sri Krishna Chaitanya Mahaprabhu, although He took Sannyasa, kept His Brahmachary name, without the title Bharati.

Prakasananada Saraswati inquired from Lord Chaitanya: "Well sir, You belong to our Sankara sect, and You are living at Benares. Why don't You mix with us? What is the reason? Another thing—You are a Sannyasi. You are supposed to engage Your time simply in Vedanta study. But we see that instead of doing that You are always engaged in chanting, dancing, and playing on musical instruments. What are the reasons? These things are done by emotional and sentimental people. But You are a qualified Sannyasi. Why should You not engage Yourself in the study of Vedanta? By Your effulgence it appears to us that You are just like the Supreme Narayana, the Personality of Godhead, but Your behavior appears to be otherwise. So we are inquisitive to know, what are the reasons?"

Lord Chaitanya replied: "My dear sir, I may inform you that My Spiritual Master saw Me as a great fool, and therefore he more or less punished Me and said that, because I am such a fool, I have no jurisdiction in the study of Vedanta. So he kindly gave Me the chanting of *Hare Krishna, Hare Krishna, Krishna Krishna, Hare Hare/Hare Rama, Hare Rama, Rama Rama, Hare Hare.* My Spiritual Master told Me: 'You go on Chanting this Krishna Mantra, and it will make You all-perfect.'"

Actually, Lord Chaitanya was neither a fool nor ignorant of the principles of Vedanta, but His purpose was to demonstrate to modern society that for fools who have no penance and austerity behind them, and simply for some recreational purpose want to study Vedanta—that is not recommended. In His *Sikshastak*, Lord Chaitanya said that one should be in a humble state of mind, should think of himself as lower than the grass on the street, more tolerant than the tree, devoid of all false sense of prestige, and ready to offer all kinds of respects to others. In such a state of mind, one can chant Vedanta philosophy or the Holy Name of God constantly. He also wanted to teach that a serious student of transcendental science should follow exactly the words of the Spiritual Master. According to the calculation of the Spiritual Master, Lord Chaitanya appeared to be a fool, so he said that He should not indulge in the study of Vedanta but should go on chanting the Krishna Mantra. Therefore, He strictly obeyed. In other words Lord Chaitanya impressed on the Mayavadis that the words of a bona fide Spiritual Master must be strictly followed. That would make one perfect in all respects.

Vedanta means that the last word of the Vedic knowledge is to understand Krishna: *Vedaischa sarvai aham eva vedyam:* Actual understanding of the Vedanta is to know Krishna, and our relationship with Krishna. And one who understands Krishna understands everything. The knower of Krishna is always engaged in the transcendental loving service of Krishna. The Lord confirms this in *Bhagavad Gita*: "I am the Source of everything, and everything emanates from Me. Therefore, one who knows Me perfectly well is fully engaged in My transcendental loving service." A living entity is eternally related with Krishna by that relationship of Master and servant, and once that service is wanting—or, in other words, when one is not situated in Krishna Consciousness—it is to be understood that his study of Vedanta is insufficient. When one does not understand what is Krishna Consciousness, or is not engaged in the trascendental loving service of Lord Krishna, it is to be understood that he is adverse to the study of Vedanta or understanding the Supreme Personality of Godhead.

The path shown by Lord Chaitanya in the matter of studying Vedanta philosophy, as explained in this connection, should be followed by all. A person who is puffed up over his so-called education, has no humility and therefore does not seek after the protection of a bona fide Spiritual Master, thinks that he does not require a bona fide Spiritual Master, and, rather by his own effort, he can achieve the highest perfection. Such persons are not eligible for the study of *Vedanta Sutra*. Those who are under the spell of the material energy, instead of following the instructions of the disciplic succession, try to manufacture something of their own, and thereby step outside the sphere of Vedanta study. A bona fide Spiritual Master must always condemn such independent mental speculators. If the bona fide Spiritual Master directly points out the foolishness of a disciple, that should not be taken otherwise. In other words, a person who is completely innocent in the Science of God is actually not learned. And, more or less, everyone who is not in Krishna Consciousness is subject to that foolishness.

Sometimes we display our foolishness by accepting somebody who is barely even educated as our Spiritual Master. That is another sign of our foolishness. It is our duty to understand the Supreme Personality of Godhead, Whose Lotus Feet are worshipped by all the Vedas. One who does not understand that Supreme Personality of Godhead, and is proud of his false understanding of Vedanta, is actually a fool. Mundane attempts at academic knowledge are another foolishness. So long as one cannot understand the cosmic manifestation as a representation of the three modes of material Nature, one must be considered in the darkness of inebriety and caught in the duality of this material world. Actually, a person who is in perfect knowledge of the Vedanta becomes a servitor of the Supreme Lord, Who is the Maintainer and Sustainer of the whole cosmic manifestation. So long as one is not transcendental to the service of the limited, he cannot be a person with Vedanta knowledge.

So long as one is in the limited jurisdiction of fruitive activities, or involved in mental speculation, he is perhaps eligible for studying or instructing on the theoretical knowledge of *Vedanta Sutra*, but he cannot be on the platform of understanding the Supreme, Eternal, transcendental (completely liberated) vibration of *Hare Krishna, Hare Krishna, Krishna Krishna, Hare Hare/Hare Rama, Hare Rama, Rama Rama, Hare Hare.* In other words, anyone who has achieved his perfection in chanting the transcendental vibration *Hare Krishna* does not have to learn separately the philosophy of *Vedanta Sutra*.

Persons who are not eligible by thorough understanding of the transcendental vibration as nondifferent from the Supreme, and who try to become Mayavadi philosophers and expert in *Vedanta Sutra*, are all fools according to the teaching of Chaitanya Mahaprabhu, or the bona fide Spiritual Master. To study *Vedanta Sutra* by the ascending process is another sign of foolishness. On the other hand, he who has attained the taste for chanting the transcendental vibration is actually situated at the conclusion of Vedanta. In this connection there are two verses of *Srimad Bhagwatam* which are very instructive: The purport of the first is that, even if a person is born in the family of the lowest of human beings, but is engaged in chanting the transcendental vibration, then it is to be understood that he has already performed all kinds of renunciation and austerities, and has performed all kinds of sacrifices, and has studied all the *Brahma Sutras*—so that he is now able to chant *Hare Krishna, Hare Krishna, Krishna Krishna, Hare Hare/Hare Rama, Hare Rama, Rama Rama, Hare Hare.* The purport of the second verse is that a person who is chanting the two syllables *Ha-re* (ray) must be considered as having studied all the Vedas: the *Rig Veda, Atharva Veda, Yaju Veda* and *Sama Veda*.

On the other hand, there are many so-called devotees who think that Vedanta is meant for a particular class of men, and is not meant for the devotees. They do not know that Vedanta is the only plaform of pure devotees. All the great Acharyas of the four Sampradayas of the Vaishnava sect have made their commentaries on the *Vedanta Sutra*, but the so-called devotee class, who are known as *Prakrita Sahajia*, carefully avoid the study of *Vedanta Sutra*. The *Prakrita Sahajia* misunderstand the pure devotees and Vaishnav Acharyas as being mental speculators or fruitive actors. As a result of such a conclusion, they themselves become Mayavadis, and leave the service of the Supreme Lord.

Understanding the *Vedanta Sutra* by academic knowledge never qualifies a man for understanding the value of the transcendental vibration. Such persons who are entangled in academic knowledge are conditioned souls who are confused about the facts of *I* and *My understanding*. As such, they are unable to detach their minds from the external energy.

When a person actually attains transcendental knowledge, he becomes free from this duality and becomes engaged in transcendental loving service of the Supreme Lord. The transcendental loving service of the Supreme Lord is the only means for being detached from material activities. A person properly initiated by a bona fide Spiritual Master, and engaged in chanting *Hare Krishna, Hare Krishna, Krishna Krishna, Hare Hare/Hare Rama, Hare Rama, Rama Rama, Hare Hare*, gradually becomes freed from the conception of I and Mine, and therefore becomes attached to the transcendental loving service, in one of the five different transcendental relationships. Such transcendental service is not subject matter for the gross and subtle bodies. When, however, one can understand that there is no difference between the Supreme and His Name, at that time only can he be situated in Krishna Consciousness. At that time he has no longer any necessity for grammatical adjustment of the language. Rather, he becomes more interested in the subject matter of the address: *Hare Krishna*—O my Lord, O energy of the Lord, please engage me in Your service!

Lord Chaitanya explained all this to Prakasananda Saraswati and told him that He had heard it from His Spiritual Master in these words. He informed Prakasananda Saraswati that His Spiritual Master had taught Him that the actual commentary on the *Vedanta Sutra* is *Srimad Bhagwatam*, as it is stated in the *Srimad Bhagwatam* by Vyasadeva, the Author of *Vedanta Sutra*.

The perfection of a student is to understand the identity of the Holy Name and the Supreme Lord. And, without being under the shelter of such a realized Spiritual Master, one's understanding of the Supreme is simply foolishness. One can, however, fully understand the transcendental by service and devotion. When Lord Chaitanya uttered *Krishna* without any offense, or when He offenselessly chanted the Krishna Mantra, or Maha Mantra, He declared that it can at once deliver a conditioned soul from the material contamination. In this Age of Kali there is no other alternative to chanting this Maha Mantra. It is stated that the essence of all Vedic literature is to chant this Holy Name of Krishna: *Hare Krishna, Hare Krishna, Krishna Krishna, Hare Hare/Hare Rama, Hare Rama, Rama Rama, Hare Hare*. He also said to Prakasananda Saraswati that, in order to convince Me about this essential fact of Vedic knowledge, he has taught Me a verse from *Brihad Naradiya Puranam:*

Harer Nama Harer Nama Harer Nama Eva Kevalam. Kalau Nasteva Nasteva Nasteva Gatir Anyatha.

"In this age of quarrel and hypocrisy, the only means of deliverance is to chant the Holy Name of the Lord—and there is no other means of success."

In three out of the four millenniums, namely the *Satya Yuga*, *Treta Yuga* and *Dvapara Yuga*, there was honor in understanding transcendence through the path of disciplic succession. In the present age, on account of Kali, people have no interest in the matter of the disciplic succession, but they have invented many paths of argument and logic. Such an ascending process of understanding transcendence is not approved according to the Vedic way. The Absolute Truth must descend from the Absolute platform. It is not to be understood by the ascending process. The Holy Name of the Lord, *Hare Krishna, Hare Krishna, Krishna Krishna, Hare Hare/Hare Rama, Rama Rama, Hare Hare* is a transcendental vibration. Therefore it comes down from the transcendental platform, the Supreme Abode of Krishna. And, because there is no difference between Krishna and His Name, therefore the Holy Name of Krishna is as pure, as perfect, and as liberated as Krishna Himself. For understanding the transcendental nature of the Holy Name of God, the academic scholars have no entrance by their logic and argument. The single path to understanding the transcendental nature of *Hare Krishna, Hare Krishna, Krishna Krishna, Hare Hare/Hare Rama, Hare Rama, Rama Rama, Hare Hare,* is to chant these Names with faith and adherence. Such chanting will release one from the designated conditions of gross and subtle bodies.

In this age of logical argument and disagreement the chanting of *Hare Krishna* is the only means for self realization, and because this transcendental vibration alone can deliver the conditioned soul, therefore it is the essence of the *Vedanta Sutra*. In the material conception there may be duality and differences between the Name, Form, quality, emotion and activities of a person and the person himself; but so far as this transcendental vibration is concerned, there is no such limitation, because it descends from the Spiritual World. In the Spiritual World there is no such difference between the Name of the Person Whose Name is a Quality, and the Person of the Quality. There is no such difference as there is in the material world. The Mayavadi philosophers cannot understand this, and therefore they are not eligible to utter the transcendental vibration.

Lord Chaitanya then said to Prakasananda Saraswati that, because He got that order from His Spiritual Master, therefore He was constantly engaged in chanting *Hare Krishna, Hare Krishna, Krishna Krishna, Hare Hare/Hare Rama, Hare Rama, Rama Rama, Hare Hare.*

"As a result of this chanting, sometimes I become impatient and cannot restrain Myself from dancing and laughing or crying or singing—just like a madman. When I first wondered whether I had become a madman by chanting this *Hare Krishna, Hare Krishna, Krishna Krishna, Hare Hare/Hare Rama, Hare Rama, Rama Rama, Hare Hare,* I approached My Spiritual Master and informed him that by chanting this *Hare Krishna, Hare Krishna, Krishna Krishna, Hare Hare/Hare Rama, Hare Rama, Rama Rama, Hare Hare,* 'I am becoming just like a madman, so what is my actual position?'"

In the *Narada Pancharatra* it is stated that all the Vedic rituals and Mantras and understanding are compressed into the eight words *Hare Krishna, Hare Krishna, Krishna Krishna, Hare Hare.* Similarly, in the *Kalisantra Upanishad,* it is stated that *Hare Krishna, Hare Krishna, Krishna Krishna, Hare Hare/Hare Rama, Hare Rama, Rama Rama, Hare Hare*—these sixteen words—are especially meant for counteracting the contamination of Kali. To save oneself from the contamination of Kali there is no other alternative than these sixteen words.

Lord Chaitanya informed Prakasananda Saraswati that when His Spiritual Master understood Him, the Spiritual Master said: "It is the transcendental nature of the Holy Name of *Hare Krishna, Hare Krishna, Krishna Krishna, Hare Hare/Hare Rama, Hare Rama, Rama Rama, Hare Hare* to transport a man into spiritual madness. Anyone who sincerely chants this Holy Name is actually elevated very soon onto the platform of love of God, and therefore he becomes mad after Him. This madness of love of God is the first perfectional stage of the human being." Generally the human being is after religiousness, economic development, sense gratification, and liberation. But this love of God is above all such perfections of life. The process is that a bona fide Spiritual Master chants the Holy Name, *Hare Krishna, Hare Krishna, Krishna Krishna, Hare Hare/Hare Rama, Hare Rama, Rama Rama, Hare Hare,* and the transcendental sound vibration enters into the ear of the disciple. If the disciple follows in the footsteps of his Spiritual Master and chants the Holy Name with equal respect, that becomes the worship of the transcendental Name.

When the transcendental Name becomes worshipped by the devotee, the Name Himself spreads His Glories within the heart of the devotee, and when he is perfectly qualified in chanting such transcendental vibration of the Holy Name, he is quite fit to become a Spiritual Master for delivering all the people of the world. The chanting of the Holy Name is so powerful that, gradually, it establishes its supremacy above all in the world. And the devotee who chants it becomes transcendentally situated in ecstasy, and sometimes he laughs and cries and dances in his ecstasy. Sometimes less intelligent persons put some hindrances in the way of the chanting of Hare Krishna, or the Maha Mantra; but one who is situated on the platform of love of Godhead chants the Holy Name loudly for the benefit of all persons concerned. As a result of that, everyone becomes initiated in chanting the Holy Name, Hare Krishna, Hare Krishna, Krishna Krishna, Hare Hare/Hare Rama, Hare Rama, Rama Rama, Hare Hare. By the chanting and hearing of the Holy Name of Krishna, a person can remember the Forms and Qualities of Krishna.

CHAPTER NINETEEN

The Goal of Vedanta Study

The transcendental ecstatic attachment for Krishna by perfectly understanding that Krishna the Person and Krishna the Name are identical is called *Bhava*. One who has achieved such Bhava is certainly not in the contamination of material Nature. He actually enjoys transcendental pleasure from such Bhava. And, when Bhava is more intensified, it is called love of Godhead. The Holy Name of Krishna is called the Maha Mantra (Great Chanting): therefore Lord Chaitanya explained to Prakasananda Saraswati that the Holy Name of Krishna has a specific influence on anyone who chants It and he can attain the stage of love of Godhead, or intensified Bhava. Such love of Godhead is the ultimate goal of human necessity. When one compares this love of Godhead with the other necessities of the human society, namely, religiousness, economic development, sense gratification, and liberation, they are seen as most insignificant. When one is absorbed in temporary designative existence, one hankers after sense gratification, or else after liberation. But love of Godhead is the eternal nature of the soul; it is unchangeable, without beginning, and it has no end; therefore, temporary sense gratification or a desire for liberation cannot compare with the transcendental nature of love of God. This love of God is called the fifth dimension in the human goals of life. Compared with the ocean of love of transcendental pleasure, the impersonal Brahman conception cannot measure as even one drop of water.

Lord Chaitanya now explained that His Spiritual Master had confirmed the ecstatic situation of His chanting the Holy Name of God, and had confirmed that the essence of all Vedic literature is the attainment of love of Godhead. His Spiritual Master said that Lord Chaitanya was fortunate enough to have attained such a stage of love of Godhead. By attainment of such transcendental love of Godhead, one's heart becomes very anxious to attain direct contact with the Lord; and with that transcendental sentiment he sometimes laughs, sometimes cries, sometimes sings, sometimes dances like a madman, and sometimes he traverses hither and thither.

There are various ecstatic symptoms of the body: crying, changing the color of the body, madness, bereavement, silence, feeling proud, ecstasy, gentleness, and, often, the person in love of Godhead dances. Such dancing puts him into the ocean of the nectar of love of Krishna.

Lord Chaitanya's Spiritual Master said to Him: "It is very good that You have attained such a perfectional stage of love of Godhead, and by Your attainment I am very much obliged to You."

The father becomes more enlightened when he sees his son advance beyond himself. Similarly, when the Spiritual Master sees a disciple advancing, he takes more pleasure in that than in his own advancement. Lord Chaitanya's Spiritual Master blessed Him, telling Him to "dance, sing and propagate this Samkirtan movement, and by instructing people about Krishna, try to deliver them from the nescience."

His Spiritual Master taught Him a very nice verse from *Srimad Bhagwatam* which is from the Eleventh Canto, Second Chapter: "A person who is constantly engaged in devotional service to Krishna by chanting His Holy Name becomes so transcendentally attached to the chanting that his heart becomes softened without any extraneous endeavor. In such a condition of softened heart he exhibits transcendental ecstasies, sometimes by laughing, sometimes by crying, sometimes by singing, sometimes by dancing—not exactly in an artistic way, but just like a madman."

Lord Chaitanya informed Prakasananda Saraswati, "I have full faith in my Spiritual Master's words, and therefore I am always engaged in the matter of chanting *Hare Krishna, Hare Krishna, Krishna Krishna, Hare Hare/Hare*

Rama, Hare Rama, Rama Rama, Hare Hare. I do not know how I have become just like a madman, but the Name Krishna Himself induces Me to become so. I realize that the transcendental pleasure derived from chanting *Hare Krishna, Hare Krishna, Krishna Krishna, Hare Hare/Hare Rama, Hare Rama, Rama Rama, Hare Hare,* is just like an ocean and, in comparison, all other pleasures, including the pleasure of the impersonal conception, are like shallow water in channels."

It appears from the talks of Lord Chaitanya that a person who cannot keep his faith in the words of the Spiritual Master and thus acts independently cannot ever attain the desired success in the matter of chanting *Hare Krishna.* In the Vedic literature it is said that, for one who has unflinching faith in the Supreme Lord, and similar faith in his Spiritual Master, the import of the transcendental literature becomes revealed. Lord Chaitanya firmly believed in this statement of His Spiritual Master, and He never stopped His Samkirtan movement by neglecting the instruction of His Spiritual Master. Therefore, the transcendental potency of the Holy Name encouraged Him more and more in chanting *Hare Krishna,* or the Maha Mantra.

Lord Chaitanya immediately informed Prakasananda that people in general in the modern age are more or less bereft of all spiritual intellect. When such persons come under the influence of Sankaracharya's Mayavadi, or impersonalist, philosophy before beginning the most confidential *Vedanta Sutras,* their natural tendency toward obediance to the Supreme is checked. The Supreme Source of everything is naturally respected by everyone, but by the impersonalist conception of Sankara, this natural tendency is hampered. Therefore, the Spiritual Master of Lord Chaitanya suggested that it is better not to study the *Sarirakabhasya* of Sankaracharya, which is very harmful to people in general. Neither has the common man the intelligence to penetrate into the jugglery of words. He is better advised to chant the Maha Mantra: *Hare Krishna, Hare Krishna, Krishna Krishna, Hare Hare/Hare Rama, Hare Rama, Rama Rama, Hare Hare.* In this quarrelsome Age of Kali, there is no alternative for self realization to the chanting of the *Hare Krishna* Maha Mantra.

After hearing the arguments and talks of Chaitanya Mahaprabhu, all the the Mayavadi Sannyasis who were present became pacified, and replied in sweet words: "My dear sir, whatever You have spoken is all true. A person who attains love of Godhead is certainly very fortunate. And undoubtedly You are very fortunate that You have attained such a stage of love of Godhead. But what is the fault in Vedanta that You do not study it, although it is the duty of a Sannyasi to read and understand Vedanta?"

According to Mayavadi philosophers, Vedanta means the *Sariraka* commentary of Sankaracharya. By "*Vedanta*" and "*Upanishads*," impersonal philosophers mean "according to the commentary of Sankaracharya," the greatest teacher of Mayavadi philosophy. After Sankaracharya came Sadananda Yogi, who said that Vedanta and *Upanishads* should be understood through the commentary of Sankaracharya. Factually, it is not so; for the Vedanta philosophy or the *Upanishads* there are many other commentaries made by the Vaishnava Acharyas, rather than those of Sankaracharya. Mayavadi philosophers influenced by Sankaracharya do not find any importance in the different Vaishnava philosophical understandings.

There are four different sects of Vaishnava Acharyas, called the *Suddhadvaita, Visistadvaita, Dvaidadvaita,* and *Achintya Bhedabheda;* and all the Vaishnava Acharyas have written commentaries on the *Vedanta Sutra,* which the Mayavadi philosophers do not recognize. Mayavadis make a distinction between Krishna and Krishna's Body, and therefore the worship of Krishna by the Vaishnava philosophers is not recognized by them.

Therefore, when the Mayavadi Sannyasis inquired from Lord Chaitanya as to why He did not study *Vedanta Sutra,* the Lord replied as follows: "My dear sir, you have inquired why I do not study Vedanta. In answer to this question I may speak something, if you won't be sorry on hearing it."

All the Mayavadi Sannyasis present said, "Now, we shall be very much pleased to hear You, because we see You are just like Narayan, and Your speeches are so nice that we are taking a great pleasure in hearing Your words. We are very much obliged to see You and hear You. Therefore, whatever You say, we shall be very glad to accept and hear patiently."

Then the Lord began to speak about Vedanta philosophy as follows: *Vedanta Sutra* is spoken by the Supreme Lord Himself. The Supreme Lord, by His incarnation as Vyasadeva, has compiled this great philosophical treatise, *Vedanta Sutra.* Vyasadeva's incarnation of the Supreme Lord means that He cannot be likened to the ordinary person, who has the four defects of material existence. The defects of the conditioned soul are: 1. he must commit mistakes, 2. he must be illusioned, 3. he must possess the tendency to cheat others, and 4. his senses must be all imperfect. When we speak of the incarnation of Godhead, we understand that He is transcendental to all these defects of the conditioned living entity. Therefore, whatever has been spoken and written by Vyasadeva is to be understood as perfect. The *Upanishads* and *Vedanta Sutra* aim at the same subject matter: the Supreme Absolute Truth; and, when we accept the import of *Vedanta Sutra* and the *Upanishads* directly, as they are stated, it becomes very glorious for us. But the commentary made by Sankaracharya is indirect, and is very dangerous for the common man, because, by understanding the import of the *Upanishad* in such an indirect, disruptive way, one becomes practically barred from spiritual realization.

According to *Skanda* and *Vayn Puranas*, "*Sutra*" means a condensed form of words, which carries meaning and import of immeasurable strength without any mistake or fault. "*Vedanta*" means the end of Vedic knowledge. In other words, any book which deals with the subject indicated by all the Vedas is called *Vedanta*. For example, the *Bhagavad Gita* is also Vedanta, because in the *Bhagavad Gita* we will find that the Lord says that the ultimate end of all Vedic research is Krishna, Therefore, *Bhagavad Gita* and *Srimad Bhagwatam*, which aim only at Krishna, are to be understood as Vedanta.

In transcendental realization there are three divisions of knowledge, and they are called *Prasthana Trai*. The department of knowledge which is proven by Vedic instruction, like the *Upanishads*, is called *Sruti Prasthan*. Authoritative books indicating the same thing and written by liberated souls like Vyasa— for example *Bhagavad Gita*, *Mahabarata* and the *Puranas*, especially the *Srimad Bhagwatam*, the *Maha Purana*—are called *Nyaaprasthana*. From the Vedas we understand that the Vedas originated from the breathing of Narayan. Vyasadeva, Who is an incarnation of the power of Narayan, has compiled the *Vedanta Sutra*. According to the Sankara commentary there appears another name, Apantartama Rishi, who is also credited with having compiled the codes of the *Vedanta Sutra*. According to Lord Chaitanya, the Codes of *Pancharatra* and the codes of Vedanta are one and the same. The *Vedanta Sutra*, being compiled by Vyasadeva, is to be understood as spoken by Narayan Himself. From the whole descriptive literature about the *Vedanta Sutra*, it is understood that there were many other *Rishis* contemporary with Vyasadeva who also discussed this *Vedanta Sutra*. The following sages—Atriya, Asmarathyk, Audulomi, Karshnajini, Kasakritsna, Jaimimi, Badari, and other sages such as Parasarikarmandi—also discussed *Vedanta Sutra*.

Actually, in the first three chapters of *Vedanta Sutra*, the relationship of the living entities with the Supreme Lord is explained, and in the Third Chapter the discharge of devotional service is explained. In the Fourth Chapter the result of the relationship of discharging devotional service is explained.

The natural commentary on the *Vedanta Sutra* is *Srimad Bhagwatam*. The great Acharyas of the four sections of the *Vaishnava* community—namely, Ramanujacharya, Madhvacharya, Vishnu Swami, and Nimbarka—have also written commentaries on the *Vedanta Sutra* in following the principles of

Srimad Bhagwatam. At present the followers of all the Acharyas have written many books following the principles of *Srimad Bhagwatam* as the commentary on the Vedanta. Sankara's commentary on the *Vedanta Sutra*, known as *Sarirakabhasya* is very much adored by the impersonalist class of scholars. But commentary on the Vedanta from the materialistic point of view is completely adverse to the transcendental loving position of devotional service to the Lord. And, therefore, Lord Chaitanya said that the direct commentary of the *Upanishad* and *Vedanta Sutra* is glorious, and anyone who follows the *Sarirakabhasya* of Sankaracharya without following the direct path is certainly doomed.

Lord Chaitanya admitted that Sankaracharya was an incarnation of Lord Shiva, and Lord Shiva is one of the greatest devotees, a *Mahajan* of the Bhagwat school. There are twelve great authorities on devotional service, and Lord Shiva is one of them. Then, why did he adopt the process of Mayavadi philosophy? The answer is given in the *Padma Purana*, where there is a statement by Lord Shiva as follows: "The Mayavadi philosophy is veiled Buddhist philosophy." In other words, the void philosophy of Buddha is more or less repeated in the Mayavadi philosophy of impersonalism, althouth the Mayavadi philosophy claims to be directed by the Vedic conclusions. Lord Shiva thus admits that this philosophy was manufactured by him in the Age of Kali as a Brahmin boy to mislead the atheist class of men: "Actually, the Supreme Personality of Godhead has His transcendental Body, but I describe the Supreme as impersonal. Similarly, I have explained the *Vedanta Sutra* also on the same principles of Mayavadi philosophy."

In the *Shiva Puranam* there is one statement by the Supreme Lord: "In the beginning of the *Dvapara Yuga*, under My order, there will be many sages who will bewilder the people in general by Mayavadi philosophy." In the *Padma Purana*, Lord Shiva personally says to Bhagavati Devi: "My dear Devi, sometimes I speak Mayavadi philosophy for persons who are engrossed in the modes of ignorance. But anyone in the modes of goodness who happens to hear this Mayavadi philosophy falls. In the Mayavadi philosophy I say that the living entity and the Supreme Lord are one and the same."

Sadanada Yogi, one of the greatest Mayavadi Acharyas, has written in his book, *Vedanta Sara*, as follows: "Absolute Truth of eternity, knowledge and bliss is *Brahman*. Ignorance and all products of ignorance are non-*Brahman*. Any products out of the three modes of material Nature are covered by ignorance, and all are different from the Supreme Cause and effect. This ignorance is manifested in a collective and individual sense. Collective ignorance is called *Visuddhasatvapradhana*. When that *Visuddhasatvapradhana* becomes manifested within the ignorance of material Nature it is called the Lord, and the Lord manifests all kinds of ignorance. Therefore Hs is known as *Sarvajna*." According to the Mayavadi philosophy the Lord is the product of this material Nature, and the living entity is in the lowest grade of ignorance. That is the sum and substance of the Mayavadi philosophy.

If, however, we accept directly the import of the *Upanishads*, it is clear that the Supreme Personality of Godhead is a Person with unlimited Potency. For example, in the *Brihadarnyak* it is stated that the Supreme Personality of Godhead is the Origin of everything, and He has multiple different potencies: "The Supreme Personality of Godhead is transcendental to the cosmic manifestation of His time through His material energy, and He is the Origin of all religiousness, and He is the Supreme Deliverer, and He is Possesser of all opulences. Let me understand the Supreme Personality of Godhead, Who is just like the Sun, profusely distributing His different energies, while beyond the cloud of this material cosmic manifestation. He is the Master of masters, and He is the Supreme of the supremes. He is known as the Greatest Lord, the Personality of Godhead. His energies and potencies are multiple, variously distributed." It is stated that Vishnu is the Supreme, and those who are saintly persons are always anxious to see the Lotus Feet of Vishnu. In the *Aitariya Upanishad* also it is stated that the Lord glanced over the material Nature, and thus the cosmic manifestation came about. This is also stated in the *Prasna Upanishad*.

When there is a negative description of the Lord in the Vedic literature, just like *Apani Pada*, such a Mantra indicates that the Lord has no material body, and that He has no material Form. But He has His Spiritual Body, He has His transcendental Body, and He has His transcendental Form. The Mayavadi philosophers misunderstand this transcendental nature of the Supreme Lord, and explain the Supreme Lord as impersonal. The Lord, His Name, Form, Quality, Entourage and Abode all being in the transcendental world—how can He be a transformation of this material Nature? Everything connected with the Supreme Lord is eternal, blissful, and full of knowledge.

So, in effect, Sankaracharya delivered this Mayavadi philosophy to bewilder a certain class of atheistic people. Actually, he never meant that the Supreme Lord, the Personality of Godhead, is impersonal, with no Body or no Form. Therefore, the intelligent persons should not attend any lecture on Mayavadi philosophy. We should understand that the Supreme Personality of Godhead

Vishnu is not impersonal. He is a transcendental Person. The basic principle of the cosmic manifestation is the energy of Vishnu. Mayavadi philosophy cannot trace the energy of the Supreme Lord, but in all the Vedic literature we have various evidences of the Supreme Lord's various mainfestations of energies. Vishnu is not the product of the material Nature, but material Nature is the product of Vishnu's potency. The Mayavadi philosopher understands that Vishnu is a product of this material Nature. If Vishnu is a product of the material Nature, He can be counted as one of the demigods. One who accepts Vishnu as one of the demigods is certainly mistaken and misled. And how he is misled is explained in the *Bhagavad Gita:* "My material energy is so powerful that it is very difficult to surpass the spell of material Nature, even for the greatest scholar."

CHAPTER TWENTY

The Mayavadi Philosophers
Are Converted

It is concluded that Lord Krishna, or Vishnu, is not of this material world, but that He belongs to the Spiritual World. Anyone considering Him as one of the demigods of the material world is a great offender. This is called blasphemy. Lord Vishnu is, therefore, not subject to perception by the material senses, and neither can He be realized by mental speculation. There is no difference between the Body and Soul of the Supreme Lord Vishnu. In the material world there is always the difference between the body and soul.

Anything material is enjoyed by the living entities because the living entities are superior in nature, whereas the material Nature is of inferior quality. Therefore, the superior quality of Nature, the living entities, can enjoy the inferior quality of Nature, matter. Because Lord Vishnu, is in no way touched by matter, He is not subject to the enjoyment of the living entities. The living entities cannot gain knowledge of Vishnu by enjoying their mental speculative habits. The infinitesimal living entities are not, therefore, the enjoyers of Vishnu, but they are enjoyed by Lord Vishnu. If somebody thinks that

Vishnu is enjoyable, then he is the greatest offender. The greatest act of blasphemy is to consider Vishnu and the living entity on the same level.

The Supreme Absolute Truth, the Personality of Godhead, is compared with the blazing fire, whereas the innumerable living entities are compared with the sparks emanating from the blazing fire. So, although both of them are fire in quality, yet there is the distinction that Vishnu the Supreme is infinite, whereas the living entities, which are sparks, are infinitesimal. The infinitesimal living entities are emanations from the original infinite spirit. In other words, in their constitutional position as infinitesimal spirits, there is no trace of matter.

The living entities are not as great as Narayan, Vishnu, Who is beyond the Creation of this material world. This is accepted even by Sankaracharya—that Narayan is beyond this material Creation. So neither Vishnu nor the living entity are of the material Creation. Somebody may then enquire: Why were such small particles of the spirit created at all? The answer is that the completeness of perfection of the Supreme Absolute Truth is possible when He is both infinite and infinitesimal. If He is simply infinite and He is not infinitesimal, then He is not perfect. The infinite portion is the *Vishnu Tattwa*, or the Supreme Absolute Personality of Godhead; and the infinitesimal portion is the living entity.

By the infinite desires of the Supreme Personality of Godhead there is the existence of the Spiritual World, and by the infinitesimal desires of the living entities there is this material world. When the infinitesimal living entities are engaged in their infinitesimal desires for material enjoyment, they are called *Jiva Shakti;* but when they are dove-tailed with the infinite, they are called liberated souls. There is no question, therefore, as to why God created the infinitesimal portions. It is the complementary and supplementary side of the Supreme. It is essential, without any doubt, that the infinite must have the infinitesimal portions. They are inseparable parts and parcels of the Soul.

And, because they are infinitesimal parts and parcels of the Supreme, there is a reciprocation of feelings between the infinite and the infinitesimal. Had there been no infinitesimal living entities, then of course the Supreme Lord would have been inactive, and there would have not been any variegatedness in spiritual life. As there is no meaning of a king if there is no subject, therefore there is no meaning of the Supreme God if there are no infinitesimal living entities. There would have been no meaning of the word "Lord," if there were none to overlord. The conclusion is that the living entities are counted as expansions of the energy of the Supreme Lord, and the Supreme Lord, the Personality of Godhead, Krishna, is the Energetic.

In all the Vedic literature, such as *Bhagavad Gita* and *Vishnu Purana*, there is innumerable evidence for this distinction between the energy and the Energetic. In *Bhagavad Gita*, Seventh Chapter, 5th verse, it is clearly stated that earth, water, fire, air and sky are five principal gross elements of the material world. Mind, intelligence and false ego are elements of the subtle matter. The whole material Nature is considered to be divided into these eight elements, which are the inferior quality of Nature. Another name for this inferior quality of Nature is *Maya*, or illusion. Beyond these eight kinds of inferior Nature there is another superior quality of Nature, which is called *Paraprakriti*. That *Paraprakriti* is the living entity, and the entities are found all over this material world. The purport is that the Supreme Lord is the Absolute Truth, the Energetic, and that He has energy also. That energy, when not properly manifested, or when covered by some shadow, is called *Maya Shakti*. The cosmic manifestation is a product of that covered *Maya Shakti*.

The living entities are factually beyond this covered inferior energy. The living entities have their pure spiritual existence, and their pure identity, and they have their pure mental activities. And all of them are beyond the manifestation of this cosmic world. The living entity, his mind, his intelligence, and his identity are beyond the range of this material world, but when he enters into this material world by his desire to lord it over matter, then his original mind, intelligence, and body become covered by the material energy. When he is again uncovered from these material or inferior energies, he is called liberated. And when he is liberated he has no false ego, but his real ego comes again into existence.

Foolish mental speculators think that after liberation even the identity is lost, but that is not so. Because we are eternally part and parcel, the living entity, when liberated, revives his original, eternal part-and-parcel identity. *Aham Brahmasmi* (I am not this body) does not mean that I lose my identity. At the present moment I say that I am matter, but in my liberated state I will understand that I am not matter, I am spirit soul, as part of the infinite. So to become Krishna conscious or spiritually conscious and to be engaged in this loving transcendental service of Krishna is the sign of the liberated stage.

In the *Vishnu Purana*, Sixth Chapter, 7th verse, it is very nicely and clearly stated: "The energy of the Supreme Lord is divided into three: *Para*, *Kshetrajna* and *Avidya*." *Para* energy is actually the energy of the Supreme Lord; the *Kshetrajna* energy is called the living entities; and the *Avidya* energy is called this material world, or Maya. It is called *Avidya*, or ignorance, because under the spell of this material energy one forgets his actual position and his relationship with the Supreme Lord. It is concluded, therefore, that the living entities represent one of the energies of the Supreme Lord. Such an infinitesimal part and parcel of the Supreme Lord is called *Jiva*. If the Jiva is artificially put onto the same level with the infinite Supreme—because both of them are Brahman, or *spirit*—that will certainly lead to bewilderment.

The Mayavadi philosophers are perplexed before a learned Vaishnava philosopher because the Mayavadi cannot explain the cause of bondage of the living entities. They simply say: "It is out of ignorance," but they cannot explain why the Supreme is covered by this ignorance. The actual solution is that the living entities, although qualitatively one with the Supreme are infinitesimal, and are not infinite. Had they been infinite there would not have been any possibility of being covered by ignorance. But, because the living entities are infinitesimal, they are covered by another, an inferior, energy. We can see their foolishness and ignorance when they try to explain that the infinite is covered by ignorance. It is an offensive attempt to qualify the infinite as subject to the spell of ignorance.

Sankara, although he attempted to cover the Supreme Lord by his Mayavadi philosophy, was doing so only by the order of the Supreme Lord. It is to be understood that his teaching was a timely necessity, but not a permanent fact. In the *Vedanta Sutra* this distinction between energy and the Energetic is accepted from the very beginning. In that *Brahma*, or *Vedanta*, *Sutra* the first aphorism, *Janmadyasya*, is a clear explanation that the Supreme Absolute Truth is the Origin or Source of all emanation. Therefore the emanations are His energy, whereas He is the Energetic. Sankara has falsely put his argument in this way: that if the transformation of energy is accepted, then the Supreme Absolute cannot remain immutable. But that is not true; in spite of unlimited energy being generated, why not accept that the Supreme Absolute Truth remains always the same, even though there is the emanation of unlimited energies from Him? Sankaracharya has therefore incorrectly and wrongly established the theory of illusion.

In this connection Ramanujacharya has discussed the point very nicely as follows: "If you argue that before the creation of this material world there was only one Absolute Truth, then how is it possible that the living entity emanated from Him? If He was alone, how could He produce or generate the infinitesimal living entities?" In reference to this question the *Vedas* state that everything is generated from the Absolute Truth, everything is being maintained by the Absolute Truth, and, after annihilation, everything enters into Him. From this statement of the *Upanishads*, it is clear that the living entities enter into the Supreme Existence in their liberated state without changing their original constitutional position of activity.

We must always remember that the Supreme Lord has His creative function; and, similarly, the infinitesimal living entities have also a creative function. When they are liberated and enter into the Supreme after the dissolution of this material body, their creative function is not lost. On the contrary, the creative function of the living entity becomes properly manifested in the liberated stage. If the living entity's activities are definitely manifested when he is in this material condition, then how is it possible that when he is in his spiritual liberated stage his activities can be stopped? *Entering* is therefore understood in the sense that the bird enters into the trees, or the animals enter into the forest, or the flying vehicle enters into the sky.

While explaining Code Number One of the First Chapter of *Vedanta Sutra*, Sankara has most unceremoniously tried to explain that Brahman or the Supreme Absolute Truth is impersonal. Similarly, he has tried to twist most cunningly the doctrine of by-product into the doctrine of state of change. Actually, there is no change of state for the Supreme Absolute. It is simply by His inconceivable power of doing things that there comes a by-product. A relative truth produced out of another truth is called the transformation of a by-product. For example, when a sitting chair is produced out of crude wood it is the transformation of a by-product. Similarly, the Supreme Absolute Truth, Brahman, is immutable, and when we find a by-product—the living entity or this cosmic manifestation—it is called a transformation of that by-product of the Supreme. Another example can be cited in this connection: that of milk and yogurt. Yogurt is a transformation of milk. In this way, if we study the living entities and the cosmic manifestation, it will appear that they are not different from the original Absolute Truth.

But from the Vedic literature we understand that the Absolute Truth has various multiforms of energy, and therefore the living entities and the cosmic manifestation are only a demonstration of His various energies. As energies are non-separable from the Energetic, therefore this transformation of the living entity and the cosmic manifestation is an inseparable truth which is part of the same Absolute Truth. Such a conclusion about the Absolute Truth and the relative truth should not be unacceptable to any sane man.

The Supreme Absolute Truth has His inconceivable potency, and out of that potential energy this cosmic manifestation has been effected. In other words, the Supreme Absolute Truth is the ingredient and the living entity and the cosmic manifestation are by-products. In the *Taittiriya Upanishad* it is clearly stated: *Yato va imani bhutani jayande*. This clearly states that the Absolute Truth is the original reservoir of all ingredients, and this material world of the living entities is produced out of those ingredients.

Less intelligent persons who cannot understand the doctrine of by-products cannot grasp how this cosmic manifestation and the living entity are simultaneously one and different from the Absolute Truth. Without understanding this truth, if, out of unnecessary fear, one concludes that this cosmic manifestation and the living entity are false, by putting forward the example of mistaking a rope for a snake, as Sankaracharya does, or mistaking the oyster shell for gold, surely that sort of argument is simply cheating. The examples of mistaking a rope for a snake and the oyster shell for gold, mentioned in the *Mandukya Upanishad*, have their different applications, and can be understood as follows: the living entity in his original constitution is pure spirit. And when a human being identifies himself with this material body, that is a case of accepting the rope as a snake, or the oyster shell as gold. The doctrine of transformation of state is accepted when one thing is mistaken for another. Actually, the body is not the living entity; and to accept the body as the living entity is the doctrine of transformation of state. *Every conditioned soul is undoubtedly contaminated by this doctrine of transformation of state.*

This conditional state of the living entity is a diseased condition. Originally, the living entity and the Original Cause of this cosmic manifestation are certainly not in this state of transformation. But mistaken thoughts and arguments can overcome a person when he forgets about the inconceivable energies and activities of the Supreme Lord. Even in the material world there are many examples: the Sun is producing unlimited energies from time immemorial, and so many by-products result from the Sun; yet there is no change in the heat and temperature of the Sun itself. If the Sun can maintain itself in its original state of temperature—although it is a material product—in spite of producing so many by-products, then is it very difficult to understand that the Supreme Absolute Truth, in spite of His producing so many by-products by His inconceivable energy, is not changed at all? Therefore, there is no question of the transformation of His state.

It is learned from the Vedic literature that there is a material product which is called touchstone which, simply by touch, can transform iron into gold. The touchstone can produce an unlimited quantity of gold, and still the touchstone itself does not change its state. Therefore, to suppose that this cosmic manifestation and the living entities are false or illusory, as advocated by the Mayavadi philosopher, is ignorance. No sane man should impose ignorance

and illusion upon the Supreme Absolute Truth, Who is Absolute in everything. There is no possibility of change or ignorance or illusion with Him.
Supreme Brahman is transcendental and completely different from any sort
of material conception. Therefore, in the Supreme Absolute Truth, there is
every possibility of inconceivable potential energy.

In the *Svetasvetara Upanishad* it is stated that the Supreme Absolute Personality of Godhead is full of inconceivable energies, and no one else has such
energy. By the misunderstanding of such inconceivable energies of the
Supreme, one may conclude that the Supreme Absolute Truth is impersonal,
but this is false. Such a conclusion is only a delusion experienced by a living
being when he is in an acute stage of disease. In *Srimad Bhagwatam* also there
are statements that the Supreme *Atma*, the Lord, has got inconceivable, innumerable potencies. In the *Brahma Samhita* also it is stated that in the Supreme
Spirit there are many variegated, inconceivable energies.

In the Absolute Truth there is no possibility of ignorance. Ignorance and
knowledge are conceptions of this world of duality, but in the Absolute there
cannot be any ignorance. Therefore it is simply foolishness to consider that the
Absolute becomes covered by ignorance. If the Absolute Truth has the possibility of ignorance, how can it be said to be Absolute?

Understanding of the inconceivable energy of the Absolute is the only
solution to the question of duality. In other words, the inconceivable energy
of the Absolute is the cause of the doctrine of duality. By such inconceivable
energy, the Supreme Absolute Truth, without being changed, can produce
this cosmic manifestation and the living entities, just as the touchstone can
produce unlimited quantities of gold without being changed. Because the
Absolute Truth has such inconceivable energy, the material quality of covering
by ignorance cannot be applied to the Absolute Truth. True variegatedness
in the Absolute Truth is therefore a product of that inconceivable energy.
It can be safely concluded that this cosmic manifestation is by-product of that
inconceivable energy. And when we accept the inconceivable energy of the
Supreme Lord, then there is no duality at all.

The expansion of the energy of the Supreme Lord is as true as the Supreme
Lord. In the manifestation of the Supreme energy there is no question of
transformation of state. The same example of the touchstone can be cited
again: that, in spite of producing unlimited quantities of gold, the touchstone
remains the same. (We hear, therefore, some sages say that the Supreme is
the Ingredient or Cause of this cosmic manifestation.)

The example of accepting the rope as the snake is also not irregular. When we accept the rope as the snake it is to be understood that one has previous experience of the snake. Otherwise, how can one mistake the rope as a snake? Therefore, the conception of the snake is not untrue or unreal. It is the question of application. When, by mistake, we impose our conviction on the rope as being a snake, that is ignorance. But the very idea of the snake is not itself ignorance. Similarly, when we accept a mirage of water in the desert, there is no question of water being a false concept. Water is a fact, but the application of water in the desert is a mistake.

Therefore, this cosmic manifestation is not false, as is stated by Sankara. There is nothing false here. To consider this material manifestation as false is another ignorance. The Mayavadi theory that this world is false is ignorance. The conclusion of Vaishnava philosophy is that this cosmic manifestation is a by-product of the inconceivable energy of the Supreme Lord.

The principal word in the Vedas, *Pranava Omkara*, is the sound representation of the Supreme Lord. Therefore *Omkara* should be taken as the sound Supreme. Sankara has falsely preached *Tatvamasi* as the Supreme vibration in the Vedas, instead of Omkara. Omkara is the reservoir of all the energies of the Supreme Lord. The accent on the word *Tatvamasi* by Sankara, as the Supreme vibration of the Vedas, is wrong, because this word *Tatvamasi* is a secondary word only. This word suggests only a partial representation of the Vedas. In the *Bhagavad Gita* the Lord has in many places given importance to Omkara. The importance of Omkara is mentioned in the Eighth Chapter, 13th verse, Ninth Chapter, 17th verse, and Seventeenth Chapter, 23rd verse. Similarly, the importance of Omkara is stated in the *Atharva Veda*. Similarly, we get the importance of Omkara vibration in the *Mandukya Upanishad*.

Srila Jiva Goswami has given great importance to the word Omkara in his *Bhagavat Sandarbha*. He says: "Omkara is the most confidential sound representation of the Supreme Lord." The sound representation or Name of the Supreme Lord is as good as the Supreme Lord. By vibration of such sound as Omkara, or of *Hare Krishna, Hare Krishna, Krishna Krishna, Hare Hare/Hare Rama, Hare Rama, Rama Rama, Hare Hare*, one can be delivered from the contamination of this material world. And, because such vibrations of transcendental sound can deliver a conditional soul, it is known as *Tarak*, or deliverer.

The sound vibration of the Supreme Lord is identical with the Supreme Lord. In the *Narada Pancharatra* also it is stated that when sound vibration is practiced by the conditioned soul, the Supreme Lord is present on the tongue of such a vibrating person. In the *Mandukya Upanishad* the same importance is given, in that whatever is seen as spiritual, with the addition of Omkara, is perfect spiritual vision. In the Spiritual World or in the spiritual vision there is nothing except Omkara, or the one alternate, *Om*. Unfortunately, Sankara has given up this chief word, Omkara, and he has whimsically accepted *Tatvamasi* as the Supreme vibration of the Vedas. By accepting such a secondary word of the Vedas as *Tatvamasi*, leaving aside the principal word Omkara, he has given up direct interpretation in favor of his own indirect interpretation of the Scripture.

CHAPTER TWENTY-ONE

Further Talks With Prakasananda

Sripad Sankaracharya has unceremoniously obscured the Krishna Consciousness described in the *Purusa Vedanta Sutra* by manufacturing an indirect interpretation, and giving up the direct interpretation. But unless we take all the statements of *Vedanta Sutra* as self-evident, there is no need to study *Vedanta Sutra*. To interpret the verses of *Vedanta Sutra* according to one's own whimsy is the greatest disservice to the self-evident *Vedas*.

So far as *Omkara Pranava* is concerned, He is considered the sound incarnation of the Supreme Personality of Godhead; as such Omkara is eternal, unlimited, transcendental, supreme, and indestructible. He is the beginningless, and He is the beginning, middle and end. When one understands the Omkara as such, then he becomes immortal. One should know Omkara as a representation of the Supreme situated in everyone's heart. Anyone who understands Omkara and Vishnu as one and the same and all-pervading, never laments in the material world, nor does he remain anymore as a Sudra.

Although He (Omkara) has no material Form, He is unlimitedly expanded, and has unlimited Form. By understanding the Omkara one can become free from the duality of the material world and be placed in Absolute Knowledge. Therefore, Omkara is the most auspicious representation of the Supreme Lord. Such is the description of the *Mandukya Upanishad*. One should not foolishly interpret such a description of the *Upanishad*, and say that because the Supreme Personality of Godhead "cannot" appear Himself in this material world in His own Form, therefore the sound representation Omkara is here. By such a false interpretation, Omkara comes to be considered as something material, and the eulogizing of Omkara is misunderstood as simply *an exhibition* of His value. Actually, Omkara is as good as other incarnations of the Supreme Lord.

The Lord has innumerable incarnations, and Omkara is one of them, as an incarnation of the alphabet. As stated in the *Bhagavad Gita:* "Amongst the letters I am Omkara". This means that Omkara is non-different from Krishna—that is the right interpretation. The impersonalist, however, gives more importance to the Omkara than to the Personality of Godhead, Krishna. In fact, however, any representational incarnation of the Supreme Lord is non-different from Him. Such an incarnation or representation is as good spiritually as the Supreme Lord. Omkara is therefore the ultimate representation of all the Vedas. The Vedic Mantras or hymns have transcendental value because they are prefixed by the pronoun Omkara. The Vaishnavas, however, interpret Omkara as follows: By the letter O, Krishna the Supreme Personality of Godhead is indicated; by the letter U, Krishna's eternal consort Srimati Radharani is indicated; and by the letter M, the eternal servitor of the Supreme Lord, the living entity, is indicated. Sankara has not given so much importance to the Omkara. It is found, however, in the *Vedas* and in the *Ramayana* and in the *Puranas* and in the *Mahabarata*, from the beginning to the end, and in the middle—everywhere. Thus the glories of the Supreme Lord, the Supreme Personality of Godhead, are declared.

Thus Lord Chaitanya condemned the attempt at indirect interpretation of the *Vedanta Sutra*, and the Sannyasis present were all struck with wonder by His explanation. After hearing the direct interpretation of the *Vedanta Sutra* from Lord Chaitanya, one of the Sannyasis in the meeting immediately declared, "O Sripad Chaitanya, whatever You have explained by condemning the indirect interpretation of Omkara is not at all a useless argument. Only the fortunate persons can accept Your interpretation as the right one. Actually, every one of us now knows that the interpretations given by Sankara are all artificial and imaginary, but because we belong to the sect, therefore we took it for granted to be the right interpretation. We shall be very glad to hear You if You explain further the *Vedanta Sutra* by direct interpretation."

After this, Lord Chaitanya explained each and every verse of the *Vedanta* by direct interpretation. He thus explained the word *Brahman*. Brahman means the greatest, and the direct interpretation of greatest is the Supreme Personality of Godhead. Greatest means full with six opulences. The Supreme Personality of Godhead is the Reservoir of all wealth, all fame, all strength, all beauty, all knowledge, and all renunciation. When Lord Krishna was present Personally on the Earth, He exhibited these six opulences in full. Nobody was richer than Lord Krishna, nobody was more learned than Krishna, nobody was more beautiful than Krishna, nobody was stronger than Krishna, nobody was more famous than Krishna, and nobody was more renounced than Krishna. Therefore the Supreme Personality of Krishna is the Supreme Brahman. This is confirmed in the *Bhagavad Gita*, Tenth Chapter, when Arjuna thus addressed Him: "You are *Param Brahman*," the Supreme Brahman. Therefore, Brahman means the Greatest, and the greatest means the Supreme Personality of Godhead, Krishna. He is the Shelter of the Absolute Truth, *Para Tattwa*, because He is Param Brahman. But, at the same time, in all His opulences and exhibitions of wealth, fame, strength, beauty, knowledge and renunciation, there is nothing material. Everything spiritual and transcendental in all the Vedic verses and hymns indicates that Supreme Personality of Godhead, Krishna. Wherever, therefore, the word *Brahman* appears in the *Vedas*, it should be understood to indicate Krishna, the Supreme Personality of Godhead. The intelligent person at once replaces the Name *Krishna* wherever there is the word *Brahman*.

The Supreme Personality of Godhead is transcendental to the material modes of Nature, but He is fully qualified with transcendental qualities. To accept the Supreme as impersonal is to deny the manifestation of spiritual energies. When the Supreme Personality of Godhead, Brahman, is full with spiritual energies, and somebody simply accepts His impersonal exhibition of spiritual energy, then he does not accept this Absolute Truth in full. To accept It in full means to accept the spiritual variegatedness also, which is transcendental to the material modes of Nature. Therefore, failing to indicate the Supreme Lord, the impersonalist conception is incomplete.

The approved method of understanding the Supreme Personality of Godhead, Krishna, is the path of devotional service, as is confirmed in every Vedic

Scripture. The devotional service of the Lord begins by hearing about Him. There are nine different methods in devotional service, of which hearing is the basic one. Hearing, chanting, remembering, worshipping—all these are the process of attaining the highest perfection of understanding the Supreme Personality of Godhead. This process of understanding the Supreme Personality of Godhead is known as *Abhidheya*, or practice of devotional service within our conditional life.

In practice it is also experienced that anyone who takes to Krishna Consciousness does not like to deviate to any other consciousness. This Krishna Consciousness is a development of love for Krishna, the Supreme Personality of Godhead. And this development of love of Godhead is called the fifth dimensional interest of the human being. When one takes to this process of transcendental devotional service, or love of Godhead, he relishes his relationship with Krishna directly, and by such reciprocation in relishing transcendental dealings with Krishna, Krishna becomes gradually a Personal associate of the devotee. The devotee eternally enjoys blissful life. Therefore, the purport of the *Vedanta Sutra* is to re-establish the lost relationship of the human being with the Supreme Lord Krishna, to execute devotional service, and ultimately to achieve the highest goal of life, love of Godhead. These three principles of transcendental life are described in the *Vedanta Sutra*, and nothing more.

After this explanation of *Vedanta Sutra* by direct interpretation of the verses. one of the disciples of Prakasananda Saraswati, considered to be the chief amongst all his disciples, stood up in the assembly and began to praise Lord Chaitanya as Personally the Supreme Personality of Godhead, Narayan. He very much appreciated the explanation of *Vedanta Sutra* by Lord Chaitanya, and said publicly that the direct explanation by Lord Chaitanya of the meaning of the *Upanishad* and *Vedanta Sutra*, "is so pleasing that we forget ourselves, and forget that we belong to the Mayavadi sect." It must be admitted herewith that the explanations by Sankaracharya of the *Upanishads* and *Vedanta Sutra* are all imaginary. We sometimes accept such imaginary explanations for the sake of sectarian feuds, but actually such an explanation does not satisfy us. Simply by accepting the order of *Sannyasa* one does not become free from material entaglements. Actually, if we understand the explanation given by Lord Chaitanya, that will help us. Sri Krishna Chaitanya has very nicely explained the meaning of *Harer Nama Harer Nama Harer Nama Eva Kevalam*— and we are all very much pleased. There is no alternative to devotional service.

Without devotional service nobody can become liberated from the material clutches. Especially in this age, when simply by chanting *Hare Krishna, Hare Krishna, Krishna Krishna, Hare Hare/Hare Rama, Hare Rama, Rama Rama, Hare Hare,* one can achieve the highest liberation."

In the *Srimad Bhagwatam,* Tenth Canto, Fourteenth Chapter, it is stated that, for a person who gives up the path of devotional service and simply undergoes some labor of life for knowledge, there is no other profit than taking the trouble to understand what is matter and what is spirit. It is considered useless labor to try to get grains from the husks which are empty. Similarly, in the Tenth Canto, Second Chapter, it is also said that a person who gives up the transcendental loving service of the Supreme Lord and artificially considers himself liberated, never attains to actual liberation. On the contrary, with great labor of austerity and penances he may be elevated to the status of liberation, but for want of shelter unto the Lotus Feet of the Supreme Lord, he falls down again into the material contamination.

The Supreme Brahman cannot be accepted as impersonal. Otherwise the six opulences, meaning the Supreme Personality of Godhead, will not be acceptable in the concept of Brahman. All the *Vedas* and the *Puranas* affirm that the Supreme Personality of Godhead is full of spiritual energies. Foolish persons do not accept the energy of the Supreme Personality of Godhead, and therefore His Pastimes and His Activities are derided by them. They misinterpret the transcendental Body of Krishna as a creation of the Material Nature, and this is the greatest offense and sinful act. One should, therefore, accept the words of Chaitanya just as He explained in this assembly.

The individual Personality of the Supreme Absolute Truth is explained in the *Srimad Bhagwatam,* Third Canto, Ninth Chapter: "O my Supreme Lord, the transcendental Form which I am just seeing is simple transcendental pleasure without any change and without any contamination of the material modes. It is full of effulgence and there is no greater manifestation of the Absolute Truth than this. O Soul of everyone, You are the Creator of this cosmic manifestation with all the material elements, and I surrender unto You, Your transcendental Form, O Krishna! O Most Auspicious Universe! You advent Yourself in Your Original Personal Form for the Purpose of being worshipped by us. We perceive You either by meditation or by worshipping directly. Foolish persons, mostly contaminated by the material Nature, do not give much importance to Your transcendental Form, and therefore they are understood to be gliding down to hell."

The same statement is confirmed in the *Bhagavad Gita,* Ninth Chapter,

11th verse: "Only the foolish persons mock at Me because I am here just like human being. Such foolish persons do not know the intrinsic value of this transcendental Form, that I am the Proprietor, I am the Master, I am the Lord of All Creation."

For such foolish, demoniac persons, hell is also confirmed in the *Bhagavad Gita*, Sixteenth Chapter, 19th verse: "Such deriding persons who are envious of Me and My devotee, I put into this material world in the most degraded species of life, and being thus situated in such degraded forms, the demoniac persons have no chance to understand the Supreme Personality of God."

The doctrine of by-product, *Parinamavada*, is ascertained from the very beginning of the *Vedanta Sutra*, but Acharya Sankara has artificially tried to hide it and to establish the doctrine of transformation of state, *Vivartavata*, and he has the audacity to say that Vyasa is mistaken. All the Vedic literature, including the *Puranas*, confirm that the Supreme Lord is the center of Spiritual energy and variegatedness. The Mayavadi philosopher, however, is puffed up, in his own incompetence, and cannot understand variegatedness in spiritual energy. He therefore falsely conceives that the spiritual variegatedness is no more than material variegatedness. Deluded by this false belief, he derides the Pastimes of the Supreme Personality of Godhead. Such foolish persons, being unable to understand the spiritual activities of the Supreme Lord, consider Krishna as one of the products of this material Nature. This is the greatest offense which can be committed by any human being. Lord Chaitanya therefore establishes that Krishna is *Sat Chit Ananda Vigraha*, the Form of Eternity, Knowledge and Bliss, and is always engaged in His transcendental Pastimes of spiritual variegatedness.

The student of Prakasananda summarized the explanation of Lord Chaitanya and concluded: "We have practically given up the actual path of spiritual realization. We simply engage in nonsense talk. The Mayavadi philosophers who are serious about attaining benediction should engage in the devotional service of Krishna, but instead they take pleasure only in useless talk. We admit herewith that by the explanation of Sankara the actual import of Vedic literature is hidden. Only the explanation given by Chaitanya is acceptable, and all other interpretations are useless."

After thus explaining his position, that particular student of Prakasananda Saraswati engaged himself in the chanting of *Hare Krishna, Hare Krishna, Krishna Krishna, Hare Hare/Hare Rama, Hare Rama, Rama Rama, Hare Hare*. Prakasananda Saraswati saw that his chief student was engaged in chanting *Hare Krishna*, and he too admitted the fault of Sankaracharya, and spoke as follows: "Acharya Sankara wanted to establish the doctrine of monism, and therefore he had no other alternative than to interpret the *Vedanta Sutra* in a different way. If he accepts the Supreme Personality of Godhead, then the doctrine of monism cannot be established. Therefore, by his illusory scholarship, he has tried to cover the actual meaning of the *Vedanta Sutra*. Not only Sankara, but any author who wants to give his own views must curtail and misinterpret the *Vedanta Sutra*."

The Lord therefore gave the direct meaning of the *Vedanta Sutra*. No Vedic Scripture can be used for indirect speculation; not only Sankara, but other materialistic philosophers like Kapila, Gautama, Astavakra, Patanjali —every one of them has tried to put forward philosophical speculations in a different way. The philosopher Jaimina and his other followers, who are all more or less logicians, have given up the real meaning of the *Vedas*, devotional service, and have tried to establish the Absolute Truth as subject to the material world. It is their opinion that if we do our material activities nicely, then if there is any God He will be pleased and give us the desired result. Similarly, the atheist Kapila has tried to establish that there is no God Who is the Creator of this material world. But he (Kapila) has analyzed the material world's elements and their combination as the cause of creation. He has tried to establish this. Similarly, Gautama and Kanad have given stress to the material elements, and have tried to establish that atomic energy is the origin of creation. Similarly, the impersonalists and monists like Astavakra have tried to establish the impersonal effulgence of the *Brahmajyoti* as the Supreme. Similarly, Patanjali, one of the greatest authorities on the *Yoga* system, has tried to conceive an imaginary Form of the Supreme Lord.

To summarize their philosophy, it is understood that all these materialistic philosophers have tried to avoid the Supreme Personality of Godhead, as they wanted to put forward their own mentally concocted philosophies. But Vyasadeva, the learned sage and incarnation of Godhead, has thoroughly studied all these philosophical speculations of different sages; and to answer all of them he has compiled the *Vedanta Sutra*, which simply indicates the relationship with the Supreme Personality of Godhead, execution of devotional service, and ultimate achievement of love of Godhead. In the very beginning of the *Vedanta Sutra*, the verse *Janmadyasa yata* appears and is explained in his *Srimad Bhagwatam* in which Vyasa establishes at the very beginning that the Supreme Source of everything is a cognizant, Transcendental Person.

The impersonalist tries to explain that the impersonal effulgence of the Supreme Lord, or *Brahmajyoti*, is beyond these material modes of Nature, but at the same time he wants to establish the Supreme Personality of Godhead as contaminated by the modes of material Nature. The *Vedanta Sutra* establishes that the Supreme Personality of Godhead is not only transcendental to the material modes of nature, but also that He has innumerable transcendental qualities and energies. All these speculative philosophers are one in denying the existence of the Supreme Lord Vishnu, and they are very much enthused to put forward their own theories to be recognized by the people. Unfortunate persons become enamoured of these atheistic philosophers, and thus they can never understand the real nature of the Absolute Truth. It is better for them, therefore, to follow in the footsteps of great souls who are called *Mahajans*. According to *Srimad Bhagwatam* there are twelve *Mahajans* or great souls. They are: 1. Brahma, 2. Lord Shiva, 3. Narada, 4. Vaivasvata Manu, 5. Kapila (not the atheist, but the original Kapila), 6. the Kumaras, 7. Prahlada, 8. Bhisma, 9. Janaka, 10. Bali, 11. Sukadeva Goswami, 12. Yamaraj.

According to *Mahabharata* there is no use of arguing about the Absolute Truth. Because there are different kinds of Vedic Scriptures and philosophical understandings, and no philosopher is agreeable to another philosopher. Everyone is trying to give us his own point of view, rejecting the other. Therefore, to understand the prime necessity of religious principles is very difficult. It is better to follow in the footsteps of the great *Mahajans*, Great Souls, as above mentioned. One is then able to achieve the desired success. Lord Chaitanya's teaching is just like nectar, and it holds whatever you need. The best way to take to this path, is to follow.

CHAPTER TWENTY-TWO

The *Srimad Bhagwatam*

After this incident of the conversion of the Mayavadi Sannyasis into the path of Chaitanya Mahaprabhu, many many scholars and inquisitive persons used to visit Lord Chaitanya at Benares. All of them could not see Chaitanya Mahaprabhu at His residence, and therefore they used to stand in line to see Lord Chaitanya as He used to pass on His way to the temple of Viswanath and Bindumadhav. One day He visited the temple along with His associates—Chandra Sekhar Acharya, Paramananda, Tapan Mishra, Sanatan Goswami, etc. He was singing,

> *Hari haraye namah Krishna Yadavaya namah*
> *Gopala Govinda Rama Sri Madhusudana*

—and while He was singing like that, chanting and dancing, thousands of people gathered around Him, and there was a roaring following the vibration of Chaitanya Mahaprabhu. This vibration was so tumultuous that Prakasananda Saraswati, who was sitting nearby, came immediately along with his disciples, and as soon as he saw the beautiful Body of Lord Chaitanya and

His nice dancing, along with His associates, he also joined and began to sing with Him:

Hari! Hari!

All the inhabitants of Benares were struck with wonder by seeing the dancing of Lord Chaitanya in ecstasy. Lord Chaitanya, however, checked Himself in His continuous ecstasy, and stopped His dancing when He saw that the Mayavadi Sannyasis were also present. As soon as He stopped His chanting and dancing, Prakasananda Saraswati fell at the feet of Lord Chaitanya. Lord Chaitanya tried to stop him and said: "Oh, you are the Spiritual Master of the whole world, Jagat Guru, and I am not equal even to your disciple. You should not therefore worship an inferior like Me, Who is not even equal to the disciple of your disciple. You are exactly like Supreme Brahman, and if you fall down at My Feet it is a very great offense on My part. Although you have no vision of duality, still for the teachings of the people in general you should not do this."

Prakasananda Saraswati replied, "Previously I spoke ill of You many times. Therefore, in order to free myself from the result of my offense, I fall down at Your Feet." He quoted in this connection a verse of Vedic literature in which it is stated that when even a liberated soul commits offense to the Supreme Lord he becomes again a victim of the material contamination. He quoted another verse from *Srimad Bhagwatam*, from the Tenth Canto, Thirty-fourth Chapter, in connection with Nanda Maharaj and the attack of a serpent who was previously Vidyadhavarehita. This serpent, being touched by the Lotus Feet of Krishna, regained his previous body and thus he was freed from the reaction of his sinful activities.

Lord Chaitanya, after hearing the equation of himself with Krishna, mildly protested against such behavior. The fact is, He wanted to warn people in general not to compare the Supreme Lord with any living entity. Although He was the Supreme Lord Himself, still, to teach us, He protested against this comparison, and said that nobody should be compared with the Supreme Lord Krishna—that is the greatest offense. Lord Chaitanya always maintained that Vishnu, the Supreme Personality of Godhead, is great and the living entities, however great they may be, are not the infinite, but are infinitesimal. He quoted, in this connection, a verse from *Vaishnava Tantra*, in the *Padma Purana*, where it is stated: "Any person who compares the Supreme Lord even with the greatest of demigods like Brahma and Shiva, must be considered a number one atheist."

Prakasananda replied, "I can understand that You are the Supreme

Personality of Godhead, Krishna, but even though You present Youself as a devotee, still You are worshippable by me, because You are greater than all of us in education and in realization. Therefore, by blaspheming You, we committed the greatest offense and You should excuse us."

How a devotee becomes the greatest of all transcendentalists is stated in the *Srimad Bhagwatam*, Sixth Canto, Fourteenth Chapter: "There are many liberated souls, and there are many perfected souls; but out of all such liberated and perfected souls, one who is a devotee of the Supreme Personality of Godhead is the best. Such devotees of the Supreme Personality of Godhead are always calm and quiet, and their perfection is very rarely to be seen even in millions of persons."

Prakasananda quoted another verse from the Tenth Canto, Fourth Chapter, in which it is stated that duration of life, prosperity, fame, religiousness, and the benediction of higher authorities—everything gained, becomes lost by transgressing the respect of a devotee. He quoted another verse from *Srimad Bhagwatam*, Seventh Canto, Fifth Chapter, in which it is stated that the touch of the Lotus Feet of the Supreme Personality of Godhead causes the disappearance of all kinds of misgivings of the conditioned soul. But this facility of touching the Lotus Feet of the Supreme Lord is not possible unless one receives benediction by the dust of the Lotus Feet of a pure devotee of the Lord. In other words, nobody can become a pure devotee of the Supreme Personality of Godhead without being favored by another pure devotee of the Lord.

Prakasananda Saraswati spoke further: "Now I am taking shelter of Your Lotus Feet, for I want to be elevated to be a devotee of the Supreme Lord."

After talking in this way, both Prakasananda Saraswati and Lord Chaitanya sat together and Prakasananda Saraswati began to enquire from the Lord as follows: "Whatever You have said in pointing out discrepancies in the Mayavadi philosophy is known to us also, because we know that all the commentaries on Vedic Scriptures by Mayavadi philosophers are in error by interpretation—especially those by Sankaracharya, whose interpretation of *Vedanta Sutra* is all his own imagination. You have not explained the codes of *Vedanta Sutra* and *Upanishad* by Your imagination, but You have explained them as they are, and by hearing Your explanation, all of us are very pleased. Such explanations of the codes of *Vedanta Sutra* or *Upanishads* could not be given by anyone else except the Supreme Personality of Godhead, and You have all the potencies. Kindly explain further about the *Vedanta Sutra*, so that I may be benefitted."

Lord Chaitanya again protested against His being called the Supreme Lord, and He said, "My dear sir, I am an ordinary living entity. I cannot know the meaning of *Vedanta Sutra*, but Vyasadeva, Who is an incarnation of Narayan, knows the real meaning of the *Vedanta Sutra*. No ordinary living being can interpret the *Vedanta Sutra* with his mundane education. In order to curb commentary on *Vedanta Sutra* by unscrupulous persons, the author, Vyasadeva Himself, has already commented on the *Vedanta Sutra* by writing *Srimad Bhagwatam*." In other words, if the author himself explains the purport of his book, that is excellent. Nobody can understand the author's mind unless the author himself discloses the purport of his language. Therefore *Vedanta Sutra* should be understood by the commentary of the Author Himself, which is *Srimad Bhagwatam*.

Pranava or Omkara is the divine substance of all the *Vedas*. Omkara is explained further in the *Gayatri Mantra*, as exactly explained in the *Srimad Bhagwatam*. There are four verses in this connection. These verses are explained to Brahma, and Brahma explained them again to Narada, and Narada explained them to Vyasa. Therefore the purport of the verses in the *Srimad Bhagwatam* comes down in disciplic succession. It is not that anyone and everyone can make his own commentary on the *Vedanta Sutra* foolishly, and mislead the readers. Anyone who wants to understand *Vedanta Sutra* must read *Srimad Bhagwatam* carefully. Under the instruction of Narada Muni, Vyasadeva compiled *Srimad Bhagwatam* with the purpose of explaining the *Vedanta Sutra* codes. *Vedanta Sutra* was written before *Bhagwatam*. After hearing from Narada Muni, Vyasadeva commentated on the *Vedanta Sutra*. By writing *Srimad Bhagwatam* He collected all the essence of the *Upanishads*, the purpose of which was explained also in the *Vedanta Sutra*. *Srimad Bhagwatam* is therefore the essence of all Vedic knowledge. That which is stated in the *Upanishads* and stated in the *Vedanta Sutra* is explained very nicely in the *Srimad Bhagwatam*.

There is a passage from *Isho Upanishad*, similiar to one in the *Srimad Bhagwatam*, Eighth Canto, First Chapter, the purport of which is that whatever one sees in the cosmic manifestation, everywhere, is the Supreme Lord's energy, which is non-different from Him. Therefore, He is the Controller of all living entities, and the Friend and Maintainer of everyone. We should live by the mercy of God, and by the things allotted to our particular living condition. Thus one enjoys life, and nobody should encroach on any other's property.

In other words, the purpose of the *Upanishad* and *Vedanta*, and that of *Srimad Bhagwatam*, are one and the same. If anyone studies *Srimad Bhagwatam* carefully, he will find that all the *Upanishads* and *Vedanta Sutra* codes are nicely explained there. In *Bhagwatam* also the subject matter is divided into three: to establish the eternal relationship with the Supreme Lord, how to act in that relationship, and, lastly, how to achieve the highest benefit from it.

The four verses dealing with *Ahameva asam agrey* are the gist of the whole *Bhagwatam*, and this is very nicely explained as follows: "I am the Supreme Center of relationship of all living entities, and My knowledge is the Supreme Knowledge, and the process by which I can be achieved by the living entity is called *Abhidheya*. And, by the *Abhidheya* process, one attains to the highest perfection of life, love of Godhead. When one attains that stage of life, love of Godhead, then his life becomes perfect." The explanation of these four verses is given in the *Srimad Bhagwatam*.

In this connection Lord Chaitanya gave a short description of the principles of the four slokas of *Srimad Bhagwatam* as follows: Nobody can understand the consitutional position of the Supreme Lord—how He is situated, what are His transcendental qualities, what are His transcendental activities, how He is full with six kinds of opulences. These things cannot be understood by mental speculators or by one's academic education. These things are to be understood by the mercy of the Lord, as has been stated in the *Bhagavad Gita*: one who is fortunate enough to be favored by the Supreme Lord can understand all these explanations by the mercy of the Lord.

The Lord existed before the material Creation; therefore the material ingredients and Nature and the living entities all emanated from Him, and again after dissolution they rest in Him. When the Creation is correct it is maintained by Him; at the same time, whatever manifestation we see, that is only a transformation of the external energy. When the external energy is withdrawn by the Supreme Lord, then everything enters into Him. In the first verse of *Ahameva*, the word, *Aham*, I, is mentioned three times. That is to stress that the Supreme Personality of Godhead is full with all opulences. For anyone, therefore, who cannot understand or does not believe in the transcendental Nature and Form of the Supreme Lord, and who says He is without any Form—*Aham* is stated three times just to chastise him.

The Lord possesses His internal energy, besides His external, marginal and relative energies, as well as the manifestation of His cosmic world and the living entities. The external energy is manifested by the qualitative modes, or gunas, of material Nature. One who can understand the nature of the living entity in the Spiritual World can actually understand *Vedyam*, or perfect knowledge. One cannot understand the Supreme Lord simply by seeing the material energy and the conditioned soul. But when one is in perfect knowledge, then he is free from the influence of the external energy. Just as the Moon is the reflection of the Sun, and without the existence of the Sun the Moon cannot illuminate, so this material cosmic manifestation is something like the reflection of the Spiritual World.

When one is actually liberated from the spell of the external energy, he can understand the constitutional nature of the Supreme Lord. Devotional service to the Lord is the only means for attaining Him. And this devotional service of the Lord can be accepted by everyone and anyone, in any country, in any atmosphere, and under any circumstance. Devotional Service is above the four principles of religiousness, or above the understanding of liberation. Even the preliminary process of executing devotional service is transcendental to the highest subject matter of liberation in the ordinary course of religiousness.

One should, therefore, approach a bona fide Spiritual Master, irrespective of caste, creed, color, country and place, and he must hear from that bona fide Spiritual Master everything about devotional service. The real purpose of life is to revive our dormant love of God. That is our ultimate necessity. How that love of God can be achieved is explained in the *Srimad Bhagwatam*. There is theoretical knowledge and specific, or realized knowledge. The perfect, realized knowledge, is obtained in realization of the teaching received from the Spiritual Master.

CHAPTER TWENTY-THREE

Why Study the *Vedanta Sutra?*

Knowledge means information gathered from the Scriptures, and science means practical realization of the knowledge gathered from the Scriptures. It is scientific knowledge when it is gathered from the Scriptures through the practical application of the bona fide Spiritual Master, but when interpreted by mental concoction it is personal. By scientific understanding of the information from the Scripture, through the bona fide Spiritual Master, one learns, by one's own realization, each actual conception of the Supreme Personality of Godhead. The transcendental Form of the Supreme Personality of Godhead is different from material manifestation and different from the reactions of matter. Therefore, without scientific understanding of the Spiritual Form of the Personality of Godhead one becomes an impersonalist. The sunshine is itself an illumination, but that illumination is different from the Sun. Yet the Sun and the sunshine are not differently situated; without the Sun there is no sunshine, and without the sunshine there is no Sun.

Unless one is freed from the influence of material energy, one cannot understand the Supreme Lord and His different energies. One who is captivated by the spell of material energy cannot understand the Spiritual Form of the Supreme Lord. *Unless there is realization of the transcendental Form of the Supreme Personality of Godhead, there is no question of love of Godhead.* Without realization of the transcendental Form of the Supreme Lord, love of Godhead is fictitious, and without realization of love of Godhead there is no perfection of human life. Such realization of the Supreme Personality of Godhead is as follows: it is just like the five gross elements of Nature, namely earth, water, fire, air and ether: they are both within and without all living beings in this world. Similarly, those who are devotees of the Supreme Lord can realize the Personality of Godhead both inside and outside this existence.

Pure devotees know very well that they are meant to serve the Supreme Personality of Godhead, and all things that exist are the means for service to the Supreme Lord. Because a devotee has been blessed by the Supreme within the core of his heart, therefore, wherever he looks, he can see the Supreme Lord and nothing more. *Srimad Bhagwatam* confirms this type of relationship between the devotee and the Supreme Personality of Godhead in the Eleventh Canto, Second Chapter, as follows: "For a person whose heart is always tied to the Lotus Feet of the Supreme Lord by the rope of love of Godhead, the Lord does not leave him even if remembrance is not very carefully done; such a person is called a first class devotee." An example of this is described in the *Bhagavata Tasumskunda:* The Gopis were assembled for the *Rasa* Dance with Krishna, but Krishna left them, and so the assembled Gopis began to chant the Holy Name of Krishna. They became overwhelmed with madness, and began to inquire from the flowers and creepers in the forest about Krishna, Who is compared with the sky and Who is situated everywhere.

Study of *Bhagwatam*, therefore, means to be informed about our eternal relationship with the Supreme Lord, the procedure for how to regain Him, and the ultimate realization, which is love of Godhead.

Lord Chaitanya next explained to Prakasananda Saraswati how to achieve the Supreme Personality of Godhead by devotional service. He quoted in this connection a verse from *Srimad Bhagwatam*, from the Eleventh Canto, Fourteenth Chapter, in which the Lord says He can be realized only through devotional service, with faith and the love of the devotee, and it is devotional service only which purifies the heart of the devotee and elevates him into the ultimate realization of faith and service unto the Supreme Lord. Even though he is born of a low family such as a *Chandala*—one who eats dogs—yet by realization of the Supreme stage of love of Godhead one becomes full with transcendental symptoms.

These symptoms are described in the *Srimad Bhagwatam*, Eleventh Canto, Third Chapter, as follows: "When devotees discuss the subject of the Supreme Lord, Who can cleanse the heart of a devotee from all kinds of sinful reaction, they become overwhelmed with ecstasies of different symptoms, *on account of their devotional service;* and, as such, when they chant the Holy Name of the Supreme Lord, due to their spontaneous attachment for Him, they sometimes cry, sometimes laugh, sometimes dance, sometimes sing, without caring for any social convention."

We should understand, therefore, that *Srimad Bhagwatam* is the real explanasion of the *Brahma Sutra*, and it is compiled by the Author Himself. In the *Guru Purana* it is said: "The *Srimad Bhagwatam* is the actual explanation of *Brahma Sutra*, and is a further explanation of *Mahabarata*. It is the explanation of the *Gayatri Mantra* and the essence of all Vedic knowledge. This *Srimad Bhagwatam* contains 18,000 verses, and is known as the explanation of all Vedic literature." In the First Canto of *Srimad Bhagwatam* there is an enquiry by the sages of Naimisharanya to Suta Goswami, on how to know the essence of Vedic literature. In answer to the enquiry, Suta Goswami presented *Srimad Bhagwatam* as the essence of all the *Vedas* and histories and other Vedic literature. In the Twelfth Canto, Thirteenth Chapter of *Srimad Bhagwatam*, it is clearly stated the *Srimad Bhagwatam* is the essence of all Vedanta knowledge, and one who relishes the knowledge from the *Srimad Bhagwatam* has no taste for studying any other literature. In the very beginning of *Srimad Bhagwatam*, the meaning and purpose of the *Gayatri Mantra* is also described: "I am offering my obeisances unto the Supreme Truth." This is the first introductory verse on the Supreme Truth, described in the *Bhagwatam* as the Source of creation, maintenance, and dissolution of the cosmic manifestation.

Obeisances unto the Personality of Godhead, Vasudeva, directly indicate Lord Sri Krishna, Who is the Divine Son of Vasudeva and Devaki. The fact will be more explicitly presented later in the text of the *Srimad Bhagwatam*, by the direct statement of the Author, in His assertion that Sri Krishna is the Original Personality of Godhead, and all others are either His direct or indirect plenary portions, or portions of the portion. Srila Jiva Goswami has later on still more explicitly developed this subject matter in his *Krishna Sandarva*, and Brahmaji, the original living being, has explained the subject of Sri Krishna substantially in his treatise, called *Brahma Samhita*. In the *Samveda Upanishad* it is also said that Lord Sri Krishna is the Divine Son of Devaki.

Therefore, in this prayer of the Author of *Bhagwatam*, the first proposition is that Lord Sri Krishna is the Primeval Lord, and if any transcendental nomenclature for the Absolute Personality of Godhead has to be understood, it must be the Name indicated by the word *Krishna*, the All-attractive. In the *Bhagavad Gita* in many passages the Lord has affirmed Himself as the Original Personality of Godhead, and it is confirmed by Arjuna, with the authorized statements of great sages like Narada, Vyasa, and many others. In the *Padma Puranam* also it is said that, of innumerable Names of the Lord, the Name of Krishna is the principal Name. Therefore, although Vasudeva indicates the plenary portion of the Personality of Godhead, and although all the different Forms of the Lord are identical with Vasudeva, in this text Vasudeva is principally meant to indicate the Divine Son of Vasudeva and Devaki. Sri Krishna is always meditated upon by the *Paramhansas*, or the most perfect of the renounced order of life. This Vasudeva, or Lord Sri Krishna, is the Cause of all causes. Everything that exists is an emanation from the Lord, and how this so happens is explained in later chapters of *Srimad Bhagwatam.*

The *Bhagwat Puranam* (*Srimad Bhagwatam*) is described by Mahaprabhu Sri Chaitanya as the spotless *Puranam*, because It contains the transcendental narration of the Personality of Godhead Sri Krishna. The history of *Srimad Bhagwatam* is also very glorious. It was compiled by Sri Vyasadeva from His mature experience of transcendental knowledge under the instruction of Sri Naradaji, His Spriritual Master. Vyasadeva compiled all the Vedic literature, namely the four divisions of the *Vedas*, the *Vedanta Sutra* or *Brahma Sutras*, the *Puranas*, and the *Mahabarata*. But He was still not delighted in His mind. This was observed by His Spiritual Master, and thus Narada advised Him to write on the transcendental activities of the Lord, Sri Krishna. The transcendental activities of Lord Sri Krishna are described specifically in the Tenth Canto of the Book, which is considered to be the substance. But, in order to reach the substance of the Tenth Canto, one has to approach gradually by developed knowledge of the categories.

Generally, a philosophical mind is inquisitive to know what is the Origin of all creations. He sees the night sky and naturally asks what are the stars, how are they situated, who lives there, and so on. All these inquiries are quite natural for a human being, because he has a more developed consciousness than the animals. And to answer at once such a sincere inquirer, the Author of the *Srimad Bhagwatam* says that the Lord is the Origin of all creations. He is not only the Creator, but He is also the Maintainer of the cosmic situation, and He is also the Destroyer. The manifested Cosmic Nature is created at a certain period by the will of the Lord, it is maintained for some time, and then it is annihilated by His Will; and as such He is the Supreme Will behind all these activities.

There are atheists of various categories who do not believe in the conception of a Creator, but that is due only to their poor fund of knowledge. The modern scientist has created a sputnik, and by some arrangement or other the sputnik is thrown into outer space to fly on for some time at the control of a scientist who is far away from the flying sputniks. All the Universes, with innumerable planets within them, are similar to the sputniks, and are controlled by the Personality of Godhead.

In the Vedic literature it is said that the Absolute Truth, the Personality of Godhead, is the Chief amongst the living personalities. All living beings, from the first created being, Brahmaji, down to the smallest ant, are all individual living beings. And, above Brahmaji, there are many other living beings with individual capacities, and the Personality of Godhead is also a similar living being, as individual as the other living beings. But the Supreme Lord, or the Supreme Living Being, has the greatest mind, with the supermost inconceivable energies of different varieties. If a man's mind can produce a sputnik, we can very easily imagine that minds higher than man's can produce similar other wonderful things far superior to the man-made sputniks. A reasonable person will easily accept this argument, but there are stubborn, obstinate ones who may not believe in these reasonable statements.

But Srila Vyasadeva at once accepts the Supreme Mind as the *Parameswara*, the Supreme Controller. He proposes to offer His respectful obeisances unto the Supreme Personality of Godhead. And that Parameswara is Sri Krishna, as is stated in the *Bhagavad Gita* and all other Scriptures delivered by Srila Vyasadeva, and specifically in the *Srimad Bhagwatam*. In the *Bhagavad Gita* the Lord says that there is no other *Paratattwa* (*Summum bonum*) than Himself. Therefore, the Author at once worships the *Paratattwa*, Sri Krishna, Whose transcendental activities are described in the Tenth Canto.

Unscrupulous persons go at once to the Tenth Canto, and especially the five chapters where a description of the Lord's *Rasa* Dance is kindly given. This portion of the *Srimad Bhagwatam*, however, is the most confidential part of the great literature. Unless one has thoroughly accomplished himself in the transcendental knowledge of the Lord, one is sure to misunderstand the Lord's worshippable transcendental Pastimes in the form of *Rasa* Dance, and His love affairs with the Gopis. The subject matter is highly spiritual and technical, and only liberated persons who have gradually attained to the stage of *Paramhansa*, as referred to before, can transcendentally relish the worshippable *Rasa* Dance.

Srila Vyasadeva, therefore, gives us the chance for gradual development of spiritual realization before we can actually relish the essence of the Pastimes of the Lord, He therefore purposely invokes the Gayatri Mantra, "Dheemahi." This Gayatri Mantra is meant for the spiritually advanced people. When one has attained success in the matter of chanting the Gayatri Mantra he can enter into the transcendental position of the Lord. One must acquire the Brahminical qualities, or be perfectly situated in the quality of goodness of the modes of material Nature, in order to chant the Gayatri Mantra successfully, and then attain to the stage of transcendentally realizing the Lord, His Name, His Fame, His Qualities, etc. *Srimad Bhagwatam* is the narration of the *Swarupa* or Form of the Lord, manifested by His internal potency; and this potency is distingushed from the external potency, which has manifested the cosmic world which is within our experience. Srila Vyasadeva makes a clear distinction between the two in the 1st verse of the First Chapter.

He says there that the manifestation of the internal potency is factual reality, whereas the external manifested energy in the form of material existence is temporary and illusory, no more real than the mirage in the desert. In the mirage of the desert there is no actual water. By the interaction of something else there is the appearance of water. Real water is somewhere else. Similarly, the manifestive cosmic Creation appears like reality, but the true reality, of which this is but a reflection only, is somewhere else in the Spiritual World, in which there are no mirages. Absolute Truth is there, and not here. Here everything is relative truth, one seeming truth depending on another. This cosmic Creation is an interactory resultant of the three modes of Nature, and the temporary manifestations are so created as to present an illusion of reality to the bewildered mind of the conditioned soul, appearing as so many species of life, including the higher demigods like Brahma, Indra, Chandra, etc. In fact there is no reality in the manifested world, but it appears so on account of the True Reality in the Spiritual World, where the Personality of Godhead eternally exists with His transcendental paraphernalia.

The chief engineer of a complicated construction does not personally take part in the construction, but it is he only who knows all the nooks and corners of the construction, because everything is done by his direction only. He knows everything about the construction directly and indirectly. Similarly, the Personality of Godhead, Who is the Supreme Engineer of this cosmic Creation, knows very well what is happening in the nooks and corners of the cosmic Creation, although the things are apparently done by someone else. From Brahma down to the insignificant ant, nobody is independent in material Creation, and everywhere there is the Hand of the Supreme Lord. All material elements as well as spiritual sparks are but emanations from Him only. And whatever is created in this material world is but the interaction of the two energies, material and spiritual, or the Absolute Truth, the Personality of Godhead, Sri Krishna (Vasudeva).

A living entity called a chemist can manufacture water in the chemical laboratory by mixing hydrogen and oxygen gases, but in reality the living entity works in the laboratory under the direction of the Supreme Lord, and the materials with which the chemist works are also supplied by the Lord. As such, the Lord knows everything directly and indirectly, and He is cognizant of all the minute details of everything, and He is fully independent. He is compared with the mine of gold, and the cosmic creations in different forms are compared with the gold rings and necklaces, etc. The gold ring and the gold necklace are qualitatively one with the gold in the mine, but quantitatively the gold in the mine and the gold in the earring or necklace are different. The whole philosophy of the Absolute Truth is, therefore, that *It is simultaneously one and different*. Nothing is absolutely equal to the Absolute Truth, but at the same time nothing is independent of the Absolute Truth.

Conditioned souls, beginning from Brahma, the engineer of this particular Universe, down to the insignificant ant, are all creating something, but none of them are independent of the Supreme Lord. The materialist wrongly thinks that there is no Creator save and except his own good self, and this is called *Maya*, or illusion. On account of his poor fund of knowledge the materialist cannot see beyond the purview of his imperfect senses, and thus he thinks that matter automatically takes its own shape without a conscious background. This is refuted in the 1st verse of the *Bhagwatam* by Srila Vyasadeva, Who is a liberated soul and compiled this book of authority after His mature spiritual perfection. The Complete Whole, or the Absolute Truth, being the Source of everything, nothing is independent of the Whole Body. Any action and reaction on the body becomes a cognizable fact to the embodied Whole. Similarly, if the whole Creation is the Body of the Absolute Whole, then nothing is unknown to the Absolute, directly or indirectly.

In the *Sruti Mantra* it is also stated that the Absolute Whole, or Brahman, is the Ultimate Source of everything. Everything emanates from Him, and everything is maintained by Him, and at the end everything enters into Him only. That is the law of Nature. In the *Smriti Mantra* also the same thing is confirmed. It is said there that at the beginning of Brahma's millennium the Source from which everything emanates—and, at the end of that millennium, the reservoir that everything enters into—is the Absolute Truth, or Brahman. Material scientists haphazardly take it for granted that the ultimate source of all the planetary systems is the Sun. But they are unable to explain the source of the Sun. Herein the ultimate Source is explained. According to the Vedic literature, Brahma is the creator of this Universe, and yet he also had to meditate to get inspiration for such creation. Therefore Brahma, or the Sun, is not the ultimate creator.

It is stated here in the 1st verse of *Srimad Bhagwatam* that Brahma was taught the Vedic knowledge by the Personality of Godhead. One may argue that Brahma is the original living being within this Universe, and who could then give him inspiration, as there was no second being at that time? In the 1st verse of *Srimad Bhagwatam* it is said that the Supreme Lord inspired the secondary creator, Brahma, who then could go on with the creative functions. What we have already mentioned above about the supervising engineer is applicable here. The Real Mind behind all creative agents is the Absolute Personality of Godhead, Sri Krishna. In the *Bhagavad Gita* Lord Sri Krishna has Personally admitted that it is He only Who superintends over the creative energy, *Prakriti*, or the sum total of matter. Sri Vyasadeva, therefore, worships neither Brahma nor the Sun, but the Supreme Lord Who guides both Brahma and the Sun in their different activities of creation.

In the 1st verse of *Srimad Bhagwatam* the particular Sanscrit words *Avijna* and *Swarat* are significant. These two words distinguish the Lord from all other living entities. No living entity other than the Supreme Being, the Absolute Personality of Godhead, is either *Avijna* or *Swarat*—i.e., none of the entities are either fully cognizant, or fully independent. Everyone has to learn from the superior all about knowledge. Even Brahma, who is the first living being within this material world, has to meditate upon the Supreme Lord and take help from Him in order to create. When Brahma, or the Sun, cannot create anything without acquiring required knowledge from the superior, then what to speak of the material scientists who are fully dependent on so many things? Jagadish Chandra Bose, Isaac Newton, Prof. Einstein, etc. of the modern scientists who may be boastful of their respective creative energies, were also dependent on the Supreme Lord for so many things. After all, the respective, highly intelligent brains of these gentlemen were certainly not the products of any human being. The brain is created by another agent, other than the celebrated scientists themselves. If brains like that of Jagadish Bose or of Isaac Newton could have been manufactured by any human being, then they would have produced many such brains instead of eulogizing the brains of these scientists. Even the scientists could not manufacture a similar brain, what to speak of other foolish atheists who defy the authority of the Lord?

Even the Mayavadi impersonalists who flatter themselves that they have become the Lord are not *Avijna* or *Swarat*, fully cognizant or fully independent. Such Mayavadi monists undergo a severe process of austerity and penances to acquire the knowledge of becoming one with the Lord, but ultimately they become dependent on some rich follower who supplies them the requisite paraphernalia to conduct a great establishment in the form of monastery and temples. Atheists like Ravana and Hiranya Kashipu had to undergo severe penances before they could flout the authority of the Lord, and ultimately they were so helpless that they could not save themselves when the Lord appeared before them as cruel Death. The same is applicable to the modern atheists also who dare to flout the authority of the Lord. Such atheists will be dealt similar awards as were meted out to the past great atheists like Ravana and Hiranya Kashipu. History repeats itself and so what was accorded in the past, will recur again and again whenever there is such necessity. Whenever there is negligence of the authority of the Lord, the penalty by the laws of Nature is always there.

That the Supreme Lord, the Personality of Godhead, is All-perfect is confirmed in all *Sruti Mantras*. It is said in the *Sruti Mantras* that the All-perfect Lord glanced over matter, and thus He created all living beings. The living beings are parts and parcels of the Lord, and He impregnates the vast material Nature with the seeds of spiritual sparks, and thus the creative energies are set in motion for so many wonderful creations. One atheist friend argued that God is no more expert than the manufacturer of a subtle watch which moves by delicate machineries. We had to reply to the atheist friend that God is still a greater mechanic than the watchmaker in the sense that He creates one machine in duplicate male and female forms. The male and female forms of different grades of machinery go on producing innumerable quantities of similar machines without the further attention of God. If a man could manufacture such sets of duplicate machines to produce further machines without any attention from the original manufacturer, then of course a man could equal the intelligence of God. But that is not possible. Each and every one of the imperfect machines have to be handled individually by the mechanic, for nobody can be equal in intelligence to God. Another Name of God is there-fore *Asmaurdha.* Nobody is equal to or greater than Him. Everybody has his equal or superior in intelligence, and nobody can claim that he has neither. This fact is corroborated in the *Sruti Mantras,* where it is said that before the Creation of the material Universe, there was the Lord, Who is the Master of everyone. The Lord instructed Brahma in the Vedic knowledge. That Per-sonality of Godhead has to be obeyed in all respects. Anybody who wants to become free of the material entanglement must, therefore, surrender unto Him. This is confirmed in the *Bhagavad Gita* also.

Unless one surrenders unto the Lotus Feet of the Supreme Personality of Godhead it is sure and certain that one must be bewildered, even if he happens to be a great mind. When the great minds surrender unto the Lotus Feet of Vasudeva and know fully that Lord Vasudeva is the Cause of all causes, as is confirmed in the *Bhagavad Gita,* then only can such great minds become *Mahatmas* or the truly broad-minded. But such a broad-minded *Mahatma* is rarely seen. Only the *Mahatmas,* however, can understand the Supreme Lord, Who is the Absolute Personality of Godhead, the Primeval Cause of all crea-tions. He is *Parama,* or Ultimate Truth, because all other truths are relatively dependent on Him. And because He is the Source of everyone's knowledge He is omniscient, and for Him there is no illusion as there is for the relative knower.

Some scholars of the Mayavadi school argue that *Srimad Bhagwatam* was not compiled by Sri Vyasadeva, and some of them suggest that this book is a creation in the modern age of somebody by the name of Bopedeva. Srila Sridhar Swami, in order to refute this meaningless argument, says that there is reference to the *Bhagwatam* in many other of the oldest *Puranas.* The first *Sloka,* or verse, of the *Srimad Bhagwatam* is begun with the *Gayatri Mantra,* and there is reference to this as the *Matsya Puranam* (the oldest *Puranam*). In that *Puranam* it is said, with reference to the context of *Gayatri Mantra* in the *Bhagwatam,* that there are many narrations of spiritual instructions, begin-ning with the *Gayatri Mantra,* and also the history of Vitrasura is in *Gayatri Mantra.* Anyone who makes a gift of this great work on the full moon day, attains to the highest perfection of life by going back to Godhead. Similarly, there is a reference to this *Bhagwatam* in other *Puranas* where it is said that the work consists of twelve cantos and 18,000 *Slokas.* In the *Padma Puranam* also there is reference to the *Bhagwatam,* during the conversation of Goutam and Maharaj Amburish. The king was advised therein to read regularly *Srimad Bhagwatam* if he at all desired liberation from the material bondage. Under the circumstances, there is no doubt regarding the authority of *Srimad Bhag-watam Puranam.* Within five hundred years from the present era, many scholars, even after the time of Lord Sri Chaitanya Mahaprabhu, have made elaborate commentaries on the *Bhagwatam Puranam* with unique scholarship; and the serious student will do well to make an attempt to go through them, to relish more happily the transcendental messages from the *Bhagwatam.*

Srila Viswanath Chakravarty Thakur specifically deals with the original and pure sex psychology (*Adirasa*) devoid of all mundane inebriety. *The whole material world is turning on the basic principle of sex life.* In the modern human civilization, sex life is the central point of all activities. Wherever we may turn our face we see a great prominence of sex life. Therefore, sex life is not unreal. Its true reality is experienced in the Spiritual World. Material sex life is but a perverted reflection of the original. The original, therefore, is in the Absolute Truth; and the Absolute Truth cannot be impersonal and have a sense of pure sex life. The impersonal monist philosophy has given an indirect impetus to the abominable mundane sex life, because it has given too much stress to the impersonality of the Ultimate Truth. The result is that men who lack knowledge have accepted the perverted sex life as all-in-all without any information about the actual spiritual form of sex. There is a distinction between sex life in the diseased condition of material life and that in the spiritual exist-ence. The *Srimad Bhagwatam* will gradually elevate the unbiased reader to the highest perfectional stage of transcendence, above the three modes of material activities, namely fruitive actions. speculative philosophy, and worshipping the functional deities as they are inculcated in the Vedic verses.

Srimad Bhagwatam is the embodiment of devotional service to the Supreme Personality of Godhead, Krishna. It is therefore situated in a superior position over all other Vedic literature.

The term religiousness includes four primary subjects: namely, (1) pious activities, (2) economic development, (3) satisfaction of the senses, and (4) liberation from the material bondage. Religious life is distinguished from the irreligious life of barbarism, and human life begins from the life of religious-ness. The four principles of animal life—eating, sleeping, defending and mating —are common both to the animals and the human beings. Religion is the extra concern of the human being, and without religion the so-called human life is no better than that of the animal. Therefore, in real human society there is some form of religion aiming at self realization, with reference to the eternal relationship with God.

In the lower stage of human civilization there is always a competition in lording it over material Nature; or in other words, there is a continuous rivalry for satisfying the senses. And, driven by this consciousness of sense gratification, religiousness is performed. Pious activities or religious functions are performed with an aim generally for some material gain. If such material gain is obtainable in another way, then the so-called religiousness is neglected, as we can see in the modern human civilization. The economic desires being seemingly fulfilled in another way, nobody is interested in religion now. The church, mosque, or the temple is practically always a vacant place, and people are more interested in the factories, shops, and cinemas than in the religious places formerly erected by the forefathers of different paths of religiousness. This proves definitely that religiousness is performed for economic development, and economic development is needed for sense gratification. And where one is baffled in the matter of sense gratification, he takes to the cause of salvation in order to become one with the Supreme Whole. Therefore, all these stages are different examples of the same aim of life, namely sense gratification.

In the Vedas, the above-mentioned four activities are prescribed in a regulative way so that there may not be any undue competition for the purpose of sense gratification. But *Srimad Bhagwatam* is transcendental to all these sense gratifying activities of the material world. It is purely transcendental literature, understandable by a particular class of men known as devotees of the Lord, who are above the competitive field of sense gratification. In the material world there is keen competition between the animals, between men, communities, or even nations in this sense gratifying activity, but the devotees of the Lord are above this. Devotees have nothing to compete for with the materialists because they are on the path back to Godhead, where everything is eternal, full, blissful. Such transcendentalists are a hundred per cent nonenvious, and therefore pure in heart. In the material world everyone is envious of everyone and therefore there is competition. But the transcendentalists or devotees of the Lord are not only freed from all material enviousness, but they are kind to everyone, endeavoring to establish *a competitionless society, with God in the center.*

The socialist idea of society is artificially competitionless, because even in the socialistic state there is competition for the post of dictator. The fact is, therefore, that the state of sense gratification is the order of materialistic life, take it either from the Vedas or from the common human activities. As mentioned above, there are three divisions of the Vedas, namely the stage of fruitive activities for getting advancement to better planets like heaven, etc. And, above this, there are the activities of worshipping different demigods with the same intentions—of getting advanced into the different planets of the different types of demigods. And, lastly, there are the activities of reaching the Absolute Truth in His impersonal Feature, to become One with Him.

The impersonal aspect of the Absolute Truth is not the last word. Above the impersonal Feature is the *Paramatma*, or Supersoul, aspect, and above that there is the Personal quality of the Absolute Truth. *Srimad Bhagwatam* gives us information about the Absolute Truth in His Personal quality, beyond the impersonal aspect. It is therefore greater than the topics of impersonal philosophical speculations, and as such, *Srimad Bhagwatam* is given higher status than the *Jnanakanda* division of the Vedas. It is higher than the *Karmakanda* division as well as the *Jnanakanda* division and it is above the *Upashanakanda* division, because *Srimad Bhagwatam* recommends the worship of the Supreme Personality of Godhead, Sri Krishna, the Divine Son of Vasudeva. In the *Karmakanda* of the Vedas there is competition for supremacy in reaching the heavenly planets for better sense gratification. And the same competition is there in the *Jnanakanda* or *Upashanakandas*. But *Srimad Bhagwatam* is above all of them because It aims at the Supreme Truth, the Substance or the Root of all categories. In other words, from *Srimad Bhagwatam* we can know the Substance as well as the relativities in the true sense and prespective. The Substance is the Absolute Truth, the Supreme Personality of Godhead, and all emanations from Him are relativities in different forms of energies. The living entities are also related to all different types of His energies, and therefore nothing is different from the Substance. But, at the same time, the energies are different from the Substance. This concept is not self-contradictory. *Srimad Bhagwatam* explicitly deals with this simultaneously one and different philosophy of the *Vedanta Sutra*, which begins with the *Janmadyasya Sutra*.

Such knowledge of the simultaneously one and different nature of the Absolute Truth is really for the well-being of the knower. Otherwise the mental speculators mislead the people wrongly establishing the energy as Absolute. When it is understood, the truth becomes more pleasing than the imperfect concept of monism or dualism. Development of this consciousness leads one at once to the stage of freedom from the threefold miseries. The threefold miseries are 1. in relation to the body and the mind, 2. in relation to our dealings with other beings, and 3. in relation to the acts of providence, over which we have no control.

Srimad Bhagwatam begins from the surrender of the living entity *unto the Absolute Person, with clear consciousness of the devotee's oneness with the Absolute, and, at the same time, his awareness of his eternal position of servitorship toward the Lord.* In the material conception of his life he thinks of himself falsely as the lord of all he surveys, and therefore he is always troubled with the above-mentioned threefold miseries of life. But, as soon as he comes to know his real position of transcendental servitude, he at once becomes freed from all the above-mentioned miseries. The servitor position of the living being is wasted in the material concept of his life. With a false sense of overlordship, the living being must offer his service to the relative energies of matter. When this servitorship is transferred unto the Lord in pure consciousness of spiritual identity, the living entity at once becomes freed from the encumbrances of material affliction.

Over and above this, *Srimad Bhagwatam is the Personal commentary on the Vedanta Sutra by the great Author Himself*—and that also in the mature stage of His spiritual realization, through the mercy of Narada. Sri Vyasadeva is the authorized incarnation of Narayan, the Personality of Godhead. Therefore, there is no question about His Authority. He is the Author of all other Vedic literature; but, surpassing all of It, He recommends the study of *Srimad Bhagwatam.* In other *Puranas* there are different methods of worshipping the demigods, but in the *Bhagwatam* only the Supreme Personality of Godhead is mentioned. The Supreme Personality of Godhead is the Whole Body, and the demigods are the different parts of the body. As such, by worshipping the Supreme Lord there is no need to worship the demigods, because the Supreme Lord is at once fixed in the heart. Lord Chaitanya Mahaprabhu has recommended this *Srimad Bhagwatam* as the spotless *Puranam*, as distinguished from all other *Puranas.*

The mode of receiving the transcendental message is to get it through the ears by submissiveness. No challenging mode can help the receiver in getting or realizing the transcendental message. Therefore, in the 1st verse of *Srimad Bhagwatam*, one particular word is used for our proper guidance. This particular word is *Shushrusu:* one must be anxious to hear about the transcendental message. And this qualification of hearing with interest is the prime qualification for assimilating transcendental knowledge.

Unfortunately, some persons are not interested in giving patient hearing to the message of *Srimad Bhagwatam.* The process is simple, but the application is difficult. Unfortunate persons will find enough time to hear ordinary social, political, and all sorts of idle talks, but when they are invited to attend a meeting of the devotees assembled to hear *Srimad Bhagwatam*, the unfortunate creatures will either be reluctant to attend such a meeting, or they will indulge in hearing the portion they are unfit to enter into. Professional readers of the

Bhagwatam indulge in the confidential topics of the Pastimes of the Supreme Lord, which seemingly appear to be sex literature. *Srimad Bhagwatam* is meant to be heard from the beginning, and the class of persons who are fit to assimilate it is also mentioned in *Srimad Bhagwatam* I/1/2: A bona fide audience for hearing the *Srimad Bhagwatam* is generated after many pious deeds. But an intelligent person, by thoughtful discretion, can believe in the assurance of the great sage Vyasadeva, and give patient hearing to the message of *Srimad Bhagwatam*, in order to realize directly the Supreme Personality of Godhead. And without undergoing the different Vedic stages, one can at once be lifted to the position of *Paramhansa*, simply by agreeing to receive patiently the message of *Srimad Bhagwatam*. The sages at Naimisharanya confirmed before Suta Goswami that they were increasing in their intense desire to understand the *Srimad Bhagwatam*. They were hearing from Suta Goswami about Krishna, the Supreme Personality of Godhead. They were never satiated by such discussion, because persons who are really attached to Krishna never cease to want to hear more and more about Krishna.

Lord Chaitanya therefore advised Prakasananda Saraswati, "Always read *Srimad Bhagwatam* and try to understand each and every verse, and you will actually understand the *Brahma Sutra*. You say you are very anxious about the study of *Vedanta Sutra*, but you cannot understand *Vedanta Sutra* without understanding *Srimad Bhagwatam*." He also advised Prakasananda Saraswati to always chant Hare Krishna, Hare Krishna, Krishna Krishna, Hare Hare/Hare Rama, Hare Rama, Rama Rama, Hare Hare. "And, by doing that, very easily you will be liberated. And after liberation you'll be eligible to achieve the highest goal of life, love of Godhead."

The Lord then recited many verses from authoritative Scriptures like *Srimad Bhagavad Gita* and *Srimad Bhagwatam*, and *Nrishingha Tapani*. He quoted a verse from *Bhagavad Gita*, Eighteenth Chapter, 54th verse, that when one actually becomes self-realized, knowing he is Brahman, he becomes happy and joyful, and has no more cause for lamentation and hankering. Such a person sees all living entities on an equal level, and he becomes a pure devotee of the Supreme Personality of Godhead. Similarly, in the *Nrishingha Tapani* it is said that when a person is actually liberated, then he can understand the transcendental Pastimes of the Supreme Lord, and thus become engaged in His devotional service. He also quoted a verse from the Second Canto of *Srimad Bhagwatam*, in which Sukadeva Goswami admits that, although he was elevated to the liberated stage and free from the clutches of Maya, still, he was attracted by the transcendental Pastimes of Krishna. And, as such, he studied

Srimad Bhagwatam from his great father Vyasadeva.

He also quoted another *sloka* from *Srimad Bhagwatam*, Third Canto, Fifteenth Chapter, about the Kumaras. When the Kumaras entered the temple of the Lord they were attracted by the odor of flowers and *tulsi* leaves offered to the Lotus Feet of the Supreme Lord with pulp of sandalwood, And, simply being incensed by the aroma of such flowers and *tulsi*, their minds became inclined to the service of the Supreme Lord, although they were already liberated souls. Therefore, according to *Srimad Bhagwatam*, First Canto, Seventh Chapter, even if one is a liberated soul and is actually free from material contamination, still he becomes attracted to the devotional service of the Supreme Lord without any cause, and without being hampered by any material propensities. God is so attractive—therefore He is called *Krishna*.

Lord Chaitanya was discussing the *Atmarama* verse from *Srimad Bhagwatam* with Prakasananda Saraswati. His admirer, the Maharastrian Brahmin related in the assembly that the Lord has already explained the verse in 64 different ways. All the people assembled there were very eager to hear again from the Lord about the different versions of the *Atmarama Sloka*, and as they were so eager, Lord Chaitanya explained the *Atmarama Sloka* again, in the same way that He had explained it before to Sanatan Goswami. All the people assembled there heard the explanation of the *Atmarama Sloka* from the Supreme Lord, and they were amazed and considered that the Lord was nobody else than Sri Krishna Himself.

CHAPTER TWENTY-FOUR

Talks with
Sarbabhouma Battacharya

When Lord Chaitanya met Sarbabhouma Bhattacharya at Jagannath Puri, Bhattacharya, as the great logician of the day, also wanted to teach Him Vedanta. Bhattacharya was an elderly man of the age of Lord Chaitanya's father, and therefore he took compassion on the young Sannyasi; he requested that He should learn *Vedanta Sutra* from him, otherwise it would be difficult to continue as a young Sannyasi. When the Lord agreed to learn Vedanta philosophy from Bhattacharya, he began to teach Him in the temple of Jagannath. Bhattacharya spoke to the Lord about *Vedanta Sutra* continually for seven days, and the Lord silently heard him without speaking a word. On the eighth day of teaching, Sarbabhouma Bhattacharya enquired from the Lord, "You are hearing *Vedanta Sutra* from me for the last week, but You do not inquire or say anything as to whether I am explaining it nicely. So I cannot tell whether You understand me or not."

The Lord replied as follows: "I am a fool, I have no study of *Vedanta Sutra*, but you asked Me to hear you, and therefore I am trying to hear you.

You said that it is the duty of every Sannyasi to hear *Vedanta Sutra*, so I simply hear; but the meaning which you create—that I cannot understand." In other words, the Lord was explaining that in the Mayavadi Sampradaya there are many so-called Sannyasis who are even illiterate and have not sufficient intelligence but just as a matter of formality they hear *Vedanta Sutra* from their Spiritual Master, although they do not understand anything. So far as Lord Chaitanya was concerned, He did not understand the explanation of Bhattacharya because He did not approve of the explanation of Mayavadi philosophy.

When He said that He was an uneducated fool Who could not follow, Bhattacharya replied to Him, "If You do not follow what I am saying, how is it that You do not inquire, but simply sit down silently? It appears that You do have something to say about my explanation."

Then the Lord replied, "My dear sir, so far as the *Vedanta Sutra* or the codes of the Vedanta are concerned, I can understand the meaning very nicely, but the explanation which you are promoting is not understandable by Me. There is nothing difficult about the meaning of the original codes of *Vedanta Sutra*. But the way you were explaining them appears to be obscuring the real meaning of the codes. You do not elucidate the direct meaning of the *Vedanta Sutra*, but you imagine something and hide the true meaning. I think you have a particular doctrine, and you are trying to expound it through the codes."

According to *Mukti Upanishad*, there are 108 Upanishads. Some of them are: 1. Iso, 2. Kena, 3. Katha, 4. Prasna, 5. Mund, 6. Mandukya, 7. Tittirih, 8. Aitriya, 9. Chhandogya, 10. Brihadaranoyakam, 11. Brahma, 12. Jaivalya, 13. Javala, 14. Svetsva, 15. Hansa, 16. Arunih, 17. Garbha, 18. Narayana, etc. These 108 *Upanishads* contain all knowledge about the Absolute Truth. Sometimes people inquire about the meaning of these 108 prayer beads, but we think because there are 108 *Upanishads* which contain full knowledge of the Absolute Truth, therefore 108 beads are accepted. Sometimes, on the other hand, the Vaishnava transcendentalists think there are 108 companions of Lord Krishna in His *Rasa* Dance, and therefore 108 beads are accepted.

Lord Chaitanya protested against misinterpretations of the statements of the *Upanishads*, and so any explanation which did not follow the direct meaning of the *Upanishad* He did not accept. The direct interpretation is called *Abhidavritti*, whereas the indirect method is called *Lakshnavritti*. The indirect meaning, or *Lakshnavritti*, serves no purpose. There are four kinds of understanding, called: (1) direct understanding, (2) hypothetical understanding,

(3) historical understanding, and (4) sound understanding. Out of these four kinds of understanding, to receive knowledge by sound understanding, the understanding from the Vedic Scriptures (which are the sound representation of the Absolute Truth), is the best. The traditional Vedic students accept this sound understanding as the best.

For example, the stool and bone of any living entity is considered the most impure thing by the Vedic literature; but, at the same time, the Vedic literature asserts that cow dung and the conch shell are the purest of all. Apparently these statements are contradictory, but because cow dung and the conch shell have been called pure in the Vedic literature, although they are the stool and bone of living entities, they are accepted as pure without any argument. They cannot be changed by our mundane arguments added to the statements of the Vedas. If we want to understand the statements by indirect interpretation under some hypothesis, then we challenge the evidential quality of the Vedic statement. In other words, Vedic statements cannot be accepted by our imperfect interpretation; they must be accepted *as they are*. Otherwise there is no authority in the Vedic statement.

According to Lord Chaitanya, persons who try to always find some interpretation of the Vedic statements are not at all intelligent. They mislead their followers by some innovation of their own interpretation. In India there is a class who are known as *Aryasamajist*, who say that they accept only the original Vedas and no other Vedic literature. But their purpose is only to make their own interpretation, and according to Lord Chaitanya such interpretation is not accepted. Neither are they Vedic. Lord Chaitanya then said that the Vedic statements of the *Upanishads* are just like sunlight; as in the sunlight everything is clear and very distinct, so the statements in the Vedas are distinct and clear. The Mayavadi philosophers cover the sunlight with the cloud of their misinterpretation.

He then said that all Vedic statements of the *Upanishads* aim at the truth, known as *Brahman*. The meaning of the word *Brahman* is "the greatest," and when you speak of the greatest we must immediately understand that greatest means the Supreme Personality of Godhead, the Source of all emanations. Unless the greatest is filled with six opulences it cannot be the greatest; therefore the greatest, with the fullness of six opulences, means the Supreme Personality of Godhead. In other words, the Supreme Brahman is the Supreme Personality of Godhead. In the *Bhagavad Gita* also, in the Tenth Chapter, the Supreme Personality of Godhead, Krishna, is accepted as the Supreme

Brahman. The conceptions of the impersonal Brahman and the localized Supersoul are contained within the understanding of the Supreme Personality of Godhead.

Whenever we speak of the Supreme Personality of Godhead, we add the word "Sri": this means that He is full with six opulences, and, in other words, He is eternally a Person. Otherwise the six opulences cannot be present in fullness. Therefore, if we say that the Supreme Absolute Truth is impersonal, it means that He is not a Person of this material world. To distinguish His transcendental Body from the material body, some have explained Him as materially impersonal. In other words, material personality has been denied and Spiritual Personality has been established. In the *Svetasvatara Upanishad*, Third Chapter, 19th verse, it has been clearly explained that the Absolute Truth has no material legs and hands, but still He has spiritual hands by which He accepts everything which we offer to Him. He has no material eyes, but He has spiritual eyes by which He can see everything and anything. He has no material ears but He can hear everything and anything. He has perfect senses—therefore He knows past, future and present. He knows everything, but nobody can understand Him, because by material senses He cannot be understood. He is the Origin of all emanations and therefore He is the Supreme, the greatest, the Personality of Godhead.

There are many such Vedic hymns which definitely establish that the Supreme Absolute Truth is a Person, but that He is not a Person of this material world. In the *Hayasirsa Pancharatra* there is a nice verse which explains that, in each and every *Upanishad* the Supreme Brahman is first viewed as impersonal, but at the end there is acceptance of the Personal Form of the Supreme Lord. Another example, in the *Isa Upanishad*—the 15th Mantra—runs as follows:

Hiranmayena patrena satysya apihitam mukhm
Jat tvam pusan, apavrinu satya dharmaya dri staye

This verse indicates that everyone should be engaged in devotional service to the Supreme Lord; "O my Lord, the Supreme Personality of Godhead, You are the Maintainer of the whole Universe. Everyone is sustained by Your mercy. Therefore, devotional service unto You is the true religion of life. I am therefore engaged in such devotional service, and I expect that You will please maintain me, and ever increasingly engage me in Your transcendental service. For the Supreme Personality of Godhead is the eternal Form of *Sat-Chit-Ananda*, and Your effulgence is spread all over the Creation, just like the sunshine. Where the sun disc is covered by the glaring sunshine, similarly Your transcendental Form is covered by the *Brahmajyoti*. I desire to find You within the *Brahmajyoti*—therefore please remove this glaring effulgence."

In this verse of *Isa Upanishad* it is clearly stated that the eternal, blissful, cognizant Form of the Supreme Lord is to be found within the glaring effulgence of *Brahmajyoti*. *Brahmajyoti* is the emanation from the Personal Body of the Supreme Lord. Therefore the Personal Body of the Personality of Godhead is the source of the *Brahmajyoti* as it is described in the *Bhagavad Gita*. The impersonal Brahman is dependent on the Supreme Personality. This is stated in the *Hayasirsa Pancharatra;* and, in any Upanishad or Vedic Scripture, wherever there is talk first of the impersonal Brahman, the Supreme Personality is finally established at the end. Just as we have quoted above from the *Isa Upanishad*, the Supreme Absolute Truth is both impersonal and Personal eternally, but His Personal aspect is more important than the impersonal concept.

The Mantra in the *Taetreia Upanishad* is: *Yato va imani bhutani jayante.* According to this Mantra this cosmic manifestation is an emanation from the Supreme Absolute Truth, and it rests also in the Supreme Absolute Truth. So the Absolute Truth becomes the ablative and causative and locative Performer. Therefore, as Performer, He is the Supreme Personality of Godhead. These are the symptoms of Personality. This Absolute Truth being ablative Performer of this cosmic manifestation, it is to be concluded that He has thinking, feeling and willing. Without these three psychic symptoms there is no possibility of such a nice arrangement and design of the cosmic manifestation. Then again He is causative: He is the Original Designer of the cosmic manifestation. And He is locative: everything is resting in His energy. These are the clear symptoms of His Personality.

Then again, in the *Chandyago Upanishad*, when the Supreme Personality of Godhead desires to become many, He turns over the material Nature. As it is confirmed in the *Taiitariya Upanishad*, "The Lord glanced over the material Nature." There was no existence of the cosmic manifestation before His glancing, and therefore this glancing does not mean that He has a glancing or seeing power which is materially contaminated. His seeing power existed before the material Creation, and therefore His body is also not material. His thinking, feeling and acting are transcendental. In other words it is to be concluded that the mind by which the Lord thinks, feels and wills, is transcendental; the eyes by which He glances over the material Nature are also transcendental. All of His senses existed before the material Creation, and so He has His transcendental Body, transcendental Mind, and transcendental thinking, feeling and willing, This conclusion is the purpose of all the Vedic literature. In all the *Upanishads*, the word *Brahman* is found everywhere. In the *Srimad Bhagwatam*, Brahman, Paramatma and the Supreme Personality of Godhead are together calculated as the Absolute Truth. Therefore the Brahman conception and Paramatma realization also are grades or stages, and when ultimate realization is reached, that realization is the Supreme Personality of Godhead. This is the conclusion of all Vedic literature.

So, by the evidences of the different Vedic Scriptures, the Supreme Lord Krishna is accepted as the ultimate Goal of Brahman realization. *Bhagavad Gita* confirms that there is nothing superior to Krishna. The great Acharya of Brahma's disciplic succession, Madhva Acharya, has described—in connection with his explanation of the *Vedanta Sutra*—that everything can be seen through the authorities of the Scriptures. He has quoted a verse from the *Bhobishya Purana* in which it is stated that *Rig Veda, Sam Veda, Atharva Veda, Mahabharata, Pancharatracum,* and the original *Ramayan,* are actually evidential Vedic literature, and the *Puranas* which are accepted by the Vaishnavas are also accepted as evidential Vedic literature. Whatever is spoken in that literaute should be taken without any argument as the ultimate conclusion, *and in all that literature it is found that Krishna is the Supreme Personality of Godhead.*

CHAPTER TWENTY-FIVE

Personal and
Impersonal Realization

The *Puranas* are called the supplementary Vedic literature, because sometimes in the original Vedas the subject matter is too difficult to be understood by the common man. The *Puranas*, therefore, explain things nicely by different stories and historical incidents. So, in the *Srimad Bhagwatam* it is stated in the Tenth Canto, Fourteenh Chapter, that Maharaj Nanda and the cowherd men and inhabitants of Vrindaban generally are very fortunate because the Supreme Brahman, the Personality of Gobhead, full of bliss, is now engaged there in His eternal Pastimes as their Friend.

According to *Svetasvatara Upanishad*, the *Mantra* of *Apanipado javano grahita* comfirms that although Brahman has no materially created hands and legs, still He walks very stately, and He accepts everything offered to Him. These words suggest that He has transcendental limbs of the body, and therefore He is not impersonal. The person who does not understand the Vedic principles simply stresses the impersonal material features of the Supreme Absolute Truth, and thus unceremoniously calls the Absolute Truth impersonal. Although the impersonalist Mayavadi philosophers want to establish the Absolute Truth as impersonal, yet the Vedic literature itself does not confirm this. Vedic literature confirms that the Supreme Absolute has multiple energies, and still the Mayavadi impersonalists want to establish that the Absolute Truth has no energy. The Absolute Truth is therefore full of energy and He is a Person. He cannot be established as impersonal.

According to the *Vishnu Purana*, the living entities are considered as *Kshetrajna* energy. Although the living entity is part and parcel of the Supreme Lord, and is fully cognizant, still he becomes entrapped in the material contamination, and therefore suffers all the miseries therein. Such living entities live in different positions in proportion to their entanglement in material Nature. The purport is that the original energy of the Supreme Lord is spiritual and non-different from the Supreme Absolute Personality of Godhead. The living entity is called the marginal energy of the Supreme Lord, whereas the material energy is called inferior. On account of possessing inert and material inebriety, the living entity, although in the marginal position, becomes entangled with the inferior energy, matter. At that time he forgets his spiritual significance and identifies himself with the material energy and therefore becomes subjected to threefold miseries. When he is, however, free from that material contamination, he proportionately becomes situated in different standards of life.

According to the Vedic instruction, everyone should understand the constitutional position of the living entity, the Lord, and the material energy in their inter-relation. First of all, one should try to understand the constitutional position of the Supreme Lord, the Personality of Godhead. That Supreme Personality of Godhead has eternal, cognizant, blissful Body; His spiritual energy is distributed as eternity, knowledge, and bliss. In His blissful identity there is His pleasure potency, and in His eternal identity He is the Cause of everything, and in His cognizant identity He is the Supreme Knowledge. *Krishna* means that Supreme Knowledge. In other words, the Supreme Personality of Krishna is the Reservoir of all knowledge, all pleasure, and all eternity. That Supreme Knowledge of Krishna is exhibited in three different energies; they are called internal energy, marginal energy, and external energy. By internal energy, He exists in Himself with His spiritual paraphernalia, by marginal existence He exhibits Himself as the living entities, and by His external energy He exhibits Himself as the material energy. In each and every exhibition of His different energies there is the background of eternity, pleasure potency, and cognizance potency.

The conditioned soul is the marginal potency, overpowered by the external potency. When the marginal potency, however, comes under the spiritual potency, the marginal potency becomes eligible for love of Godhead. The Supreme Lord enjoys with six kinds of opulences and nobody can establish that He is Formless or that He is without energy. If somebody says that, it is completely against the Vedic instruction. Actually, the Supreme Personality of Godhead is the Master of all energies. The living entity, being an infinitesimal part and parcel, becomes overpowered by the material energy.

In the *Mundaka Upanishad* it is stated that two birds of the same feather are sitting on one tree. One of them is eating the fruit of the tree, and the other is not eating the fruit of the tree, but is witnessing the activities of the other bird. When the bird eating the fruit of the tree looks on the other bird, he becomes freed from all anxieties. This is the position of the infinitesimal living entity. So long as he is forgetful of the Supreme Personality of Godhead, he is subjected to the threefold miseries; but when he looks to the Supreme Lord, or becomes a devotee of the Supreme Lord, he becomes free from all anxieties and miseries of material existence.

This position of the living entity means that he is eternally subordinate to the Supreme Lord. The Supreme Lord is always the Master of all energies, whereas the living entities are always under the energies of the Supreme Lord. The living entity, although qualitatively one with the Supreme Lord, has a tendency to lord it over the material Nature; but, being infinitesimal, the living entity has the tendency to be controlled by material Nature. This qualification of the living entity is called marginal potency. Because the living entity has a tendency for being controlled by the material Nature, he cannot at any stage of life become One with the Supreme Lord. If a living entity were equal to the Supreme Lord then there would be no chance of his being controlled by the material energy. In *Bhagavad Gita*, the living entity has been described as one of the energies of the Supreme Lord. Energy, although inseparable from the energetic, is still energy, and cannot be equal with the energetic. In other words, the living entity is simultaneously one and different from the Supreme Lord. The *Bhagavad Gita*, in the Seventh Chapter, verses 4–5, clearly states that earth, water, fire, air, ether, mind, intelligence, and false ego are the eight different elementary energies of the Supreme Lord. All these energies are of inferior quality, whereas the living entity has energy of superior quality. Therefore Vedic instruction confirms the transcendental Form of the Supreme Lord as eternal, blissful, and full of knowledge.

The conception of impersonalism is the opposite of the transformations of the material modes of Nature. The form beyond the modes of material Nature is not exactly like the form of this material world, but there is form, which is called spiritual form. That spiritual form cannot be compared with any one of these material forms. Anyone, therefore, who does not agree to accept the spiritual Form of the Supreme Lord, is counted among the atheists. Lord Buddha did not accept these Vedic principles, and therefore the Vedic teachers considered Him an atheist. Although Mayavadi philosophers do pretend to accept the Vedic principles, they indirectly preach the Buddhist philosophy or atheistic philosophy, without acceptance of the Supreme Personality of Godhead. This philosophy is inferior to Buddha's philosophy, which directly denies the Vedic authority; for the Mayavadi philosophy is disguised as Vedanta philosophy, and is thus more dangerous than Buddhism or atheism.

Vedanta Sutra is purely compiled by Vyasadeva for the benefit of all living entities in order to understand the philosophy of *Bhakti Yoga*. Unfortunately, the Mayavadi commentary, *Sarirakabhasya*, has practically defeated the purpose of the *Vedanta Sutra*. In the Mayavadi commentary, the spiritual, transcendental Form of the Supreme Personality of Godhead has been denied and the Supreme Brahman has been dragged down to a level equal with the individual Brahman, the living entity. Both of them have been denied the spiritual form of individuality, although it is clearly stated that the Supreme Lord is the One Supreme Living entity, and the living entities are many. Therefore, to consider the commentary of the Mayavadi philosophy on the *Vedanta Sutra* is always dangerous. The danger is in the false understanding of the living entity as equal to the Supreme Lord. A living entity can thus be falsely directed; and as a result he can never come to his actual position, his eternal activity in Bhakti Yoga. In other words, the Mayavadi philosophy has rendered the greatest disservice to humanity by promoting the impersonal view of the Supreme Lord. These philosophers are depriving human society of the real message of the *Vedanta Sutra*.

From the very beginning of the *Vedanta Sutra* it is accepted that the cosmic manifestation is a display of the energy of the Supreme Lord. In the very beginning, *Janmadyasya*, it is described that the Supreme Brahman is That from Whom everything is taking appearance. Everything is being maintained and everything is dissolved in Him. The Absolute Truth is the Cause of Creation, Maintenance, and Dissolution. The cause of the fruit is the tree. When the tree produces a fruit it does not mean that the tree is impersonal. The tree produces many hundreds and thousands of fruits but it remains as it is. The fruit is produced, developed, stays for some time, dwindles, and then vanishes. That does not mean that the tree has vanished. From the very beginning, therefore, the purpose of the *Vedanta Sutra* is the exposition of the doctrine of by-products. These activities of production, maintenance and dissolution are going on by the inconceivable energy of the Supreme Lord. The cosmic manifestation is a transformation of the energy of the Supreme Lord, although the energy of the Supreme Lord and the Supreme Lord Himself are non-different and inseparable. An example is the touchstone which produces great quantities of gold by contact with iron—but still the touchstone remains as it is. The Supreme Lord, therefore, in spite of His producing the huge material cosmic manifestation, is always in His transcendental Form.

Mayavadi philosophy has the audacity to decline acceptance of the purpose of Vyasadeva, as explained in the *Vedanta Sutra*, and has tried instead to establish transformation of the Supreme: a doctrine of transformation by imagination. According to Mayavadi philosophy, the cosmic manifestation is a transformation of the Absolute Truth, and the Absolute Truth has no separate existence. This is not the message of the *Vedanta Sutra*. This transformation has been explained by Mayavadi philosophers as false; but it is not false—it is temporary. Mayavadi philosophy says that the Absolute Truth is the only truth, and this manifestation of the world is false, Actually it is not so. The material contamination is not false; it is relative truth, and therefore it is temporary.

Pranava or *Omkara* is the chief indication of Vedic hymns, and Omkara is considered as the sound Form of the Supreme Lord. From Omkara, all Vedic hymns have emanated, and the world has also emanated from the Omkara sound. The world *Tatvamasi*, picked up from the Vedic hymns, is not the chief word, but it is an explanation of the constitutional position of the living entity. The meaning of this *Tatvamasi* is that the living entity is a spiritual particle of the Supreme spirit; but this is not the chief motif of the Vedanta or Vedic literature. The chief sound representation of the Supreme is Omkara.

All these faulty explanations of *Vedanta Sutra* are atheism. The Mayavadi philosophers do not agree to accept the eternal, transcendental Form of the Supreme Lord and they are therfore unable to be engaged in real devotional service. The Mayavadi philosopher is ever bereft of Krishna Consciousness and Krishna's devotional service. The pure devotee of the Personality of Godhead never accepts the Mayavadi philosophy as an actual path to transscendental realization. The Mayavadi philosophers are hovering on the moral and immoral material atmosphere of the cosmic world; they are always engaged in rejecting and accepting material enjoyment. They have falsely accepted the nonspiritual as the spiritual. As a result of this misconception they have forgotten the spiritual, eternal Form of the Supreme Personality of Godhead, His Name, Quality and Entourage. They consider the transcendental Pastimes, Name, Form and Quality of the Supreme as a product of material Nature, and so the Mayavadi is eternally subjected to the material miseries because of his acceptance or rejection of material pleasure and misery.

The actual devotees of the Lord are always different from the Mayavadi philosophers. Impersonalism cannot be a representation of eternity, blissfulness, and knowledge. Being situated in imperfect knowledge of liberation, the Mayavadi decries eternity, knowledge, and blissfulness, under a misconception of materialism. They reject devotional service. Therefore they are less intelligent men. They are unable to understand the effect of devotional service. Their jugglery of words for amalgamating knowledge and the knowable and the knower into one has proved their very existence as a less intelligent class of men. The doctrine of by-product is the real purport of the beginning of *Vedanta Sutra*. The Lord is empowered with innumerable unlimited energies, and as such He displays the by-products of such energies in different ways. Everything is under His control. The Supreme Controller is called the Supreme Personality of Godhead, and He is manifested in innumerable energies and expansions.

CHAPTER TWENTY-SIX

Bhattacharya Is Converted

For the impersonalist and void philosophers the next world is senseless eternity and bliss. The void philosophers want to establish that ultimately everything is senseless, and the impersonalists want to establish that the next world is simply knowledge without any activities. In other words, less intelligent salvationists want to carry imperfect knowledge into the perfect sphere of spiritual activity. The impersonalist, having experienced a great disadvantage in material activity, wants to establish spiritual life without activity. He cannot understand the activities of devotional service. Spiritual activity in devotional service is not intelligeble to the void phiolsophers and impersonalists. The Vaishnava philosophers know perfectly well that the Absolute Truth, the Supreme Personality of Godhead, having the power of innumerable potencies, can never be impersonal or void. He can present Himself in multiple Forms with innumerable energies, and still He remains Himself as the Absolute Supreme Personality of Godhead. He is competent Himself to maintain His transcendental position in spite of His becoming expanded in multiple Forms and diffused by His innumerable multiple Forms of energy.

Thus Lord Chaitanya showed many defects in the Mayavadi philosophy, and although Bhattacharya wanted to establish himself with various juggleries of words and logic, Lord Chaitanya was able to maintain Himself from such attacks, and He established that the Vedic literature is meant for three things: to understand our relationship with the Absolute Supreme Personality of Godhead, to act according to that understanding, and at the end to achieve the highest perfection of life, love of Godhead. Anybody who wants to prove something other than the above-mentioned three purposes must be the victim of his own imagination.

The Lord then quoted some verses from the *Puranas*, by which He wanted to establish that Sankaracharya was meant to do his teaching by the Supreme order of the Personality of Godhead. He quoted a verse from *Padma Purana* in which it is stated that the Lord ordered Mahadeva Lord Shiva to present some imaginary interpretation of the Vedic literature, and thus try to distract persons from the actual position of the *Veda*. "By such activity you try to make them atheists, and after that they can be engaged in producing more population." In the same *Padma Purana* it is also said that Lord Shiva explained to his wife, Parvati, that in the Age of Kali, in the form of a Brahmin, he would preach the imperfect explanation of the *Veda*, known as *Mayavadi*, which is actually a second edition of the atheist philosophy of Buddha.

By such explanations of Lord Chaitanya, Bhattacharya was overwhelmed. And, hearing the explanation of Mayavadi philosophy from Lord Chaitanya, he could not speak, and simply remained silent for some time. Lord Chaitanya asked him, "My dear Bhattacharya, don't be hampered with this explanation. Please take it from Me that the devotional service of the Supreme Lord is the highest perfectional stage of human understanding. Devotional service of the Lord is so attractive that even persons who are already liberated become devotees of the Lord by the inconceivable potency of the Supreme Personality of Godhead." There are many instances of this in the Vedic literature, such as in the *Srimad Bhagwatam*, First Canto, Seventh Chapter: therein is the famous *Atmarama* verse for persons who are attached to self-realization, and liberated from all material attachment. Such liberated impersonalist sages become attracted to devotional service by the various activities of Lord Krishna. That is the transcendental Quality of the Supreme Personality of Godhead.

Actually, the pure consciousness of the living entity is to understand himself as the eternal servant of the Supreme Lord. Under the spell of illusion, a less intelligent person accepts the gross body and the subtle body as his self; such a conception is the basis of the doctrine of transference. Actually the part and parcel of the Supreme is not subjected eternally to such a false conception of gross and subtle bodily life. The covering of the living entity by the gross and subtle body is not his eternal form, but can be changed; or, the living entity can become free from such existence. While he is in the conception of the body and mind he has certainly transferred his position from spirit to matter. Mayavadi philosophers, of course, take advantage of this doctrine of transference: they say that the living entity under the wrong impression thinks himself as part and parcel, but he is the Supreme Himself. This doctrine cannot be tenable.

Bhattacharya then asked Lord Chaitanya to explain the famous *Atmarama* verse, as he desired to hear it from the Lord, Lord Chaitanya replied to him that, first of all, he should explain the verse according to his own understanding, and then Lord Chaitanya would explain it by His own understanding. Bhattacharya then began to explain the *Atmarama Sloka* with his method of logic and grammar. He explained the *Atmarama Sloka* in nine different ways. The Lord appreciated his erudite scholarship in explaining the verse, and said: "My dear Bhattacharya, I know that you are personally a representation of the learned scholar, like Brihashpati, and you can explain any portion of the Shastras in such a nice way. And yet your explanation is more or less based on academic education only. But there is another explanation, beside the academic, scholarly explanation."

Then, at the request of Bhattacharya, Lord Chaitanya explained the *Atmarama Sloka* thus: On the basis of the analytical parts of the verse, the verse is explained as follows: 1. *Atmarama*, 2. *Cha*, 3. *Munayah*, 4. *Nirgranthah*, 5. *Api*, 6. *Urukrama*, 7. *Kurvanti*, 8. *Ahaituki*, 9. *Bhaktim*, 10. *Itthambhutagunah*, 11. *Harih*. (This verse is already explained in connection with the Lord's teachings to Sanatan Goswami). Lord Chaitanya did not touch the nine different explanations of Bhattacharya, but He explained on the basis of 11 analyses of the verse, and each analytical basis He divided into five and six and, in this way, He expounded a total of 61 different explanations of the *Atmarama* verse. It is summarized, then, that the Supreme Personality of Godhead is full of innumerable potencies: nobody can estimate how many transcendental qualities are possessed by Him. They are always inconceivable, and any process of self-relization generally inquires into these inconceivable potencies of the Supreme Personality of Godhead, His energies, and His qualities. But those who are devotees at once accept this inconceivable position of the Supreme Lord. He explained that even great liberated souls like the Kumaras and Sukadeva Goswami also become attracted to the transcendental qualities of the Supreme Lord.

Bhattacharya then appreciated the explanation of Lord Chaitanya, and he concluded that Lord Chaitanya is none other than Krishna Himself. And he began to deprecate his own position. He related that at first he had considered Lord Chaitanya as an ordinary human being, and therefore he felt that he had been offensive to the identity of Lord Chaitanya. He fell down at the Lotus Feet of Lord Chaitanya, deprecating his own position, and requested Lord Chaitanya to show His causeless mercy upon him. Lord Chaitanya appreciated the humbleness of such a great learned scholar. He therefore exhibited His own Form, first with four hands, and then the six-handed form called *Sadabhuj*. Sarbabhouma Bhattacharya then repeatedly fell down on the Lotus Feet of the Lord and began to pray with various kinds of prayers composed by himself. He was a great scholar undoubtedly, and after receiving the causeless mercy of the Lord he was empowered to explain the Lord's activities in different ways—such as being able to express the benefit of chanting *Hare Krishna, Hare Krishna, Krishna Krishna, Hare Hare/Hare Rama, Hare Rama, Rama Rama, Hare Hare.*

It is said that Sarbabhouma Bhattacharya then composed 100 verses in appreciation of the Lord's activities, and those verses are so important that even Brihashpati, the learned scholar in the heavenly planet, could not compose such nice verses. The Lord was very much pleased by hearing his composition of 100 verses, and He embraced Bhattacharya. By His touching, Bhattacharya became overwhelmed with ecstasy, and practically became unconscious. He was crying, sometimes trembling, sometimes shivering, sometimes perspiring, sometimes dancing, sometimes singing, and in this way he fell at the Lotus Feet of Lord Chaitanya. His brother-in-law, Gopinath Acharya, and the devotees of the Lord, were surprised to see the condition of Bhattacharya as he was transformed into a great devotee.

Gopinath Acharya addressed the Lord and began to thank Him: "Sir, it is by Your grace only that Bhattacharya has been transformed from his stonelike position into such a devotee." Lord Chaitanya replied to Gopinath Acharya that, due to a devotee's favor upon others, a stonelike man can be transformed to a mild flower-like devotee. Actually, Gopinath Acharya, the brother-in-law of Bhattacharya, had sincerely desired that such a scholar as Bhattacharya should become a devotee of the Lord. He had sincerely desired that the Lord show favor to Bhattacharya, and was glad to see his desire fulfilled by Lord Chaitanya. In other words, a devotee of the Lord is more merciful than the Lord Himself. When a devotee desires to show his mercy to a person, the Lord accepts, and by His grace such a person becomes a devotee.

Lord Chaitanya pacified Bhattacharya and asked him to go home. Bhattacharya again began to praise the Lord and said, "You have descended Yourself to deliver all the fallen souls of this material world. That project is not so difficult for You, but You have turned a stonehearted man like me, and that is Your wonderful act. I am very expert at logical arguments and grammatical explanations of the Vedic process. I am as hard as a lump of iron. But Your influence and temperature is so strong that You could melt away even hard iron like me."

Lord Chaitanya then returned to His place and Bhattacharya, through Gopinath Acharya, sent various kinds of *Prasadam* from Jagannath temple. The next day, the Lord went to see the temple of Jagannath early in the morning, which is called *Mongalarati*. The priests in the temple brought Him a garland from the deity and offered Him various kinds of *Prasadam*. The Lord was very much pleased to receive them, and He at once went to the house of Bhattacharya, taking the *Prasadam* and the flowers to present to Bhattacharya. It was early in the morning, and Bhattacharya understood that the Lord had come and was knocking on his door. He at once rose up from his bed and began to say *Krishna, Krishna!*, which was heard by Lord Chaitanya. And at once he came to the door and opened it and saw the Lord standing there. He was so pleased to see the Lord early in the morning, and wanted to receive Him with all care. He again offered Him a nice seat, and both of them sat there and Lord Chaitanya offered him the Prasadam which He had received in the temple of Jagannath. Bhattacharya was very glad to receive Prasadam from the hand of Lord Chaitanya, and without taking his bath and without performing his daily duties or washing his teeth he began immediately to eat the Prasadam. Actually, he was now freed from all contamination of material attachment; and he cited a verse from *Padma Purana* as he began to eat the Prasadam.

In the *Padma Purana* it is stated that when Prasadam is brought or is received, even if it has become very dry or it is even very old or brought from a distant place, as soon as it is received it must be eaten immediately, without following any of the rules or duties of one's daily activities. It is enjoined in the Shastras that Prasadam should be immediately taken, and there is no restriction of time and space—that is the order of the Supreme Personality of Godhead. In other words, there are restrictions in accepting foodstuff from different kinds of people, but there are no such restrictions in accepting Prasadam from different kinds of people—neither a restriction as to time, place, or atmosphere. Prasadam is always transcendental, and it can be taken under any condition.

Lord Chaitanya was very much pleased to see that Bhattacharya, who always obeyed rules and regulations, could accept Prasadam without following any such rules and regulations. Being so pleased Himself, Lord Chaitanya. embraced Bhattacharya. Both of Them began to dance in transcendental ecstasy. In that ecstasy, Lord Chaitanya explained: "My mission in Jagannath Puri is now fulfilled because I have converted a person like Sarbabhouma Bhattacharya."

The Lord continued: "I shall be able now to attain Vaikuntha without fail." The missionary activity of a devotee is to convert one person to become a pure devotee. Then admission to the Spiritual Kingdom is guaranteed. The Lord was so much pleased with Bhattacharya's philosophy that He began to bless him repeatedly: "Dear Bhattacharya, now you are a completely pure devotee of Lord Krishna, and Krishna is now very much pleased with you. From today you are free from the contamination of this material body, and from today you are free from any entanglement under the spell of material energy. You are now fit to go back to Godhead, back to Home." He then cited one nice verse from the *Srimad Bhagwatam*, Second Canto, Seventh Chapter: "Anyone who takes complete shelter of the Lotus Feet of the Supreme Lord is favored by the Supreme Lord, Who is known as Unlimited. And such a person gets permission to cross over the ocean of nescience. Anyone who is under the misconception that this material body is himself, cannot have appreciation or causeless mercy from the Supreme Personality of Godhead."

After this incident, Lord Chaitanya returned to His place, and Bhattacharya became a pure devotee without any faults. Since he was formerly an academic scholar, this conversion of Bhattacharya was possible only by the causeless mercy of Chaitanya Mahaprabhu. From that day forward he never explained any Vedic literature without an explanation of devotional service. Gopinath Acharya, his brother-in-law, was very much pleased to see the condition of Bhattacharya, and he began to dance in ecstasy, vibrating the transcendental sound, *Hare Krishna, Hare Krishna, Krishna Krishna, Hare Hare/Hare Rama, Hare Rama, Rama Rama, Hare Hare.*

The next day, after visting Jagannath temple early in the morning, Bhattacharya came to the place of Lord Chaitanya and offered his respects by falling down before the Lord; and he began to explain his past undesirable behavior. He asked the Lord to say something about devotional service, and the Lord began to instruct him on the verses of *Brihadnaradia Purana*, in which is stated *Harer Nama Harer Nama*. Lord Chaitanya explained the meaning of this verse very explicitly. After hearing the explanation of the *Harer Nama* from Lord Chaitanya, Bhattacharya became more and more ecstatic. Seeing his condition, his brother-in-law, Gopinath Acharya, addressed him and said, "My dear Bhattacharya, what I stated before—'when he is favored by the Supreme Lord he will understand about the techniques of devotional service' —I am today seeing fulfilled."

Bhattacharya offered him his due respect and replied, "My dear Gopinath Acharya, it is through your mercy that I have the mercy of the Supreme Lord." The mercy of the Supreme Personality of Godhead can be achieved through the agency of the pure devotee. Lord Chaitanya's mercy was bestowed upon Bhattacharya because of Gopinath Acharya's endeavor.

Bhattacharya said to his brother-in-law: "You are a great devotee of the Lord, and I was simply blind with my academic education. So I have achieved the mercy of the Lord through your agency only." The Lord was very much pleased to hear from Bhattacharya that a man can achieve the mercy of the Lord through the agency of the devotee, and he appreciated the verses and embraced Bhattacharya, confirming his statement.

The Lord then requested Bhattacharya to go and see Jagannath temple. Bhattacharya then started out for Jagannath temple, accompanied by Jagadananda and Damodar, two principal associates of Lord Chaitanya. He returned to his home after seeing Jagannath temple, and brought with him much nice Prasadam purchased from the temple. He sent all this Prasadam to Lord Chaitanya through his Brahmin servant, and also dispatched two verses written by him on palm tree leaves, and requested Jagadananda to do this favor and deliver them. All of them again came back to Lord Chaitanya and offered Him the Prasadam and the verses on the palm leaf. But before reaching the Lord, Mukunda Datta, who also undertook the delivery of the written palm leaf, had noted the verses down in his book. Lord Chaitanya read those verses and tore them into pieces, because He never liked to be praised by anyone. But his devotees had the verses written by Sarbabhouma Bhattacharya, from the notes of Mukunda Datta.

The purport of the verses written by Sarbabhouma Bhattacharya was praise of the Lord, the Supreme Original Personality of Godhead. He—Lord Chaitanya—has descended to preach detachment and transcendental knowledge along with devotional service to the people in general. Lord Chaitanya is the Original Personality of Godhead, and is compared with the ocean of mercy. "Let me surrender unto that Lord Chaitanya Mahaprabhu." The other verse states, "The Lord, seeing that devotional service was absent, descended Himself in the Form of Lord Chaitanya to preach that devotional service. Let us all surrender unto His Lotus Feet to learn from Him what is actual devotional service." These two important verses are taken by the devotees of the Lord in disciplic succession, as the most important jewels, and Sarbabhouma Bhattacharya has become highest amongst the devotees because of these famous verses.

Sarbabhouma Bhattacharya was thus converted to become one of the important devotees of the Lord, and he had no other interest than to serve the Lord. His only concern was to think of Lord Chaitanya constantly, and this meditation and chanting became the main purpose of his life. One day Sarbabhouma Bhattacharya came before the Lord, and after offering his respects he began to read a verse from the *Srimad Bhagwatam*. This verse is stated in the Tenth Canto, Fourteenth Chapter, in connection with Lord Brahma's prayer to the Lord. Sarbabhouma Bhattacharya wanted to change two letters in the last portion of the verse, where the word *Muktipade* occurs. Sarbabhouma Bhattacharya wanted to change it into *Bhakti*. The purport of the verse is: A person who devotes his mind, body and speech to the service of the Lord, even in the midst of miserable life due to past misdeeds, is assured of liberation. And Bhattacharya wanted to change the *Mukti*, to *Bhakti*— devotional service.

The Lord inquired from Bhattacharya, "Why have you changed the original verse? The word is *Mukti*, and why have you changed it into *Bhakti?*" Bhattacharya replied that *Mukti* is not so valuable as *Bhakti*; and therefore *Mukti* is a sort of punishment for the pure devotee. He had therefore changed the word from *Mukti* to *Bhakti*. He began to explain his realization of *Bhakti*, and said, "Any person who does not accept the transcendental Personality of Godhead and His transcendental Form cannot know the Absolute Truth.

Anyone who does not understand the transcendental nature of the Body of Krishna becomes His enemy and decries or fights with Him. And for such enemies of the Lord, the destination is to merge into the Brahman effulgence of the Lord. Such kind of *Mukti* or liberation is never befitting the devotees of the Lord. Although there are five kinds of liberation, as, (1) getting admission to the same planet in which the Lord resides, (2) being able to associate with the Lord, (3) having a transcendental body like the Lord, (4) having opulence like the Lord, and (5) merging into the existence of the Lord, a devotee is satisfied being engaged in the transcendental loving service of the Lord, without any particular interest for any one of the above mentioned kinds of state of liberation. Specifically, a devotee is most averse to merging into the existence of the Lord, and becoming without any individual identity. A devotee considers oneness with the Lord as worse than hell, even though he may accept one of the other four kinds of liberation in consideration of being engaged in the service of the Lord. Of the two possibilities for merging in the Transcendence, namely, (1) becoming one with the Impersonal Brahman effulgence, and (2) becoming one with the Personality of Godhead, the latter is still more abominable to a devotee. The devotee has no other aspiration than to be always engaged in the transcendental loving service of the Lord. On hearing this, Lord Chaitanya informed Bhattacharya that there is another purport of the word *Mukti*. *Muktipada* means directly the Personality of Godhead. That is to say, the Personality of Godhead has innumerable liberated souls engaged in His transcendental loving service, or He is the ultimate Resort for the ninth subject, called liberation. So, in either of the above mentioned im port, Krishna becomes the ultimate Shelter. Sarvabhouma replied, "In-spite of such import, I prefer *Bhakti* to *Mukti*. Although according to You, there are two kinds of imports of the word *Mukti*, still, because this sound is equivocal, I shall prefer directly *Bhakti* to *Mukti* because by direct perception, *Mukti* refers to the context of becoming one with the Supreme. I therefore hate to utter the word *Mukti*, and I feel enthusiastic in uttering the word *Bhakti*." At this, Lord Chaitanya laughed very loudly, and embraced the Bhattacharya with great love.

Thus the same Bhattacharya who took pleasure in explaining Mayavadi philosophy became a staunch devotee, so much so that he hated to utter the word *Mukti*. This is only possible by the causeless mercy of Lord Sri Chaitanya, and by His Grace He can turn iron into gold, like a touchstone. After this incident, all persons marked a great change in the Bhattacharya and they concluded that this was possible only by the inconceivable power of Lord Chaitanya. And they took it for granted that Lord Chaitanya was none other than Lord Krishna Himself.

Ramananda Roy Talking on High Level Krishna Consciousness with Lord Chaitanya

Lord Chaitanya and Ramananda Roy

The author of *Chaitanya Charitamrita* has described Lord Chaitanya Mahaprabhu as the ocean of transcendental knowledge, and Sri Ramananda Roy as the cloud which is produced from the ocean. Ramananda Roy was a greatly advanced scholar in devotional service, and by the grace of Lord Chaitanya he gathered all such transcendental conclusions, just as the cloud achieves its existence from the water of the ocean. As the cloud appears from the ocean and redistributes water all over the world, and then again goes back to the ocean, so by the grace of Lord Chaitanya Ramananda Roy achieved his higher knowledge in devotional service, and thus he again went to Lord Chaitanya at Puri after retirement from service.

When Lord Chaitanya was visiting the southern part of India, He first of all visited the great temple Bisakhapattan, the temple known as Jiayar Nrishingha Kshetra. It is situated at a place known as Singachalam, five miles from the railway station Bisakhapattan. The temple is situated on the top of a hill, and there are many temples in that quarter, but Jiayar Nrishingha

Kshetra temple is the biggest of them all. The temple is full of beautiful sculpture, still wonderful for many students; and, on account of its popularity, it is a very rich temple. There is an inscription in the temple which states that the king of Vijynagar formerly decorated this temple with gold, and smeared the body of the deity with gold. For facilitating attendance at the temple there are free apartments for the visitors. The temple is managed by priests who belong to the sect of Ramanujacharya.

When Lord Chaitanya visited this temple He praised the deity, and He quoted a verse from *Srimad Bhagwatam:* "Although Lord Nrishingha is very servere to the demons and the non-devotees, He is very kind to His submissive devotees like Prahlad." Lord Nrishingha appeared as an incarnation of Krishna when Prahlad, a boy devotee of the Lord, was too much harassed by his father, Hiranya Kasipu. As the lion is very ferocious to other animals, but is very kind and submissive to his cubs, so Lord Nrishingha, although He appeared ferocious to Hiranya Kasipu, was very kind to Prahlad, His devotee.

After visiting the temple of Jiayar Nrishingha, the Lord proceeded farther south into India, and ultimately He reached the bank of the Gudabudee. On the bank of the Gudabudee the Lord remembered the Yamuna of Vrindaban, and the nice trees on the bank were considered by Him the forest of Vrindaban; so He was in ecstasy there. After taking His bath on the bank of the Gudabudee, the Lord was sitting a little off from the bank and was chanting *Hare Krishna, Hare Krishna, Krishna Krishna, Hare Hare/Hare Rama, Hare Rama, Rama Rama, Hare Hare.* Sitting in that way, the Lord saw that the governor of the province, Sri Ramananda Roy, had reached the bank of the river accompanied by his associates, many Brahmins, and a band party. The Lord had asked about Ramananda Roy, the governor of this province, from Sarbabhouma Bhattacharya, and the Lord was requested by Sarbabhouma Bhattacharya to see the great devotee Ramananda Roy at Kabur.

The Lord could understand that this man approaching was Ramananda Roy, and He wanted to see him immediately. But, because He was in the renounced order of life, He restrained Himself from seeing a person of political affairs. But Ramananda Roy, as a great devotee, was attracted by the Features of Lord Chaitanya as a Sannyasi, and he himself came to see Him. Ramananda Roy, on reaching Chaitanya, prostrated himself to offer Him obeisances and respect. Lord Chaitanya received him by vibrating *Hare Krishna, Hare Krishna, Krishna Krishna, Hare Hare/Hare Rama, Hare Rama, Rama Rama, Hare Hare.* When Ramananda Roy presented his credentials, Lord Chaitanya embraced him, and both of them became overwhelmed with ecstasy. The Brahmins who accompanied Ramananda Roy were surprised that these two persons were overwhelmed with transcendental ecstasy simply by embracing. The Brahmins were all stalwarts of the rituals, and they could not understand the meaning of these devotional symptoms. They were rather surprised to see that a great Sannyasi could touch a Sudra, and they were also surprised that Ramananda Roy, who was a great governor, and practically king of that province, was crying simply by touching a Sannyasi. While the Brahmins were considering this, Lord Chaitanya understood the unfavorable situation, and He pacified Himself.

After this, Lord Chaitanya and Ramananda Roy both sat down together, and Lord Chaitanya informed him that, "Sarbabhouma Bhattacharya has spoken very highly of you, so I have come to see you."

Ramananda Roy replied, "Sarbabhouma Bhattacharya considers myself as one of his devotees, and therefore he very kindly recommended You to see me." Ramananda Roy very much appreciated the Lord's behavior for His touching a man of wealth. A king or governor or any politician is always absorbed in thoughts of political affairs and pounds-shilling-pence; therefore, such persons are avoided by a Sannyasi. But Lord Chaitanya knew Ramananda Roy to be a great devotee, and so He did not hesitate to touch and embrace him. Ramananda Roy was surprised by the behavior of Lord Chaitanya, and he cited a nice verse from *Srimad Bhagwatam*, in which it is stated that, "The great personalities and sages appear in the houses of worldly men just to show them mercy."

Lord Chaitanya's special treatment of Ramananda Roy indicated that, although Ramananda Roy was born of a family who were not Brahmins, still he was far, far advanced in spiritual knowledge and activity. Therefore he was more respectable than a Brahmin who happens to born in a Brahmin family. Although Sri Ramananda, out of his meek and gentle behavior, accepted himself as born of a lower Sudra family, still Lord Chaitanya considered him to be situated in the highest transcendental stage of great devotion. The devotees never advertize themselves as being great, but the Lord is very anxious to advertize the glory of the devotee. Ramananda Roy and Lord Chaitanya, just acquainted for the first time that morning at the bank of the Gudabudee, separated, and there was an engagement made that Ramananda Roy would come in the evening to see the Lord.

In the evening, when the Lord was seated after taking His bath, Ramananda Roy came to see Him with a servant. He offered his respects and sat down before the Lord. Before Ramananda Roy could ask the Lord anything about advancement of spiritual knowledge, the Lord Himself inquired, "Please quote some verses from Scripture about the ultimate goal of life for the human being."

Sri Ramananda Roy at once replied to the Lord that, "A person who is sincere in his occupational duty will gradually develop the sense of God consciousness." In this connection he quoted a verse from the *Vishnu Purana*, in which it is stated that the Supreme Lord is worshipped by following the principles of one's occupational duty, and there is no other alternative for satisfying the Supreme Lord from the formalities of performing one's occupational duties. The purport is that human life is meant for understanding one's relationship with the Supreme Lord and acting in that way. Any human being can dovetail himself with the service of the Lord by discharging his prescribed duties or occupational performances.

For this purpose, human society may be divided into four classes: namely, the intelligent class, or the Brahmins, the administrative class, or the Kshatriyas, the merchantile, or productive class, called Vaishyas, and the laborer class or the helping class, the Sudras. For each division of human society there are prescribed rules and regulations and occupational functions. The prescribed duties of the four classes or four divisions of human society are very nicely described in the *Bhagavad Gita*, Eighteenth Chapter, 42–44 verses. An organized, civilized society of humanity should follow such prescribed rules and regulations for particular divisions. At the same time, for spiritual advancement, they must follow the four stages of *Ashrama:* namely, the student life, which is called *Brahmachary* life; then householder's life, then retired life, and then renounced life.

Ramananda Roy stated that persons who are strictly following the rules and regulations of these eight divisions of human society are the best, and they are actually satisfying the Supreme Lord. One who does not follow the principles of the social division and the rules of spiritual advancement is certainly spoiling his human form of life and gliding down towards hell. One can peacefully execute the goal of his human life simply by following the rules and regulations which apply to himself. The character of a particular person becomes developed by following the principles of regulation according to his birth and association and education. The divisions of society are so designed that many persons of different characteristics can be regulated under them, for the peaceful administration of social life and spiritual advancement. The social divisions of human society may be divided as follows: 1. One who has taken as the aim of his life to understand the Supreme Lord, the Personality of Godhead, and for which aim he has devoted himself to the learning of the Vedas and similar literatures, is called a Brahmin. 2. A person who has taken to the occupation of showing his force and of administering the government is called a Kshatriya. 3. One who is engaged in agriculture and herding cows and trade and business is called a Vaishya. 4. Persons who have no special knowledge but are satisfied by serving the three other higher social divisions are called Sudras. If one faithfully discharges his prescribed duties, it is surely an advancement toward perfection. Therefore, regulated life is the source of perfection for everyone. This regulated life, when culminating in devotional service to the Lord, attains its perfection. Otherwise it is a useless waste of time.

Therefore, Lord Chaitanya, after hearing from Ramananda Roy about the proper execution of regulated life, said that this is external. Indirectly, He asked Ramananda to state something which is better than this external exhibition of life. Formal execution of this ritualistic life or religious life is not very congenial unless it attains the perfection of devotional service. Actually. Lord Vishnu is not satisfied simply by the ritualistic performance of Vedic instructions, but He is actually pleased when one attains the stage of devotional service.

The verse cited by Ramananda Roy in reply to Lord Chaitanya means that, by the divisional ritualistic performances, one can rise up to the point of devotional service. In the *Bhagavad Gita* we find that Lord Sri Krishna, Who appeared Himself for the deliverance of all classes of people, has mentioned that the human being can attain the highest perfectional stage of life by worshipping the Supreme Lord, from Whom everything has emanated, by dint of his occupational duties. It is stated in the *Bhagavad Gita*: "A person duly engaged in his occupational duties attains the highest perfection." This perfectional process is followed by great devotees like Bodhyana, Tanaka, Dramida, Guhadeva, Kapardi, Bharuchi—all these great personalities have followed this particular path of perfection of the human life. The Vedic injunctions also aim at this point of life. Ramananda Roy wanted to present this fact before the Lord. But, apparently, simply discharging the ritualistic duties is not perfection. Therefore Lord Chaitanya said that it is external. Lord Chaitanya's purport was that a man having a material conception of life, even if he follows the ritualistic regulations, cannot attain the highest perfection.

CHAPTER TWENTY-EIGHT

Relationship with
the Supreme Lord

The reason Lord Chaitanya rejected the statement of the *Vishnu Purana* made by Ramananda Roy is that He thus rejected a class of philosophers who are called *Karmamimsat*. *Karmamimsat* philosophers accept God as being subject to one's work. If one works nicely, God is bound to give them good results: that is their conclusion. Therefore, from the statement of the *Vishnu Purana* as enunciated by Ramananda Roy, the meaning is sometimes drawn that Vishnu, the Supreme Lord, has no independence. He is bound to award a certain kind of result to the worker. Such a non-independent Supreme Personality of Godhead becomes subjected to the worshipper, and the worshipper accepts the Supreme Lord as *he wishes*, both impersonal and Personal, although they give more or less stress to the impersonal Feature of the Supreme Absolute Truth.

Lord Chaitanya did not like this idea of impersonalism, and therefore He rejected it. He said: "Tell Me if you know of something beyond this conception of the Supreme Absolute Truth."

Therefore Ramananda Roy stated that it is better to give up the result of fruitive activities. Ramananda Roy understood the purpose of Lord Chaitanya. He quoted a verse from *Srimad Bhagavad Gita*, Ninth Chapter, 37th verse. The Lord says there that, whatever one does, whatever one eats, whatever one sacrifices, whatever one gives or whatever austerity one undergoes for a certain achievement—everything should be dedicated to the service of the Supreme Lord. *Srimad Bhagwatam* also, Eleventh Canto, Second Chapter, 36th verse, has a similar passage, in which it is stated that one should submit everything, the result of his fruitive activities, either by his body, by his speeches, by his mind, by his senses, by his intelligence, by his soul, or by his practical natural modes of Nature—everything should be surrendered to the Supreme Personality of Godhead, Narayan.

Lord Chaitanya rejected this second statement of Ramananda Roy, and He said, "If you know something higher, state it." The instructions of the *Bhagavad Gita* and the *Srimad Bhagwatam*, to offer everything to the Supreme Personality of Godhead, is a better proposal than the impersonal idea of the Supreme Lord, and making the Supreme Lord subject to our work. But it is still short of surrendering activities to the Supreme Lord. The worker's identification with material existence is not changed without proper guidance. Such activity of the fruitive worker will continue his material existence. He is simply instructed here to offer the fruitive result of his work to the Supreme Lord, but he has no idea of how to get out of the material entanglement. Therefore Lord Chaitanya rejected this proposal.

After this second rejection by Lord Chaitanya, Ramananda proposed that one should forsake his occupational activities, and by such detachment rise to the transcendental plane. This is, in other words, renunciation of one's worldly life. In this connection Ramananda Roy gave two evidences from the *Shastras*: in the *Srimad Bhagwatam*, Eleventh Canto, Eleventh Chapter, the Lord says, "In the religious Scriptures I have described ritualistic principles, and how one becomes situated in devotional service. That is the highest perfectional stage of religiousness." Similarly, in the *Bhagavad Gita*, Eighteenth Chapter, 67th verse, the Lord says: "You give up all kinds of religiousness and just surrender unto Me, the Supreme Personality of Godhead. I shall protect you from all sinful reactions, and you have nothing to be aggrieved over."

On hearing this from Ramananda Roy, Lord Chaitanya rejected it again. By rejecting Ramananda Roy's third proposal, Lord Chaitanya wanted to demonstrate that simple renunciation is not sufficient. There must be positive engagement. Without positive engagement the highest perfectional stage cannot be attained. Generally, in the renounced order of life, there are two kinds of philosophers: the goal of one is *Nirvana*, and of the other, the impersonal quality of the Brahman effulgence. They cannot conceive that they can reach beyond, or that there is a Spiritual Sky with Vaikuntha Planets. Because such mentalities cannot have any conception of the Spiritual Planets and activities, therefore Lord Chaitanya rejected the proposal of renunciation.

Ramananda Roy then gave evidence from *Bhagavad Gita*, Eighteenth Chapter, 54th verse, wherein the Lord says as follows: "When a person realizes himself as not different from the Supreme Absolute Truth by cultivation of knowledge, he becomes joyful and freed from all kinds of lamentation and material desires. At that time he perfects his Brahman realization by looking at everyone on the same spiritual level. This stage of Brahman realization can elevate one to the transcendental stage of devotional service." The purport is that Ramananda Roy first suggested devotional service with renunciation of fruitive results from one's work; but better than that stage of life is devotional service with full knowledge and spiritual realization.

Lord Chaitanya again rejected this proposal because in that stage of simply renouncing material results in Brahman realization there is no realization of the Spiritual World and the spiritual activities. Although in the Brahman realization stage there is no material contamination, yet, because there is no positive engagement in spiritual activity, it is not perfectly cleansed. It is still on the mental plane, and therefore external. The pure living entity is not liberated unless he has the complete spiritual idea and is engaged in spiritual activity. When one is absorbed in impersonal thought, or void thought, then his entrance into eternal life, blissful life, and life of knowledge is not complete. When spiritual knowledge is not complete, people will hinder you in your attempt to vacate the mind of all material variegatedness. Impersonalists are hindered in such attempts to make the mind void by artificial meditation. It is very difficult to make the mind void of material conceptions. In the *Bhagavad Gita* it is stated that those who indulge in such voidness or impersonal meditation make very difficult spiritual advancement, and what they attain is not complete liberation. Therefore Lord Chaitanya rejected it.

After rejection of this fifth proposal, Ramananda Roy said that devotional service without any attempt at cultivation of knowledge or mental speculation is the highest stage of perfection. In this connection he gave evidence from *Srimad Bhagwatam*, Tenth Canto, Fourteenth Chapter, in which Lord Brahma says to the Supreme Personality of Godhead: "My dear Lord, one should give up monistic speculation and the cultivation of knowledge altogether. He should begin his spiritual life in devotional service by receiving the information of the activities of the Lord from a realized devotee of the Lord. If one prosecutes his spiritual cultivation by following these two principles and keeping himself rightly in the honest path of living, then, although Your Lordship is never conquerable You become conquered by him by such a process."

When this prescription was presented by Ramananda Roy to Lord Chaitanya, the Lord at once said, "Yes, this is right." In other words, the mission of Lord Chaitanya is as follows: In this age there is no possibility of acquiring spiritual knowledge by renunciation, or by mixed devotional service, or by fruitive results in mixed devotional service, or by the culture of knowledge. Because the people are not so advanced, and in fact most of them are fallen, and because there is no time to elevate them in a general process, the best thing, Lord Chaitanya prescribed, is to let them remain in whatever condition they are—but let them be engaged in hearing about the activities of the Lord, as they are explained in the *Bhagavad Gita* and *Srimad Bhagwatam*. Such messages should be received by aural reception from realized souls. By this principle a person may live in whatever condition he is in, and still make progress in spiritual advancement. He will advance surely and certainly, so much so that he will be a fully realized soul of the Supreme Personality of Godhead.

Lord Chaitanya accepted these principles, but He requested Ramananda Roy to go further in advanced devotional service. Lord Chaitanya gave Ramananda Roy a chance to develop gradually the advancement from the principles of Varnashram Dharma (caste and the four orders of spiritual life); and, further, offering the results of all fruitive activities. Then he recommended discussion of spiritual knowledge. Lord Chaitanya rejected all of these, because in the field of executing pure devotional service there is very little use for such principles. Artificial methods of devotional service without self realization cannot be accepted as pure devotional service. Self-realized pure devotional service is completely different from all other kinds of transcendental activities. The highest stage of transcendental activities is always free from all material desires and fruitive activities, and speculative attempts at knowledge. The highest stage concentrates on a simple, favorable execution of pure devotional service.

Ramananda Roy could understand the motive of Lord Chaitanya, and therefore he stated that attainment of pure love of Godhead is the highest perfectional stage. There is a very nice verse in *Padya Vali* which is understood to be composed by Ramananda Roy himself. The purport of the verse is: "So long as there is hunger within the belly and one has a feeling for eating and drinking—so long, by taking anything eatable, one becomes happy. Similarly, there may be much paraphernalia for worshipping the Supreme Lord, but when that is mixed with pure love of Godhead, it becomes an actual source of transcendental happiness." There is another verse in that connection composed by Ramananda Roy, in which it is stated that even after millions and millions of births one cannot achieve a sense of devotional service. But if, somehow or other, one becomes desirous of achieving the stage of devotional service, the association of a pure devotee will help such a strong desire for serving the Lord to become prominent. One should try to have such a strong desire to become engaged in devotional service, if it is available from any source. In these two verses, Ramananda Roy has described first the regulative principles, and, second, the developed love of Godhead. Lord Chaitanya wanted to bring him up to this stage of developed love of Godhead, and to speak from that basis. Therefore, the discussion between Ramananda Roy and Lord Chaitanya will now proceed on the basis of love of Godhead:

If love of Godhead becomes elevated to personal affinity, that is called *Prema Bhakti*. In the beginning of *Prema Bhakti* there is no establishment of a particular relationship between the Supreme Lord and the devotee, but when this stage of *Prema Bhakti* develops further, there is manifested, in different transcendental flavors, a relationship with the Supreme Lord. The first stage is called servitude—to accept the Supreme Lord as the Master, and the devotee as the eternal servitor. When Lord Chaitanya accepted this process, Ramananda Roy described the relationship of the servitor and the Master. As cited in the *Srimad Bhagwatam*, Ninth Canto, Fifth Chapter, Durbasamuni was a great mystic Yogi and considered himself to be very elevated. Yet he envied Maharaj Amburish, who was known as the greatest devotee of the time. Durbasamani wanted to harass Maharaj Amburish, and as a result he met with great catastrophe, and Durbasamani was defeated by the Sudarsan Chakra of the Lord. The Yogi admitted his fault and said, "For pure devotees who are always engaged in the transcendental loving service of the Lord, nothing is considered impossible to obtain, because they're engaged in the service of the Supreme Personality of Godhead, hearing Whose very Name is sufficient for liberation."

Yamunacharya has composed various verses in his book, *Strotraratna*. In this *Strotraratna*, Yamunacharya writes a nice verse, the purport of which is as follows: "My Lord, persons who are keeping themselves independent of Your service are helpless. They're working on their own account, and they have no support from superior authority. Therefore I long for the time when I shall be fully engaged in Your transcendental loving service, without any desire for material satisfaction or hovering over the mental plane. When I shall be engaged in such unalloyed devotional service I shall enjoy actual spiritual life."

On hearing that statement of Ramananda Roy, the Lord requested him to go still further.

CHAPTER TWENTY-NINE

The Transcendental Pastimes of Radha and Krishna

When Lord Chaitanya said that that was accepted, and that he might advance further, Ramananda Roy said that fraternal relationship with Lord Krishna is a still higher transcendental position. Ramananda Roy's purport in saying this is that, when the relationship with Krishna is increased by a more affectionate tendency, then the mood of fearfulness, the consciousness of the extra-superiority of the Supreme Personality of Godhead, becomes diminished; and there is the development of a mood of faithfulness. And this faithfulness is called friendship. In this friendly relationship, there is a sense of equality between Lord Krishna and His friends.

In this connection, Ramananda Roy quoted a nice verse from *Srimad Bhagwatam*, Tenth Canto, 12th Chapter, where Sukdeva Goswami describes Lord Krishna's lunch with His friends in the forest where they went to play with the cows. It is said there that the cowherds boys who went to play in the forest with Krishna enjoyed transcendental friendship with the Supreme Personality of Godhead, Who is considered the Impersonal Brahman by great sages, considered the Supreme Personality of Godhead by the devotees; and, for the ordinary man, He is considered an ordinary human being.

Lord Chaitanya appreciated this statement by Ramananda Roy very much, but still He said, "You can advance further." At the request of Lord Chaitanya, Ramanada Roy stated that the relationship with Krishna as son and father, the relationship of parenthood, is a still higher transcendental position.

Ramananda Roy's meaning was that the friendly attitude toward Krishna, increased by still more affection becomes the relationship between parents and their children. In this connection Ramananda Roy quoted a nice verse from *Srimad Bhagwatam*, Tenth canto, 8th chapter, where it is stated that the King inquired from Sukdeva Goswami as to the magnitude of righteous activities which had been performed by Yasoda, the mother of Krishna, for which the Supreme Personality of Godhead called her "mother," and sucked at her breast. And he quoted still another verse from *Srimad Bhagwatam* (Tenth Canto, 9th Chapter), in which it is stated that Yasoda, the wife of Nanda, a cowherd man, received mercy from the Supreme Personality of Godhead which is incomparable, even by the mercy which is received by Brahma, the first created living being, or Lord Shiva, or even the Goddess of Fortune, Lakshmi, who is always situated on the chest of Lord Vishnu.

Lord Chaitanya asked Ramananda Roy to proceed further, to come to the point of conjugal love. Ramananda Roy, understanding the mind of Lord Chaitanya, immediately answered that the relationship of conjugal love with Krishna is the highest position. In other words, intimate relationship with Krishna develops from an ordinary conception of the Supreme Personality of Godhead, to the conception of Master and servant. And when it has become confidential, it develops into a friendly relationship, and when it is further developed, it is the relationship between parents and the children; and when it is developed to the highest point of complete love and affection, it is known as conjugal love with the Supreme Personality of Godhead.

In this connection, Ramananda Roy quoted a nice stanza from the *Srimad Bhagwatam*, Tenth Canto, 47th Chapter, in which it is stated that the transcendental mode of ecstasy which was exhibited during the Rasa Dance of the Gopis with Krishna was never relishable even by the Goddess of Fortune, who is always situated on the chest of the Lord in the spiritual kingdom. What to speak of the experience of ordinary women?

Ramananda Roy then explained the gradual process of the development of pure love with Krishna. He stated that a person who is related to the Supreme

Personality of Godhead in any one of the different modes of affection is in the relationship just suitable for him. But actually a relationship with the Supreme Lord begins with the relationship of Master and servant, and further develops into friendship, and further develops into paternal love, and further develops into conjugal love. Anyone who is situated in his particular relationship with the Supreme Personality of Godhead is in the best relationship for him, but when we study all these different flavors of transcendental taste in relationship with the Supreme Personality of Godhead, we can see that the first stage is *Brahmabuta*, or the neutral stage of realization of the Supreme Lord. The state accompanying the conception of accepting the Lord as Master and oneself as His servant is better; and the more developed conception of that relationship is as a friend; and still further as a father; this is the superior quality of development. From friendship to paternal love, the relationship is advanced and of superior quality, and the further advance to conjugal love is the supreme relationship with the Supreme Lord.

Self realization with the sense of servitude is certainly a transcendental development. And the mode of Master and servant, with fraternity added, is a further development. And with progressive affection, it develops into parenthood. But the highest development is conjugal love in relationship with the Supreme Lord. In this connection, Ramananda Roy quoted a verse from *Bhakti Rasamrita Sindhu*. It is stated there that the development of spiritual affection for the Supreme Lord is in all categories transcendental, but that the specific aptitude of a devotee to a particular state is more relishable by him than others.

Such a transcendental relationship with the Supreme Lord cannot, however, be manufactured by the mental concoction of a pseudo devotee. In this connection, Rupa Goswami in his *Bhakti Rasamrita Sindhu*, has stated that devotional service without reference to the Vedic Scriptures as well as to Vedic literature, following the principles of Vedic Scripture, can never be approved. Sri Bhakti Siddhanta Saraswati Goswami Maharaj remarks that those who are professional spiritual masters, professional *Bhagwatam* reciters, professional performers of *Kirtan*, or persons who are engaged in so-called devotional service of their own mental concoction, cannot be accepted. There are different kinds of professional communities known as *Aul, Vaul, Kartabhaza, Nada Darbesa, Snai, Atibibadi, Chudadhari, Gaurnaganagari*. A member of the *Ventor Goswami* society, or the caste called *Goswami*, cannot be accepted as the descendent of the six original Goswamis. Similarly, so-called devotees who manufacture different kinds of songs in connection with Lord Chaitanya, or those who are professional priests or paid recitors, cannot be accepted in this connection. One who does not follow the principle of *Pancharatra*, and one who is an impersonalist, and one who is addicted to sex life, cannot be compared with persons who have dedicated their lives to the service of Krishna.

A pure devotee who is always engaged in Krishna Consciousness can sacrifice everything for the service of the Lord. A person who has dedicated his life to the service of Lord Chaitanya and Krishna and the Spiritual Master, or a person who is following the principles of householder life, and similarly those who are following the principles of the renounced life in the order of Chaitanya Mahaprabhu, are devotees and cannot be compared to the professional men.

When one is freed from all material contamination, any one of the relationships with Krishna is relishable transcendentally. Unfortunately, those who are inexperienced in the transcendental science cannot appreciate these different stages of relationship with the Supreme Lord, and they think that all such different stages of relationship with the Supreme Lord, and all these explanations, are due to Maya. But in *Chaitanya Charitamrita*, the author has given a very nice practical example of this matter. He states that earth, water, fire, air, and ether are the five elements, and these five elements develop from the subtle form to the grosser form. For example, in the ether there is a characteristic which is called sound. But in the air, there is the characteristic of ether, sound, plus a sensation of touch. When one comes to the fire, there is the characteristic of ether plus the characteristic of air, plus the characteristic which is called form. So, in fire there are three characteristics; similarly, when we come to water, there are four characteristics—namely sound, touch, form and taste. When you go to earth, there are five characteristics, namely sound, touch, form, taste, and smell. As there is a development of different characteristics, beginning from ether down to earth, so, if we analyze the different relationships with Lord Krishna and the devotee, we find that all the five characteristics of the devotional attitude are present in the relationship of conjugal love. Therefore, the relationship with Krishna in conjugal love can only be accepted as the highest perfectional stage of love of God.

There is a nice verse from the Tenth Canto, 82nd Chapter of *Srimad Bhagwatam*, which can be cited here: "Devotional service for the Supreme Personality of Godhead is the life of every living entity." And the Lord, addressing the damsels of Vraja, informed them that their love for the Supreme Personality of Godhead is the only cause of their achieving the association of the Lord. It is said that Lord Krishna, in relationship with His devotees, accepts all kinds of devotional service according to the aptitude of each particular devotee, and Krishna also responds to such a devotee in a reciprocal way. For anyone who wants the relationship with Krishna of Master and servant, He plays the part of the perfect Master. For anyone who wants Krishna as his Son, in the parental relationship, Krishna plays the part of the perfect Son. Similarly, if a devotee wants to worship Krishna in conjugal love, Krishna plays the part of husband or paramour in perfection. But He has admitted that His loving relationship with the damsels of Vraja in conjugal love is the highest perfectional stage.

In *Srimad Bhagwatam*, Tenth Canto, 32nd Chapter, Krishna addressed the Gopis and said, "My dear Gopis, your relationship with Me is completely transcendental, and in exchange for your love, it is not possible for Me to offer anything, even after many births. You have been able to give up all attachment for material enjoyment, and you have searched after Me. I am unable to repay your love; and therefore, be pleased with your own activities."

Srila Bhakti Siddhanta Saraswati Goswami Maharaj has remarked that there is a class of common men who say as follows: Anyone and everyone can worship the Supreme Lord according to his particular invention of some mode of worship, and he will still achieve the Supreme Personality of Godhead. One may try to approach the Supreme Personality of Godhead, either by fruitive activities or by speculative knowledge or by meditation or by austerity—any one of the methods accepted will help one to reach the perfectional stage. They generally give the example that if anyone wants to reach a certain destination he can accept one of many different paths, and still reach the same place. Similarly, they say the Supreme Absolute Truth may be worshipped either as the Goddess Kali, or the Goddess Durga, or Lord Shiva, or Ganesha, or Rama, or Hari, or Brahma—any way that the Absolute Truth is addressed, it is all one and the same. They give an example in this connection that a man might have different names, but if he is called by any of those names he will answer.

Such explanations by mental concoction might be very pleasing to the ordinary person, but they are full of misconceptions of transcendental life. One who worships different demigods conducted by material lust cannot achieve the Supreme Personality of Godhead. The external energy of the Supreme Lord can award them some result for worshipping the particular demigods, as is stated in the *Bhagavad Gita:* "One who does not worship the Supreme Personality of Godhead directly cannot achieve His association by worshipping the demigods." The Supreme Personality of Godhead awards the benediction of His association only to persons who worship the Supreme Personality of Godhead, and not via the demigods. It is not a fact, therefore, that everyone and anyone can reach the Supreme Personality of Godhead by worshipping material demigods. It is surprising, therefore, how a man can imagine he will become perfect by worshipping the demigods. The result of devotional service in full Krishna Consciousness cannot be compared with the result of worshipping different demigods or by functioning in fruitive activities or by mental speculation. The results of fruitive activities are that, either one can go to the heavenly planets, or one can go to hell.

CHAPTER THIRTY

Pure Love For Krishna

The difference between executing ordinary religious procedures and devotional service is very great. By executing religious rituals one can achieve the stage of the perfection of material gain, economic development, sense gratification, or liberation—being merged into the existence of the Supreme. But the result of transcendental devotional service is completely different from such temporary benefits of the material condition. Devotional service of the Lord is evergreen, and it is increasingly transcendentally pleasing. Therefore, there is a gulf of difference between the result of devotional service and the result of the four goals of the religious rituals. The great spiritual energy known as *Jagatdhatri*, or the Superintendent of the material world, or *Mahamaya*, and the material executive departmental directors, the demigods, and all of the products of the external energy of the Supreme Lord, are perverted reflections of the opulence of the Supreme Lord. They are, practically, order carriers of the Supreme Lord in the material creation and its management. In the *Brahma Samhita* it is stated that the working of the supremely powerful superintendent, Durga, is just like a shadow indication of the Supreme Lord. The sun works just like the eye of the Supreme Lord. Brahma works just as reflected light of the Supreme Lord. In this way, all these demigods, and the external energy herself, Durgadevi, and different departmental directors are servants of the Supreme Lord in the material world.

In the Spiritual World there is another energy, the superior spiritual energy, or internal energy, which acts under the direction of Yogamaya. Yogamaya means the internal potency of the Supreme Lord. She also works under direction, but in the Spiritual World. When the living entity puts himself under the direction of this Yogamaya instead of Mahamaya, the result is that he becomes gradually, causelessly, a devotee of Krishna. On the other hand, those who are after material opulence and the advancement of material happiness put themselves under the care of the material energy, Mahamaya, or under the care of material demigods such as Lord Shiva and others. In the *Srimad Bhagwatam* it is found that when the Gopis of Vrindaban desired to have Krishna as their husband, they prayed for the gratification of their desire before the spiritual energy, Yogamaya. And in the *Shapta Shati* it is found that King Shurath and another merchant of the name Samadi, wanted opulence of material existence according to their material mode of Nature—and they worshipped Mahamaya. Therefore, one should not mistakenly equalize Yogamaya and Mahamaya.

There is no difference between the Holy Name of the Supreme Lord and the Supreme Lord Himself. Because the Lord is on the Absolute platform, there is no difference between His Name and Himself. There are different Names of the Supreme Lord, such as Paramatma, the Supersoul, Brahman the Supreme Absolute, Shristikarta the Creator, Narayan the Transcendental Lord, Rukminiraman the husband of Rukmini, Gopinath the Enjoyer of the Gopis, and Krishna. The Lord has different Names, and they have different purposes. When one understands the Supreme Lord as the Creator, He is different from the aspect of the Lord as Narayan. Some of the Names of the Lord as the Creator are the conception of the materialistic men. One cannot fully realize the essence of the Supreme Personality of Godhead by understanding the name of the Creator, because this material creation is the function of the external energy of the Supreme Lord. Such a conception of God includes only the external feature of the Supreme Lord.

Similarly, when we call the Supreme Lord *Brahman*, we cannot have any understanding of the six full opulences of the Supreme Lord. In the Brahman realization of the Supreme Lord there is no realization of His six opulences in full. Therefore, Brahman realization is not complete understanding of the Supreme Lord, not recognition of eternity, bliss, and knowledge. When we speak of the Supersoul, that is also not a full realization of the Supreme Personality of God; we understand the Supreme Lord by His All-Pervading Nature as a partial representation of His opulence. In our transcendental relationship also, one who is a devotee of Narayan in Vaikuntha, cannot realize the nature of the relationship with Krishna in Goloka Vrindaban. Nor do devotees of Krishna relish the devotional service to Narayan, because devotional service to Krishna is so attractive that such devotees do not desire to worship other forms.

Again, the Gopis of Vrindaban do not like to see Krishna as the Husband of Rukmini, neither do they address Him as Rukminiraman. In Vrindaban, Krishna is addressed as Radha-Krishna, or Krishna the Property of Radharani. In the ordinary sense, although the Husband of Rukmini and Radha's Krishna are on the same level, still in the Spiritual World the Names are different understandings of different aspects of this Transcendental Personality. If somebody equalized Rukminiraman and Radharaman and Narayan and any other Name of the Supreme Lord as all on the same level, there is the fault of overlapping tastes, which is techically called *Rasabhasa*. Those who are expert devotees do not accept such amalgamation of different conceptions and aspects of the Supreme Personality of Godhead. It is against the conclusion of pure devotional service. But when the conceptions are scrutinizingly discriminated, many less intelligent men understand such discrimination as bigotry.

Although Sri Krishna, the Supreme Personality of Godhead, is Superexcellence and beauty, still, when He is amongst the damsels of Vraja, He is known as Gopijanaballabh; then He becomes the highest perfectional stage for devotees. The devotees cannot relish the beauty of the Supreme Lord more than this. In the *Srimad Bhagwatam* it is confirmed, in the Tenth Canto, 33rd Chapter, that although Krishna the Son of Devaki is Superexcellence and the last word of beauty, still, when He is amongst the Gopis, it appears that He is a sublime Jewel set amongst divine golden craftsmanship.

Lord Chaitanya accepted this statement of the highest realization of the Supreme Lord as conjugal lover. Still, He requested Ramananda Roy to advance further.

At this request, Ramananda Roy remarked that this was the first time that he was requested to go still further than the Gopis in the matter of understanding Krishna. It has been described that there is certainly a transcendental intimacy between the damsels of Vraja and Krishna, but out of all the Gopis the relationship of Sri Radharani with Krishna in conjugal love is the most perfect stage. No common man can understand the ecstasy of transcendental love between Radharani and Krishna. Neither can he understand the transcendental flavor of the transcendental love between Krishna and the Gopis. But if anyone tries to follow in the footsteps of the Gopis, there is the possibility of becoming situated in the highest stage of such transcendental love. Anyone who wants to be elevated to such a transcendental stage of perfection should follow in the footsteps of the damsels of Vraja as the assistant maid servant of such Gopis. Lord Chaitanya exhibited the mood of Srimati Radharani when She is delegated from Dwarka by Sri Krishna.

Such a mode of transcendental love is not possible for any common man. Therefore, one should not imitate the highest perfectional stage of the loving attitude exhibited by Chaitanya Mahaprabhu. But, if somebody desires to be in that association, they may follow in the footsteps of the Gopis. In the *Padma Purana* it is stated that, as Radharani is dear to Krishna, similarly the *Kunda*, known as *Radhakunda*, is also very dear to Krishna. Radharani is the only selected Gopi who is dearer to Krishna than all the other Gopis. In the *Srimad Bhagwatam*, Tenth Canto, 30th Chapter, it is also stated that Radharani and the Gopis render the highest perfectional loving service to the Lord, and that the Lord is so pleased with them that He does not wish to go anywhere else to leave the company of Srimati Radharani.

When Lord Chaitanya heard from Ramananda Roy about the loving affairs of Krishna and Radharani, still He requested, "You may go further, on and on." The Lord said that He was enjoying the description of the loving affairs between Krishna and the Gopis very relishingly, "As if the river of nectar is flowing from your lips." When Krishna danced amongst all the Gopis, He thought that, "I am not giving any special attention to Radharani." So, because amongst the other Gopis, Radharani was not so much an object of special love, Krishna stole Her away from the area of the Rasa Dance, and thus exhibited His special favor for Her.

When this was explained by Lord Chaitanya, Ramananda Roy replied, "Now let us relish the transcendental loving affair between Krishna and Radha to which there is no comparison in this material world." When there was a performance of Rasa Dance, Radharani all of a sudden left the area, as if She was angry that there was no special favor shown to Her. Krishna was desirous to see Radharani in order to fulfill the purpose of the Rasa Dance, but in the absence of Radharani He was sorry, and He went to search Her out. In the *Gita Govinda* there is a nice verse in which it is stated that the enemy of Kansa,

Krishna, also wanted to be entangled in love affairs with women, and thus He simply took Radharani, away, and left the company of the other damsels of Vraja.

Krishna was much afflicted by the absence of Radharani and being thus distressed in mind, He began to search out Radharani along the banks of the Yamuna. Failing to find Her, He entered into the bushes of Vrindaban, and began to lament for Radharani. Ramananda Roy said that when we discuss the purport of these two special verses from *Srimad Bhagwatam*, we can relish the highest nectar of Krishna and Radha's loving affairs.

Although there were many Gopis to dance with Krishna, still Krishna was pleased to dance with Radharani especially. In the Rasa Dance Krishna placed Himself between each two Gopis, but He was present especially with Radharani.

Radharani was not pleased with the behavior of Krishna, which is described in *Ujjal Nilmoni* as follows: "The path of loving affairs is just like the movement of a snake; amongst the young lovers there are two kinds of mental features, causeless and causal." So, when Radharani, out of Her anger for not being treated specially, left the area of the Rasa Dance, Krishna was very sorry not to see Her in the presence of the other Gopis. The perfection of the Rasa Dance was considered to be complete on account of the presence of Radharani, and in Her absence Krishna thought that the Rasa Dance was now disturbed, and therefore He left the arena to search Her out.

After wandering in several places, when He could not find Radharani, He was very distressed in mind; therefore it is understood that Krishna could not enjoy His pleasure potency in the midst of all the Gopis; but in the presence of Radharani He was satisfied.

This transcendental love between Radharani and Krishna was described by Ramananda Roy. Lord Chaitanya admitted that, "I came to you for understanding about the transcendental loving affairs of Krishna and Radha, and I am very much satisfied that you have described it so nicely. I can understand now from your version that this is the highest loving state between Krishna and Radha." Lord Chaitanya still requested him to try something more: What are the transcendental features of Krishna and the transcendental features of Radharani, and what are the transcendental features of the reciprocation of Their feelings, and what is the love between Them? If you will kindly describe all this to Me, I think I shall be very much obliged, because I know that except for you, nobody can describe such things."

Ramananda Roy in all humility replied, "I do not know anything, but whatever You are causing me to say I am saying. I know You are Krishna Himself, but still You are relishing hearing about Krishna from me. Therefore, You will excuse me for my faulty expression. I am just trying to express whatever You are causing me to express."

Lord Chaitanya said, "I am a Mayavadi Sannyasi. I have no knowledge of the transcendental features of devotional service. By the grace of Sarbabhouma Bhattacharya My mind is now clear and I am trying to understand the nature of devotional service to Lord Krishna. He recommended that I see you for understanding Krishna, and he said that Ramananda Roy is the only person who knows something about love of Krishna. I have come to you recommended by Sarbabhouma Bhattacharya, so you should not hesitate to relate to Me all the confidential affairs of Radha and Krishna."

The example Lord Chaitanya set, before Ramananda Roy, was actually to take the subordinate position. And this has a very great significance. The purport is that, if anyone is serious about understanding the transcendental nature of Krishna, he should approach a person who is actually enriched with Krishna Consciousness. One should not be proud of his material birth, material opulence, material education, and material beauty and thereby try to conquer the mind of an advanced student of Krishna Consciousness. Somebody who goes thus to such an advanced Krishna conscious person, so that he will be induced favorably toward him, is under a misconception regarding this science.

One should approach a Krishna conscious person with all humility, and put relevant questions to him, and not challenge him. If anyone goes to challenge him, such a highly elevated Krishna conscious person will not be available for any tangible service. A challenging, puffed-up person will not be able to gain from a Krishna conscious man, and will continue to remain in the material conception of life. Although Lord Chaitanya was born of a high Brahmin family, and was situated in the highest perfectional stage of Sannyas, still He showed by His behavior that even an elevated person did not hesitate to take lessons from Ramananda Roy, although he appeared to be a householder, and situated in social status beneath that of a Brahmin.

Lord Chaitanya clearly showed that a sincere student never minds whether his spiritual master may be born of a very high grade Brahmin family, or of a Kshatriya family; or he may be a high grade Sannyasi, or a Brahmachary, or whatever status of life. Whoever can teach him about Krishna Science is his *Guru*.

CHAPTER THIRTY-ONE

The Supreme Perfection

Whatever he may be, whatever position he may have, if a person is fully conversant with the science of Krishna, Krishna Consciousness, he can become a bona fide Spiritual Master, initiator, or teacher of the science. In other words, the capability of becoming a bona fide Spiritual Master depends on his sufficient knowledge of the science of Krishna, Krishna Consciousness; it does not depend on a particular position in society or of birth. This conclusion of Lord Chaitanya Mahaprabhu is not against the Vedic injunction. On the strength of this conclusion, Lord Chaitanya, previously known as Viswambhar, accepted a Spiritual Master, Iswara Puri, who was a sannyasi. Similarly, Lord Nityananda Prabhu also accepted as his Spiritual Master Madavendra Puri, another sannyasi. This Madhavendra Puri is also known as Laksmipati Tirtha. Sri Adwaita Acharya also accepted this Madhavendra Puri as his Spiritual Master. Similarly, another great Acharya, Sri Rasikananda, accepted as his Spiritual Master Sri Shymananda, who was not born of a Brahmin family. So also Ganganarayana-chakravarty accepted as his Spiritual Master Das Gadadhar. In ancient days there was a hunter whose name was Dharma. He also became the Spiritual

Master of many persons. There are plain instructions in *Mahabharata* and *Srimad Bhagwatam* (Seventh Canto, 11th Chapter) in which it is stated that a person should be accepted—either a Brahmin or a Kshatriya or a Vaishya or a Sudra—by his personal qualification, and not by birth.

And, if such personal qualifications become applicable to a person who is born in a family outside the ordinary field of his actual qualification, he should be accepted by his personal qualification alone. For example, if a man is born of a Brahmin family but his personal qualification is that of a Sudra, then he should be accepted as a Sudra. Similarly, if a person is born of a Sudra family but his personal characteristics are those of a Brahmin, he should be accepted as a Brahmin. All Shastric injunctions, and the version of great sages and authorities—and their practical behavior as well—establish that a bona fide Spiritual Master is not necessarily of the caste Brahmin class. The only qualification is that he must be conversant in the science of Krishna, Krishna Consciousness. That will make him perfectly eligible to become a Spiritual Master. That is the conclusion of Sri Chaitanya Mahaprabhu in His discussions with Ramananda Roy.

In the *Hari Bhakti Vilasa* there is the statement that, if there is a bona fide Spiritual Master born of a Brahmin family, and another who is qualified but born of a Sudra family, one should accept the Spiritual Master who is born of the Brahmin family, and not of the Sudra family. This statement is somewhat of a compromise to social understanding; but is not meant for spiritual understanding. For persons who prefer to count social status as more important than spiritual status, this injunction of the *Hari Bhakti Vilasa* is applicable. But not for the persons who are spiritually serious. For a person spiritually serious, the instruction of Chaitanya Mahaprabhu is that anyone—never mind what he is—if he is conversant with Krishna science must be accepted as the Spiritual Master.

There are many injunctions in the *Padma Purana* which state as follows: a highly elevated, spiritually advanced devotee of the Lord is always a first class devotee, and therefore he is a Spiritual Master. But a highly elevated person born in a Brahmin family, who is not a devotee of the Lord, cannot be a Spiritual Master. A person born in a Brahmin family may be conversant with all the rituals of the Vedic Scripture, but if he is not a pure devotee of the Lord, he cannot be a Spiritual Master. In all the *Shastras*, the chief qualification of a bona fide Spiritual Master is that he must be a qualified person conversant in the science of Krishna.

Lord Chaitanya therefore requested Ramananda Roy to go on teaching

Him, and not to hesitate about speaking on the science of Krishna because Lord Chaitanya Mahaprabhu was a sannyasi in the renounced order of life. He requested him to go on speaking on the Pastimes of Radha and Krishna.

Ramananda Roy then humbly submitted: "Because You are asking me to speak on the Pastimes of Radha and Krishna, of course I must obey Your order, and whatever You would like me to say, I will speak in that way." Ramananda Roy humbly submitted himself as a puppet, and Lord Chaitanya was the puppeteer. So, he wanted to dance according to the will of Chaitanya Mahaprabhu. He expressed that his tongue was just like a string instrument, and "You are the player of the string instrument." So, as Lord Chaitanya would play, Ramananda Roy would vibrate the sound.

He said that Lord Krishna is the Supreme Personality of Godhead, the Source of all incarnations, and the Cause of all causes. There are innumerable Vaikuntha planets, and there are innumerable incarnations and expansions of the Supreme Lord, and there are innumerable universes also. Of all these existences the Supreme Lord Krishna is the only Source. His transcendental Body is composed of eternity and blissfulness and knowledge, and He is known as the Son of Maharaj Nanda, or as the Inhabitant of Goloka Vrindaban; He is full with six opulences—namely, all wealth, all strength, all fame, all beauty, all knowledge, and all renunciation.

In the *Brahma Samhita*, Fifth Chapter, 1st verse, it is confirmed that Krishna is the Supreme Lord, He is the Lord of all lords, and His transcendental Body is Sat-chit-ananda. And no one is the Source of Krishna, but Krishna is the Source of everyone. He is the Supreme Cause of all causes. He is Resident of Vrindaban, and very attractive, just like Cupid. One can worship Him by *Kam Gayatri Mantra*.

The description of Vrindaban is stated in the *Brahma Samhita* as follows: the transcendental land of Vrindaban is always spiritual. That spiritual land is full of Goddesses of Fortune, who are known as Gopis; and they are all beloved of Krishna, and Krishna is the only Lover of all those Gopis. The trees of that land are all desire trees: you can have anything you want from any tree. The land is made of touchstone, and the water is nectar, and all speech is song, and all walking is dancing, and the constant companion is the flute. Everything is self-illuminated, just as we experience the sun and the moon in this material world.

The human form of life is meant for understanding this transcendental land of Vrindaban, and one who is fortunate should cultivate knowledge of Vrindaban and the residents of Vrindaban.

In that Supreme Abode, there are the *Surabhi* cows, who are overflooding the land with milk. In that land, the Supreme Abode of Krishna, even a moment is not misused. Therefore, there is no past, present or future. An expansion of that Vrindaban, the Supreme Abode of Krishna, is here also on this Earth. Superior devotees worship this earthly Vrindaban as being as good as the Supreme Abode Vrindaban. Nobody can appreciate Vrindaban without being highly elevated in spiritual knowledge, Krishna Consciousness. Vrindaban in ordinary experience appears to be just like ordinary land; but in the eyes of a highly elevated devotee, it is as good as the original Vrindaban. A great saintly person, an Acharya, has expressed this in his song: "When will my mind be cleared of all dirty things, and when shall I be able to see Vrindaban as It is? And when shall I be able to understand the literature left by the Goswamins—so that I will be able to understand the transcendental Pastimes of Radha and Krishna?"

The loving affairs in Vrindaban between Krishna and the Gopis are also transcendental. They appear to be like the ordinary lust of this material world, but there is a gulf of difference between the moods of Vrindaban and this material world. In the material world there may be the temporary awakening of lust, but it disappears after so-called satisfaction. But in the Spiritual World the love between the Gopis and Krishna is constantly going on, and it is increasing at every moment. That is the difference between the love of the transcendental world, and the lust of the material world. The lust of so-called love arising out of this body, is as temporary as the body itself. But the love in the Spiritual World is on the spiritual platform, and the spirit soul is eternal. And so that love is also eternal. Therefore, Krishna is addressed as the evergreen Cupid.

Lord Krishna is worshipped by the *Gayatri Mantra*, and the specific *Mantra* is called *Kamagayatri*. The explanation of the *Kamagayatri Mantra* is stated in the Vedic literature: that sound vibration which can elevate one from mental concoction is called *Gayatri*. The *Kamagayatri Mantra* is composed of $24\frac{1}{2}$ syllables, and is stated as follows:

Klim kamadevaya vidmahe puspavanaya dheemahi tanna' nanga prachodayat.

This *Kamagayatri* is received from the Spiritual Master when a disciple is far advanced by chanting *Hare Krishna, Hare Krishna, Krishna Krishna, Hare Hare/Hare Rama, Hare Rama, Rama Rama, Hare Hare.* In other words, this *Kamagayatri Mantra* and *Sanksar*, or reformation of a perfect Brahmin, are offered by the Spiritual Master to a student when he sees that the disciple is advanced in spiritual knowledge. Even such *Kamagayatri* is not uttered under certain circumstances. Still, the chanting of *Hare Krishna* is sufficient to elevate one to the highest spiritual platform.

In the *Brahma Samhita* there is a nice description of the flute of Krishna. The purport of the description is thus: "When Krishna began to play on His flute, the sound vibration entered into the ear of Brahma as the Vedic Mantra, OM. This OM is composed of three letters: A, U, and M, or a description of our relationship with the Supreme Lord. It describes our activities to achieve the highest perfection of love, and the actual position of the loving condition in the spiritual platform. When the sound vibration of Krishna's flute became expressed through the mouth of Brahma, it became *Gayatri*. Therefore, being influenced by the sound vibration of the flute of Krishna, Brahma, the supreme creature and first living entity of this material world, was initiated as a Brahmin.

This remark on Brahma's becoming a Brahmin, initiated by the flute of Krishna, is confirmed by Srila Jiva Goswami. When Brahma was enlightened by the *Gayatri Mantra* through the flute of Krishna, he became possessed of all Vedic knowledge. He acknowledged the benediction offered to him by Krishna, and thus he became the original Spiritual Master of all living entities.

The word *Klim* added to the *Gayatri Mantra* is explained in *Brahma Samhita* as the transcendental seed of love of Godhead, or the seed of the *Kamagayatri*. The object is Krishna, Who is the evergreen Cupid. And, by utterance of *Klim Mantra*, Krishna is worshipped. In the *Gopal Tapini Upanishad*, it is further stated that when we speak of Krishna as Cupid we should not misunderstand that He is the Cupid of this material world. As we have explained, Vrindaban is the Spiritual Abode of Krishna, and so this word *Cupid* is also spiritual and transcendental. One should not misunderstand the material Cupid and Krishna as being on the same level. Material Cupid is the attraction of this external flesh and body, but the spiritual Cupid is the attraction of the Supersoul upon the individual soul.

Actually, lust and the sex urge are there in spiritual life, but because the spirit soul is now embodied in material elements, that spiritual urge is expressed through this material body; and therefore it is pervertedly reflected. When one becomes actually conversant in the science of Krishna Consciousness, he can understand that his material affection of sex life is abominable, whereas spiritual sex life is desirable.

Spiritual sex life is of two kinds: one completely in the constitutional position of the self, and the other according to the object. When one has understood the truth about this life but is not completely out of the material contamination, then, although there is an understanding of spiritual life, he is not factually situated in the transcendental Abode, Vrindaban. When, however, one becomes free from all bodily sex urges, he is actually situated in the Supreme Abode of Vrindaban. When one is situated in that stage of life, the *Kamagayatri* and *Kamavija Mantra* can be uttered by the student.

Ramananda Roy then explained that Krishna is Attractive both for men and women, for the movable and the immovable—for all living entities. Therefore, He is called the transcendental Cupid. And He quoted a verse from *Srimad Bhagwatam*, Tenth Canto, 32nd Chapter, where the Lord appeared before the damsels of Vraja just like Cupid, while smiling and playing His flute.

There are different kinds of devotees of the Lord, and they have different aptitudes and relationships with the Supreme Lord. Any kind of relationship with the Supreme Lord is as good as any other, because the central point is Krishna. In the *Bhakti Rasamrita Sindhu* there is a nice verse in this connection, which states as follows: "Krishna is the Reservoir of all pleasure, and by the spiritual luster of His Body, He is always attracting the Gopis, especially Taraka, Pali, Shyama, and Lalita. Krishna is very dear to Radharani, the foremost Gopi." Like Krishna, the Gopis were glorified by His Pastime activities. In other words, there are different kinds of specific relationships with Krishna, and anyone who is attracted to Krishna by a particular flavor is glorified.

Krishna is so beautiful and transcendental, and so attractive, that sometimes He becomes attractive to Himself. There is a very nice verse in *Gita Govinda*: "My dear friend, do you see how Krishna is enjoying His transcendental Pastimes in the springtime, by expanding the beauty of His Personal Body? And, just like the most beautiful moon, His soft legs and hands are being used on the bodies of the Gopis, and He is embracing them by different parts of the body, and thus He is so beautiful! Krishna is so beautiful that He is attractive even to Narayan, and not only to Narayan—He is also attracting the Goddesses of Fortune who associate with Narayan."

In *Srimad Bhagwatam* there is a nice verse in this connection. The Bhuma Purusa said to Krishna, "My dear Krishna and Arjuna, just to see You I have brought the *Brahmins* before You." This is in connection with Arjuna's attempt to save some youths, who he heard had died untimely at Dwarka. And when he failed to save them, Krishna took him to the Bhuma Purusa, and when the Bhuma Purusa brought forth those dead bodies as living entities he expressed his feelings in the following words: "Both of You appeared for the preservation of religious principles in this world, and to annihilate the demoniac persons." In other words, the Bhuma Purusa was also attracted by the beauty of Krishna, and under some pretext He wanted to see Krishna and this Pastime was invented by him. There is another nice verse in the *Srimad Bhagwatam*, Tenth Canto, 16th Chapter, in which it is stated, "My dear Lord, we cannot estimate how this fallen snake got the opportunity of being kicked by Your Lotus Feet, for which even the Goddess of Fortune underwent austerities for several years—just to see You." This was spoken by the wife of Kaliya, in connection with Kaliya's punishment by Krishna.

How Krishna is attracted by His own beauty is also stated in the *Laleeta Madhav*, Eighth Chapter, 20th verse. Krishna, by seeing His own picture, is lamenting, "How nice this picture is, how glorious this picture is. I am also becoming attracted just like Radhika is attracted by this picture." Krishna was attracted as much as Radhika, or Radharani, was when She saw the picture.

Thus, Ramananda Roy explained about the beauty of Krishna in summary. He again began to speak about the spiritual energy of Krishna, headed by Srimati Radharani. It is said that Krishna has immense expansions of energy, out of which three energies are predominant: one is called internal energy, the second is called external energy, and the third is called marginal energy, or the living entity. This is confirmed in the *Vishnu Purana*, 6th Chapter: Vishnu has one energy, which is called spiritual energy, and it is manifested in three ways. When spiritual energy is overwhelmed by ignorance, that is called marginal energy. So far as spiritual energy is concerned—because Krishna is a combination of eternity, bliss, and knowledge, the spiritual energy is also exhibited in three forms. So far as Krishna's bliss and peacefulness are concerned, His spiritual energy is manifested as pleasure-giving potency, His eternity is manifestive energy, and His knowledge is manifested as spiritual perfection. It is confirmed in the *Vishnu Purana*, First Canto, 12th Chapter: "The pleasure potency of Krishna can give Krishna transcendental pleasure and bliss." Therefore, when Krishna wants to enjoy pleasure, He exhibits His own spiritual potency, known as Alhadini.

Krishna in His Spiritual From enjoys the spiritual energy, and that is the sum and substance of the Radha Krishna Pastime. These Radha Krishna Pastimes can be understood by elevated devotees only. From the ordinary platform one should not try to understand this Radha Krishna Potency, and their Pastimes. People only misunderstand it as being material.

When the pleasure potency is further condensed, it is called *Mahabhava*. Srimati Radharani, the eternal Consort of Krishna is a personification of that Mahabhava. This Mahabhava representation is explained by Rupa Goswami in his book *Ujjal Nilmoni* in the Second Canto, 2nd Sloka. It is stated there, that although there were two competitors in love of Krishna, Radharani and Chandravali; still, by comparison, it appears that Radharani is the best, and She is possessed of the *Mahabhava Svarupa*. Therefore, this Mahabhava Svarupa, or personification, is applicable to Radharani only, and no one else.

Mahabhava is full of the pleasure potency, and is an exhibition of the highest attitude of love towards Krishna. She is therefore known throughout the world as the Most Beloved of Krishna. And Her name is always associated with Krishna, as *Radha Krishna.*

Brahma Samhita also confirms this: Krishna expands Himself by His pleasure potency in the Spiritual World, and the potencies are all non-different from Krishna in the Absolute. Krishna, although He is always enjoying the company of His expansions of the pleasure potency, is All-pervading. Therefore, Brahma offers his respectful obeisances to Govinda, the Cause of all causes.

As Krishna is the highest emblem of spiritual perfection, so Radharani is the highest emblem of the spiritual pleasure potency meant for satisfying Krishna. Krishna is unlimited, and so Radharani is also unlimited, for His satisfaction. Krishna is satisfied by seeing Radharani, but Radharani also expands Herself in such a way that Krishna still wants to enjoy more. And, because Krishna was unable to estimate the pleasure potency of Radharani, He wanted to accept the role of Radharani. That combination is called *Sri Chaitanya Mahaprabhu.*

Ramananda Roy then began to explain that Radharani is therefore the supreme emblem of the pleasure potency of Krishna. And Radharani expands Herself into different forms, known as *Lalita Visakha* and Her confidential associates. The Characteristics of Srimati Radharani are explained by Rupa Goswami in his book *Uljal Nilmoni,* and they can be understood as follows: The body of Radharani is an evolution of transcendental pleasure. That body is decorated with flowers and fragrant aromas, complete with transcendental love for Krishna. That is the personification. That transcendental body takes birth three times: first in the water of mercy, second in the water of useful beauty, and third in the water of youthful luster. After taking birth three times in that way, covered with shining garments and decorated with His Personal beauty, which is compared with cosmetics (Her beauty being the highest artistry) Her body is decorated with ornaments of the ecstasies of spiritual emotion—trembling, tears, checking of the body in transcendental pleasure, stopping of all functions of the body, perspiration, choking of the voice, blood pressure, madness, and stumbling.

There are nine symptoms of decorative transcendental pleasure potency.

Five are by Her expansion of personal beauty, decorated with garlands of flowers; and Her patient calmness is compared with a covering of cloths, cleansed by camphor. Her confidential agony for Krishna is the knot of Her hair, and the mark of telok on Her forehead is Her fortune. The hearing of Radharani is fixed on Krishna's Name and Fame, eternally. By chewing betel nuts the lips become reddish. Similarly, the complete attachment of Radharani to Krishna has blackened the border of Her eyes. It can be compared to ointment, due to Nature joking with Radha and Krishna. Her smiling is just like the taste of camphor. The garland of separation moves on Her body when She lies down on the bed of pride, within the room of aroma. Her breast is covered by the blouse of anger, out of ecstatic affection for Krishna; and a stringed instrument is Hers for Her reputation of being the best amongst all the girlfriends of Krishna. She puts Her hand on the shoulder of His youthful posture. Although She possesses so many transcendental qualities, still She is always engaged in the service of Krishna.

Srimati Radharani is decorated with Suddipta Sattvik emotions, which include sometimes tribulation, sometimes pacification. All these transcendental ecstasies are symptoms of the body of Srimati Radharani. Suddipta Sattvik emotion is when a lover is overwhelmed with certain kinds of feelings which he or she cannot check. Radharani has another emotion which is called *Kilakinchita*. This *Kilakinchita* emotion has twenty different manifestations. Such manifestations are partly due to the body, due to the mind, and due to habit. So far as the bodily emotions are concerned, they are called posture and movement. So far as the emotions of the mind are concerned, they are the exposition of beauty, luster, complexion, mellows, talking, magnanimity and patience. As far as habitual emotions are concerned, they are pastimes, enjoyment, preparation, forgetfulness.

There is the fortune telok on the forehead of Srimati Radharani, and She has a locket of *Premvaichittya*. *Premvaichittya* is the symptom of a lover that occurs when the lover and the beloved meet together, and still have a fear of separation.

Srimati Radharani is fifteen days younger than Krishna. She always keeps Her hand on the shoulder of Her friends; and She is always talking and thinking of Pastimes with Krishna. She always offers Krishna, by Her sweet talks, a kind of intoxication. She is always prepared to fulfill all the desires of Sri Krishna. In other words, She is the supply source for all the demands of Sri Krishna, and She is qualified with unnatural or uncommon qualities for the satisfaction of Krishna.

There is a nice verse in the *Govinda Lilamrita* in which is stated as follows: "Who is the breeding ground of Krishna's affection? The answer is, it is only Srimati Radhika. Who is the most dear lovable object of Krishna? The answer is, it is only Srimati Radhika, and nobody else." Sheen in the hair and a moistness in the eyes, and firmness in the breast—all these qualities are there in Srimati Radhika. Therefore only Srimati Radhika is able to fulfill all the desires of Krishna, and nobody else can.

Sottabhama is another competitor of Srimati Radharani, but she always desires to come to the standard of Srimati Radharani. Srimati Radharani is so expert in every affair that all the damsels of Vraja come and learn all those arts from Her. She is so extraordinarily beautiful that even the Goddess of Fortune and Parvati, the wife of Lord Shiva, also desire to be elevated to the standard of Srimati Radharani's beauty. Arundhuthi, who is known as the most chaste lady in the universe, desires to learn the standard of chastity from Srimati Radharani. Even Lord Krishna cannot estimate the highly transcendental qualities of Srimati Radharani; and therefore it is not possible for any ordinary man to estimate those qualities.

Lord Chaitanya, after hearing from Sri Ramananda Roy about the qualities of Srimati Radharani and Krishna, desired to hear from him about the reciprocal exchange of love between Radharani and Krishna. Krishna is described by Ramananda Roy as *Dhirlalita*, and He is always engaged in love affairs with Radharani. *Dhirlalita* describes a person who is very cunning and youthful, and always expert in joking, without any anxiety, and always subservient to his girlfriend. This Krishna is always engaged in the bushes of Vrindaban to enjoy lusty activities with Radharani, and thus He successfully carried out the instincts of lust.

In the *Bhakti Rasamrita Sindhu* there is a very nice verse in connection with the dealings of Radha and Krishna, and it is said there: "This Krishna, by His impudent and daring talks about sex indulgence, obliged Srimati Radhika to close her eyes and taking the opportunity of the closed eyes of Srimati Radharani, Krishna painted many pictures on the breasts of Radharani, which was the subject matter for joking for the friends of Radharani. Krishna was always engaged in such lustful activities, and thus He made successful His primary youthful life."

On hearing of these transcendental activities between Radha and Krishna, Lord Chaitanya said, "My dear Ramananda, what you have explained about the transcendental Pastimes of Sri Radha and Krishna is perfectly right, but still there must be something more I should like to hear from you."

On hearing this, Ramananda Roy said, "It is very difficult for me to express anything beyond this. But I can only say that there is an emotional activity which is called *Prembilasa Bivarta*. I may try to explain the *Prembilasa*. I do not know whether You will be happy to hear it, but I must explain it to You." In the *Prembilasa* emotion there are two kinds of emotional activities, which are called separation and meeting. That transcendental separation is so acute that it becomes more ecstatic than meeting. Ramananda Roy was expert in understanding such highly elevated dealings between Radha and Krishna, and he composed a very nice song which he narrated to the Lord. The purport of that song is as follows: the lover and the beloved, before their meeting, by the exchange of their transcendental activities, generate a kind of emotion. That emotion is called *Raga*, or attraction. Srimati Radharani expressed Her willingness, that "This attraction and affection between Ourselves has risen to the highest extent"—but the cause of such attraction is Radharani Herself. "Whatever the cause may be, that affection between Yourself and Myself," said Radharani, "has mixed Us in oneness. Now it is the time of separation, so I cannot see the history of the evolution of this love between You and Me. There was no other cause or mediator in Our love, the only cause was Our meeting and visionary exchange of feelings."

This exchange of feelings between Krishna and Radharani is very difficult to understand, unless one is elevated onto the pure platform of goodness. Such transcendental reciprocation between Radha and Krishna is not possible to understand even on the platform of material goodness. One has to transcend even material goodness in order to understand. Such an exchange of feelings between Radha and Krishna is not any subject matter of the material world. Even the highest mental speculators cannot understand this, directly or indirectly. Material activities are manifested either for the gross body or the subtle mind, but this exchange of feeling between Radha and Krishna is beyond such intellectual mental speculation. This transcendental subject matter can be understood by purified senses, freed from all the designations of the material world.

Purified senses can understand these transcendental features, but those who are impersonalists, who have no knowledge of spiritual senses, can simply discriminate within the scope of the material senses, and cannot understand the spiritual exchange or spiritual-sensual activities. Persons who are elevated in experimental knowledge can simply satisfy their blunt material senses, either by gross bodily activities or by mental speculation. Everything generated from the body or the mind is always imperfect and perishable, but transcendental spiritual activity is always bright and wonderful. Pure love on the transcendental platform is the symbol of purity—this means without any material affection, or completely spiritual. Affection for matter is perishable, therefore the inebriety of sex is there in the material world, but there is no such inebriety in the Spiritual World. Hindrances in the performance of sense satisfaction are the cause of material distress, and that is not exactly comparable with spiritual separation. In spiritual separation there is no inebriety or ineffectiveness as with matter.

Lord Chaitanya admitted that this is the highest position of transcendental loving reciprocation, and He said to Ramananda Roy, "By your grace only I have been able to understand such a high transcendental position. This transcendental position cannot be achieved without the performance of transcendental activities; so would you kindly explain to Me how I can raise Myself to this platform?"

Ramananda replied, "It is similarly difficult for me to make You understand, but so far as I am concerned, I can speak what You would like me to say before You. For no one can escape Your Supreme Will. There is nobody in the world who can surpass Your Supreme Will, and although I appear to be speaking, I am not actually the speaker—You are speaking. Therefore, You are both the speaker and the audience. Let me speak as You will me to speak, about the performance required to achieve this highest transcendental position." Ramananda Roy then began:

The transcendental activities of Radha and Krishna are very confidential. They are not to be understood in the emotional relationship of master and servant, friend and friend, or parent and son to the Supreme Lord. This confidential subject matter can be understood in the association of the damsels of Vraja, because such confidential activities have arisen from the feelings and emotions of those damsels. Without the association of Vraja, no one can nourish or cherish such transcendental understanding. In other words, these confidential Pastimes of Radha and Krishna have expanded through the mercy of the damsels—and without their mercy we cannot understand. One has to adopt this life, to follow in the footsteps of the damsels of Vraja, and then one can understand.

When one is actually situated in that understanding, he is eligible to enter into the confidential Pastimes of Radha and Krishna. There is no other alternative way to understand this confidential part of the Pastimes of Radha and Krishna. This is confirmed in the *Govinda Lilamrita*, in a verse which reads as follows: "The emotional exchanges of Radha and Krishna, although manifest and very happy and expanded and unlimited, are limited for understanding to the damsels of Vraja only, or to their followers." As no one can understand the expansion of spiritual energy of the Supreme Lord without the causeless mercy of the Supreme Lord, similarly, no one can understand the transcendental sex life between Radha and Krishna without following in the footsteps of the damsels of Vraja. There are different names for the associates of Radharani: they are called *Shaktis*, or personal associates, and also the *Manjarys*, the near assistants.

It is very difficult to express their dealings with Krishna, as they have no desire to mix with or to enjoy Krishna Personally. But they are always ready to help Radharani be with Krishna. Their affection for Krishna and Radharani is so pure that they are simply satisfied when Radha and Krishna are together, and they simply enjoy the transcendental pleasure of seeing Radha and Krishna combined, united. The actual form of Radharani is just like a creeper embracing the tree of Krishna. The damsels of Vraja, the associates of Radharani, are just like the leaves and flowers of the creeper. And when the creeper embraces the tree, automatically the leaves and flowers also take the opportunity to embrace the tree, along with the creeper.

This is confirmed in the *Govinda Lilamrita* as follows: Radharani is expressed as the expansion of the pleasure potency of Krishna. As She is compared with the creeper, Her associates, the damsels of Vraja, are just like the flowers and and leaves of that creeper. When Radharani and Krishna enjoy Themselves, the damsels of Vraja enjoy the pleasure more than Radharani Herself. Although the associates of Radharani do not expect any personal attention from Krishna, still Radharani is so pleased with Her associates that She arranges a meeting of Krishna and the damsels of Vraja, individually. By many transcendental maneuvers, Radharani tries to combine or unite the associates with Krishna. Radharani takes more pleasure in these meetings than in Her own affairs. And, when Krishna sees that both Radharani and Her associates are pleased by His association, He becomes more satisfied. Such association and reciprocation of love has nothing to do with material lust, but because it resembles such unification between man and woman, or the similarity to the combination of man and woman is there, therefore sometimes it is called, in transcendental language, *transcendental lust*.

In *Goutamiyatantra* this combination of Radharani and Her relationships with Krishna is explained as follows: "Lust means that one is attached to one's personal sense gratification. But, so far as the associates of Radharani and Radharani Herself are concerned, They had no desire for Their personal sense gratification. They want only to satisfy Krishna." In the *Srimad Bhagwatam* this is further confirmed in the Tenth Canto, 31st Chapter, when the Gopis or damsels of Vraja were talking among themselves, as follows: "My dear Friend, Krishna, You are now roaming in the forest with Your bare feet, which You may sometimes keep on our breasts, and although we keep Your Foot on our breasts, still we think that our breasts are so hard, and Your sole is so soft. Now You are wandering in the forest, traversing over the particles of stones; and we do not know how You are feeling, because You are our life and soul. And so Your displeasure in travelling over the rough stone is giving us much distress." Such feelings of the damsels of Vraja, are the highest emotions of Krishna Consciousness, and anyone who becomes captivated by Krishna Consciousness approaches this highest level of the Gopis.

There are sixty-four kinds of devotional service, and by performing these regulative principles one can rise up to the stage of this unconditional devotion of the Gopis. Affection for Krishna exactly on the level of the Gopis is called *Raganuga*, spontaneous love. In that spontaneous loving affair with Krishna, there is no necessity of following the Vedic rules and regulations.

There are different kinds of personal devotees of Lord Krishna in the transcendental Abode. For example, the servants of Krishna known as Raktak and Bhadrak are friends of Krishna, just like Sridham and Subhad; and there are parents of Krishna, just like Nanda and Yasoda, who are also engaged in the service of Krishna in their different transcendental emotions. One who desires to enter into the Supreme Abode of Krishna may take shelter of one of the above transcendental servitors, and then execute loving service in such a way as to achieve the highest result of transcendental affection with Krishna at the end. In other words, the devotee in this material world who executes loving service in pursuance of the activities of those eternal associates of Krishna also achieves the same post when he is perfect.

The sages who are known in the *Upanishads* and in Sruti also desire the post of the Gopis, and they also follow in the footsteps of the Gopis in order to achieve that highest goal of life. This is confirmed in the *Srimad Bhagwatam*, Tenth Canto, 86th Chapter, as follows: The sages practice Pranayam, a trance, by controlling the breathing process and the mind and the senses, by the mystic Yoga practice. And thus try to enter into the Supreme Brahman, or be merged into the Supreme. The same thing is also obtained by persons who, atheist by Nature, fight the principle of the existence of God; if they are killed by an incarnation of the Supreme Personality of Godhead, they also achieve the same result, or merging into the Brahman existence of the Supreme Lord. But the damsels of Vrindaban worship Sri Krishna, being bitten by Him as a person is bitten by a snake, because Krishna's body is compared with the body of a snake. The snake's body never goes straight but it always curling, and as Krishna stands always in three-curved postures, He is compared to the snake. This snake, Krishna, had bitten the Gopis with transcendental love, and they were in a better position than all the mystic Yogis or the persons who desired to merge into the Supreme Brahman. Therefore, the sages of Dundakarannya also follow in the footsteps of the damsels of Vraja, in order to achieve a similar position. By a simple execution of the regular principles one cannot achieve that position; not unless and until one is seriously following the principles of the Gopis. This is confirmed in the *Srimad Bhagwatam*, Tenth Canto, 9th Chapter, by a verse in which it is stated that Lord Sri Krishna, the Son of Srimati Yasoda, is not so easily available to persons following the principles of mental speculation. But He is very easily available for all kinds of living beings who follow the path of devotional service.

There are many pseudo devotional parties claiming to belong to Lord Chaitanya Mahaprabhu's sect. Such pseudo devotional parties in the sect of Lord Chaitanya Mahaprabhu, dress themselves up artificially as the damsels of Vraja. This sort of dressing is not approved by advanced spiritualists or advanced students of devotional service. Such dressing of the outward material body is another foolishness of the concept of the body being the soul. They are mistaken in considering that the spiritual body of Krishna and Radharani and their associates, the damsels of Vraja, are of material Nature. One should know perfectly that all such manifestations are expansions of eternal bliss and knowledge in the transcendental world. They have nothing to do with this material body. Therefore, the body, the dress, the decoration, and the activities of the damsels of Vrindaban do not belong to this material cosmic manifestation. Such damsels of Vrindaban are not subject matter for the attraction of persons who are in the material world. They are the transcendental attraction for the All-Attractive. Krishna is All-Attractive—therefore His name is "Krishna." But the damsels of Vrajabhumi, Vrindaban, are attractive even to Krishna. Therefore, they are not anything of this material world.

If somebody wrongly thinks that this material body is as perfect as the spiritual body, and thus begins to worship by imitating the damsels of Vrindaban, he becomes part and parcel of the Mayavadi or impersonal philosophy. The impersonalists also recommend a process of *Aham Grahapasana*. This process recommends that one should worship his own body as the Supreme. By this material way of thinking, the pseudo transcendentalists dress themselves as the damsels of Vraja; but they are to be taken as the Aham Grahapasana, and are not acceptable in devotional service.

Srila Jiva Goswami, the most authentic Acharya of the *Gaudiya Sampradaya*, has condemned this attempt by imitators. The process of transcendental realization is to follow in the footsteps of the associates of the Supreme Lord, Krishna. And so, to think of oneself as one of the direct associates of the Supreme Lord is also condemned. The process, according to authorized *Vaishnava* principles, is that one should follow a particular devotee and not think of himself an associate.

Sri Ramananda Roy explained, therefore, that one should accept the mood of the damsels of Vraja. In *Chaitanya Charitamrita* it is clearly said that one should accept the emotional activities, and not imitate the dress, of the associates of Krishna, the damsels of Vraja. One should always think within himself about the dealings of Radha and Krishna in the transcendental world. He should think of Radha and Krishna all twenty-four hours, and be engaged in Their service within himself; not externally change his dress only. This is called the mood of the associates of friends of Radharani; and, by following the associates of Radharani, one can ultimately achieve the perfectional stage of being transferred to Goloka Vrindaban, the transcendental Abode of Krishna.

This mood of emotional pursuit of the Gopis is called *Siddhadeha*. Siddhadeha means the pure spiritual body which is beyond the senses, mind, and intelligence. Siddhadeha is the purified soul; and is just suitable for serving the Supreme Lord. No one can serve the Supreme Lord as His associate without being situated in that perfectly pure spiritual identity. That identity is completely free from all material contamination. It is stated in the *Bhagavad Gita* that a person materially contaminated transmigrates to another material body by material consciousness. At the time of death he thinks in that way, and therefore is transferred to another material body. Similarly, when one is situated in his pure spiritual identity, and thinks of spiritual loving service rendered to the Supreme Lord, he is transferred into the Spiritual Kingdom, to enter into the association of Krishna. In other words, to think of Krishna and His associates in the spiritual identity is the qualification for transference to the Sprritual Kingdom.

No one can contemplate or think of the activities of the Spiritual Kingdom without being situated in pure spiritual identity. That pure spiritual identity is called Siddhadeha. Ramananda Roy therefore expressed himself to the effect that, without attending to that Siddhadeha, no one can become an associate of the damsels, or render service directly to the Personality of Godhead, Krishna, and His eternal consort, Radharani. He quoted, in this connection, a nice verse from the *Srimad Bhagwatam*, Tenth Canto, 47th Chapter, in which is stated the following: "Neither the Goddess of Fortune, Lakshmi, nor even the damsels of the Heavenly Kingdom could attain the facilities of the damsels of Vrajabhumi—and what to speak of others?"

Lord Chaitanya was very satisfied upon hearing this statement from Ramananda Roy, and He embraced him. Both of them began to cry in ecstasy in that transcendental realization. Both the Lord and Ramananda Roy discussed throughout the whole night the transcendental Pastimes of Radharani and Krishna, and in the morning They separated. Ramananda left to go to his place, and the Lord went to take His bath.

At the time of separation, Ramananda Roy fell down at the feet of Lord Chaitanya and prayed as follows: "My dear Lord, You have come just to deliver me from this mire of nescience. Therefore I request that You may remain here at least for ten days, and You can purify my mind of this material contamination. There is nobody else who can deliver such transcendental love of God."

The Lord replied, "I have come to you to purify Myself by hearing from you of the transcendental Pastimes of Krishna and Radha; and I am so fortunate, for you are the only teacher of such transcendental Pastimes. I do not find anyone else in this world who can realize this transcendental loving reciprocation between Radha and Krishna. You are requesting Me to stay here for ten days, but I feel that I wish to remain with you for the rest of My life. Please come to Jagannath Puri, My headquarters, and We may remain together for the rest of My life, and I can pass My remaining days in understanding Krishna and Radha by your association."

Sriman Ramananda Roy came to see the Lord the next day in the evening, and there were discourses on this transcendental subject matter. And the Lord again began to inquire from Ramananda Roy, as follows: "What is the highest standard of education?" Ramananda Roy immediately replied that the highest standard of education is to know the science of Krishna. The standard of material education is sense gratification, but the standard of spiritual education, especially the highest standard, is to know the science of Krishna. In the *Srimad Bhagwatam*, Fourth Canto, 29th Chapter, 47th verse, it is stated that work which pleases the Supreme Personality of Godhead is the highest standard of work, and the science or knowledge which places one in full Krishna Consciousness is the highest standard of knowledge. Similarly, Prahlad Maharaj, while instructing his childhood friends at school, also stated that hearing or chanting of the Lord, remembering, worshipping, praying, serving, making friendship with Krishna and offering everything to Him, is to be understood as the highest standard of spiritual knowledge. Then Lord Chaitanya asked Ramananda Roy, "What is the highest standard of reputation?" Ramananda Roy immediately replied that if a person is famous by a reputation of Krishna Consciousness, he is to be called the most famous man in the world. In other words, if a man is known as Krishna conscious, he is the greatest, most famous of men.

CHAPTER THIRTY-TWO

Conclusion

One who is famous as the man of Krishna Consciousness has eternal fame. In the material world, everyone is after three things: he wants his name to be perpetuated, he wants his fame to be broadcast all over the world, and he wants some profit out of his material activities. But he does not know that all this material name, fame, and profit belong to this temporary body; and, as soon as the body is finished, all name, fame and profit are finished. Due to ignorance, everyone is after name, fame and profit in connection with this body. But to become very famous in connection with this body, or to become known as a man of spiritually developed consciousness, without any knowledge of the Supreme Spirit, Vishnu, must be deprecated. Real fame is if one attains Krishna Consciousness in this very life.

According to *Srimad Bhagwatam*, there are twelve authorities. They are famous because they were all great devotees of the Lord—Brahma, Narada, Lord Shiva, Manu, Kapila, Prahlad, Janaka, Bhisma, Sukadeva Goswami, Bali, Jamaraja and the Kumaras. All these great stalwarts are devotees of the Lord, and therefore they are still remembered.

In the *Garuda Purana* there is a verse in which it is said that, instead of becoming a demigod such as Brahma or Lord Shiva, if one becomes a famous devotee of the Supreme Lord in this Age of Kali, that is very rare. Yudhisthira also, in connection with talks between Narada and Pundarik, said, "After many, many births, if somebody comes to understand that *he is the servant of Vasudeva*, that person is the most famous, and can deliver all others. Similarly, in the *Bhagavad Gita* it said, "Anyone who understands that Vasudeva is everything and surrenders to Him is the most learned and wise man." In the *Agni Puranam* it is said that liberation or transcendental life follows all the devotees of Godhead. In the *Vrihat Naradia Purana*, it is also stated that even personalities like Brahma and the other demigods do not know the value of a devotee of the Supreme Personality of Godhead. In the *Garuda Purana* also it is stated that, out of many thousands of Brahmins, one is prominent who is expert in performing sacrifices; and out of thousands of such Brahmins who are expert in the performance of sacrifice, one Brahmin who is expert in the *Vedanta Sutra* is the most famous; and out of many, many thousands of Vedantists, one person who is a devotee of Lord Vishnu is the most famous. There are many devotees of Vishnu, and out of them, one who is an unflinching devotee is eligible to enter into the Kingdom of God. In *Srimad Bhagwatam*, Third Canto, 13th Chapter, it is also stated that there are many students of the *Vedas*, but one who is always thinking of the Supreme Personality of Godhead within his heart is the best. In the Narayan prayers it is said that even Brahma if not a devotee of the Lord, He is therefore insignificant, whereas even a bacteria who is a devotee of the Lord is famous.

Lord Chaitanya at this point inquired from Ramananda Roy, "What are the most valuable riches in this world?" Ramananda Roy replied that one who has love for Radha Krishna has the most valuable jewel, the greatest riches. One who is too much addicted to material sense gratification, or to material wealth, has no such value. When one comes to the spiritual platform in Krishna Consciousness he can understand that there are no more valuable riches than love of Radha Krishna. In the *Srimad Bhagwatam*, Maharaj Dhruva sought out the Supreme Lord because he wanted to get some land, but when he saw Krishna he said, "I am so pleased that I don't want anything." In the *Bhagavad Gita* it is also stated that if one takes shelter of the Supreme Personality of Godhead, or is elevated to the Supreme State of love of Godhead, then there is nothing more to aspire to. Although such devotees can obtain anything they desire from the Personality of Godhead, still, a pure devotee does not ask anything from God.

When Lord Chaitanya asked Ramananda Roy what is the most painful existence, Ramananda Roy replied that separation from a pure devotee is the most painful existence in human society. In other words, where there is no known devotee of the Lord, society becomes painful, and association also becomes painful. In the *Srimad Bhagwatam*, Third Canto, 30th Chapter, it is stated that if somebody tries to become happy simply in association with society, friendship, and love—without Krishna Consciousness—he is in the most distressed condition, bereft of the association of a pure devotee.

Lord Chaitanya then inquired from Sri Ramananda Roy: "Out of so many so-called liberated souls, who is actually liberated?"

Ramananda replied that the person who is completely saturated with devotional love of Radha and Krishna is to be considered the best of all liberated persons. In the *Srimad Bhagwatam*, Fifth Canto, it is stated that the association of a pure devotee is more desirable than life itself, and in separation from the association of the devotee, not even a second is passed happily. Similarly, it is stated in the *Srimad Bhagwatam*, Sixth Canto, 14th Chapter: a devotee of Narayan is so rare that you can find only one out of millions and millions.

Chaitanya Mahaprabhu inquired from Sri Ramananda Roy: "There are many songs; which song do you think the best of all?"

Ramananda replied that any song which describes the Pastimes of Sri Radha and Krishna is the best song. The conditioned soul is such that everyone is captivated by sex life; all the material fiction—dramas and novels—are descriptions of love between a man and woman. As people have so much attraction for this literature, Krishna therefore appeared on this material world and displayed His transcendental loving affairs with the Gopis, and there is an immense literature dealing with the transactions between the Gopis and Krishna. Anyone who takes shelter of this story of Radha and Krishna enjoys actual happiness. In the *Srimad Bhagwatam*, Tenth Canto, 33rd Chapter, it is said that the Lord, in order to show His actual life, displayed His Pastimes at Vrindaban; and any intelligent person who tries to understand the Pastimes of Radha and Krishna is the most fortunate. And that sort of song and story is the highest in the world.

Lord Chaitanya then inquired from Sri Ramananda Roy, "What is the most profitable thing in this world, the essence of all auspicious events?"

Ramananda Roy replied that there is nothing so profitable as the association of pure devotees.

Lord Chaitanya inquired: "What do you recommend a person think of?"

Ramananda Roy replied that one should always think of the Pastimes of Krishna. This is Krishna Consciousness. Krishna has multiple activities, and they are described in so many Vedic Scriptures. One should think of all those Pastimes, always; that is the best meditation, and the highest ecstasy.

In the *Srimad Bhagwatam*, Second Canto, 2nd Chapter, it is confirmed by Sukadeva Goswami that people should always think of the Supreme Personality of Godhead; not only think of Him—one should hear and chant the Name, Fame, and Glories of the Supreme Lord.

Lord Chaitanya now inquired of Ramananda Roy: "What is the best type of meditation?"

And Ramananda replied, "One who always meditates upon the Lotus Feet of Radha and Krishna is the best meditator."

Srimad Bhagwatam confirms this in the First Canto, 2nd Chapter, wherein it is stated: "It is only the Supreme Personality of Godhead Who is the Master of all devotees, Whose Name we should always be chanting, and Who should be always thought of in meditation, and worshipped regularly."

Lord Chaitanya inquired from Ramananda Roy, "Where should a person live, giving up all other pleasures?"

And Ramananda Roy replied that one should give up all other pleasures and should live in Vrindaban, the place where Lord Krishna had so many Pastimes. In the *Srimad Bhagwatam*, Tenth Canto, 47th Chapter, it is said by Uddhava that it is best to live at Vrindaban, even as one of the plants or creepers of the land; where the Supreme Lord was, and where the Gopis went, worshipping the Supreme Lord, the ultimate Goal of all Vedic knowledge.

Chaitanya Mahaprabhu now asked, "What is the best subject to hear of?"

And Ramananda Roy replied, "The best subject matter to hear of is the Pastimes of Radha and Krishna." Actually, when the Pastimes of Radha and Krishna are heard from the right source, one becomes at once a liberated soul. But sometimes it happens that people do not hear the Pastimes of Radha and Krishna from a person who is a realized soul. And they are therefore sometimes misguided. It is stated in the *Srimad Bhagwatam*, Tenth Canto, 30th Chapter, that one who hears about the Pastimes of Krishna with the Gopis will attain to the highest platform of devotional service, and he will be freed from the material lust which is overwhelming everyone's heart. In other words, the actual result of hearing the Pastimes of Radha and Krishna is to get rid of all material lust. If one does not become freed from material lust, then he should not indulge in hearing the Pastimes of Radha and Krishna. Unless we hear from the right source, the Pastimes of Radha and Krishna will be misrepresented, and we shall think that it is an ordinary affair between a man and woman, and we shall be misguided.

Chaitanya Mahaprabhu next inquired from Ramananda Roy: "Who is the most worshippable deity?"

And Ramananda Roy immediately replied that the transcendental couple, Sri Radha and Krishna, is the ultimate Object of worship. There are different kinds of worshippable objects, just as the impersonalists worship the impersonal *Brahmajyoti*. But the result of such worship is that one becomes bereft of his living activities, and becomes just like the tree and other unmoving entities. Those who are worshippers of the Void also attain such a result. And those who are *Bhukti*, who are after material enjoyment, worship demigods and achieve the planets of the demigods, and in that body they enjoy material happiness.

Lord Chaitanya inquired about those who are after material happiness, and liberation from this material bondage. Where do they ultimately go? Ramananda Roy replied that ultimately, some of them become as good as the standing tree, and some of them achieve the heavenly planets to enjoy material happiness.

Ramananda Roy went on to say that those who have no taste for Krishna Consciousness or spiritual life are just like crows who take pleasure in eating the bitter margosa fruit, while the poetic cuckoo eats the seeds of the mango. Similarly, the unfortunate transcendentalists are simply speculating on dry philosophy, whereas the transcendentalists who are in love with Radha Krishna enjoy, just like the cuckoo. Therefore, those who are devotees of Radha and Krishna are the most fortunate persons in the world. Ramananda Roy compared mental speculation with the bitter margosa fruit, which is not at all edible; simply full of dry speculation, and so fit for the crowlike philosophers; however, mango seeds are very relishable, and those who are in the devotional service of Krishna and Radha are like those mango-tasting cuckoos.

Thus Ramananda Roy and Chaitanya Mahaprabhu talked together for the whole night, sometimes dancing, sometimes singing, sometimes crying. In this way the night was passed, and at dawn Ramananda Roy went to his own place, and again in the evening he came back to see Chaitanya Mahaprabhu. The next day, after talking and discussing Krishna for some time, Ramananda Roy fell at the feet of Chaitanya Mahaprabhu and began to submit: "My dear Lord, You are so kind upon me that You have spoken to me about the science of Krishna, about the science of Radharani and Their loving affairs, and Their affairs of the Rasa Dance, and Their Pastimes—I never thought that I should be able to speak on this subject matter. So have You taught me, as You formerly taught Brahma the Vedas."

This is the system of instruction from the Supersoul. Externally He is not to be seen. Yet, internally, He speaks to the devotee, and that is confirmed in the *Bhagavad Gita:* to anyone who is sincerely engaged in the service of the Lord, the Lord from within dictates, and He acts in such a nice way that he ultimately achieves the Supreme goal of life. When Brahma was born there was nobody else to instruct him. Therefore, in the Vedic literature, we find that the Supreme Lord Himself instructed Brahma about the Vedic knowledge through his heart. The same thing is also confirmed in the *Srimad Bhagwatam*, Second Canto, 4th Chapter, by Sukadeva Goswami: the *Gayatri Mantra* was first of all instructed by the Supreme in the heart of Brahma. Similarly, Sukadeva Goswami prayed to the Lord to also help him in speaking *Srimad Bhagwatam* before Maharaj Parikshit.

The first verse of the First Canto of the *Srimad Bhagwatam* describes the Supreme Absolute Truth, Who instructed Brahma through the heart. It is stated there by Vyasadeva, the author of *Srimad Bhagwatam:* "Let me offer my respectful obeisances to Sri Krishna, the Supreme Personality of Godhead, Who is the Cause of cosmic manifestation, its maintenance, and its dissolution." If we scrutinizingly try to understand the Supreme Truth, we can understand that He knows everything directly and indirectly. He is the only Supreme Personality fully independent, and it is He only, alone, Who instructed Brahma as the Supersoul from within. Even the greatest learned scholar becomes bewildered about understanding the Supreme Truth, because the whole perceivable cosmic manifestation is situated in Him. Although this material manifestation is a byproduct of fire, water, and earth, still it appears just like the truth. But it is in Him only that the spiritual manifestation, the material manifestation, and the manifestation of the living entities—*everything*—rests. Therefore He is the Supreme Truth.

Sri Ramananda Roy continued to speak to Lord Chaitanya: "Sir, first of all I saw You as a Sannyasi, and again I saw You as a cowherd Boy. Further, I see before You a golden doll. Due to the presence of that golden doll, Your complexion has become gold, and yet I see Your complexion to be black, as a cowherd boy. Will You kindly explain why I am seeing You with such different complexions? Will You kindly explain to me without any reservation?"

Lord Chaitanya replied, "It is the nature of highly elevated devotees to see Krishna in everything. Whenever they see anything, they do not see the form of that particular thing, but they see Krishna." This is confirmed in *Srimad Bhagwatam*, Eleventh Canto, 2nd Chapter: that a person who is highly elevated in devotional service sees the Supersoul, Krishna, Who is the Soul of all individual souls. A similar passage is found in the Tenth Canto, 35th Chapter, in which it is stated that all the creepers, plants and trees, full with flowers and fruits, were bent over on account of the ecstasy of love for Krishna, because Krishna was the Soul of their soul; and those trees and plants, after Krishna manifested before them, were growing thorny.

Lord Chaitanya then continued to speak, addressing Ramananda: "You have the highest conception of the Pastimes of Radha and Krishna, and you are therefore seeing Radha Krishna everywhere."

In reply to this Ramananda Roy said, "Sir, I may request that You don't try to hide Yourself. I understand that You have accepted the complexion and mode of thinking of Srimati Radharani, so that You are trying to understand Yourself from the viewpoint of Radharani; and You are advented to take this point of view. Your incarnation is chiefly for understanding Your Own Self, but, side by side, You are distributing love of Krishna to the world. You have personally come here to deliver me. Now don't try to deceive me, I request You, it is not good for You."

Lord Chaitanya became very satisfied, and He smiled and showed Ramananda His real form. In other words, the Form which Lord Chaitanya manifested as the combination of Sri Radha and Krishna was first shown to Ramananda Roy. Lord Chaitanya was, therefore, Sri Krishna Himself, with the external features of the mode of Srimati Radharani. This transcendental ability of one becoming two and two becoming one is possible, and was seen by Sri Ramananda Roy. Persons who are fortunate enough to understand Lord Chaitanya as well as the Pastimes at Vrindaban of Radha and Krishna can be able, by the mercy of Sri Rupa Goswami, to know about the real identity of Sri Krishna Chaitanya Mahaprabhu.

Seeing this unique feature of Lord Chaitanya, Ramananda Roy fainted and fell down flat on the floor. While he was unconscious, Lord Chaitanya touched him, and he came to his senses. Ramananda Roy was surprised to see Lord Chaitanya in His dress of a mendicant. Lord Chaitanya then embraced him and pacified him and informed him that nobody had seen this Form except himself. "You have understood the purpose of My incarnation, and therefore you are privileged to see this particular feature of My Personality." Lord Chaitanya continued: "My dear Ramananda, I am not a different person with fair complexion known as Gaura Purusa. I am the Selfsame Krishna—Son of Maharaj Nanda, and due to contact with the body of Srimati Radharani I have now assumed this Form. Srimati Radharani does not touch anyone else but Krishna, and therefore Srimati Radharani has influenced Me with Her complexion, mind and words, and I am just trying to understand the transcendental flavor of Krishna's relationship." No one should therefore eliminate Lord Chaitanya from Sri Krishna.

The fact is that both Krishna and Lord Chaitanya are the Original Personality of Godhead. In His Form of Sri Krishna He is the Supreme Enjoyer, in His Form of Lord Chaitanya He is the Supreme Enjoyed. No one can be more superexcellently attractive than Sri Krishna, and except for Krishna no one can be the Enjoyer of the Supreme Form of Devotion, Srimati Radharani. Except Sri Krishna, all other Vishnu Forms are lacking this quality.

This is explained in the Govinda description of *Chaitanya Charitamrita*, where it is said that Srimati Radharani is the only personality who can infuse Sri Krishna with transcendental pleasure. Therefore, Srimati Radharani is the chief of all the damsels of Vraja who love Govinda, the Supreme Personality of Godhead, Sri Krishna.

"Please take it from Me that I have nothing to hide from you. And even if I do try to hide from you, you are such an advanced devotee that you can understand everything of My secret. I request that you plese keep this secret, and do not disclose it to anyone. It would be considered that I am a madman. The facts which are disclosed to you cannot be understood by any materialistic person. When they hear all this description they will laugh at Me. You can understand yourself, and keep it for yourself. As a devotee becomes mad in his ecstasy of love for Krishna, so from the materialistic point of view, both yourself and Myself are the same as madmen. Therefore, don't disclose these facts to the ordinary men, or they will laugh at Me."

Lord Chaitanya then passed ten nights with Ramananda Roy, and enjoyed his company in discussing the Pastimes of Krishna and Radha. The discussion between Sri Chaitanya and Sri Ramananda Roy was on the highest level of love of Krishna. Some of the talks are described, but most of them could not be described. This has been analyzed in the *Chaitanya Charitamrita* as an examination in metallurgy. The comparison is that the discussion proceeds just like metals being studied: first copper, then bronze, then silver, gold, and at last touchstone. The preliminary discussions between Lord Chaitanya and Ramananda Roy are considered copper, and a higher discussion is considered gold. But the fifth dimension of the discussion between Ramananda Roy and Lord Chaitanya is considered to be touchstone. If, however, one is very eager to progress higher and higher to the position of the highest metallurgist, then he can understand—beginning with inquiring into the difference between copper and bronze, and then silver, and so on.

The next day, Lord Chaitanya asked Ramananda Roy to allow Him to go back to Jagannath Puri, "So that the rest of Our lives We can remain together at Jagannath Puri, and We can pass Our time in discussing Krishna." Lord Chaitanya thus embraced Ramananda Roy and sent him to his own place. In the morning He started His further journey. Ramananda Roy and Lord Chaitanya met on the river bank where there was a deity, a temple of Hanuman. After seeing the temple of Hanuman He left that place. So long as Chaitanya Mahaprabhu remained at Kavur, all kinds of people met Him, and by His Grace everyone became a devotee of the Supreme Lord.

After the departure of Lord Chaitanya, Ramananda Roy became overwhelmed by separation from the Lord, and he decided to retire from service just to meet the Lord again at Jagannath Puri. This discussion of Ramananda Roy with Lord Chaitanya is the most concentrated form of devotional service, and by hearing the discussion of Ramananda Roy and Lord Chaitanya one can understand the Pastimes of Sri Radha and Krishna. One can also understand the confidential part played by Lord Chaitanya. If one is fortunate enough, he can place his faith in this discussion, and can enter into the transcendental association of Radha and Krishna.